6/13/16

The Power of Pills

The Power of Pills

Social, Ethical and Legal Issues in Drug Development, Marketing, and Pricing

Edited by
Jillian Clare Cohen, Patricia Illingworth,
and Udo Schüklenk

Pluto Press

LONDON • ANN ARBOR, MI

First published 2006 by Pluto Press
345 Archway Road, London N6 5AA
and 839 Greene Street, Ann Arbor, MI 48106

www.plutobooks.com

British Library Cataloguing in Publication Data
A catalogue record for this book is available from the British Library

hardback
ISBN-10   0 7453 2403 7
ISBN-13   978 0 7453 2403 6
paperback
ISBN-10   0 7453 2402 9
ISBN-13   978 0 7453 2402 9

Library of Congress Cataloging in Publication Data applied for

10 9 8 7 6 5 4 3 2 1

Designed and produced for Pluto Press by
Chase Publishing Services Ltd, Fortescue, Sidmouth, EX10 9QG, England
Typeset from disk by Stanford DTP Services, Northampton, England
Printed and bound in India

Contents

Part III: The social, ethical, and political challenge: neglected diseases

Part IV: Patents and access to medicines

Part V: Research ethics

Part VI: Political activism and treatment access

Part VII: National responsibilities

List of abbreviations

AARP	American Association of Retired Persons
ABC	Abstinence, Be Faithful, Use Condoms
ACM	Advanced Market Commitments
ACP	American College of Physicians
ADAA	Anxiety Disorders Association of America
ADE	Adverse Drug Event
AGAO	African Growth and Opportunity Act
AGDFAT	Australian Government Department for Foreign Affairs and Trade
AHRQ	Agency for Healthcare Research and Quality
AMA	American Medical Association
AMC	Advanced Market Commitments
ANC	African National Congress (South Africa)
ANDAs	Abbreviated New Drug Applications
APC	Advanced Purchase Commitment
API	Active Pharmaceutical Ingredients
ARC	Australian Research Council Grant
ART	Anti-retroviral Therapy
ARV	Anti-retroviral
AUSFTA	Australia–US Free Trade Agreement
AZT	Azidothymidine (first retroviral approved for treatment of HIV)
BC	British Columbia
BCG	Boston Consulting Group
BOP	Buy-Out Price
BUMED	Bureau of Medicine and Surgery
CAFTA	Central American Free Trade Agreement
CBD	Convention on Biological Diversity
CBO	Congressional Budget Office
CCIC	Canadian Council for International Cooperation
CCOHTA	Canadian Coordinating Office for Health Technology Assessment
CEDAC	Canadian Expert Drug Advisory Committee
CEP	Clinical Evaluation Packages
CESCR	Committee on Economic, Social and Cultural Rights
CfA	Commission for Africa
CGD	Center for Global Development
CHAI	Clinton Foundation HIV/AIDS Initiative

CH(A)LN	Canadian HIV/AIDS Legal Network
CHR	Commission on Human Rights
CIA	Central Intelligence Agency
CIGB	Centro de Ingeniería Genética y Biotecnología (Cuba: Center for Genetic Engineering and Biotechnology)
CIOMS	Council for International Organization of Medical Sciences
CIPIH	Commission on Intellectual Property, Innovation and Public Health
CIPR	Commission on Intellectual Property Rights
CLASS	Celecoxib Long-Term Arthritis Safety Study
CMA	Canadian Medical Association
COO	Chief Operating Officer
COX-2	Cyclooxygenase 2
CPA	Central Procurement Agency
CPI	Consumer Price Index
CPIX	Consumer Price Index – excluding certain interest rates
CRBPC	Canada's Research-Based Pharmaceutical Companies
CSPL	Committee on Standards in Public Life
CSR	Corporate Social Responsibility
DBSA	Development Bank of South Africa
ddI	didanosine
DEFEND	Developing Economies' Fund for Essential New Drugs
DFAIT	Department of Foreign Affairs and International Trade
DFID	Department for International Development
DMD	Doha Ministerial Declaration
DMF	Drug Master File
DNA	Deoxyribonucleic Acid
DNDI	Drugs for Neglected Diseases Initiative
DND-WG	Drugs for Neglected Diseases Working Group
DoC	Department of Commerce
DoH	Department of Health
DOTS	Directly Observed Treatment, Short-course
DPCO	Drug Price Control Authority (India)
DQT	Drug Quality and Therapeutics Committee
DRA	Drug Registration Authority
DTC(A)	Direct to Consumer (Advertising)
DTI	Department of Trade and Industry
DUR	Drug Utilization Review
EC	European Community
ECDS	Eastern Caribbean Drug Service
ED	Erectile Dysfunction
EDL	Essential Drugs List
EFTA	European Free Trade Agreement
EMA	European Medicines Agency

EU	European Union
FDA	Food and Drug Administration
FDCs	Fixed-Dose-Combination/Fixed Dose Combination Medicines
FHC	Female Health Company
FMSAE	French Ministries of Social Affairs and Economy
FTA	Free Trade Agreement
FTAA	Free Trade of the Americas Agreement
G8	Group of Eight: Canada, France, Germany, Italy, Japan, UK, USA, Russian Federation
GATB	Global Alliance for TB Drug Development
GB	Great Britain
GDF	Global TB Drug Facility
GDP	Gross Domestic Product
GFATM	Global Fund to Fight HIV, TB, and Malaria
GFHR	Global Forum for Health Research
GMP	Good Manufacturing Practices
GRRF	Genetic Recognition Resources Fund
GTAG	Global Treatment Access Group (Canada)
HALE	Healthy Life Expectancy (WHO)
HDI	Human Development Index
Health GAP	Health Global Access Project
HIV	Human Immunodeficiency Virus
HoC	House of Commons
HSPH	Harvard School of Public Health
HUGO	Human Genome Organization
IAVI	International Aids Vaccine Initiative
ICC	International Criminal Court
ICESCR	International Covenant on Economic, Social & Cultural Rights
ICTSD	International Center for Trade and Sustainable Development
IFPMA	International Federation of Pharmaceutical Manufacturers Associations
IFRC&RCS	International Federation of Red Cross and Red Crescent Societies
IHR	Institutes of Health Research
ILO	International Labour Organization
IMS	IMS Health, Inc.
IoM	Institute of Medicine
IOWH	Institute for OneWorld Health
IP	Intellectual Property
IPR	Intellectual Property Rights
IRB	Institutional Review Board
IRC	International Red Cross
JAMA	*Journal of the American Medical Association*
LDC	Least Developed Country
LDL	Low-density lipoprotein

LP	Liberal Party (of Canada)
MCP	Marginal Cost of Production
MCSRTA	Mubarak City for Scientific Research and Technology Applications
MDG	Millennium Development Goals
MDR	Multi-Drug Resistant
MINEFI	Ministry of Economy, Finance and Industry
MLJ	Ministry of Law and Justice
MMAS	Massachusetts Male Aging Study
MMV	Medicines for Malaria Venture
MoH	Minister/Ministry of Health
MoI	Ministry of the Interior
MPDIMA	Medicare Prescription Drug Improvement and Modernization Act
MRDT	Medical Research and Development Treaty
MSA	Ministry of Social Affairs
MSF	Médecins Sans Frontières
MSH	Management Sciences for Health
NBAC	National Bioethics Advisory Commission
NCB	Nuffield Council on Bioethics
NCE	New Chemical Entity
NDA	New Drug Application
NDP	National Drug Policy
NGO	Non Governmental Organization
NHS	National Health Service
NIC	National Intelligence Council
NICE	National Institute of Clinical Excellence
NIEHS	National Institute of Environmental Health Sciences (NIH, DHHS)
NIH	National Institutes of Health
NIHCM	National Institute for Health Care Management
NME	New Molecular Entity
NPV	Net Present Value
NRTI	Nucleoside Reverse Transcriptase Inhibitor
NSAID	Non-Stereoidal Anti-Inflammatory Drug
NTE	National Trade Estimate
NVNB	Non-Violation Nullification of Benefits
OCGPDT	Office of the Controller General of Patents, Designs and Trademarks
OECD	Organization for Economic Cooperation and Development
OIG	Office of Inspector General (Department of Health & Human Services)
OPV	Oral Polio Vaccine
OTA	Office of Technology Assessment
PBAC	Pharmaceutical Benefits Advisory Committee
PBPA	Pharmaceutical Benefits Pricing Authority
PBS	Pharmaceutical Benefits Scheme
PEC	President of the European Commission

PEDFAR	President's Emergency Plan for AIDS Relief
PhRMA	Pharmaceutical Research and Manufacturers of America
PMPRB	Patented Medicines Prices Review Board
PNGIMR	Papua New Guinea Institute of Medical Research
PoC	Parliament of Canada
PPH	Primary Pulmonary Hypertension
PPP	Public–Private Partnership
PPRS	Pharmaceutical Price Regulation Scheme
QALYs	Quality Adjusted Life Years
RCT	Research on Clinical Trials
R&D	Research and Development
RDS	Respiratory Distress Syndrome
RTAM	Round Table on Access to Medicines
Rx&D	Canada's Research-Based Pharmaceutical Companies Association
SA	South Africa
SACU	Southern African Customs Union
SARS/SRS	Severe Acute Respiratory Syndrome
SC	Supreme Court
SCRP (KFPE)	Swiss Commission of Research Partnership with Developing Countries (Kommission des CASS für Forschungspartnerschaften mit Entwicklungsländern)
SSRI	Selective Serotonin Reuptake Inhibitor
TAC	Treatment Action Campaign (South Africa)
TAC/ALP	Treatment Action Campaign and the AIDS Law Project
TAM	Treatment Access Movement (Pan-African)
TB	Tuberculosis
TDR	The Special Program for Research and Training in Tropical Diseases
TGA	Therapeutic Goods Administration
TRIPS	Trade-Related Aspects of Intellectual Property Rights
UDHR	Universal Declaration of Human Rights
UKP	United Kingdom Parliament
UNAID	The Joint United Nations Program on HIV/AIDS
UNCESCR	United Nations Committee on Economic, Social and Cultural Rights
UNCHR	United Nations Commission on Human Rights
UNCTAD	United Nations Commission for Trade and Development
UNDP	United Nations Development Program
UNESCO	United Nations Education, Scientific and Cultural Organization
UNICEF	United Nations International Children's Emergency Fund
UNIDO	United Nations Industrial Development Organization
UNIFEM	United Nations Development Fund for Women
UNRISD	United Nations Research Institute for Social Development
USAID	United States Agency for International Development
USC	United States Congress

USDoC	United States Department of Commerce
USFDA	US Food and Drug Administration
USTR	United States Trade Representative
VHA	Veterans and Health Administration
WHO	World Health Organization
WMA	World Medical Association
WTO	World Trade Organization

The Power of Pills

Introduction

Pharmaceutical policy lies at the intersection of a diverse range of disciplines. Although this makes pharmaceutical policy immensely interesting, it also makes it challenging to understand, for the student, the policymaker, and even the educator. We were motivated by the pressing need for an interdisciplinary approach to pharmaceutical policy. No doubt our different disciplinary backgrounds helped us meet this ambitious goal. To that end, we have assembled a collection of thoughtful papers that illuminate many of the wide range of issues that pharmaceutical policy embraces. In the pages that follow, we include contributions of a social, ethical, and legal nature in an effort to develop more comprehensive thinking on the subject.

Health is a necessary precondition for all in our attempts to live satisfying, happy lives. In a global world, each of us has an interest in the health of others, including those who live in the developing world. The common concern of most contributors to this volume is that today's main approaches to drug research and development are suboptimal. Diseases that do not provide sufficient profit incentives to multinational pharmaceutical companies are disregarded. Those most affected by this response are the developed world's poor and hundreds of millions of people living in the developing world. Our authors analyze the international trade frameworks that determine these undesirable outcomes from legal, ethical, and policy perspectives. They provide a critique as well as constructive responses designed to tackle these problems. Contributions reflect on both international and national regulatory frameworks, fundamental issues such as the moral sustainability of intellectual property rights-based incentives for drug research and development, as well as the equitable sharing of benefits derived from research undertaken in developing countries. Long overdue critical analysis is also applied to recent high-profile attempts at wedding non-profit initiatives to market-driven solutions.

Although our focus is the pharmaceutical industry, this should not be interpreted to mean that we believe that changes to that industry will magically solve global health problems. We realize that the global poor face public health problems that go beyond what pharmaceutical companies can address. Nonetheless, it is necessary for each stakeholder to do what it can to alleviate the health problems that face the global poor.

Part I offers a wider perspective on the pharmaceutical industry. Joel Lexchin's chapter introduces many of the criticisms the industry faces. He discusses how pharmaceutical companies are motivated to increase their profits rather than focus on the healthcare needs of populations. He identifies a number of strategies firms use to increase profits that can lead to unethical practices. These include setting research priorities on "blockbuster" drugs, suppressing unfavorable results from post-marketing studies, and drug promotion practices which include direct-to-consumer advertising (DTCA) as well as drug promotion to physicians, which ignore the possible serious side-effects of a drug while overstating the drug's benefits.

Kristina M. Lybecker focuses on the tensions inherent in the socioeconomic construct that is today's pharmaceutical industry. On the one hand, it has a social contract to develop medicines that enhance the health of the public, but on the other it seeks to maximize profit. Lybecker explains the major challenges facing the industry today, such as longer drug development times, rising R&D costs, generic competition, and parallel importation.

Ann Mills, Patricia Werhane, and Michael Gorman, in a provocative essay, discuss how the pharmaceutical industry needs a new framework so that health needs in developing countries are addressed. The authors note that the patent system may be perceived as a prerequisite for business development for richer countries, but developing countries view it as an enormous obstacle to improving access to drugs. Mills et al. suggest alternatives which could help remedy this situation, including strengthening the ability of governments to require universities to grant non-exclusive licenses.

Warren Kaplan argues that we should expect hybrid structures to appear in the pharmaceutical industries of the important middle-income producers of generic medicines (e.g., India). Notwithstanding the possible effect of these structures on pharmaceutical innovation in middle-income countries, this restructuring is likely to have important consequences for access to affordable medicines. The effect of these hybrid structures on real pharmaceutical innovation in the established pharmaceutical industry and in the newer public–private initiatives is still unclear.

Next, Ian Marshall examines the relationship between physicians and the pharmaceutical industry and the issue of gift-giving to physicians. He enumerates several codes that are in place to regulate the relationship and notes that one major deficiency is that they are not being vigorously enforced.

Finally in Part I, Robert Freeman provides an industry perspective. He answers some of the criticisms directed at the pharmaceutical industry, particularly those concerning drug prices. For instance, in response to the criticism that the industry has excessive expenditures for marketing and sales of drugs, which from the public's perspective makes the industry seem profit-driven, Freeman argues that it is important for a company to develop various marketing tools because new drugs will not be prescribed by physicians in the absence of constant, repetitive communication through marketing. In contrast to the majority of the contributors to this volume, Freeman emphasizes that the pharmaceutical industry is aware of its corporate social responsibility to communities and countries in which they operate.

In Part II, we include a diverse group of chapters that address the normative and legal implications of the view that medicines are global public goods. Wendy Parmet points out that even though pharmaceuticals are not "classical" public goods insofar as they do not fulfill the criteria of being non-excludable or non-rivalrous, they are partial public goods because of their impact on public health. Parmet gives a number of examples drawn from the history of public health, including herd immunity, which is activated when the rate of vaccination is sufficiently high to interrupt the chain of transmission of a particular disease for everyone, including those who have not received the vaccination. Parmet also points out that medicines have not only a public nature, but also a global one. Given that the conditions of ill health are global, she argues that, from a normative point of view, we ought to share the medications that will reduce those illnesses. From a public policy perspective, and in the name of global public health, it is imperative that each nation adopts laws and policies that will facilitate the use of these medicines by the global community.

The demands of global justice are further explored by David Resnik. Resnik believes that international justice depends not on individuals, but primarily on nations because they stand to have the greatest impact. In view of international justice goals, global health inequalities need to be considered. Resnik looks at the implications of the main theories of justice and what our international obligations of justice are. He begins with Rawlsian egalitarianism and then considers the implications of utilitarianism in relation to questions about international justice.

In "Pharmacogenetics and Global (In)Justice" Søren Holm explains the effects of pharmacogenetics on global justice. The moral problem with pharmacogenetics is that it seems unlikely that there will be a trickle-down effect. He reasons in the following way. According to the trickle-down theory, the benefits of pharmaceutical R&D eventually trickle down to the poor once they become generics. While it is questionable whether this happens to a sufficient extent in practice, the question that concerns Holm is how pharmacogenetics will impact the poor. Holm considers two possible scenarios and concludes that on both the implications for the poor are dismal. Problems of global justice will thus be exacerbated.

In Part III, our contributors focus on the moral, social, and political issues surrounding the apparently intractable problem of neglected diseases, offering analysis and potential solutions. Nathan Ford outlines the reasons why some diseases are neglected, explaining that this phenomenon cannot easily be accounted for on the basis of a lack of knowledge, but is more readily explained by the fact that R&D in pharmaceuticals is driven by the markets of wealthy countries. The patent system fails to stimulate innovation for neglected diseases. Ford argues that adequate drug development should be viewed as a government responsibility and not as solely that of private philanthropy.

The next chapter focuses on more practical matters. James Orbinski and Barry Burciul discuss the efforts of the Drugs for Neglected Diseases Working Group (DND-WG) to find creative solutions to the problems of neglected diseases. For this group any solution or recommendation had to be "sustainable, affordable, need driven and involve input and active engagement of developing countries." In a short time, the working group created the Drugs for Neglected Diseases Initiative (DNDI). DNDI focused not only on funding and conducting R&D itself, but also on strengthening the R&D efforts of others. The authors draw an important distinction between neglected diseases and most-neglected diseases. The former may affect a few people in wealthy countries while the latter are exclusively the diseases of those in developing countries. Because of the poverty in developing countries, they offer no market to pharmaceutical companies for R&D. Orbinski and Burciul also examine various efforts to generate R&D for neglected diseases. They pose the important question: "Does a country's membership in the community of nations not entitle it to make certain demands of the rest of humanity?"

Aidan Hollis continues the discussion about neglected diseases and illuminates how research can foster R&D for neglected diseases. He makes the important point that poor countries not only face the problem of neglected diseases, but also must usually contend with a number of other problems, including a lack of doctors, nurses, clinics, hospitals, and equipment.

One of the more promising approaches to neglected diseases to surface in recent years, embraced by many government and non-government organizations (NGOs), are advanced purchase commitments (APC) in which large donors create markets for vaccines or medicines, thus generating R&D. After identifying significant moral and practical problems with this approach, Donald Light explores some of the social and political impetus behind the somewhat surprising international support for APCs.

Thomas Pogge, in "Harnessing the Power of Pharmaceutical Innovation," provides a good example of a workable pull mechanism. As with many contributors to this volume, Pogge finds the present patent system morally troubling as it pits the vital needs of impoverished patients against the desire of pharmaceutical companies to recoup their investment. He recommends rewarding pharmaceutical research in proportion to its impact on the global disease burden. Such an approach would have the advantage of both reducing the impact of neglected diseases on the poor and stimulating new profitable research for pharmaceutical organizations.

In Part IV, we turn to the issue of patents and pharmaceuticals. Adam Mannan and Alan Story argue that drug access could be improved if product patents were abolished. They argue that even if a process patent is present, competitors can find alternative processes or uses for the chemical compound and create price competition. To further support their argument, the authors explain how the patent system was created not because it had to create conditions for sustainable innovation, but for market protection. They note that, until recently, few countries even recognized pharmaceutical product patents and some countries, such as India, were able to develop a thriving industry as a result of the absence of product patents.

Michael Selgelid and Elin Sepers argue that there is a need to "incentivize" pharmaceutical firms to undertake research for diseases of the developing countries. They highlight and analyze the costs and benefits of a select number of international proposals, including those advanced by Thomas Pogge and the Consumer Project on Technology and Health. They conclude soberly that each proposal requires political will and substantial funding from wealthy developed nations. On each of these schemes the funds for pharmaceutical innovation would need to be assured upfront, and the vast majority of funds would need to come from NGOs, charities, and national governments.

Finally in this part, Kevin Outterson's thoughtful and comprehensive essay argues that low-income populations should not pay any patent appropriation rent for essential pharmaceuticals because to do so is both cruel and unnecessary – cruel in that people will die if a treatment is available yet unaffordable to them; unnecessary because low-income populations would never have contributed much toward global pharmaceutical rent extraction. Drugs used to treat global diseases, he argues, should be exempt from appropriation by providing generic drugs to the poor without undermining innovation from the pharmaceutical company. He concludes by proposing four new paradigms that could help resolve drug access issues.

In her paper, Lisa Forman demonstrates how bilateral and regional free trade agreements are imposing rigorous intellectual property law obligations on developing countries. This has in turn created TRIPS-plus standards for countries, which has potentially dire consequences on access to medicines in these countries. These trade agreements have effectively undercut countries' capacity to use flexibilities within the TRIPS Agreement to support public health objectives.

In Part V, we examine research and ethics. Increasingly, clinical research is undertaken in multi-center studies involving numerous countries and jurisdictions. Argentinian bioethicist Florencia Luna, a past president of the International Association of Bioethics, introduces one of the major issues debated in recent years in international research ethics in this context, namely the question of what constitutes appropriate standards of care for participating patients. The line taken by the U.S. National Institutes of Health and many American bioethicists has been that it is acceptable for developed world sponsors of such trials to provide less than the best proven therapeutic means of treatment to the trial participants. Developed world-based bioethicists do not always agree and Luna explains why.

Steve Miles takes this discussion further by asking how it can be ensured that the benefits of human genomic research that is undertaken in the developing world are equitably shared with the peoples living there. Miles argues that the socioeconomic gap between rich and poor nations is likely to grow unless developing countries establish research capacity prioritizing the health needs of their peoples. He takes a strong stance against the Human Genome Organization's view that the human genome should be seen as the collective property of humankind and should be freely explored by anyone so interested. Such an interpretation would primarily serve developed nations and compound the injustice committed against developing nations over centuries.

Next, in Part VI, we offer some insights into political activism and treatment access. Given market failures in drug access and R&D, activists in developed and developing countries are working on sustainable answers to the moral challenges posed to the patent system. Richard Elliott describes how Canadian civil society groups came together and began – successfully – lobbying their government about the TRIPS (Trade-Related Aspects of Intellectual Property Rights) Agreement and its relationship to access to essential medicines. The primary target of this coalition of civic society organizations was to see legislation introduced that would permit producers of generic drugs to obtain compulsory licenses for products under patent protection in Canada for the purpose of producing affordable medicines for export to developing countries.

Similarly, Brook K. Baker, in his passionate contribution, argues that treatment access activists should focus on placing access to essential drugs on the human rights agenda. Baker bases his arguments on the health-related provision in the 1948 UNDHR, and the UN's ICESCR. They effectively make provision of access to essential medicines a fundamental duty of all member states of the UN system. Baker acknowledges theoretical and historical concerns about human rights-based strategies, but maintains that important policy objectives in the realms of women's reproductive rights, labor, and environmental rights for instance, and on health-related rights have been realized by means of rights-based campaign tactics. He warns that human rights declarations are stillborn in the absence of civic society organizations and responsive states.

In Part VII we look at the role of governmental or national responsibilities. South African pharmacist João L. Carapinha addresses these issues from his country's perspective. Carapinha proposes a comprehensive public–private sector response to the treatment access challenge. He comes out strongly in favor of an interventionist government, noting the need for the developing country to intervene in the manufacturing sector and to direct it to produce affordable medications.

In line with reasons developed by Baker and Carapinha, Kinsley Wilson and colleagues also accept the premise that the state is primarily responsible for ensuring access to essential medicines. They suggest that countries should develop a National Drug Policy (NDP) and accompanying implementation plans. Countries need to establish adequate processes as far as the registration, selection, procurement, and distribution of drugs are concerned.

Thomas A. Faunce from Australia's National University explores appropriate policy options in response to pharmaceutical industry lobbying designed to undermine regulatory systems. He proposes the establishment of a global, socially responsive, cost-effective pharmaceutical pricing system. Faunce describes how currently employed national regulatory processes variably include encouraging generic competition, issuing compulsory licenses, and limiting pharmaceutical companies' profits, amongst others. He suggests that it is desirable to establish a "gold standard" global cost-effectiveness evaluation for pharmaceuticals.

As the chapter summaries demonstrate, this volume may help us to foster conditions in which our biomedical R&D capacities are truly serving the majority of people living on this planet. More R&D development must be undertaken to achieve this. Strong political will – in other words, resolute commitment by governments – is required. Lastly, we hope this volume inspires you to think differently about some of these topics if you are already familiar with them. If you are not, we hope it helps you to better understand them. For that, no matter how trivial, is a vital first step in helping to improve access to medicines globally.

Invariably, a book such as this relied on the assistance of many people to allow it to come to fruition. We are grateful to Neil McPherson for his outstanding help with research and manuscript preparation. Audrey Capuano helped with administration and research. We benefited enormously from her standards of excellence and good-natured disposition. We also wish to thank Anjali Lilani for her help with citations. She brought a lawyer's eye for detail even while working in India. We thank her for her care and dedication. We are also grateful to Nela Suka who provided wonderful support with manuscript preparation.

We worked very closely with David Castle of Pluto Press. He has been a wonderful editor and we are grateful to him for all his help. Pluto Press has been a welcoming publisher. We thank them for bringing their expertise to this book.

Finally, a word in defense of our decision to make extensive use of abbreviations in this book. Space constraints motivated us to create a register of acronyms and make extensive use of abbreviations. This is likely to require you to check occasionally for abbreviations with which you might be unfamiliar. We thank you for your understanding in this regard.

Jillian Clare Cohen, Toronto, Canada
Patricia Illingworth, Boston, USA
Udo Schüklenk, Glasgow, UK

Part I

Pharmaceutical industry profits and obligations

1 The pharmaceutical industry and the pursuit of profit

Joel Lexchin

For over 30 years profit levels in the pharmaceutical industry have outstripped profits in other industries by a wide margin, and the gap has been growing. Based on data from *Fortune* magazine, during the 1970s drug companies averaged 8.9 per cent profit as a percentage of revenue compared to 4.4 per cent for all Fortune 500 industries. In the 1980s, drug companies increased their margin by earning 11.1 per cent compared to 4.4 per cent for all Fortune 500 companies during the 1990s, the gap grew to 15.1 per cent compared to just 4.1 per cent (Public Citizen 2002). In the past couple of years, the pharmaceutical industry has fallen from first place in the Fortune rankings, but even at third place it still outpaces nearly all other industries in profitability (Fortune 500 2005).

Drug companies frequently claim that their profits are overstated because traditional accounting measures count R&D as an expense rather than an investment. This method reduces taxes, because all the R&D is deducted immediately instead of being spread over several years as other investments (e.g. machines and buildings) are. The firms really don't have much choice about how to handle these matters for tax purposes. But when it comes to calculating the return on investment – which is more a policy matter than a tax matter – the odd way in which R&D is handled creates a problem. Because R&D is left out of investment, the ratio of profits to total investment is distorted; the denominator is artificially small. That makes the return on investment look larger than it really is (Calfee 2004).

In the early 1990s, the OTA investigated this issue in depth for the period 1976–87. The accounting profit rate for the pharmaceutical companies was 4–6 percentage points per year higher in the study period (1976–87) than for the control firms, selected to be similar to pharmaceutical companies over a range of financial characteristics. Using alternative methodology, the OTA concluded that, after adjusting for differences in risk, returns to the pharmaceutical industry as a whole over the twelve-year period were 2–3 percentage points per year higher than returns to non-pharmaceutical firms (USC 1993). Therefore, although the drug industry remained above average in terms of profitability, there may be some merit to its defense.

This debate on the correct way to measure profits raises the much wider issue of what is an acceptable level of profit. The British have answered this through their PPRS, which sets a profit range for the industry at 17–21 per cent based on sales of pharmaceuticals to the NHS (DoH 2003). The rational for using this is somewhat murky. What is a fair profit is a question that will elicit a wide variety of responses depending on the point of view that is being adopted: industry might say "high enough to attract the capital needed for research and development," but the Treasury Department, which is paying the bills, might say "too high" to any figure.

Rather than continue a fruitless debate about "appropriate profit levels," this chapter takes the approach of looking at the activities that the industry engages in to achieve its profits, regardless of what they may be, and the consequences of those actions. Specifically I will examine the industry's priorities around how it directs its R&D money, how research is conducted, and ultimately how it is reported to both regulators and in medical journals. Part of this analysis will involve parsing the industry's argument that high profits are necessary because R&D is enormously expensive. Another major thrust will be an assessment of the incremental therapeutic value of new drugs. Next, I will look at tactics that industry uses to encourage sales of its products focusing on DTCA, promotion to physicians and off-label promotion, and the effect of these different types of promotion on prescribing and drug use. The following section will show how expanding the use of a drug is not confined to off-label promotion but includes widening indications for the product and loosening the boundaries around those indications. Safety issues can significantly affect the sales of products and an examination of how companies treat safety will be the topic of the penultimate section. Finally, I will examine the use of IPR, especially as drugs approach the end of their patent life.

Most of the material in this chapter is based on data from the U.S., which is the home of most of the multinational pharmaceutical companies as well as being by far the single largest market for drugs. Where necessary I also draw on information from other settings, such as Canada and Europe. I also utilize specific case histories to illustrate general points.

The research agenda

Pharmaceutical companies have never denied that they are motivated by profit, but the caveat has always been that there is no contradiction between profit-seeking behavior and delivering medications that satisfy healthcare needs. At present, in order to meet shareholder expectations on rates of return, the industry has increasingly been adopting a blockbuster mentality, meaning that it is looking for drugs that will generate annual sales in the order of at least US$500 million and preferably US$1 billion. What such a focus means is that drugs with low revenue potential will not be developed.

In a report by MSF, of 1,223 new chemical entities marketed between 1975 and 1997, only 13 (1 per cent) were specifically for tropical diseases, and just four could be considered to be products resulting directly from research activities of the pharmaceutical industry (Pécoul et al. 1999). More recently, the DND-WG and the HSPH sent questionnaires to the world's top 20 pharmaceutical companies to assess the level of R&D activity in five neglected diseases: sleeping sickness, leishmaniasis, Chagas disease, malaria and tuberculosis. Thirteen companies responded, eleven of which completed the questionnaire. In fiscal 2000, eight of the eleven spent nothing on

R&D for sleeping sickness, leishmaniasis and Chagas disease; only two spent anything on malaria research; and seven spent less than 1 per cent of their R&D budgets on any of the five diseases or failed to respond to the question (DND-WG 2001).

Even in the developed world market, size and the contribution a medication is expected to make to the bottom line play the largest role in determining whether companies invest in R&D on new molecules. In the mid- to late 1980s, 43 per cent of the terminations in the development of new compounds were for economic reasons versus 31 per cent for efficacy issues and 21 per cent for safety problems (DiMasi 1995). Companies do not hesitate to terminate ongoing clinical trials if their commercial priorities change, despite the fact that this means that there will be no meaningful results from these trials (Psaty and Rennie 2000).

Another indication of research priorities comes from an examination of the therapeutic value of new medications. Based on figures from the Canadian PMPRB only 14 out of 111 new chemical entities that were marketed in 1999–2003 were major therapeutic gains compared to the other 97, which were rated as having moderate, little, or no therapeutic advantage over existing treatments (PMPRB 2004). This assessment of the value of new drugs is echoed by evaluations done by the French drug bulletin *La revue Prescrire* between 1981 and 2004. In that time, the journal looked at almost 3,100 new products or new indications for existing drugs; out of that total 10 per cent were considered to be moderate to significant advances and another 15 per cent were rated as "possibly helpful", but over 68 per cent fell into the "nothing new" category (*La revue Prescrire* 2005). Garattini and Bertele noted that new anti-cancer drugs reaching the European market in 1995–2000 offered few or no substantial advantages over existing preparations yet in some cases cost an order of magnitude more (Garattini and Bertele 2002). This type of investment pattern makes rational economic sense from an industry whose prime motivation is profit-seeking as opposed to producing medications that meet the greatest health needs.

The outcome of clinical research

The outcome of clinical research on new drugs can have profound effects on the financial gains from the products. Trials with results that are unfavorable to the sponsor – that is, trials that find the drug to be less clinically or cost-effective or less safe than other drugs used to treat the same condition – have the potential to pose significant financial risks to companies. Pressure to produce results showing an association between the drug and a favorable outcome can potentially result in biases in the outcome of industry-sponsored research. The question of bias has recently been investigated by a number of authors. Lexchin and colleagues combined the results of 15 studies (18 different comparisons between industry- and non-industry-funded research) using meta-analytic techniques (Lexchin et al. 2003). The summary odds ratio for favorable outcomes for research with industry sponsorship was 4.05 (95 per cent CI, 2.98, 5.51). Their results applied across a wide range of disease states, drugs, and drug classes, over a period spanning at least two decades and regardless of the type of research being assessed – pharmacoeconomic studies, clinical trials, or meta-analyses of clinical trials.

Subsequently, three similar articles have appeared. In one of these, Als-Nielsen et al. (2003) analyzed 370 RCTs in 25 meta-analyses in the Cochrane Library. The experimental drug was recommended as treatment of choice in 16 per cent of trials funded by non-profit organizations and in 51 per cent with for-profit sponsorship. Trials funded by the latter type of organization had a 5.3 times greater chance (95 per cent CI, 2.0, 14.4) of recommending the product being tested as the treatment of choice compared to trials with non-profit sponsorship.

Suppression of unfavorable results

Besides biasing the results, companies have also suppressed unfavorable research. GlaxoSmithKline did not publish results that showed that paroxetine (Paxil™) was ineffective for the treatment of depression in children and adolescents because, according to an internal company memo, "It would be commercially unacceptable to include a statement that efficacy had not been demonstrated, as this would undermine the profile of paroxetine" (Kondro and Sibbald 2004: 783). The *Wall Street Journal* claims that "internal Merck e-mails and marketing materials as well as interviews with outside scientists show that the company fought forcefully for years to keep safety concerns from destroying the drug's [Vioxx's] commercial prospects" (Mathews and Martinez 2004: A1).

Biases in publication

Just as research results may have economic consequences, so too will published results. Companies try to ensure that what is published will reflect favorably on their products. One set of researchers obtained access to the data that were submitted to Swedish regulatory authorities as part of the approval process for a number of SSRIs and then compared these studies with the ones that were eventually published (Melander et al. 2003). Three types of bias were identified: multiple publication of single trials; selectively publishing studies showing positive effects as stand-alone publications; and using analytic techniques that were more likely to produce favorable results. All three types have the effect of making the product look more effective or safer. Multiple publication of industry-funded trials has been documented in other clinical areas as well (Gøtzsche 1989; Huston and Moher 1996). Redundant and fragmented publications may give an artificially inflated impression of the value of a product and, if unrecognized, may be counted multiple times in a meta-analysis. The end result will be higher sales.

The CLASS study published in *JAMA* in 2000 appeared to confirm the gastrointestinal protective effects of celecoxib (Celebrex™) over traditional NSAIDs after six months of treatment (Silverstein et al. 2000). However, material on the website of the FDA revealed a number of discrepancies between the data as published in *JAMA* and those submitted to the FDA. The published trial actually combined the results of two trials, one that continued for twelve months and the second which ran for 16 months. At 12–16 months there was no difference in gastrointestinal adverse effects between the celecoxib and traditional NSAID groups (Hrachovec and Mora 2001; Wright et al. 2001).

Drug companies are also frequently accused of ghostwriting, the practice of writing an article favorable to one of their products and then seeking a well-known clinician to sign it. Fugh-Berman (2005) recounts her experience with an article describing interactions between herbal preparations and anticoagulants; Healy analyzes publications on the anti-depressant sertraline (Zoloft™) (Healy and Cattell 2003); and the *Hartford Courant* describes how Wyeth-Ayerst amended manuscripts to remove unfavorable data about its diet medication fenfluramine (Pondimin™) (Kauffman and Julien 2000).

Drug prices

Nearly all developed countries, with the exception of the U.S., exercise some control over drug prices. In the absence of price controls, pharmaceutical manufacturers set U.S. prices for brand-name products at levels that are, in general, 30–40 per cent higher than those in Canada and Europe (Danzon and Furukawa 2003) making drugs unaffordable, especially for the one third of American seniors who lack drug insurance (Poisal and Chulis 2000). In order to protect its ability to set prices without government interference the industry used its lobbying power to ensure that the U.S. federal government would not be able to negotiate price discounts when the new Medicare drug benefit came into effect in 2006. Over a ten-year period this benefit is expected to cost American taxpayers US$400 billion. Out of that total, according to one estimate, as much as US$139 billion will be net profits for drug companies (Sager and Socolar 2003).

Companies justify these prices as necessary to generate profit levels sufficient to attract the capital necessary for researching and developing the next generation of drugs. A widely cited article by DiMasi and colleagues puts the figure for bringing a new drug to market at US$802 million (DiMasi, Hansen, and Grabowski 2003).

There is serious debate about the accuracy of DiMasi et al.'s calculations. To begin with their figure does not apply to all new drugs, just NCEs (drug molecules that have never been marketed before). Only 36 per cent (467 out of 1,284) of new drugs approved in the U.S. between 1990 and 2004 were NCEs; all the others were new formulations, or combinations, of existing drugs (USFDA 2005). DiMasi et al. invited 24 companies out of 33 members in PhRMA to submit data on drug development costs; only twelve accepted and data from two were not useable. The data that the companies supplied could not be independently audited and therefore there was no way of knowing exactly what was counted as a research cost. Only drugs that were developed in-house were included, therefore products produced in conjunction with the NIH, charities, or other institutions would have been excluded. Based on other data, that restriction would have excluded as many as 33 per cent of drugs made by the sample firms (DiMasi et al. 1991). Finally, DiMasi et al. did not deduct tax credits that companies receive for doing research from the total, arguing strenuously that an after-tax figure is "inadequate for our purposes and potentially misleading" (DiMasi, Hansen, and Grabowski 2003: 174). However, elsewhere this is precisely what DiMasi and others did – use an after-tax figure for R&D costs. By doing so they reduced the pre-tax estimate of US$686 million by 30 per cent to US$480 million (Grabowski, Vernon, and DiMasi 2002).

Estimates of total industry R&D spending, and therefore the profit levels necessary to generate that level of spending, also need to be questioned. In 2000, PhRMA reported that the industry spent US$21,364 billion on in-house and contracted out research (PhRMA 2004), but the amount from the survey done by the NSF was US$15,451 billion (NSF 2003), leaving a gap of almost US$6 billion to be explained.

Drug promotion

In order to encourage the rapid uptake of new high-priced drugs and, the industry would say, to inform physicians and consumers about improved medications, the industry spends billions marketing its products. DTC advertising of prescription drugs represents the most rapidly escalating portion of promotion expenses, rising from US$791 million in 1996 to US$3,235 billion in 2003 (IMS 2005). This level of promotion can have serious negative consequences.

Many serious side-effects come to light only after a drug has been marketed. Lasser and colleagues looked at 548 NCEs introduced in the U.S. between 1975 and 1999. Fifty-six of these were withdrawn or needed a new, FDA mandated safety warning (the so-called black box warning) post-marketing (Lasser et al. 2002). Often, optimal doses of new drugs are not known at launch and have to be reduced for safety reasons. Out of 354 NCEs approved by the FDA between 1980 and 1999, 58 had their recommended doses cut due to safety concerns (Cross et al. 2002). It is new drugs, whose ultimate safety profile is unknown, that are being subjected to the heaviest DTC marketing.

Pre-marketing trials are usually done on highly selected groups of patients – usually the middle-aged who are not taking other medications, do not have any other major medical problems, and who have definite diagnoses. When drugs are marketed and heavily advertised they are going to be used on a much wider range of people than they were initially tested on, with unknown results. Consider the example of Merck and rofecoxib (Vioxx™), a COX-2 inhibitor used to treat inflammation. In 2001, Merck spent US$135 million on DTC advertising of this product (Yuan and Duckwitz 2002) helping to contribute to its use by 20 million Americans and annual sales of US$2.5 billion. However, many of the people who received rofecoxib (and other COX-2s) were at low risk for the complications from traditional NSAIDs and could have safely used these much less expensive products. According to estimates, this inappropriate use accounted for more than 63 per cent of the growth of COX-2s between 1999 and 2002 (Dai, Stafford, and Alexander 2005). At the same time, it is also undoubtedly true that a relatively large number of people who received these drugs were elderly and therefore at high risk for cardiovascular disease. As a result of this widespread use, partly fueled by DTCA, there was an estimated 88,000–140,000 excess cases of serious coronary artery disease in the U.S. (Graham et al. 2005).

Although the industry claims that DTCA has educational value, an analysis of print and broadcast advertisements reveals significant information gaps in both. Most print ads did not contain basic elements of information a person might need to assess the usefulness of a treatment, such as how a drug works (missing in 64 per cent) or the likelihood of treatment success (missing in 91 per cent). Only 29 per cent of advertisements mentioned any treatment alternatives and very few provided educational content on the treated health condition beyond its name and, in 60 per cent of ads, one or more symptoms. Ninety-one per cent of the ads did not discuss any myths or misconceptions about the disease(s) the drug was designed to treat (Bell, Wilkes, and Kravitz 2000). Broadcast advertisements were no better: 83 per cent presented risk information in one continuous segment, rather than interspersing the information throughout the ad; 70 per cent did not provide any information about risk factors or symptoms that might raise awareness amongst undiagnosed people; only 34 per cent informed consumers that the drug might not work for everyone; and only one directed consumers to seek information about the portrayed indication (Kaphingst and DeJong 2004).

The amount of money spent by the industry promoting drugs to physicians dwarfs the amount spent on DTCA by almost an order of magnitude at US$22 billion (IMS 2005). Most of that money goes to two types of promotion – drug sampling and the expenses related to visits by pharmaceutical sales representatives. As with DTCA the vast majority of the money goes to promoting new drugs, with potentially the same consequences from overuse. Accepting drug samples has been associated with inappropriate prescribing for hypertension (Boltri, Gordon, and Vogel 2002). Analyses of interactions between sales representatives and doctors done in Australia, Finland, and France show that detailers rarely spontaneously mention safety information about their products and frequently overemphasize their products' benefits (Lexchin 1997; La revue Prescrire 1999). Probably as a result of the selective information that doctors receive, studies in various countries have consistently found that the more they rely on information they receive from detailers, the less appropriate is their prescribing (Bower and Burkett 1987; Berings, Blondeel, and Habraken 1994; Caudill et al. 1996; Powers et al. 1998). Besides promoting drugs through sampling and visits from sales representatives, companies may try to increase sales through what is termed off-label promotion. Drugs can legally be promoted only for uses for which they have received official FDA approval. However, there are well-documented cases where companies have aggressively promoted products for indications that have not received FDA approval. One recent example of this as reported by the *Boston Globe* involves the anti-epilepsy drug gabapentin (Neurontin™), initially marketed by Parke-Davis and then by Pfizer after it bought Parke-Davis (Kowalczyk 2002; Harris 2004).

Expanding the market

Drugs that can successfully be promoted for a widening range of conditions, or where the boundaries of the condition can be expanded, represent an attractive market for companies looking for larger sales and profits.

Market expansion is particularly prevalent in so-called "lifestyle diseases." In the late 1990s, SmithKlineBeecham received approval to market paroxetine (Paxil™) for the treatment of social phobia. This disorder can be distressing and disabling for those who suffer from it, limiting their ability to interact with the outside world. But what we risk now is an extension of the definition of social phobia to include "shyness," given the cultural acceptance of an extrovert norm. In the U.S., there is a coalition of non-profit groups, the ADAA, partially funded by SmithKlineBeecham, which has built a public awareness campaign for social phobia around the slogan "Imagine Being Allergic to People." This campaign was being orchestrated by SmithKlineBeecham's public relations firm. Some of this work was being done *pro bono* and the rest was paid for directly by the drug company. In July 1999 as part of its effort, the ADAA held a press conference to publicize the findings of a study that purported to quantify the high economic cost of anxiety disorders. The study in question was underwritten by a group of drug manufacturers (Lexchin 2001).

A month after 9/11, GlaxoSmithKline (the product of a merger of SmithKlineBeecham with Glaxo Wellcome) attempted to play on people's fears to further increase the sales of paroxetine. The company used an advertisement of a woman walking on a crowded street, her face strained, in a crowd otherwise blurred. The caption read "Millions suffer from chronic anxiety. Millions could be helped" (Mintzes 2002: 908).

Pfizer has turned sildenafil (Viagra™) from a very useful drug for a limited population – men with erectile dysfunction due to conditions like spinal cord injury, diabetes, and peripheral vascular disease – into something that generates more than a billion dollars a year in sales. The company lumps together statistics for minimal, moderate, and complete erectile dysfunction to come up with a figure that 30 million Americans aged between 40 and 70 suffer from the condition and, implicitly, require treatment. It inflates the drug's success rate by quoting figures about the number of men who experience improved erections (80 per cent), not the number who are able to achieve intercourse (Pfizer 2004) which is more in the range of 50–60 per cent (Burls et al. 1998). On its website, the message from Pfizer is that Viagra is for any man who has ever had even the occasional problem with ED (Pfizer 2004).

Safety

Just as the results of clinical trials can have significant effects on sales, so can safety concerns. When confronted with a situation where a highly profitable drug has its sales threatened by safety concerns companies will at times opt to minimize the problem. Observations over the last 15 years suggest that opting for profits over safety is a recurring practice. In 1990, 30 per cent of Upjohn's healthcare sales came from psychopharmacological products, with Halcion™ (triazolam), a sleeping pill, contributing US$726 million in sales (Abraham and Sheppard 1999). When confronted with reports that triazolam was associated with amnesia, aggressiveness, agitation, and other psychiatric side-effects, a spokeswoman for Upjohn defended her company by saying, "Upjohn puts nothing ahead of patients' health. We stand by the fact that our science is sound and that Halcion remains safe and effective medication when it is used as recommended in the labelling" (Abraham and Sheppard 1999: 110). The findings of an FDA inspections report saw the situation differently. It stated that a key Upjohn study on the safety of the drug had represented a "gross and seminal failure to properly tabulate data" and that "the claim [made by Upjohn] that the overall incidence of subjects reporting adverse effects would not change is misleading. In fact, the overall incidence and other numbers did change because the report was roughly 30 per cent incomplete" (Abraham and Sheppard 1999: 109). The FDA report further states that "the firm [Upjohn] attempted to gain approval for long-term use of the drug even though available evidence indicated that long-term use was both dangerous and medically untenable" (Abraham and Sheppard 1999: 109).

A second example of the phenomenon comes from the actions that Wyeth took regarding its diet pill Redux™ (dexfenfluramine). An earlier version of dexfenfluramine, fenfluramine (Pondimin™), had been shown to cause an invariably fatal form of lung disease, PPH. Market research indicated that sales of dexfenfluramine would peak at about US$900 million in 1998 if there was just a warning about PPH on the drug's label. However, if there was a black box warning, sales would drop to US$100 million (Mundy 2001). Wyeth's vice-president for women's health noted in a 1995 memo that "if . . . Redux has a black box for PPH . . . this would likely be an extremely strong negative" (Mundy 2001: 155). As a result Wyeth strongly resisted the FDA placing a black box warning on its product and spoke frequently with the FDA about this issue and was in contact with U.S. legislators to voice its disapproval. When Wyeth finally agreed to a black box warning in 1997, it was still objecting to the wording that the FDA wanted; specifically it did not want the warning to mention dexfenfluramine by name (Mundy 2001).

Just as companies may be reluctant to acknowledge side-effects that may significantly influence the sales of highly profitable drugs, so too they seem to be averse to doing the research that might find these problems in the first place. The FDA has looked at the outcomes of post-marketing commitments that companies made in writing when they received approval for their drugs. (The FDA has no authority to require post-marketing studies to be done and not all of them were necessarily for safety issues.) Between 1991 and 2000, only 882 of 2,400 (37 per cent) commitments for pharmaceuticals and 44 of 301 (15 per cent) for biologics had been completed (USFDA 2002).

Intellectual property rights and patents

The TRIPS Agreement, one of the treaties enforced by the WTO, has set a 20-year patent life for all products, including pharmaceuticals. The clock starts when an application for a patent is filed with the appropriate national patent office. During that time companies have the exclusive right to sell the product within the national market.

In the case of pharmaceuticals, once low-cost generic competitors appear the brand-name product will lose the bulk of the market share since brand-name manufacturers do not compete on price with generic manufacturers (CBO 1998). Therefore, brand-name companies are keen to maximize the patent life of their products. Industry claims that each day that approval of a drug is delayed costs US$1.3 million. In order to further the goal of getting drugs on the market more rapidly, in 1992 the industry agreed to pay user fees to the FDA, with the proviso that the money only be used to hire additional reviewers in order to speed up new drug approvals. As of the start of 2005, about 18 per cent of the agency's US$1.7 billion budget comes from these user fees (Slater 2005) and between 1993 and 2001 approval times for standard new drugs that did not receive priority reviews dropped from 27 to 19 months (OIG 2003).

While faster approval times benefit the industry financially, a comparison of new drug approvals in the U.S. and the UK between 1971 and 1992 has shown that they are also associated with a greater number of withdrawals due to safety problems that are missed in the pre-marketing review (Abraham and Davis 2002). Supporting that position, a 2001 survey of FDA reviewers by the OIG found that 40 per cent who had been at the agency at least five years indicated that the review process had worsened during their tenure in terms of allowing for in-depth, science-based reviews (OIG 2003).

In an effort to generate more information about the use of medications in children, the U.S. agreed to grant companies an extra six months' patent protection if the companies voluntarily tested their drugs in children. While the industry has started testing many more drugs in children many of these products are not the ones that are used most frequently in pediatric practice but rather the ones that generate the largest sales for the companies. The extra patent life that Bristol-Myers Squibb will receive for testing the anti-diabetic metformin (Glucophage™) will amount to US$648; at the same time fewer than 1 per cent of prescriptions for metformin are written by pediatricians (HRG 2001). Although pediatric studies cost between US$1 million and $7.5 million each over a 20-year period the pediatric exclusivity provision will generate an additional US$29 billion in sales (HRG 2001).

Brand-name companies have also developed tactics to delay the entry of generic drugs. A report from the FTC outlined two of the most common methods (FTC 2002). A 30-month stay of FDA approval of a generic application is invoked if a brand-name company receives notice of the application and files suit for patent infringement within 45 days of that notice. Filing of the lawsuit delays FDA approval for up to 30 months. This has historically approximated the time required for FDA review. However, if a brand-name company lists an additional patent after the generic applicant has filed its application, more than one 30-month stay may be generated. The generic applicant is required to re-certify to this later-listed patent, and FDA approval can be stayed for an additional 30 months.

Conclusion

Drug companies exist within a market economy and cannot be expected to deviate from the norms of that economy. By law, corporations have a "duty to put shareholders' interests above all others and no legal authority to serve any other interests" (Bakan 2004: 36). Corporations are amoral; they need to obey the law, but beyond that their obligation is to be as profitable as possible. Corporate social responsibility or anything that reduces profitability in the long term violates the corporation's fiduciary duty to its shareholders and leaves it vulnerable to a civil lawsuit.

Drug companies embrace this logic and, as a result, undertake the type of activities that have been documented in this chapter. They tailor their research agendas to produce products that have the largest market potential regardless of medical need. They try to ensure that the results of clinical trials are as favorable as possible to the drugs being tested, and if the market for drugs is not favorable, then they terminate development of the drug. When there are negative trials companies will try to ensure that those results are not made public. Similarly, companies employ a variety of tactics that produce publications that present their products in the best possible light. In markets where they are free to set their prices, primarily the U.S., companies price drugs in order to ensure the highest rate of return. They justify this return by citing studies that show high R&D costs regardless of the validity of these studies. Medications are promoted in such a way as to push the use of the newest and most expensive version and like the positive bias in publications, advertising emphasizes the good points about the drugs and downplays or ignores safety concerns. Where there are profitable market niches to be found companies try to position their products to fill these gaps. With highly profitable drugs, companies try to minimize emerging safety issues to keep the products on the market as long as possible. Finally, the pharmaceutical industry strongly endorses intellectual property rights so as to maximize the period when brand-name companies have a sales monopoly and works to keep generics from appearing.

Through engaging in these activities companies keep profits high by any measure and also produce medications that make a profound impact on people's lives. Drugs to treat HIV/AIDS have significantly improved lives; in severe erosive gastroesophageal reflux proton pump inhibitors have proven to be major gains. Whether these achievements justify the tactics that companies use to ensure profitability is something for society at large to decide.

References

Abraham, J. and C. Davis. 2002. *Mapping the Social and Political Dynamics of Drug Safety Withdrawals in the UK and the US.* Final report to ESRC on Project R000237658. Erie, PA: Millcreek Community Hospital and the LECOM School of Pharmacy.

Abraham, J. and J. Sheppard. 1999. *The Therapeutic Nightmare: The Battle over the World's Most Controversial Sleeping Pill.* London: Earthscan Publications.

Als-Nielsen, B., W. Chen, C. Gluud, and L. L. Kjaergard. 2003. Association of Funding and Conclusions in Randomized Drug Trials: a Reflection of Treatment Effect or Adverse Events? *JAMA* 290: 921–928.

Bakan, J. 2004. *The Corporation: The Pathological Pursuit of Profit and Power.* Toronto: Viking.

Bell, R. A., M. S. Wilkes, and R. L. Kravitz. 2000. The Educational Value of Consumer-targeted Prescription Drug Print Advertising. *Journal of Family Practice* 49: 1092–1098.

Berings, D., L Blondeel, and H. Habraken. 1994. The Effect of Industry-independent Drug Information on the Prescribing of Benzodiazepines in General Practice. *European Journal of Clinical Pharmacology* 46: 501–505.

Boltri, J. M., E. R. Gordon, and R. L. Vogel. 2002. Effect of Antihypertensive Samples on Physician Prescribing Patterns. *Family Medicine* 34: 729–731.

Bower, A. D. and G. L. Burkett. 1987. Family Physicians and Generic Drugs: A Study of Recognition, Information Sources, Prescribing Attitudes, and Practices. *Journal of Family Practice* 24: 612–616.

Burls, A., W. Clark, L. Gold, and S. Simpson. 1998. *Sildenafil – an Oral Drug for the Treatment of Male Erectile Dysfunction: West Midlands Region Development and Evaluation Committee (DEC) Report.*

Calfee, J. 2004. Personal email correspondence to author, November 26.

Caudill, T. S., M. S. Johnson, E. C. Rich and W. P. McKinney. 1996. Physicians, Pharmaceutical Sales Representatives, and the Cost of Prescribing. *Archives of Family Medicine* 5: 201–206.

Congressional Budget Office (CBO). 1998. *How Increased Competition from Generic Drugs has Affected Prices and Returns in the Pharmaceutical Industry*. Washington, DC: Government Printing Office.

Cross, J., H. Lee, A. Westelinck, J. Nelson, C. Grudzinskas, and C. Peck. 2002. Postmarketing Drug Dosage Changes of 499 FDA-approved New Molecular Entities, 1980–1999. *Pharmacoepidemiology and Drug Safety* 11: 439–446.

Dai, C., R. S. Stafford, and G. C. Alexander. 2005. National Trends in Cyclooxygenase-2 Inhibitor Use Since Market Release: Nonselective Diffusion of a Selectively Cost-effective Innovation. *Archives of Internal Medicine* 165: 171–177.

Danzon, P. M. and M. F. Furukawa. 2003. Price and Availability of Pharmaceuticals: Evidence from Nine Countries. *Health Policy* July–December Supplement: W3–521–536.

Department of Health (DoH). 2003. *Pharmaceutical Price Regulation Scheme – Seventh Report to Parliament*. London: DoH.

DiMasi, J. A. 1995. Success Rates for New Drugs Entering Clinical Testing in the United States. *Clinical Pharmacology and Therapeutics* 58: 1–14.

DiMasi, J. A., R. W. Hansen, H. G. Grabowski, and L. Lasagna. 1991. Cost of Innovation in the Pharmaceutical Industry. *Journal of Health Economics* 10: 107–142.

DiMasi, J. A., R. W. Hansen, and H. G. Grabowski. 2003. The Price of Innovation: New Estimates of Drug Development Costs. *Journal of Health Economics* 22: 151–185.

Drugs for Neglected Diseases Working Group (DND-WG). 2001. *Fatal Imbalance: The Crisis in Research and Development for Drugs for Neglected Diseases*. DND-WG/MSF. Available at: http://www.accessmed-msf.org/prod/publications.asp?scntid=30112001115034&contentt ype=PARA& [Accessed January 12, 2006].

Federal Trade Commission (FTC). 2002. *Generic Drug Entry Prior to Patent Expiration: An FTC Study*. Washington, DC: FTC.

Fortune 500. 2005. How the Industries Stack Up: Most Profitable Industries. *Fortune*, April 18.

Fugh-Berman, A. 2005. The Corporate Coauthor. *Journal of General Internal Medicine* 20. DOI: 10.1111/J/1525–1497.2005.0138.x.

Garattini, S. and V. Bertele. 2002. Efficacy, Safety, and Cost of New Anticancer Drugs. *British Medical Journal* 325: 269–271.

Gøtzsche, P. C. 1989. Multiple Publication of Reports of Drug Trials. *European Journal of Clinical Pharmacology* 36: 429–432.

Grabowski, H., J. Vernon and J. A. DiMasi. 2002. Returns on Research and Development for 1990s New Drug Introductions. *Pharmacoeconomics* 20 Supplement 3: 11–29.

Graham, D. J., D. Campen, R. Hui, M. Spence, C. Cheetham, G. Levy, S. Shoor, and W. A. Ray. 2005. Risk of Acute Myocardial Infarction and Sudden Cardiac Death in Patients Treated With Cyclo-oxygenase 2 Selective and Non-selective Non-steroidal Anti-inflammatory Drugs: Nested Case-control Study. *Lancet* 365: 475–481.

Harris, G. 2004. Pfizer to Pay US$420 Million in Illegal Marketing Case. *New York Times*, May 14.

Health Research Group (HRG). 2001. *Pediatric Exclusivity: Changes Needed to Assure Safety and Effectiveness of Medications for Children and More Affordable Drugs for Seniors*. Washington, DC: Public Citizen.

Healy, D. and D. Cattell. 2003. Interface between Authorship, Industry and Science in the Domain of Therapeutics. *British Journal of Psychiatry* 183: 22–27.

Hrachovec, J. B. and M. Mora. 2001. Reporting of 6-month vs 12-month Data in a Clinical Trial of Celecoxib. *JAMA* 286: 2398.

Huston, P. and D. Moher. 1996. Redundancy, Disaggregation, and the Integrity of Medical Research. *Lancet* 347: 1024–1026.

IMS. 2005. *Total US Promotion Spend by Type, 2003*. Plymouth Meeting, PA: IMS Health. Available at: http://www.imshealth.com/ims/portal/front/articleC/0,2777,6599_44304752_ 44889690,00.html [Accessed April 20, 2005].

Kaphingst, K. A. and W. DeJong. 2004. The Educational Potential of Direct-to-consumer Prescription Drug Advertising. *Health Affairs* 23, no. 4: 143–150.

Kauffman, M. and A. Julien. 2000. Scientists Helped Industry to Push Diet Drug Medical Research: Can We Trust It? *Hartford Courant*, April 10.

Kondro, W. and B. Sibbald. 2004. Drug Company Experts Advised Staff to Withhold Data About SSRI Use in Children. *CMAJ* 170: 783.

Kowalczyk, L. 2002. Use of Drug Soars Despite Controversy: Neurontin Maker Faces Probes into Marketing. *Boston Globe*, November 25.

Lasser, K. E., P. D. Allen, S. J. Woolhandler, D. U. Himmelstein, S. M. Wolfe, and D. H. Bor. 2002. Timing of New Black Box Warnings and Withdrawals For Prescription Medications. *JAMA* 287: 2215–2220.

Lexchin, J. 1997. What Information Do Physicians Receive from Pharmaceutical Representatives? *Canadian Family Physician* 43: 474–478.

——. 2001. Lifestyle Drugs: Issues for Debate. *CMAJ* 164: 1449–1451.

Lexchin, J., L. A. Bero, B. Djulbegovic, and O. Clark. 2003. Pharmaceutical Industry Sponsorship and Research Outcome and Quality: Systematic Review. *BMJ* 326: 1167–1170.

Mathews, A. W. and B. Martinez. 2004. Warning Signs: E-mails Suggest Merck Knew Vioxx's Dangers at Early Stage as Heart-risk Evidence Rose, Officials Played Hardball; Internal Message: 'Dodge!' *Wall Street Journal*, November 1.

Melander, H., J. Ahlqvist-Rastad, G. Meijer, and B. Beermann. 2003. Evidence B(i)ased Medicine – Selective Reporting from Studies Sponsored by Pharmaceutical Industry: Review of Studies in New Drug Applications. *BMJ* 326: 1171–1173.

Mintzes, B. 2002. Direct to Consumer Advertising is Medicalising Normal Human Experience. *BMJ* 324: 908–909.

Mundy, A. 2001. *Dispensing With the Truth: The Victims, the Drug Companies, and the Dramatic Story Behind the Battle Over Fen-phen*. New York: St. Martin's Press.

Office of Inspector General (OIG). 2003. *FDA's Review Process for New Drug Applications: A Management Review*, March. Washinton, DC: Department of Health and Human Services.

Patented Medicine Prices Review Board (PMPRB). 2004. *Annual Report 03*. Ottawa: PMPRB.

Pécoul, B., P. Chirac, P. Trouiller and J. Pinel. 1999. Access to Essential Drugs in Poor Countries: A Lost Battle? *JAMA* 281: 361–367.

Pfizer. 2004. *Viagra: Answers to Common Questions*. New York: Pfizer. Available at: http://www.viagra.com/consumer/general/commonQuestions.asp#answersEd2 [Accessed January 12, 2006].

——. 2005. *About Viagra*. New York: Pfizer. Available at: http://www.viagra.com/consumer/aboutViagra/index.asp [Accessed January 12, 2006].

Pharmaceutical Research and Manufacturers of America (PhRMA). 2004. *Pharmaceutical Industry Profile 2004*. Washington, DC: PhRMA.

Poisal, J. A. and G. S. Chulis. 2000. Medicare Beneficiaries and Drug Coverage. *Health Affairs* 19, no. 2: 248–256.

Powers, R. L., K. A. Halbritter, J. G. Arbogast, J. L. Neely, and A. J. Williams. 1998. Do Interactions with Pharmaceutical Representatives Influence Antihypertensive Medication Prescribing Practices of Family Medicine and General Internal Medicine Physicians? *Journal of General Internal Medicine* 13, Supplement: 13.

Psaty, B. M. and D. Rennie. 2000. Stopping Medical Research to Save Money: A Broken Pact with Researchers and Patients. *JAMA* 289: 2128–2131.

Public Citizen. 2002. *America's Other Drug Problem. A Briefing Book on the Rx Drug Debate*. Washington, DC: Public Citizen.

La revue Prescrire. 1999. Sales Representatives: A Damning Report by Prescrire Reps Monitoring Network. *Prescrire International* 8: 86–89.

——. 2005. A Review of New Drugs in 2004: Floundering Innovation and Increased Risk-taking. *Prescrire International* 14: 68–73.

Sager, A. and D. Socolar. 2003. *61 Percent of Medicare's New Prescription Drug Subsidy is Windfall Profit to Drug Makers*. Boston: Health Reform Program. Available at: http://www.healthreformprogram.org [Accessed January 15, 2005].

Silverstein, F. E., G. Faich, J. L. Goldstein, L. S. Simon, T. Pincus, A. Whelton, R. Makuch, G. Eisen, N. M. Agrawal, W. F. Stenson, A. M. Burr, W. W. Zhao, J. D. Kent, J. B. Lefkowith,

K. M. Verburg, and G. S. Geis. 2000. Gastrointestinal Toxicity with Celecoxib vs Nonsteroidal Anti-inflammatory Drugs for Osteoarthritis and Rheumatoid Arthritis: The CLASS Study: A Randomized Controlled Trial. *JAMA* 284: 1247–1255.

Slater, E. E. 2005. Today's FDA. *New England Journal of Medicine* 352: 293–297.

US Congress (USC). 1993. *Pharmaceutical R&D: Costs, Risks and Rewards, OTA-H-522*. Washington, DC: USC.

US Food and Drug Administration (USFDA). 2002. *Report to Congress. Reports on Postmarketing Studies [FDAMA 130]*. Washington, DC: FDA.

——. 2005. *CDER NDAs Approved in Calendar Years 1990–2004 by Therapeutic Potential and Chemical Type*. Washington, DC: FDA. Available at: http://www.fda.gov/cder/rdmt/pstable. htm [Accessed January 12, 2006].

Wright, J. M., T. L. Perry, K. L. Bassett, and G. K. Chambers. 2001. Reporting of 6-month vs 12-month Data in a Clinical Trial of Celecoxib. *JAMA* 286: 2398–2399.

Yuan, Y. and N. Duckwitz. 2002. *Doctors & DTC*. Plymouth Meeting, PA: IMS Health. Available at: http://www.imshealth.com/vgn/images/portal/cit_759/2005112345DoctorsDTC.pdf [Accessed January 12, 2006].

2 Social, ethical, and legal issues in drug development, marketing, and pricing policies: setting priorities: pharmaceuticals as private organizations and the duty to make money/ maximize profits

Kristina M. Lybecker

The pharmaceutical industry has an important social contract with the public to discover and develop medicines that have value in extending and enhancing life. Simultaneously, the industry must maintain its profitability, both to ensure the future stream of innovations and to provide investors with a return. Balancing the responsibilities to the public and to shareholders is further complicated by the inefficiencies of the global patent system, the disease burden of poor developing countries, national price control systems, and third-party payers.

The industry produces social goods characterized by high fixed costs, high information and regulatory costs, and relatively low marginal costs of production. While the existing patent system provides for limited monopoly power to reward innovation, it concurrently restricts access to medicines. Through Ramsey pricing the industry endeavors to recover the high costs of R&D, while adjusting prices across national markets to maximize consumer welfare. Although this arguably helps to enhance access to medicines, it does not help to bring drugs to market for the diseases that primarily afflict developing countries.

Both the inefficiencies and inequities inherent in the existing system have led scholars to develop alternative mechanisms for the protection of intellectual property in the pharmaceutical industry. Given the current policy environment and pressure on the industry, the current operating model must inevitably change. Preserving the incentive to invest in R&D while improving access to medicine would eliminate several of the distortions inherent in the patent system without curtailing the flow of new drugs.

Introduction

The pharmaceutical industry produces social goods characterized by high fixed costs, high information and regulatory costs, and relatively low marginal costs of production. While the existing patent system provides for limited monopoly power to reward innovation, it concurrently restricts access to medicines. The industry must balance their responsibility to provide affordable drugs to the public, while providing shareholders a return on investment. Through Ramsey pricing the industry endeavors to recover the high costs of R&D, while adjusting prices across national markets to maximize consumer welfare. Although this arguably helps to enhance access to medicines, it does not help bring drugs to market for the diseases that primarily afflict developing countries. The public debate surrounding this balance is becoming increasingly acrimonious and policymakers are more and more dissatisfied with the status quo. As a result, the pharmaceutical industry faces a number of challenges, both external and internal. The industry's objective, profitability, and the challenges to each are considered here.

Objective of the firm

As an essential player in the healthcare arena, the pharmaceutical industry has an important social contract with the public to discover and develop medicines that have value in extending and enhancing life. Simultaneously, pharmaceutical firms must maintain their profitability, to ensure the future stream of innovations and to provide investors with a return. Balancing the responsibilities to the public and to shareholders is a delicate process further complicated by the inefficiencies of the global patent system, an increasingly challenging research environment, the disease burden of poor developing countries, national price control systems, competition from generics and copycat drugs, and pharmaceutical counterfeiting.

Like most firms, pharmaceutical manufacturers seek to maximize their revenues and contain their costs. In contrast to most industries, the price-setting process has become controversial and the subject of an ugly public debate. In this industry, the structure of research, development, and manufacturing costs obfuscates pricing decisions. For a wide range of drugs, the marginal cost of production is relatively low. This would seem to suggest that drugs should be available at low prices, thereby ensuring greater access. However, the pharmaceutical industry is simultaneously characterized by high R&D costs, a global cost that must be shared across all markets. In 2004, U.S.-based pharmaceutical companies invested US$38.8 billion in R&D (PhRMA 2005).

Economic theory has established that Ramsey pricing is the most efficient mechanism for recovering this shared cost. This is accomplished by charging consumers different prices based on their price sensitivity. That is, the markup varies in proportion to the consumers' price elasticities of demand. Consumers with relatively inelastic demand, who are comparatively insensitive to price changes, will be charged a larger markup over marginal cost than consumers with more elastic demand, those who are more price-sensitive. The result is the set of prices that yields sufficient revenue to cover the shared development cost while generating the highest level of consumer welfare. The ability to price discriminate across markets is a key component in safeguarding the profitability of the industry.

Through Ramsey pricing the industry endeavors to recover the high costs of R&D, while adjusting prices across national markets to maximize consumer welfare. Although this helps to enhance access to medicines, it does not help to bring drugs to market for the diseases that primarily afflict developing countries. Unfortunately, the disease burden of the most profitable global markets does not correspond to the disease burden of developing nations. For at least 20 diseases, more than 99 per cent of the disease burden is borne by low-income countries. (Lanjouw 2001). Since the U.S. alone accounts for close to half of industry profits, diseases specific to low-income countries receive little attention and fewer research dollars. Significant demand in industrialized countries provides a sizeable incentive for investing in R&D tailored to the diseases of those markets. As a result, a disproportionate share of new drugs is developed for the maladies of the industrialized nations. Consider, for example, that in 1998, only 0.5 per cent of pharmaceutical patents issued related to the diseases that almost exclusively impact developing countries (Lanjouw 2003). This is also reflected in the region's share of pharmaceutical sales. In 2003, global pharmaceutical sales were largely focused on North America (49.2 per cent), the European Union (24.7 per cent), and Japan (11.2 per cent), with Asia, Africa, and Australia (8 per cent), Latin America (3.7 per cent) and the rest of Europe (3.2 per cent) comprising less than one sixth of global sales (Sellers 2004).

While efficiency dictates that different prices are charged in different markets, observable price differentials are not always due to reasons of economic efficiency or profit-maximization. Pharmaceutical prices are widely subject to nation-specific government regulation and a host of other factors. Bale (1998) provides a comprehensive review of potential reasons for price differences across countries. These include differences in such factors as IPR regimes, product liability laws, inflation rates, exchange rates, governmental price controls, per capita income, and regulatory systems.

The importance of IPR protection

While global price discrimination enables the pharmaceutical industry to recover their costs and maintain their profitability, it is patent protection for their intellectual property that assures their survival. Given the ease of replicating chemical and pharmaceutical innovations, IPR protection, through product and process patents, ensures that the researcher is able to appropriate the returns to R&D. This protection is disproportionately more important in the pharmaceutical and chemical industries than in most other sectors (see Cohen, Nelson, and Walsh 1996; Levin et al. 1987; a comprehensive review of such studies may be found in Lybecker 2000). This stems from both the high costs of R&D and the competitive nature of the industry. The latter has increased with the aggressive introduction of generics upon patent expiry. In a study of 18 patented brand-name drugs, Grabowski and Vernon (1990) found that generics gained close to half the market share within two years of entry.

While estimating the cost of drug development is controversial, there is no denying that pharmaceutical R&D is an expensive undertaking. Lengthy development times, extensive clinical trials and regulatory requirements, and the low probability of success, all contribute to the costly enterprise. According to a recent estimate by the Tufts Center for the Study of Drug Development, it is now close to US$800 million (Tufts 2003). While the DiMasi figures have been corroborated by a BCG study, estimates from the industry nevertheless attract considerable criticism. In contrast to the industry estimates, Love contrasts earlier DiMasi data to an examination of 58 NIH-funded clinical trials which placed the expected cost at "less than 30 per cent of the DiMasi et al. numbers" (Love 1997: 24). Regardless of the magnitude of the estimates, R&D costs have been rising rapidly due to increasing registration costs, and more demanding regulatory requests for evidence of therapeutic and economic effectiveness. For example, since 1980 the average number of clinical trials required for filing a NDA has more than doubled (Glover 2002).

Fundamentally, patents involve a trade-off between rewarding innovation and market power. Patent protection balances limit monopoly power (a static inefficiency) against the incentive to create and share new research (a dynamic efficiency). This balance also reflects the inherent tension between two public policy objectives: safe, affordable access to a variety of cutting-edge drugs and continued pharmaceutical innovation through investment in R&D. While the existing patent system provides for limited monopoly power to reward innovation, it concurrently restricts access to medicines.

Global challenges facing the pharmaceutical industry

The pharmaceutical industry is currently confronting a variety of challenges, both internal and external. The future profitability of the industry is threatened by several factors: a shrinking research pipeline, increasing R&D costs and approval times, a growing generic industry, price controls, parallel importation, and heightened pharmaceutical counterfeiting. The confluence of all these factors has reduced the profit margins of the industry and contributed to an increasingly challenging global environment.

Longer drug development times and rising R&D costs

Pharmaceutical R&D is a difficult, lengthy, and expensive process and increasingly so. Bringing a chemical compound from discovery to market is a risky process that takes more than a decade. The industry is investing more and more in R&D. Between 1980 and 2004, domestic R&D expenditures increased from US$1.55 billion to US$38.8 billion as firms searched for treatments for diseases that are increasingly complicated. At the same time, the rate of approvals fell and the regulatory requirements are increasing in number. Moreover, the amount of development time required to bring a drug from synthesis to approval is increasing. Between the 1960s and the 1990s, total drug development time increased from an average of 8.1 years to more than 14 years (PhRMA 2002). All these factors add to the cost of drug development, expose the companies to the economic risk and uncertainty of a longer development horizon, and ultimately raise the prices of innovative medicines.

Generic competition and parallel importation

The pharmaceutical marketplace has also become more crowded as innovative pharmaceutical firms compete with a growing number of generic producers as well as their own products via parallel importation. The passage of the 1984 Drug Price Competition and Patent Term Restoration Act (The Hatch–Waxman Act) intensified generic competition in the U.S., providing for an abbreviated application and expedited approval process. Since the law was passed, the generic industry's share of the U.S. prescription drug market has grown from 19 per cent to 47 per cent (PhRMA 2002). Prior to 1984, generic entry occurred three to five years following patent expiry. Many generic products now enter the market as soon as the innovator's patent expires, reducing market share and shortening the period of product exclusivity.

Beyond the generic industry, pharmaceutical firms now find that they are competing with themselves through parallel importation. According to Ganslandt and Maskus, parallel imports are "legitimately produced goods imported legally into a country without the authorisation of a trademark, copyright, or patent holder. The essential purpose of such trade is arbitrage between countries with different prices" (Ganslandt and Maskus 2001: 1). The ultimate value of a patent depends in part on the geographic reach of its protection. Parallel importation diminishes this protection and reduces the ability of the patent holder to appropriate the returns to R&D, thus potentially diminishing the incentive to innovate. Moreover, it is unclear that consumers capture the gains from parallel importation of drugs. Ganslandt and Maskus (2001) examine the effects of parallel trade in pharmaceuticals in the Swedish market. The econometric analysis shows that the rents that accrue to parallel importers, which include the costs of the activity, may exceed the gains that accrue to consumers from lower prices. Ultimately, parallel importation of pharmaceuticals may decrease global welfare.

Price controls

Government price controls for pharmaceuticals are common in both developing and industrialized nations. Price control policies enhance the government's ability to provide affordable medicines to their populations, but undermine firms' patent protection and hinder innovative firms from recovering their research investments. Again, the trade-off between access and innovation lies at the heart of the issue. In comparison to the U.S., Europe spends 60 per cent less per capita on pharmaceuticals, prices are 25–35 per cent lower, and utilization rates are 30 per cent lower per capita for new products (Gilbert and Rosenberg 2004). However, this has come at a cost. Reversing an earlier trend, fewer drugs are now launched in Europe. Between 1993 and 1997, 81 drugs were launched in Europe and 48 in the U.S., but between 1998 and 2002, 44 drugs were launched in Europe compared to 85 in the U.S. (Gilbert and Rosenberg 2004). The decline of the European pharmaceutical industry is further evidence of the impact of price controls. While R&D investment rose fivefold in the U.S., it grew by only 2.4 times in Europe between 1990 and 2001 (Moser 2003). Moreover, European firms are relocating their research operations and headquarters to the U.S. These include Novartis (Swiss, 2002), Aventis (French-German, 1999), GlaxoSmithKline (UK, 2000), and Pharmacia (Swedish, 1995) (Moser 2003).

Counterfeit drugs

Given that drugs are very high-value products relative to their bulk, and in very high demand, the profitability and proliferation of counterfeit drugs is not surprising.

Estimates of the share of drugs that are counterfeit are difficult to come by and imprecise at best. Consider the following examples from specific countries: Brazil, 20 per cent (Land 1992); Nigeria, 60–70 per cent (Alubo 1994); Indonesia, 25 per cent (PhRMA 1997); Pakistan, 50 per cent (Hajari 1998); India, 20 per cent (Gereffi 1983); Columbia, 30 per cent (Capell et al. 2001). Overall, in developing countries, 70 per cent (Stipp 1996). While the numbers vary widely, some reports set the share of counterfeit drugs in developing countries as high as 50–70 per cent (PhRMA 2001). While the magnitude of the problem is difficult to estimate, "counterfeiting has now assumed such an alarming size that it and associated activities (misbranding, substitution, adulteration, and spurious manufacture) are becoming a major threat to the industry, to future research and development, to employment, individual and community safety, and public health" (Kumar 1993: 162).

Pharmaceutical counterfeiting is detrimental to both firms and patients. For the firm, the threat extends beyond company profits to legal liability, goodwill, and reputation. For the patient, the severity of the health risk associated with fraudulent drugs can vary greatly, from inconvenience to fatality. Treatment failure is the foremost cost of fraudulent drugs, but the rise of drug-resistant strains of bacteria is perhaps the most ominous. Counterfeit drugs that contain a greatly reduced dose of the active constituent have contributed to the increase in this threat. Counterfeit pharmaceuticals can be concocted from any substance – inert or toxic – that simulates the genuine article. In addition, counterfeit pharmaceuticals result in squandered health resources, both for the individual and at the national level. Counterfeiters steal scarce funding from limited health budgets, diverting resources away from genuine treatment.

Conclusions

The pharmaceutical industry's objective is twofold. It seeks to discover and develop medicines that extend and enhance life, and aims to provide investors with a return on their investment. Fulfilling their responsibilities to the public and to their shareholders is a delicate balance. Moreover, this must be done in an increasingly challenging environment. Historically, they have focused on the most profitable segments of the global market and targeted drug development to the diseases afflicting those populations. This has been done while relying heavily on global price discrimination and strong IPR protection. While profitable, this strategy has become increasingly unpopular with the public and with policymakers. As the industry aims to strike a balance between their objectives, they are faced with new obstacles: price controls, parallel imports, increasing R&D expenses, and counterfeit drugs. Each of these has the potential to reduce the industry's profitability and change its role in the global healthcare arena.

References

Alubo, S. O. 1994. Death for Sale: A Study of Drug Poisoning and Deaths in Nigeria. *Social Science and Medicine* 38: 97–103.
Bale, H. E. 1998. The Conflicts between Parallel Trade and Product Access and Innovation: The Case of Pharmaceuticals. *Journal of International Economic Law* 1: 637–654.

Capell, K., S. Timmons, J. Wheatley and H. Dawley. 2001. What's in That Pill? *Business Week* 3737: 30.

Cohen, W. M., R. Nelson, and J. Walsh. 1996. *A First Look at the Results of the 1994 Carnegie Mellon Survey of Industrial R&D in the United States.* Unpublished manuscript.

Ganslandt, M., and K. E. Maskus. 2001. *Parallel Imports of Pharmaceutical Products in the European Union.* Policy Research Working Paper no. 2630. Washington, DC: World Bank.

Gereffi, G. 1983. *The Pharmaceutical Industry and Dependency in the Third World.* Princeton, NJ: Princeton University Press.

Gilbert, G. and P. Rosenberg. 2004. *Addressing the Innovation Divide: Imbalanced Innovation.* Munich, Germany: Bain & Company. Available at: http://www.bain.com/bainweb/PDFs/cms/Marketing/addressing_innovation_divide.pdf [Accessed December 17, 2005].

Glover, G. J. 2002. *Competition in the Pharmaceutical Marketplace.* Testimony before the Federal Trade Commission and the US Department of Justice, Antitrust Division. Washington, DC: PhRMA. Available at: http://www.ftc.gov/opp/intellect/020319gregoryjglover.pdf [Accessed December 20, 2005].

Grabowski, H. and J. Vernon. 1990. A New Look at the Returns and Risks to Pharmaceutical R&D. *Management Science* 36: 804–821.

Hajari, N. 1998. Swallowing Bitter Pills. *TIME* 151: 261–270.

Kumar, V. P. 1993. Global Syndicates and the Threat to Third World Health. In *The Pharmaceutical Corporate Presence in Developing Countries*, edited by L. A. Tavis and O. F. Williams. 161–174. Notre Dame, IN: University of Notre Dame Press.

Land, T. 1992. Combating Counterfeit Drugs. *Nature* 335: 192.

Lanjouw, J. O. 2001. A Patent Proposal for Global Diseases. *The Brookings Institution Policy Brief* 84. Available at: http://www.brookings.edu/comm/policybriefs/pb84.htm [Accessed December 19, 2005].

——. 2003. Opening Doors to Research: A New Global Patent Regime for Pharmaceuticals. *The Brookings Review* 21, no. 2: 13–17.

Levin, R. C., A. K. Klevorick, R. R. Nelson, and S. G. Winter. 1987. Appropriating the Returns from Industrial Research and Development. *Brookings Papers on Economic Activity* 3: 783–831.

Love, J. 1997. Call for More Reliable Costs Data on Clinical Trials. *Marketletter* January 13: 24–25.

Lybecker, K. M. 2000. Counterfeit Pharmaceuticals: Product Piracy and the Transition to Stronger Intellectual Property Rights in Developing Countries. PhD dissertation, University of California, Berkeley.

Moser, J. 2003. *Importation Not the Answer.* Alexandria, VA: Galen Institute. Available at: http://www.galen.org/pdrugs.asp?docID=507 [Accessed December 20, 2005].

Pharmaceutical Research and Manufacturers of America (PhRMA). 1997. *Indonesia.* Submission of the PhRMA, NTE Report on Foreign Trade Barriers. Washington, DC. PhRMA.

——. 2001. Global Intellectual Property Protection, in *Pharmaceutical Industry Profile 2001*, Washington, DC. PhRMA.

——. 2002. *Pharmaceutical Industry Profile 2002.* Washington, DC. PhRMA.

——. 2005. *R&D Investment by Pharmaceutical Companies Tops $38 Billion in 2004.* Press Release, February 18. Washington, DC. PhRMA. Available at: http://www.phrma.org/mediaroom/press/releases/18.02.2005.1128.cfm [Accessed December 19, 2005].

Sellers, L. J. 2004. Pharm Exec 50. *Pharmaceutical Executive* 24, no. 5: 60–70.

Stipp, D. 1996. Farewell, My Logo. *Fortune* 133, no. 10: 128–138.

Tufts Center for the Study of Drug Development. 2003. *Total Cost to Develop a Prescription Drug, Including Cost of Post-Approval Research, is $897 Million.* Press release, May 13. Boston, MA: Tufts Center for the Study of Drug Development. Available at: http://csdd.tufts.edu/ [Accessed December 19, 2005].

3 The pharmaceutical industry and its obligations in the developing world

Ann Mills, Patricia Werhane, and Michael Gorman

The global pharmaceutical industry interacts with research establishments, the biotech industry, and delivery systems throughout the world, including educational providers, payers, and governments, as well as altruistic organizations, NGOs, and others. It does so largely within a framework of often controversial laws and policies, both in the U.S. and in other Western countries whose goals include safety, patient health, and the promotion and protection of an important industry through patent protection of intellectual property.

But the evolution of the industry, the decisions it has made, and the consequences of these decisions have not always produced desirable results, especially in regard to developing nations and their health needs. These needs include the development and distribution of drugs specifically targeted at the diseases affecting those countries, the pricing of those drugs, and access to them.

In this chapter, we briefly discuss the market framework that supports the pharmaceutical industry. We argue that what is needed is a reformulation of pharmaceutical stakeholder obligations through the creation of a new framework – a different mental model that commits all the components of the global healthcare system to addressing the health needs of the developing countries.

The market for drugs

The constitutionally mandated purpose of the U.S. patent system is to stimulate and promote the advancement of science and the useful arts by conferring a certain amount of control over the intellectual property, production, use, and sale of a particular product or process to the patent grantee (Kitch 1986: 31–2). Control extends for 20 years from the date the application is filed, but in practice the life of the patent is generally 12–14 years (Barton 2004). This patent protection in the drug industry is justified, according to the industry, because the expenditures associated with the development and marketing of a new drug are enormous, up to US$800 million per drug, and financial incentives are necessary in order to continue to inspire companies to go into the drug business (Angell 2004). R&D costs have to be covered, and protection of patents that guarantee monopoly pricing can achieve this end. But these must be in markets that are capable of guaranteeing pricing greater than marginal costs, and the only markets capable of making such a guarantee are those associated with high-income countries.

A global view

The rest of the developed world appears to share the U.S. view that IPR should be protected to cover development costs and to provide proper incentives for market entry. But many developing countries do not share this perspective; they consider access to drugs so important that the products themselves should not be patented (Barton 2004). Indeed, in most developing countries there is no patent protection (Attaran and Gillespie-White 2001). Nevertheless, in exchange for important developed world concessions that would significantly expand their exports of agricultural and textile products, developing countries signed up to 1995 extensions of the Trade-Related Aspects of Intellectual Property Rights (TRIPS) Agreement, which requires all signatories to adhere to Western-defined standards of intellectual property protection (Boulet et al. 2000). Legal and political controversies surrounding the implementation of TRIPS (Cychosz 2004) culminated in the Doha Declaration, which affirmed the right of nations to use the exceptions of TRIPS, such as the compulsory license provision, to meet public health needs. Significantly, the public outcry that accompanied the Doha Declaration also led to the introduction of differential pricing of pharmaceuticals between the developed countries and the developing countries (Barton 2004).

In spite of the fact that most pharmaceuticals are generous to developing countries in terms of model programs, donations of drugs, and low-cost pricing, problems remain with getting the appropriate drugs at affordable prices to large populations of at-risk patients (Henry and Lexchin 2002). The infrastructure of many developing countries is inadequate to assure delivery (Attaran 2004). The manufacturing capability of most developing countries is so poor that makes it largely impossible to take advantage of the compulsory licensing provision in TRIPS (except by importing drugs from countries where products are not patented) (Correa 2002). Most importantly, the budgets of developing countries are insufficient, even at reduced pricing, to meet the needs of their populations. HIV/AIDS is just one of the diseases affecting the developing world, and these populations of patients do not even have access to drugs which have been long off-patent and which are available relatively cheaply. Moreover, because this market is so small relative to the market for the developed countries, it is insufficient to attract appropriate research interest. Public spending on drugs is at around US$239 per head per annum in OECD member states. Most developing countries, however, spend less than US$20 per year per head on *all* health programs, including drug expenditures, and this falls to less than US$6 per person in sub-Saharan Africa (Trouiller et al. 2002). A systems perspective might help to address these issues.

A systems perspective

A "system" can be defined as "a complex of interacting components together with the relationships among them that permit the identification of a boundary-maintaining entity or process" (Laszlo and Krippner 1998). Systems are connected in ways that may or may not enhance the fulfillment of one or more goals or purposes and they may be micro (small, self-contained with few interconnections), mezzo (within organizations and corporations), or macro (large, complex, consisting of a large number of interconnections).

The US Institute of Medicine (IoM), in its report *Crossing the Quality Chasm*, argued that the healthcare delivery system is a "complex adaptive system," an open system made up of human beings interacting with each other within and through organizations (Plsek 2001). Because it is a complex adaptive system, it is able to change, through its interactions, the goals of the system as well as the system itself.

A complex adaptive system has the ability to be creative and thus offer novel solutions to otherwise intractable problems. To preserve this creativity, according to the IoM report, a complex adaptive system should have a few explicit goals and be guided by a few simple rules.

Using this approach, the IoM was able to suggest that if the healthcare delivery system as a whole subscribed to one goal – that "All healthcare organizations, professional groups, and private and public purchasers should adopt as their explicit purpose to continually reduce the burden of illness, injury, and disability, and to improve the health and functioning of the people" (Committee on Quality and Health Care in America 2001) – and was guided by a few simple rules, the healthcare delivery system would be able to achieve this desirable goal.

The IoM may well be right. If a system as a whole adopts the same goal, then there is a very good chance that it will achieve that goal. But there are problems. In this case the delivery system, which includes healthcare organizations, professional groups, and private and public, *all* must adopt this goal. Moreover, the system interacts with the framework of laws and policies that governs and supports it. If we want the system to achieve its goals, the framework which governs its interactions should also be designed to encourage it to realize its goals.

Can a reframing of pharmaceutical stakeholder obligations change the goals of the system?

Let us accept the assumption that healthcare is a complex adaptive system. Let us also assume that the proper goal of any healthcare system is similar to the IoM proposal. Many, if not all, pharmaceutical companies have missions similar to the IoM statement. According to Abbott's home page, for example, their mission is "Quality Health Care Worldwide" (Abbott 2005). Merck's goal is often quoted to be, "We are in the business to cure disease" (The Business Enterprise Trust 1991). We can then apply the same logic to the pharmaceutical industry that the IoM applied to the U.S. delivery system. But pharmaceuticals are only one component of the system within which it interacts. The other components include governments, the research community, delivery systems, patients, payers, NGOs, and others. In the same way that the IoM sought to reframe the obligations of the delivery system, we must reframe the obligations of *all* of the components of global health.

Potential solutions

Despite mission statements to the contrary, it often appears that the goal of the pharmaceutical industry is to protect its interests and exploit the incentives embedded in the framework that governs and supports it. It often develops in conjunction with other research establishments, manufactures, markets, and distributes drugs that may benefit most those suffering in the developed world – not necessarily those in developing countries.

From this perspective the developing world *cannot* be said to be part of the system in which pharmaceuticals operate. If it is not part of that system, we must think of new options if we don't want to ignore the problems associated with the developing world. One option is to create parallel systems that operate differently in different economic contexts. In the next section we explore examples of parallel systems that are being created and the difficulties of creating and maintaining them.

Creating parallel systems

Without consumer or government finances, a market system for drug delivery cannot operate. But parallel systems are being created in the developing countries that are different from the standard market model. One model that has achieved some success is what Werhane and Gorman call the "Alliance" model (Werhane and Gorman 2005), the model developed by Mary Ann Leeper, COO of the Female Health Company, a for-profit company that distributes female condoms (Yemen and Powell 2003). The model was developed in response to a huge demand by women first in Zimbabwe and later in many other countries for protection against HIV infection in cultures where men are averse to condom use. The company had a fine product, a large customer demand, and adequate supplies. But, the customer base was penniless and governments in countries with high infection rates, at least in Africa, have little or no funds for this or any other product. So Leeper began finding donor organizations to support supplying this product. She solicited monies from UNAID, USAID, DFID, social marketing organizations that deeply discount products such as condoms, and other international organizations. The second challenge was getting governments in these countries to support or at least not oppose the distribution of the product. And there was a third difficulty: training villagers and local health personnel in how to use the product and how to instruct others. By working with governments and NGOs, the FHC has gradually overcome these problems through training and education, village by village, in the 100 countries where it distributes its product (Yemen and Powell 2003). This systemic approach is also used in Botswana by an alliance between Merck, the Gates Foundation, and the government of that country to attack their HIV/AIDS pandemic. But these systems are parallel to, not part of, a market system. And none has been successful, yet, in curbing the HIV pandemic in Africa (Weber, Austin, and Bartlett 2001).

Rethinking the system

If the global healthcare system is a failure, and if the proposed mission of healthcare is, as the IoM proposes, "to reduce the burden of illness ... and improve the health ... of people," a mission that is reiterated (although not always vigorously) throughout the pharmaceutical industry, we might find reason to change that system as well as the framework that supports it. Part of the initiation of that change is evidenced in the present challenges to intellectual property and patenting. Challenges to intellectual property rights emerge through copying music and other works of art without permission; generic brands of well-known drugs and other products; copying products by reverse engineering; challenges to gene patenting and genetic engineering; copying patented drugs without permission or license – for national security, in health emergencies, life-threatening epidemics, to reduce costs to end-users, or simply to make money. In addition, we see a global community increasingly skeptical of pharmaceutical companies whose business model relies on heavy funding of R&D, and we see an important constituency, the American public, increasingly impatient at having to bear the alleged R&D costs of pharmaceuticals that much of the rest of the world does not.

There are no shortages of suggestions for reform to consider in terms of restructuring the framework of the system while still preserving the basic incentives that drive it (Attaran 2004; Cychosz 2004). It might be more useful, however, to take a different world-view and conceive of the creation of a unique form of a complex adaptive system: a "trading zone."

Moving toward an alternative world-view: trading zones

The concept of "trading zones" has been used to describe the interdisciplinary communication involved in the development of complex technological systems, which required collaboration and interdisciplinary communication in the pursuit of achieving a goal against a common enemy. During the Second World War, for example, there was a need for the military, engineers, and scientists to collaborate across seemingly incommensurable paradigms in order to develop radar to defeat the enemy (Galison 1997). How does one get experts to communicate across very strongly entrenched disciplinary perspectives? Solving this problem requires a common goal. Moreover, the project will probably not succeed unless the participants develop a "creole" or other communication device that crosses these paradigm "bridges," and which is unique to the trading zone and the goal its participants seek to achieve. The development of a creole allows system component participants to understand one another. It allows their interactions to be meaningful and it allows discussion, new discoveries, and appropriate action (Gorman, Groves, and Catalano 2004; Gorman 2005).

In effect, TRIPs is an effort to establish the rules for a global trading zone around intellectual property. But the TRIPs rules create an unequal trading zone, where a large proportion of the global population in developing countries lack the resources to trade for technologies that are essential to their survival.

What is needed is a trading zone developed from a robust moral imagination. Gorman refers to this as a "shared mental model" zone, in which participants have to understand each other's perspectives. An important component of moral imagination is seeing a situation from the perspective of another (Werhane 1999). How, for example, do global IPRs look to someone who cannot afford a drug that might save her or his child's life? How do these rights look from the standpoint of a company that is giving its pharmaceuticals away, only to have them sold on the black market to those who can afford them?

Once participants in a shared mental model zone see each other's perspectives, they can work together to develop inclusive processes for achieving the shared goals, ones that take multiple situations into account. Such processes will always be subject to discussion, evaluation, and improvement. But there will be a shared commitment to working together.

Trading zones and the developing world

According to the perspective offered by the IoM, the success of complex adaptive systems depends largely on goal-sharing. By definition the participants who make up trading zones share the same goal because they perceive the same threat or opportunity. And so, in this context, we might stand the best chance for success for containing a pandemic such as HIV/AIDS by the creation of a trading zone made up of the developing and developed world government representatives, the pharmaceutical industry, the medical profession, NGOs, and international funding organizations. Each of these operates in a different paradigm and culture, and with different mental models. Nevertheless, we all face a common threat, with the shared goal of surviving a pandemic. That shared goal is to the mutual advantage of every participant in this system to contain it.

In a trading zone the participants bring their expertise and perspectives to be shared with others. In this case, the expertise brought by the developing world is their understanding of their own culture, health needs, and delivery mechanisms. The expertise brought by the developed world is their understanding of science, of manufacturing, and of management of scarce resources, including accountability and monitoring techniques. Integrating these areas of expertise might bring to the forefront solutions or stepping stones on the way to achieving the goal of the trading zone. But bridging these areas of expertise will require the development of a common language or creole and also require facilitators who can serve the role of mediating meaningful exchanges (Collins and Evans 2002).

We see the developed world and the developing world interact continuously through mechanisms such as the WHO, TRIPS, the various foundations and NGOs, the UN Global Relief Fund, and, most recently, through the development of the President's Emergency Plan for AIDS Relief (PEDFAR). In spite of all these interactions we do not yet see the development of a common creole. For instance, prevention in PEDFAR rests on the "ABC" model (Abstinence, Be Faithful, and, as appropriate, Correctly and Consistently, USE condoms) (PEDFAR 2004). This model derives from assumptions about how people *should* behave and may not be relevant to all cultures. While it is a model that may resonate with the beliefs of some in the developed world, it may fail in its application to the developing world because the model for prevention is focused less on condom use than on abstinence, and little is said about the role of empowering women in preventing infections. Because there is no common language, there is little chance of aligning the prevention model with the admonition for abstinence.

It is noteworthy that the success of trading zones is due largely to the fact that some kind of communication device was developed so that expertise could be shared. But "accountability" in PEDFAR is managerially and technologically driven according to developed world standards. Moreover, allocating resources under PEDFAR requires recipient countries to demonstrate their commitment to TRIPS and, as we have seen, developing countries do not have the protection of intellectual property rights as an important goal.

Thus, we see the beginnings of a trading zone in the biggest piece of legislation and funding offered to the developing world. We see a perception of the threat caused by the pandemic. But we see a confusion of means and we see processes to achieve goals based purely on the assumptions and values of the developed world – in this case, the United States. The expertise and cultural differences of the developing countries are not considered and there is no attempt to instigate meaningful communication with them. Without meaningful communication it is doubtful that PEDFAR will succeed efficiently. Nevertheless, PEDFAR calls for the commitment of all the components of the system, including pharmaceuticals and other nations, to help contain the pandemic. The trigger, the threat to our survival, has made us take the first step in the formation of what might, as the threat becomes more real, be a workable and sustainable trading zone.

Trading zones and the developed world

If we start with the idea that the current system is not an unmitigated success, the concept of trading zones can also serve us usefully when we think about solutions for the developed world. The same problem of incommensurable paradigms exists. Pharmaceuticals are operating according to the dictates of a framework that supports intellectual property protection while consumers, insurers, and state, local, federal, and other national governments are operating under budget constraints. But both sides are threatened. Pharmaceuticals are threatened with the collapse or dismantling of an intellectual property framework that protects their interests, and the patients who are served by these entities are threatened with decreased access to the medicines they need. Since the survival of both is in question, it is in the mutual interests of both to develop a goal that both can share, as well as a common language so that both can envision pathways to it.

Such a goal might be relatively easy to formulate. For instance, it might be that we can adapt the goal of the IoM "to relieve the burden of suffering" to include attention to costs and thus to continued profitability for pharmaceuticals. Although there will be some disruption of the industry, we might stand a chance of weeding out inefficiencies such as incentives that produce "me too" drugs and that make price rather than volume delivered more of a consideration in ascertaining returns.

Summary and conclusion

The current system is in crisis. The system has failed to address the needs of the developing world and it is in danger of failing to address the needs of the developed world too. But we know from the IoM's report on the healthcare delivery system and from observations on the way complex adaptive systems behave that all the components of a system must share a goal in order to achieve it. So we know that reframing the obligations of one component of the system, the pharmaceuticals, will not be enough to achieve the outcomes we want.

We have discussed the concept of trading zones as an alternative world-view of a seemingly intractable problem. But trading zones emerge only because of a perceived threat or opportunity. We can only conclude from PEDFAR that the perception of a threat is only just becoming real – that regardless of the pandemic, the preservation of the framework which protects intellectual property rights is deemed more important – at least to the United States – than the containment of a pandemic. Nevertheless, the trigger is real and exists in both the developed and developing worlds. Pharmaceuticals ignore it at their peril. Tragically, it appears that countless more will have to suffer and die before the trigger explodes.

References

Abbott Laboratories. 2005. Available at: http://www.abbott.com [Accessed June 22, 2005].

Angell, Marcia. 2004. *The Truth About the Drug Companies: How They Deceive and Exploit Us, And What To Do About It*. New York: Random House.

Attaran, Amir and Lee Gillespie-White. 2001. Do Patents for Antiretroviral Drugs Constrain Access to AIDS Treatment in Africa? *JAMA* 286 (15): 1886–1892.

Attaran, Amir. 2004. How Do Patents and Economic Policies Affect Access to Essential Medicines in Developing Countries? *Health Affairs* 23(3): 155–166. Available at: http://content.healthaffairs.org/cgi/content/full/23/3/155 [Accessed June 22, 2005].

Barton, John H. 2004. TRIPS and the Global Pharmaceutical Market. *Health Affairs*. 23 (3): 146–154. Available at: http://content.healthaffairs.org/cgi/content/full/23/3/146 [Accessed June 22, 2005].

Boulet, P., J. Perriens, F. Renaud-Thery, and G. Valasquez. 2000. Pharmaceutical and the WTO TRIPS Agreement. Geneva: World Health Organization. Available at: http://www.who.int/medicines/library/par/hivrelateddocs/pharmaceuticals_wto_trips.pdf [Accessed June 22, 2005].

Business Enterprise Trust, The. 1991. *Merck & Co., Inc. (A)*. Harvard Business School Publishing. 9–991–021.

Collins, H. M. and Evans, R. 2002. The Third Wave of Science Studies. *Social Studies of Science* 32: 235–296.

Committee on Quality and Health Care in America. 2001. Institute of Medicine. *Crossing the Quality Chasm: A New Health System for the 21st Century*. Washington, DC: National Academy Press.

Correa, Carlos M. 2002. Implications of the Doha Declaration on the TRIPS Agreement and Public Health. Geneva: World Health Organization. Available at: http://www.who.int/medicines/library/par/who-edm-par-2002-3/doha-implications.doc [Accessed June 22, 2005].

Cychosz, Allison. 2004. The Effectiveness of International Enforcement of Intellectual Property Rights. *John Marshall Law Review* 37: 985–1016.

Galison, Peter. 1997. *Image & Logic: A Material Culture of Microphysics*. Chicago: University of Chicago Press.

Gorman, Michael E., James F. Groves, and Robin K. Catalano. 2004. Societal Dimensions of Nanotechnology. *IEEE Technology and Society Magazine* 29 (4): 55–64.

——. 2005. Levels of Expertise and Trading Zones: Combining Cognitive and Social Approaches to Technology Studies. In Michael E. Gorman, Ryan D. Tweney, David C. Gooding, and Alexandra Kincannon, eds, *Scientific and Technological Thinking*. 287–302. Mahwah, NJ: Lawrence Erlbaum Associates.

Henry, David and J. Lexchin. 2002. The Pharmaceutical Industry as a Medicines Provider. *The Lancet* 359 (9345): 1590–1595.

Kitch, Edmund W. 1986. Patents: Monopolies or Property Rights? *Research in Law and Economics.* 8: 31–50.

Laszlo, Alexander and S. Krippner. 1998. Systems Theories: Their Origins, Foundations and Development. In J. S. Jordan, ed., *Systems Theories and a Priori Aspects of Perception.* Amsterdam: Elsevier, 47–74.

Plsek, Paul. 2001. Redesigning Health Care with Insights from the Science of Complex Adaptive Systems. In Institute of Medicine, *Crossing the Quality Chasm: A New Health System for the 21st Century.* Washington DC: National Academy Press. 310–333.

The President's Emergency Plan for AIDS Relief: U.S. Five Year Global HIV/AIDS Strategy. 2004. Available at: http://www.state.gov/s/gac/rl/or/29761.htm [Accessed June 22, 2005].

Trouiller, Patricia, P. Olliaro, E. Torreele, J. Orbinski, R. Laing, and N. Ford. 2002. Drug Development For Neglected Diseases: A Deficient Market and a Public-Health Policy Failure. *Lancet* 359 (9324): 2188–2194.

Weber, James, J. Austin, and A. Bartlett. 2001. *Merck Global Health Initiatives (B): Botswana.* Harvard Business School Case 9–301–089.

Werhane, Patricia H. 1999. *Moral Imagination and Management Decision-Making.* New York: Oxford University Press.

Werhane, Patricia H. and M. Gorman. 2005. Intellectual Property Rights, Access to Life-Enhancing Drugs, and Corporate Moral Responsibilities. *Business Ethics Quarterly* 15: 595–613.

Yemen, Gerry and Elizabeth Powell. 2003. *The Female Health Company (A) and (B).* University of Virginia: Darden Business Publishing, UVA-BC-0182–3.

4 Drug companies as organizational hybrids

Warren Kaplan

Introduction

The theory of the firm

The purpose of this chapter is to briefly review changes in the organizational structure of pharmaceutical firms and of the industry as a whole and speculate on whether or not "hybrid" organizations will increase the innovative ability of pharmaceutical R&D. The term "innovation" is highlighted because it can be defined in different ways. For our purposes, we define it as the ability of the biomedical R&D establishment – primarily biotechnology and pharmaceutical companies – to generate novel chemical entities (or versions of existing chemical entities) that have new, unexpected, or improved pharmaceutical and clinical benefits. The theory of the firm sets out to explain the nature and limitations (or boundaries) of the firm as an economic institution. The theory attempts to answer the question, why do firms exist? Answers vary but include minimizing or avoiding transaction costs, rationally maximizing profit, and dealing with market failures which arise under economies of scale and information asymmetries (Coase 1937; Arrow 1969; Arrow 1985; Cockburn 2004). All such theories can explain the organizational structure of the pharmaceutical firm.

Organizational structure of pharmaceutical firms

Prior to the 1980s, the pharmaceutical industry was characterized by a vertical structure that was essentially binary, with a clear distinction drawn between upstream, open science and a downstream, commercial sector dominated by "Big Pharma" – at that time comprising about 40 large, highly integrated firms (Cockburn 2004). Thus, for-profit pharmaceutical companies were usually large, integrated organizations that carried out all R&D from drug discovery through clinical development, drug regulatory affairs, to manufacturing, marketing, and sales. This structure allowed for control over all aspects of the product, from research to marketing to patient access. Most drug discovery lacked information about molecular biological pathways and was dominated by large-scale screening programs (Cockburn and Henderson 1996). In the upstream, not-for-profit biomedical sector, the public supported "basic" research at a small scale in government laboratories, universities, research institutes, and teaching hospitals. Research results were often shared between members of this community, and resources were allocated by competition for grants. The pharmaceutical industry made use of "upstream" science derived from research in the public sector (Cockburn 2004). Indeed, many private pharmaceutical companies have exclusively licensed in rights to make and/or market healthcare products that were originally invented with public funds. These include inventions in many HIV/AIDS drugs, such as government-owned inventions on didanosine (ddI) and public sector inventions such as stavudine (d4T), lamivudine (3TC) and Ritonavir®, as well as drugs to treat malaria and many other illnesses.

The changing structure of the pharmaceutical industry

Current pressures on the pharmaceutical industry

To meet shareholders' expectations, U.S. and European pharmaceutical companies typically focus on leveraging products to manipulate their volume, price, and marketing portfolio in ever-changing equations to boost earnings. However, current industry pressures threaten the success of these traditional strategies.

The major pharmaceutical companies have large sales forces competing for physicians' time. Opportunities to "detail" products, however, are becoming scarce. Companies reliant on volume-based strategies face the rapid introduction of competitors' "me-too" drugs, which shrink the market opportunity for exclusive drug sales (Taylor 2003). Indeed, pharmaceutical companies can no longer expect market exclusivity for the entire patent life of a product. In addition, increased competition often accompanies sales and marketing with the added pressure, rising costs, and potential public health consequences of accelerating the speed to peak sales. As the population ages and the use of high-cost drugs increases, revenue growth from price increases is meeting stiff opposition, as both public and private payers demand price reductions (Sykes 1994). The "blockbuster" model and patent expirations of blockbusters exert intense pressure on companies to replace a magnitude of lost revenues in a short period of time (Tiner et al. 2002).

Blockbuster drugs have become more difficult to develop. Despite heavy investments in new technologies to develop chemical entities, many companies are finding that the benefits from these technologies may be years away. Although companies have sought in-licensing deals to heal ailing pipelines, large pharmaceutical companies have increased the price of desirable late-stage products to potentially unprofitable levels (Angell 2000).

The major current successes of the industry – blockbuster drugs for hypertension, cholesterol, depression, ulcers, and so on – are the results of research done decades ago, under the "old" binary industry structure (Cockburn 2004). Thus, today's new drugs are the product of yesterday's R&D spending and today's R&D spending will contribute to output far in the future.

Figure 4.1 plots the temporal changes in the number of new molecular entities (U.S. FDA 2005). Although short-term trends are "noisy," there is a clear upwards trend in the data as defined by the linear regression line.

We can estimate the ratio (R&D spending per new molecular entity (NME)) as in Figure 4.2, although the question of measuring research "productivity" using easily

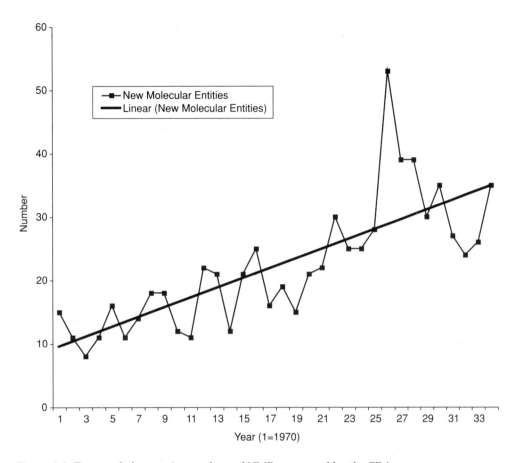

Figure 4.1: Temporal changes in numbers of NMEs approved by the FDA

measurable data is fraught with biases inherent in using aggregate data. Such estimates should be approached with caution and skepticism. Information on domestic R&D spending came from the U.S. pharmaceutical industry trade group, PhRMA, so that the spending data are from PhRMA companies and not all biomedical companies. Nearly all, if not all, of the domestic R&D expenditures of PhRMA member firms are spent on drugs which they hope will get approved in the U.S. R&D expenditures that are spent abroad on discovery, pre-clinical development, and clinical development prior to U.S. new drug approval are excluded. Finally, inflation is corrected by the GDP deflator, although corrections using the Consumer Price Index or the Producer Price Index give substantially the same results. The "opportunity" costs of R&D are not taken into account (Grabowski, Di Masi, and Hansen 2004). Figure 4.2 is based on approvals of therapeutic new molecular entities (NMEs) from all the pharmaceutical industry, not just full members of PhRMA.

Figure 4.2 shows the ratio PhRMA R&D/NME approvals over time with time-lags incorporated. For example, the five-year time-series begins with the 1982 data for NME approvals linked to the 1975 data for PhRMA R&D expenditures (Coase 1937). The data are very sensitive to time-lags between R&D spending and NME approval. Eight to twelve years is a reasonable "average" period between R&D expenditure and NME approval. At present, the cost per NME (in 2003 dollars) is between $400 and $800 million. While roughly constant at between $200 and $300 million R&D expenditure per NME during the 1980s, this index has been rapidly increasing since the early–mid-1990s. The "noise" is a function of the denominator in the index, i.e., the temporal changes in NME approvals (see Figure 4.1). The recent drop in index over the last several years (arguably an "increase" in R&D productivity) is due to the increase in NMEs over this period (Figure 4.1).

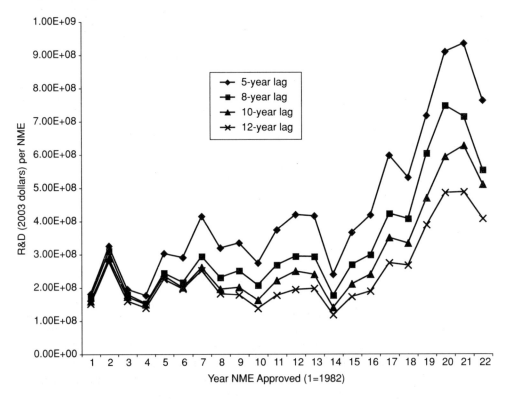

Figure 4.2: Temporal changes in the ratio R&D expenditure per NME

Industry response to pressures

In response to this nearly decade-long drop in R&D productivity, pharmaceutical firms have pursued several options: (1) enhancing their internal R&D efforts through the acquisition of smaller pharmaceutical and/or biotech companies; (2) engaging in large horizontal mergers to achieve greater economies of scale and scope in their research programs; (3) acquiring existing mature products through licensing agreements; and (4) increasing internal R&D efforts independently of consolidation with other entities

(Danzon, Epstein, and Nicholson 2003). These options are by no means mutually exclusive. In reality, companies usually simultaneously engage in a number of these activities at varying levels. For example, companies like Merck have preferred to grow without extensive mergers or acquisitions, while others such as Novartis have been more predisposed to pursue acquisitions in order to improve deteriorating pipelines. Increasingly, value is being created across structural boundaries through the creation of networks between firms (Kettler 2004).

Following the molecular biology revolution of the late 1970s and early 1980s, much of the scientific information needed for pharmaceutical R&D has grown more complex, and the industry structure has followed suit (Cockburn 2004). Gene-splicing and the ability to create molecules using recombinant DNA technology opened up new areas of research. In general, drug discovery became based on an understanding of processes at the molecular level. Molecular and computer-driven models of chemical structure drove "rational drug design" and "combinatorial chemistry" (Cockburn and Henderson 1996). Drug companies lacking such sophisticated technology were forced to rely on collaboration and exploitation of external sources of technology, through in-licensing or strategic partnerships with biotechnology companies. The pharmaceutical research-based industry increasingly relies on the research tools and product leads provided by biotechs, and 25–40 per cent of its sales are reported to come from drugs that originated in the biotech sector (Cockburn 2004). Intellectual property law allowed recombinantly derived DNA and proteins (e.g., DNA and protein sequences, monoclonal antibodies, transgenic animals and plants) to fall within the class of legally allowable and patentable "inventions." In the United States, the Bayh–Dole Act (1984) allowed more government-sponsored research to be licensed and created new tax and financial regulations.

Mergers and acquisitions

The pharmaceutical industry in industrialized countries experienced a high rate of merger and acquisition activity in the 1980s and 1990s. Most of the leading pharmaceutical firms in the OECD countries are the result of one or more horizontal mergers. For example, Pfizer is the combination of Pfizer, Warner-Lambert, and Pharmacia, which included Upjohn (Danzon, Epstein, and Nicholson 2003).

Biotech/pharma collaborations

Figure 4.3 summarizes the number of American biotech/pharmaceutical industry collaborations between 1993 and 2003, illustrating the rise in collaborative activity after 2000. Data extracted from Danzon, Epstein, and Nicholson (2003).

Transnational collaborations

Most of the collaborations in North America are R&D agreements (see Figure 4.4) but there is a significant amount of cross-border collaborative activity involving Asia (Kang and Sakai 2000; OECD 2001). The relative significance of American pharmaceutical

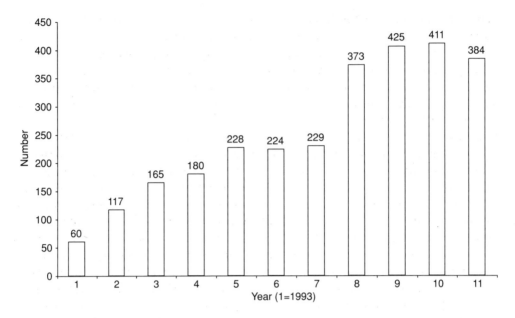

Figure 4.3: Temporal changes in the number of pharma-biotech collaborations

manufacturing deals in Asia, as compared to R&D deals, should not be a surprise given the relatively cheap labor costs in Asia. Cross-border R&D deal-making will likely increase in India and China, in particular, as these countries implement product patent protection pursuant to the TRIPS Agreement governed by the WTO.

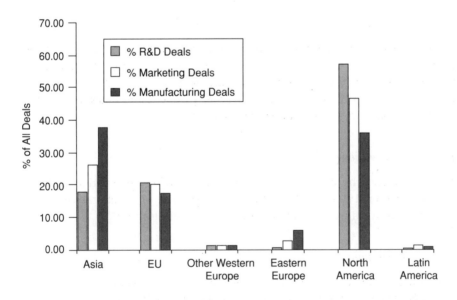

Figure 4.4: Regional distribution of cross border alliances. Source: Kang and Sakai (2000).

Consolidation/collaboration in the Indian pharmaceutical industry

The Indian pharmaceutical industry has been undergoing a major shift in its business model, starting from January 1, 2005, as the existing "process patent" regime now includes a "product" patent system, in order to comply with the TRIPS Agreement under the WTO. As a result, the Indian pharmaceutical industry is consolidating with mergers, acquisitions, and alliances (Chaudhuri 2005). The Indian research and higher education sector is very large (250 universities) (Dyer 2004) and the same dollar amounts would buy "more" research in India than in the U.S. Nonetheless, although there are many pharmaceutical firms in India, their discovery-oriented pharmaceutical R&D is small and is heavily concentrated in fewer than ten firms. Across these top players in the Indian industry in 2000–1, between 1 and 7 per cent of revenue from pharmaceutical sales was reported to be expended on R&D (Chaudhuri, personal communication, November 2004). Multinational corporations in India expend between 9 and 10 per cent of sales revenue for R&D (Ranade and Basu Das 2003).

The Indian pharmaceutical industry today exports active pharmaceutical ingredients (APIs), bulk drugs, as well as formulations to the international market. If the Indian pharmaceutical industry, over time, tends to partner with the pharmaceutical industry of the industrialized countries, then increasing support of academic and for-profit research through commercial partnerships is likely in both countries. Indeed, Indian companies were responsible for submitting nearly 21 per cent (73 of 350) of all abbreviated new drug applications (ANDAs) for generic medicines to the FDA in 2004 (Agres 2005). Indian companies also accounted for 25 per cent of submissions to FDA's Drug Master File (DMF) in the fourth quarter of 2003. DMF approval is a prerequisite for exporting a drug to the U.S. (Agres 2005).

There is considerable pharmaceutical deal-making taking place in the highly fragmented pharmaceutical markets in India. Examples of Indian companies entering into collaborative partnerships with pharmaceutical multinationals are numerous. Divi's Laboratories does custom chemical synthesis for Merck, Abbott and GSK, and makes generic anti-inflammatory and anti-arthritic formulas for other firms. Cipla and Aurobindo act as suppliers of APIs to U.S. and European generic companies (Grace 2004).

It is uncertain if these changes in the Indian pharmaceutical industry will bring about an improvement in the health status of the majority of the population. AIDS medications are not widely available to Indian patients notwithstanding the groundbreaking role of Indian companies in supplying relatively cheap generic AIDS drugs. Indian firms now undertake R&D of growing significance, but its focus and direction are shaped by the imperatives of the profit- and market-driven model of drug development, which manifestly does not meet the needs of the population in developing countries (Kaplan and Laing 2004). Public health/needs-driven discovery research or, for that matter, the supply of essential drugs as "public goods," will not be easily reconciled with success in a globally integrated pharmaceutical market.

"Organizational hybridization" within firms

In general, organizational structure tends to channel innovation and knowledge but can also constrain the creation of innovation and knowledge. Few pharmaceutical organizations have the luxury of being given a blank slate on which to design new organizational structures. Instead, they are creating hybrids that combine elements of different types of structures.

Matrices, spaghetti, and skunkworks

Consumer packaged goods firms such as Unilever, Kraft, and General Mills have been experimenting with hybrid designs since the early 1990s. Each of these firms was under pressure from forces that also exist in the pharmaceutical industry, e.g., relatively low inflation, competition from generic and private labels, new sales formats, more powerful retailers and escalating promotion costs that eat up profits.

"Hybrid" structures combine horizontal business processes with integrating and specialist functions. Cross-cutting functions such as marketing, strategy development, and human resource management provide the mechanisms for coordinating and allocating resources. Research and marketing are needed to provide technical expertise and replenish the horizontal processes with new ideas, either through insights from outside the firm or the transfer of learning across teams. Although there are many variants of the hybrid solutions to these problems, the main features of successful applications are the existence of "teams" overlaid on existing functional structure.

Within firms, the hybrid or matrix concept has become increasingly fashionable in pharmaceutical companies. Project teams are created that comprise membership from departments with specific technical, organizational, and management expertise. Such teams form and dissolve as the need arises. In principle, advantages of the matrix structure include cross-disciplinary enrichment of the team's activities and cross-fertilization of expertise. Disadvantages of the matrix system include a relative lack of professional development for specific technical expertise for each team member, the potential for cross-departmental rivalry, and competition for each team member's time based on the needs of the interdisciplinary project versus those of his/her technical "home" department (Verona and Ravasi 2003). These multi-functional teams have the potential to increase bureaucracy and delay innovation. At least on a small scale, it may be better to solve a problem with two people rather than with ten.

Some of these internal hybrids have taken on quite radical structures and have been designed as separate units with "market-like" properties such as project autonomy and incentive compensation to encourage innovation. They have been variously called "incubators" and "skunkworks." Oticon, a Danish electronics producer, became famous for radical organizational transformation in the early 1990s (Verona and Ravasi 2003). This "spaghetti organization," as it has come to be known, refers to a flat, loosely coupled, project-based organization characterized by permeable job boundaries and the ad hoc nature of delegating responsibility. Oticon abandoned this structure after some years in favor of a more conventional matrix team organization.

Open, web-based innovation structures

A few biomedical companies are exploring novel, "open" approaches to organization. Several years ago, Eli Lilly launched an innovative R&D program on the Web. The effort is intended to speed up the solution of scientific problems by soliciting the input of researchers from around the world. Several dozen problems are posted on the program's website, with prizes of up to US$100,000 for those who come up with solutions. InnoCentive LLC posts on its website scientific problems or challenges with cash incentives for an innovative solution (www.innocentive.com). These challenges have ranged from developing a new method of isolating RNA to creating a new breast cancer risk assessment tool to synthesis of new indacene derivatives.

"Organizational hybridization" among firms

University–industry hybrids

The emergence of a joint knowledge infrastructure between universities and companies is a manifestation of these technological and policy changes. Temporary collaborative R&D arrangements are in place between research organizations (mostly university departments) and innovation-oriented firms engaged in pre-competitive research of both academic and industrial relevance. The aim of establishing collaborative basic R&D settings at the interface between science and industry is to set up bridging mechanisms to reduce the barriers between academic and industrial research and creating an innovative environment for future strategic research. This structure is intended to reduce transaction costs and improves the interaction performance between scientific knowledge producers and users in the innovation system (Coase 1937; Etzkowitz 2000; Menard 2005).

"Public–private partnerships" for product development

The public sector presently leaves almost all drug development to the pharmaceutical industry. Clearly, industry incentives drive investment almost exclusively toward developing drugs that are likely to be marketable and profitable. Tax incentives and patent protection are geared towards this market-driven private investment.

Product development public–private partnerships (p-PPPs) are collaborative organizations between non-profit and for-profit organizations. They are institutionalized with public intervention and/or funding because markets are perceived as unable to adequately connect relevant resources and capabilities between science and industry in basic research. Clearly, diseases such as malaria, tuberculosis, and others that are even less well known are rampant in developing countries but are far less of a threat in most developed countries (Wheeler and Berkley 2001; Kaplan and Laing 2004). There is, therefore, little or no economic incentive to develop pharmaceutical products for these diseases (Biel 2001; Milne, Kaitin, and Ronchi 2004; Kaplan and Laing 2004). The industry's lack of enthusiasm is also a result of distribution challenges in countries with poor infrastructures and lack of awareness about these diseases in more developed countries, liability considerations, inadequate science base, and underestimation of the disease burden. Product PPPs have been developed to address this enormous and widening gap in availability of medicines (Reich 2000; Moran 2004; Ziemba 2004).

From 1986 when the first PPP for health was created until the end of 2003, 91 such partnerships have been instituted, 78 of which are still in existence. Each partnership has its own separate legal status, broad range of goals, combinations of partners from the public and private sectors, management structures and strategies (Buse and Waxman 2001; Ziemba 2004; Moran 2005). The spectrum and mix of public and private entities involved in any one partnership can range from an organization such as Drugs for Neglected Diseases Initiative, which was initially organized with no representatives of the private sector on its board of directors (Pécoul 2004), to the Pharmaceutical Security Institute whose members are research-based for-profit multinational pharmaceutical firms. (The Pharmaceutical Security Institute is a non-profit organization with the mission of protecting public health by sharing information on counterfeit pharmaceuticals and initiating enforcement activities (Pharmaceutical Security Institute 2002).) The International Trachoma Initiative is comprised of a for-profit entity, a private foundation, national governments, other private foundations, non-governmental organizations, and the World Health Organization (WHO) (Reich 2000).

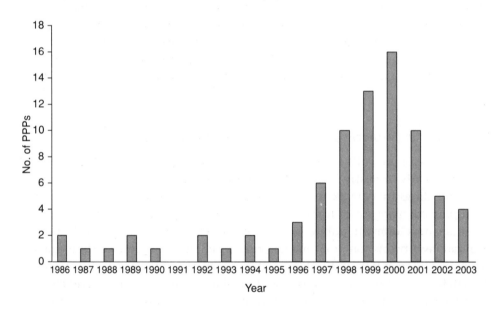

Figure 4.5: Number of all public–private partnerships created between 1986 and 2003

Of the 78 active partnerships, the number of partnerships that focus on certain diseases or health policy issues is set out in the Annex. Partnerships may deal in any combination with product distribution, product development, and/or policy and health systems issues between or among various diseases. The development of PPPs has engendered a debate over their goals, strategies, and sustainability. Table 4.1 (adapted from Foladori 2003) summarizes some of the issues.

Table 4.1: Concerns regarding PPPs in world public health

Item	Argument in favor of PPPs	Concerns	References
Basic strategy	Attack primary or neglected infectious diseases in developing countries	Reductionist, disease-by-disease approach misses the ecological relationships that see development as a way to improved health	Reductionist: (Gallup and Sachs 1998) Ecological approach: (Farmer 1996
R&D orientation	Private sector is expert in "D" and more cost-effective in bringing drugs to market	Pharma will only participate if it can patent novel medicines. Pharma will not permit low prices to reach developed markets in certain countries (India, China, Brazil). Poor people in poor countries will not be considered. Public R&D has historically been proven to develop vaccines and new medicines (polio, cancer, HIV)	(Wheeler and Berkley 2001; Biel 2001; Hardon 2001)
Sustainability	PPPs raise funds for the short term	R&D for drugs and vaccines requires a long-term budget; PPPs cannot be supported by charities	(Yamey 2001; Muraskin 2002)
Is there an alternative to PPPs?	PPPs are the best way to address global health problems	PPPs will only address diseases of interest to "big pharma"; PPPs will never take a long-term, broad approach to public health	(Muraskin 2002)

Kettler and Towse (2001) looked at intermediate indicators for PPPs, i.e., pipeline, the type and number of alliances, the reputation and reliability of the board, the amount of funds raised through public and private channels. As of 2001, PPPs have successfully raised almost a half a billion dollars, about half of their targeted R&D funds for 2005 (Kettler and Towse 2001). Significantly, there were considerable uncertainties about the ability to raise the rest of the funds and secure the deals they need, especially with large pharmaceutical companies to meet their product and cost targets. More recent assessments reveal similar findings for product development PPPs (Ziemba 2004; Moran 2005).

The product development PPPs have reported their pledged and required funding up to 2007, as shown in Table 4.2 (Ziemba 2004). This demonstrates a substantial shortfall in committed funds.

At present, the vast majority of funding for product development PPPs has been provided by major philanthropic organizations such as the Bill and Melinda Gates Foundation, the United States Agency for International Development (USAID), the United Kingdom's Department for International Development (DFID), and the Rockefeller Foundation. Multilateral donors such as the EU, UN organizations, and the World Bank have provided relatively small amounts. The international NGO Médecins Sans Frontières (MSF) has provided a five-year grant to establish and fund the new

Table 4.2: Summary of funding pledged and funding needed for product development (US$ millions)

	Cumulative funding pledged to 2007	PPP estimate of cumulative required resources to 2007	Implied shortfall
IAVA	174	1,036	862
TB ALLIANCE	35.75	249	213
DNDI	0	255	255
MMV	97	152	83
TOTAL	306.75	1,692	1,413

Drugs for Neglected Diseases Initiative (DNDI). Private sector organizations, including the major pharmaceutical companies, have made financial and in-kind donations (Ziemba 2004), but there is a substantial shortfall in the available funding. Until now, the EU member states have not provided substantial direct funding or other support to PPPs. To be fair, however, the pipelines of the Medicines for Malaria Venture (MMV) is impressive, with seven drugs in Phase I–III clinical trials and three additional medicines in pre-clinical phase and the Global Alliance for TB Drug Development as of 2004, has six compounds in pre-clinical to clinical stages. A recent comprehensive report (Moran 2005) found that at the end of 2004, over 60 neglected disease drug development projects were in progress, and fully 70 per cent of these included a PPP as an organizational structure. Assuming sufficient funding, at standard attrition rates this would be expected to deliver eight or nine drugs within the next five years, even if no further projects were commenced after the end of 2004 (Moran 2005).

However, product development PPPs, as currently constituted, actually have a limited capacity to ensure access by individuals in poor populations to any products that may emerge from their efforts. Most product development PPPs attempt to assure future access through interactions with various partners "downstream" to product development itself (Widdus 2004). Access to anticipated products of such PPPs in developing countries may not be timely if there is no way to deliver the product via the health system (e.g., for vaccines to adolescents, or microbicides to the poorest women). Certain product development PPPs have created advocacy and "access to medicines" activities as parts of their missions (Widdus 2004; Ziemba 2004).

It is still too early to tell whether PPPs will succeed with their ambitious agendas of discovering and developing new medicines for neglected diseases, but the time-frame may be less than a decade (Moran 2005). Product development PPPs face the same challenges presented by the risks inherent in the costly and time-consuming process of "big pharma" drug development. This is especially true for diseases where basic science and research has been dormant for years.

Summary

Large, vertically-oriented pharmaceutical firms have in the past been able to deal with the classic "market-based" problems of managing risk in imperfect markets, capturing knowledge spillovers, and working with distortions in symmetrical flows of information

(Cockburn 2004). Some assert that there is an assumption that vertically integrated firms are the first best solution to pharmaceutical R&D issues such as financing and management of multiple projects that are long-term, risky, and complex; dealing with activities that are costly to monitor; and dealing with substantial project-specific unrecoverable investments. It is too early to tell if changes in the structure of the pharmaceutical industry after 1990, including the increase in organizational "hybridization", will alter the relatively poor innovation track record of the pharmaceutical industry.

For so-called "neglected" diseases, new tools and approaches are not being developed in many areas and progress is being delayed by lack of targeted funding and support. For example, the U.S. is driving the tuberculosis R&D agenda, particularly for new drugs, with the preponderance of R&D now being funded by the government and American philanthropists, and with U.S.-based industry and academic groups being the main collaborators (and beneficiaries of R&D contracts) (Moran 2004).

The following areas might be considered for both PPPs and the pharmaceutical industry with regard to a public health-based agenda for pharmaceutical R&D (adapted from Moran 2004; Moran et al. 2005):

1. Application of well-established technologies to further investigate and develop known or suspected compounds including:
   - establishing consortia to prioritize and coordinate screening of known compounds in order to discover new drug leads for selected diseases;
   - outsourcing relevant development work to industry (through public funding of PPPs to cover outsourced work; or via industry incentives targeted to gaps identified by public R&D groups or PPPs). Outsourcing areas could include pre-clinical and lead optimization work, medicinal chemistry, scale-up production of screening compounds, and analogue development;
   - providing a public facility for compound screening, and possibly medicinal chemistry, available at no cost to industry and academic groups.
2. Creation of a distinctive model for R&D funding. Features of this model would be:
   - a systematic, rather than ad hoc, approach to promising R&D candidates;
   - coordinated academic research in key areas;
   - constructive use of PPPs as a conduit to identify gaps in the development pipeline, allowing R&D funding to be targeted to industry or academic groups who are active in gap areas, rather than lower-priority activities;
   - capacity to link support and rewards for industry, including biotechs and Contract Research Organizations, to activities that most closely match public health goals.

Capturing the value that ultimately derives from fundamental research is inefficient and very hard for both non-profit and for profit-oriented organizations. Unfortunately, given delays between performing basic science and measuring impacts on human health, unambiguous evidence on these issues may take some time to accumulate.
Annex: Number of partnerships with associated disease or issue

13 + 1*	HIV/AIDS (See Global Fund* below)
12 + 1*	Malaria (See Global Fund* below)
8	Health policies and systems
7	Chagas, leishmaniasis, trypanosomiasis, lymphatic filariasis – individually or in combination
6	Microbicides
5 + 1*	Tuberculosis (See Global Fund* below)
5	Vaccines of the poor
4	Onchocerciasis and/or trachoma
3	Micronutrients/Vitamin A
3	Reproductive health
2	Dengue
1	Communicable diseases – prevention through handwashing with soap
1*	The Global Fund to Fight AIDS, tuberculosis and malaria
1	Guinea worm
1	Hookworm
1	Lassa fever
1	Leprosy
1	Meningitis
1	Polio
1	Schistosomiasis
1	Tetanus

Source: Ziemba (2004). Extracted from data found on the website for Initiative on Public Private Partnerships for Health, www.ippph.org, accessed February 26, 2004.

References

Agres, T. 2005. Outsourcing Spikes Competition. *Drug Discovery and Development*. Available at: http://www.dddmag.com [Accessed May 10, 2005].

Angell, M. 2000. The Pharmaceutical Industry- To Whom is it Accountable? *New England Journal of Medicine* 342: 1902–1904.

Arrow, K. 1969. The Organization of Economic Activity. In *The Economics of Information*. Oxford: Basil Blackwell.

——. 1985. The Informational Structure of the Firm. *American Economic Review* 75: 303–307.

Biel, P. 2001. Why is There No AIDS Vaccine? *World Economics* 2: 1–16.

Buse, K. and A. Waxman. 2001. Public–Private Health Partnerships: A Strategy for WHO. *Bulletin of the World Health Organization* 79: 748–754.

Chaudhuri, S. 2005. *The WTO and India's Pharmaceuticals Industry: Patent Protection, TRIPS and Developing Countries*. New Delhi: Oxford University Press.

Coase, R. 1937. The Theory of the Firm. *Economica* 4: 386–405.

Cockburn, I. 2004. The Changing Structure of the Pharmaceutical Industry. *Health Affairs* January–February: 10–22.

Cockburn, I. and R. Henderson. 1996. Scale, Scope, and Spillovers: The Determinants of Research Productivity in Drug Discovery. *The Rand Journal of Economics* 27: 32–60.

Danzon, P., A. Epstein, and S. Nicholson. 2003. *Mergers and Acquisitions in the Pharmaceutical and Biotech Industries*. Social Science Research Network, 1–43. Available at: http://papers.ssrn.com/sol3/papers.cfm?abstract_id=468301 [Accessed May 10, 2005].

Dyer, G. 2004. A Laboratory for Globalisation: How India Hopes to Reshape the World Drugs Industry. *Financial Times* (London), August 18.

Etzkowitz, H. 2000. The Dynamics of Innovation: From National Systems and Mode 2 to a Triple Helix of University-Industry-Government Relations. *Research Policy* 29: 109–123.

Farmer, P. 1996. Social Inequalities and Emerging Infectious Diseases. *Emerging Infectious Diseases* 2: 259–269.

Foladori, G. 2003. Can PPPs in Health Cope with Social Needs? In *Knowledge Flows, Innovation, and Learning in Developing Countries*. Volume 1 of *Knowledge Flows and Knowledge Collectives: Understanding the Role of Science and Technology Policies in Development*. Global Inclusion Program, Rockefeller Foundation. Available at: http://unpan1.un.org/intradoc/groups/public/documents/APCITY/UNPAN017425.pdf [Accessed April 1, 2005].

Gallup, J. and J. Sachs. 1998. *The Economic Burden of Malaria*. Center for International Development – Harvard University, WHO Commission on Macroeconomics and Health, CMH Working Paper WG1:10. Available at: http://www.cmhealth.org/docs/wg1_paper10.pdf [Accessed May 10, 2005].

Grabowki, H., J. Dimasi, and R. Hansen. 2004. *Assessing Claims about the Cost of New Drug Development: A Critique of the Public Citizen and TB Alliance*, 1–20. Tufts Center for the Study of Drug Development. Available at: http://csdd.tufts.edu/_documents/www/Doc_231_45_735.pdf [Accessed May 10, 2005].

Grace, C. 2004. *The Effect of Changing Intellectual Property on Pharmaceutical Industry Prospects in India and China: Considerations for Access to Medicines*. Issues Paper: Access to Medicines. London: DFID Health Systems Resource Centre. Available at: http://www.dfid.gov.uk/pubs/files/indiachinadomproduce.pdf [Accessed May 10, 2005]

Hardon, A. 2001. Immunization for All? A Critical Look at the First GAVI Partners Meeting. *HAI-Lights* 6: 1–5. Available at: http://www.haiweb.org/pubs/hailights/mar2001/mar01_lead.html [Accessed May 10, 2005].

Kang, N-H. and K. Sakai. 2000. *International Strategic Alliances: Their Role in Industrial Globalization*. STI Working Paper 2000/5. Paris: OECD. Available at: http://www.oecd.org/dsti/sti.htm [Accessed January 21, 2005].

Kaplan, W. and R. Laing. 2004. *Priority Medicines for Europe and the World*. Geneva: WHO. Available at: http://mednet3.who.int/prioritymeds/Meds [Accessed April 23, 2005]. Kettler, H. 2004. Engaging Biotechnology Companies in the Development of Innovative Solutions for Diseases of Poverty. *Nature* 3: 171–176.

Kettler, H. and A. Towse. 2001. *Public Private Partnerships*. WHO Commission on Macroeconomics and Health, CMH Paper WG2:21. Available at: http://www.cmhealth.org/docs/wg2_paper21.pdf [Accessed November 5, 2005].

Menard, C. 2005. *The Economics of Hybrid Organizations*. Presidential Address, ISNIE, September 29, Massachusetts Institute of Technology. Available at: http://www.isnie.org [Accessed April 2, 2005].

Milne, C., K. Kaitin, and E. Ronchi. 2004. *Orphan Drug Laws in Europe and the US: Incentives for the Research and Development of Medicines for Diseases of Poverty*. WHO Commission on Macroeconomics and Health, CMH Working Paper Series, Paper No.WG2:9. Available at: http://www.cmhealth.org/docs/wg2_paper9.pdf [Accessed May 10, 2005].

Moran, M. 2004. Tuberculosis. In *Priority Medicines for Europe and the World*, edited by Warren Kaplan and Richard Laing. Geneva: WHO, 66–67. Available at: http://mednet3.who.int/prioritymeds/ [Accessed April 23, 2005].

Moran, M., A.L. Ropars, J. Guzman, J. Diaz, and C. Garrison. 2005. *The New Landscape of Neglected Disease Drug Development*. London School of Economics Policy Report, Pharmaceutical R&D Policy Project, 1–106. Available at: http://www.lse.ac.uk [Accessed November 4, 2005].

Muraskin, W. 2002. The Last Years of the CVI and the Birth of the GAVI. In *Public–Private Partnerships for Public Health,* edited by Michael Reich. Cambridge, MA: Harvard University Press, 115–168.

Organization for Economic Cooperation and Development (OECD). 2001. *New Patterns of Industrial Globalization: Cross Border Mergers and Acquisitions and Strategic Alliances*. Paris. Available at: http://www.oecd.org/LongAbstract/0,2546,en_2649_34557_1895829_119656_1_1_1,00.html [Accessed February 9, 2006].

Pécoul, Bernard. 2004. Interview by Elizabeth Ziemba. Drugs for Neglected Diseases Initiative, Geneva, Switzerland, March 1.

Pharmaceutical Security Institute. 2002. Available at: www.psi-inc.org [Accessed March 2, 2004].

Ranade, A. and S. Basu Das. 2003. *Sectoral Reports: Pharmaceutical Industry: Update.* Available at: http://www.abnamro.co.in/Research/pdf/pharma-apr0103.pdf [Accessed May 10, 2005].

Reich, M. 2000. Public–Private Partnerships for Public Health. *Nature Medicine* 6: 617–620.

Sykes, R. 1994. Innovation in the Pharmaceutical Industry. *British Medical Journal* 309: 422–423.

Taylor, D. 2003. Fewer New Drugs from the Pharmaceutical Industry. *British Medical Journal* 326: 408–409.

Tiner, R., L. Edwards, A. Jacobs, P. Sambrook, J. Stenmark, J. Karmali, M. Anderson, A. Karasz, P. Lurie, S. McKechnie, J. Moncrieff, P. Thomas, R. Moynihan, I. Heath, and D. Henry. 2002. The Pharmaceutical Industry and Disease Mongering. *British Medical Journal* 325: 216.

United States Food and Drug Administration. Center for Drug Evaluation and Research, CDER Approval Reports. Available at: http://www.fda.gov/cder/rdmt/default.htm [Accessed May 11, 2005].

Verona, G. and D. Ravasi. 2003. Unbundling Dynamic Capabilities: An Exploratory Study of Continuous Product Innovation. *Industrial and Corporate Change* 12: 577–606.

Wheeler, C. and S. Berkley. 2001. Initial Lessons from Public–Private Partnerships in Drug and Vaccine Development. *Bulletin of the World Health Organization* 79: 728–734.

Widdus, R. 2004. Product Development Partnerships on "Neglected Diseases": How They Handle Intellectual Property and How This May Contribute to Improving Access to Pharmaceuticals for HIV/AIDS, TB and Malaria. *ICTSD-UNCTAD Dialogue on Ensuring Policy Options for Affordable Access to Essential Medicines.* Bellagio, 12–16 October 2004. Available at: http://www.iprsonline.org/unctadictsd/bellagio/docs/Widdus_Bellagio3.pdf [Accessed May 10, 2005].

Yamey, G. 2001. Global Campaign to Eradicate Malaria. *British Medical Journal* 322: 1191–1192.

Ziemba, E. 2004. Public–Private Partnerships. In *Priority Medicines for Europe and the World*, edited by Warren Kaplan and Richard Laing. Geneva: WHO, 100–103. Available at: http://mednet3.who.int/prioritymeds/ [Accessed April 23, 2005].

5 Physicians and the pharmaceutical industry: a symbiotic relationship?

Ian E. Marshall

Since physicians are the health professionals that primarily prescribe pharmaceutical products, physicians' prescription practices are critically important to the profits of the pharmaceutical industry. Similarly, the pharmaceutical industry can be important to physicians as a source of new product information for patient treatment. Given this potentially symbiotic relationship, there is a critical need for regulation of the interaction between industry and physicians. While governments do provide a legislative framework for such regulation, most detailed regulation is currently provided by the respective codes and guidelines of the physicians and the pharmaceutical industry. Since the scope of such self-regulation is very broad, this paper restricts itself to examining the issue of gift-giving, including drug samples.

Industry interaction with physicians

The interaction between physicians and the pharmaceutical industry can be viewed in terms of supply and demand. The pharmaceutical industry has the money, which it can supply to physicians in various forms such as promotional gifts, entertainment, free drug samples, and funding for continuing medical education. The physicians have a demand for continuing education in order to discharge their professional obligations to their patients. There is an overlap or duality of interest of both the pharmaceutical industry and physicians with respect to their encouragement of the effective and responsible use of drugs in treatment and care, the monitoring of their use, and the conduct of innovative research.

Notwithstanding this overlapping of interests, physicians and the pharmaceutical industry each have a different emphasis and they focus on different stakeholders. The pharmaceutical companies' principal emphasis is the encouragement of the use of their products; the physicians' primary emphasis is effective patient care. The primary stakeholder in patient care is the patient; while the principal stakeholder in industry is the shareholder (Komesaroff and Kerridge 2002). However, the relationship between physicians and the pharmaceutical industry is often more complex, as each party may be influenced by a variety of different interests and stakeholders, e.g., community welfare.

It should not be assumed that where a duality of interest occurs between physicians and the pharmaceutical industry, there will always be a conflict of interest. Dualities of interest constitute "conflicts" only when they are associated with competing obligations that are likely to lead directly to a compromise of primary responsibilities (Komesaroff and Kerridge 2002).

One study suggested that if a physician has a relationship with a pharmaceutical company, he or she tends to prescribe more of its products (Komesaroff and Kerridge 2002). In itself, this is not evidence of wrongdoing by either party. There are many potential explanations as to why this occurs. A pharmaceutical company may inform a physician about a new product because this is the best product available for the treatment of certain of the physician's patients. In this case, the relationship may result in a "win-win" situation. The pharmaceutical company incurs costs educating the physician about the new product, but may recoup these costs and make a profit on sales prescribed by the physician. The physician may obtain information he needs to give better care to some of his patients and they may benefit accordingly.

However, problems can and often do arise because the relationship between physician and pharmaceutical company is open to varying degrees of abuse. For example, the pharmaceutical company representative may practice selective disclosure when providing information. Without all the relevant information, the physician may not be able to adequately assess the suitability of the product for his patients' use. This situation is complicated by the fact that every salesperson practices selective disclosure to some extent. It is often called "putting one's best foot forward." The difficulty lies in determining where one should draw the line.

Since the relationship between physicians and pharmaceutical companies is open to abuse in a myriad of ways, safeguards are necessary to reduce the chances of a duality of interest becoming a conflict of interest and corruption. Because abuses have occurred in the past and because positive outcomes are usually not reported or are under-reported, there is a tendency for the public to label the relationship as "bad."

The fact that both physicians and the pharmaceutical industry have instituted codes of conduct governing their relationship is evidence of their concern about the public's perception of that relationship. The physicians do not want to give the appearance of this relationship biasing their independent, professional judgement, which underlies the integrity of their fiduciary relationship with their patients. The pharmaceutical companies do not wish to be cast as corrupting one of the last professions the public still trusts. Instead, they wish to reap whatever benefits can be had from being perceived as "good corporate citizens." This is particularly important in the current environment in which the pharmaceutical industry has been subject to increasing scrutiny by NGOs, the media, and researchers.

Consequently, both physicians and the pharmaceutical industry have respectively developed codes of conduct or guidelines to govern their members in this relationship. These codes and guidelines attempt to address such issues as advertising, gift giving, drug promotions, support for travel, meeting sponsorship and medical education activities, research, and consulting. In this paper, the author has chosen to discuss the issue of gift-giving, including drug samples.

Attempting to address abuses: codes, guidelines & policies

Physicians' codes, guidelines and policies on receiving gifts and drug samples

Various approaches to self-regulation have been taken by different physicians' organizations. However, a review of these approaches reveals general themes. In most cases, the primary justification for having a direct relationship between the pharmaceutical industry and individual physicians seems to be based on the premise that an advancement of patient healthcare will occur through increased education and research. This assumes that the information provided to the physician is impartial and also disregards the capacity of physicians to keep themselves up to date about advances in drug therapy by way of medical and other academic journals.

For this reason, the AMA states, "Any gifts accepted by physicians individually should primarily entail a benefit to patients and should not be of substantial value. Accordingly, textbooks, modest meals and other gifts are appropriate if they serve a genuine educational function. Cash payments should not be accepted" (AMA 2004, Guideline 1). They also make the point that individual gifts of minimal value are permissible as long as these gifts are related to the physician's work (Guideline 2), but that no gifts should be accepted which have strings attached (Guideline 7).

The ACP *Ethics Manual* (1998) goes further by strongly discouraging the acceptance of gifts and hospitality from the healthcare industry. They argue that the acceptance of even small gifts has been documented to affect clinical judgement and heightens the perception (as well as the reality) of a conflict of interest. The *Ethics Manual* also states that while following the Royal College of Physicians' guideline "Would I be willing to have this arrangement generally known?" physicians should also ask, "What would the public or my patients think of this arrangement?" (ACP 1998).

While emphasizing patient care, the general approach used by the CMA policy on *Physicians and the Pharmaceutical Industry* (CMA 2001) is not inconsistent with that used by the AMA and the ACP. One of the general principles of the CMA policy requires the primary objective of interactions between physicians and industry to be the advancement of health of Canadians rather than the private good of physicians or industry. Another is that relationships with industry are appropriate only insofar as they do not negatively affect the fiduciary nature of the patient–physician relationship. The principles also instruct physicians to resolve any conflict of interest between themselves and their patients resulting from interactions with industry in favor of their patients. They specifically warn physicians to avoid any self-interest in their prescribing and referral practices (CMA 2001).

As outlined above, some professional organizations are more specific than others. However, the general theme appears to be that while minor gifts, entertainment, and drug samples should not be solicited they may be acceptable if they directly promote better patient care or indirectly promote education or research and, in either case, do not affect the integrity of the physician–patient relationship.

The pharmaceutical industry's codes of practice on gift-giving and drug samples

In the same way that the medical profession has recognized the need to provide its members with guidance on their relationship with the pharmaceutical industry, the pharmaceutical industry has realized that its employees need guidance as well. The industry is concerned that its employees may sully the pharmaceutical industry's reputation. The industry does not want their interactions with healthcare professionals to be perceived as inappropriate by patients or the public at large (PhRMA 2002). In order to avoid being overrun with the detailed nature of voluntary codes at the level of national associations, it is perhaps most instructive to start with the general principles contained in the IFPMA *Code of Pharmaceutical Marketing Practices* (IFPMA 2000).

The IFPMA, which has member associations in more than 55 countries, purports to represent the worldwide research-based pharmaceutical industry and the manufacturers of prescription medicines generally. The IFPMA's *Code of Pharmaceutical Marketing Practices* requires its terms to apply to any company belonging to at least one member association in all the countries of the world where that company operates. Companies entering into licensing and agency agreements are expected to require their licensees and agents to respect the provisions of the IFPMA Code.

The Code is intended to define universally applicable baseline standards of marketing practices. With respect to gift-giving and hospitality these are:

(1) Inappropriate financial benefits or material benefits, including inappropriate hospitality, should not be offered to healthcare professionals to influence them in the prescription of pharmaceutical products.
(2) Promotional items of insignificant value, provided free of charge, are permissible as long as they are related to the healthcare provider's work and/or entail a benefit to patients.
(3) Text or reference books/information and other educational material may be given to healthcare providers if they serve a genuine educational function (IFPMA 2000, sec. IV).

With respect to drug samples, the only marketing practice stated is that samples, clearly identified as such, may be supplied to the prescribing professions to familiarize them with products, to enable them to gain experience with the product in their practice, or upon request.

For the purpose of self-discipline, there is a mechanism under which IFPMA deals with complaints of alleged breaches of the Code. When a complaint is received by the IFPMA Secretariat, a summary is required to be sent to the company that is the subject of the complaint, the member association where that company has its headquarters, and the member association (if any) of the country in which the alleged breach has occurred. The relevant member associations are asked to consult the company and report back to IFPMA the results of their investigation of the case. An IFPMA decision is communicated to the complainant, the company, and the respective member associations. Where it is determined that there has been a breach of the Code, information identifying the company concerned and the complainant is immediately made public. Status Reports on the IFPMA Code, summarizing all complaints received, are also required to be published periodically and given wide circulation to government health departments, WHO, the technical press and leading medical journals, and to member associations of IFPMA.

PhRMA adopted its voluntary *PhRMA Code on Interactions with Healthcare Professionals* effective July 1, 2002. With respect to gifts, the Code concentrates on the end-use of gift items. Items primarily for the benefit of patients may be offered to healthcare professionals if they are not of substantial value (US$100 or less). Providing product samples for patient use in accordance with the Prescription Drug Marketing Act is acceptable. Items of minimal value may be offered if they are primarily associated with a healthcare professional's practice (such as pens and similar reminder items bearing the company or product logo). Items intended for the personal benefit of healthcare professionals (such as sporting event tickets) should not be offered. Payments in cash or cash equivalents (such as gift certificates) should not be offered, except as compensation for *bona fide* services. Nothing should be offered or provided in a manner or on conditions that would interfere with the independence of a healthcare professional (PhRMA 2002).

One surprising omission in the PhRMA Code is a complaints procedure. Furthermore, with regard to enforcement of the Code, each member company is only strongly encouraged to adopt procedures to assure adherence to the Code (IFPMA 2000). Unlike many other national Codes of Practice, there is no mechanism for dealing with members who violate this domestic Code. This omission encourages the perception that the Code is not being vigorously enforced.

CRBPC's *Rx&D Code of Marketing Practice* provides that member companies must not distribute service-oriented items or conduct "special promotions", which cannot be justified if subjected to scrutiny by members of the health professions and the public (CRBPC 2005). Acceptable service-oriented items are defined as items the primary goal of which is to enhance the healthcare practitioner's/patient's understanding of a condition or its treatment. When member companies provide hospitality, they must ensure that all hospitality is conducted within the limits of acceptable public and professional scrutiny, keeping in mind the need for an ethical relationship in any social interaction between healthcare professionals and pharmaceutical companies (CRBPC 2005). During such interactions, companies may provide participants with refreshments/meals that are modest in content and cost. In all instances, the provision of refreshments/meals must be clearly incidental. No other form of hospitality or entertainment is to be provided.

The Canadian Rx&D Code requires that samples (referred to as CEP) only be given to authorized healthcare practitioners who have filled out a request form for the CEP (CRBPC 2005, sec. 3.2.3(i)). However, the Canadian Code goes on to specify that all free goods (CEPs) given to a healthcare practitioner as part of an order must be included on the invoice. If no order is made when the free goods are supplied, the goods must be documented on a separate no charge invoice (sec. 3.2.3(iv)). The Canadian Code does not require that samples be limited in number, but puts the emphasis on the healthcare practitioner by allowing the distribution of as many CEPs as the healthcare practitioner believes is required for the proper evaluation of clinical response (sec. 3.2.3(v)). Provisions for storage, disposal, and auditing of CEPs held by company representatives are also included (secs. 3.2.4, 3.2.5, and 3.2.6).

One striking difference between the PhRMA Code and the Canadian Code is the latter's inclusion of provisions for enforcement. The Rx&D Marketing Practices Committee reviews complaints and can publish infractions and impose fines (sec. 15.2). There is also a right of appeal to an arbitrator selected and agreed to by the two parties involved in the complaint or, failing agreement, one appointed by the Chairman of the Board of Rx&D (sec.15.4). The decision of the arbitrator is final and the company in question must adhere to the decision as a condition of continued membership in the association (sec. 15.6).

Conclusion

In this chapter, the need to regulate physician–industry interaction has been identified. The goal of such regulation is to ensure that prescription patterns are based on the real health needs of the patient rather than industry influence. More explicitly, excerpts have been reviewed from a select number of codes offered by professional medical associations and the pharmaceutical industry as a means to regulate themselves. How can one test the efficacy of the self-regulatory regimes that these two groups have established?

The Nolan Committee on Public Standards (1995) in the United Kingdom suggested that there are seven relevant principles applying to all aspects of public life. The relationship between physicians and the pharmaceutical industry also involves duties owed to the public. Accordingly, the author used the seven Nolan Committee principles as the starting point for drafting the amended but corresponding principles described below, which are specifically applicable to the relationship between physicians and the pharmaceutical industry. To test the efficacy of the professional medical associations' and pharmaceutical industry's self-regulatory regimes, one should ask whether or not these principles are being applied to the interaction between members of their respective organizations.

Selfishness: Physicians have a duty to act in the best interests of their patients. Pharmaceutical companies have a duty not only to their shareholders, but also to the community at large. To fulfill their duty to the community, pharmaceutical companies must operate within the confines of socially acceptable behavior or risk loss of reputation, public boycotts, or legislative action. Socially unacceptable behavior by a company can ultimately lead to loss of business and become a failure in its duty to its shareholders. Both the physicians and the pharmaceutical companies or their employees must not compromise these public duties in order to gain financial or other material benefits for themselves, their families or their friends.

Integrity: Members or employees of both groups should not allow any physician to be placed in a position where he or she is under any financial or other obligation to a pharmaceutical company or its representative that might or might appear to improperly influence that physician in the performance of his or her medical duties.

Objectivity: Members or employees of both groups should strive to ensure that physicians in carrying out their medical duties, including entering into contracts with pharmaceutical companies, are able to makes choices based on scientific merit.

Accountability: Both physicians and national and international pharmaceutical industry organizations owe a duty to the public and must, through their respective organizations, provide for appropriate public scrutiny and discipline where necessary. They should also provide for appeals to qualified independent adjudicators.

Transparency: The organizations representing both groups should be as open and transparent as possible about all the decisions and actions they take. They should give reasons for their decisions and restrict information only when the wider public interest clearly demands (e.g., physician–patient privilege).

Honesty: Both physicians and employees of pharmaceutical companies should be considered to have a duty to resolve any conflicts of interest arising from their interaction in a way that protects the public interest.

Leadership: Both physicians and pharmaceutical company executives should promote and support these principles by leadership and example (available at CSPL 2005).

While existing codes and guidelines can certainly be improved, an environment of integrity still seems to be elusive. The current negative perception of the existing relationship between the pharmaceutical industry and physicians suggests that something further is required. The best code of ethics is worthless unless it is both enforced and seen to be enforced. In order to reap the benefits of such enforcement, an organization must deal with enforcement in a transparent manner. A recent case involving AstraZeneca Canada Inc., one of Canada's largest drug companies, provides an interesting case study.

In a private letter addressed to the Chief Executive Officers of Rx&D's member firms, the Rx&D president stated: "It is my obligation to inform you of a serious situation regarding one of our member companies, and of the industry as a whole, as a result of repeated non-compliance with the code of conduct. AstraZeneca Canada Inc. has reached an unprecedented number of infractions recorded in a second consecutive 12-month period" (Blackwell 2005). The company was put on six months' probation and an Rx&D spokesperson later stated that if it did violate the code again while on probation, it could be expelled. The organization also ordered AstraZeneca to communicate the action to healthcare professionals involved in the infractions and requested its CEO to appear before the Rx&D's board. No such measures have ever been taken before according to an Rx&D spokesperson (Blackwell 2005).

While these unprecedented actions are commendable in themselves, they are still less than what the public has a right to expect. One wonders why AstraZeneca wasn't put on probation after the first 12-month period? Why weren't such measures taken earlier? Why didn't Rx&D publicly announce the action it was taking, instead of only responding to later media reports? Why aren't all infractions and enforcement responses the subject of Rx&D press releases?

These omissions undermine the industry's credibility to regulate itself. An Rx&D spokesperson said: "We are sending out a clear message ... There will be no tolerance of non-compliance. This is serious" (Blackwell 2005). However, pharmaceutical industry organizations must not only "talk the talk", but "walk the walk". Strong leadership is necessary to achieve adequate transparency and to take effective action against industry members, when and where necessary. To do otherwise is to encourage the public's belief that pharmaceutical companies are conspiring to protect themselves at the public's expense. If this belief becomes strong enough, there will be great pressure to replace the self-regulatory regime with mandatory legislation. Such pressure can best be countered by bringing light through transparency to the enforcement process.

A symbiotic relationship has been defined as a "mutually advantageous" relationship (Barber 1998). To achieve a truly symbiotic relationship between physicians and the pharmaceutical industry, the light of transparency is required to dispel the darkness where conflict of interest, conspiracy, and corruption can thrive.

References

American College of Physicians. 1998. *Ethics Manual*. 4th edn. Available at: http://www.acponline.org/ethics/ethicman.html [Accessed November 14, 2005].

American Medical Association. 2003. *E-Addendum II: Council on Ethical and Judicial Affairs Clarification of Gifts to Physicians from Industry (E-8.061)*. Available at: http://www.ama-assn.org/ama/pub/category/4263.html [Accessed November 14, 2005].

Barber, K., ed. 1998. *The Canadian Oxford Dictionary*. Toronto: Oxford University Press.

Blackwell, T. 2005. Drug Firm's Violations of Ethics "Unprecedented." *National Post*, March 19.

Canada's Research-Based Pharmaceutical Companies (CRBPC). 2005. *Rx&D Code of Marketing Practices*. Available at: http://www.canadapharma.org/home_e.htm [Accessed November 15, 2005].

Canadian Medical Association. 2001. *CMA Policy: Physicians and the Pharmaceutical Industry Update 2001*. Available at: http://www.cma.ca [Accessed November 15, 2005].

Committee on Standards in Public Life (CSPL). 2005. *The Seven Principles of Public Life*. Available at: http://www.public-standards.gov.uk/about_us/seven_principles.htm [Accessed November 17, 2005].

International Federation of Pharmaceutical Manufacturers Associations. 2000. *IFPMA Code of Marketing Practices*. Available at: http://www.ifpma.org/News/news_market.aspx [Accessed November 16, 2005].

Komesaroff, P. A. and I. H. Kerridge. 2002. Ethical Issues Concerning the Relationships between Medical Practitioners and the Pharmaceutical Industry. *The Medical Journal of Australia* 176: 118–121.

Pharmaceutical Research and Manufacturers of America. 2002. *PhRMA Code on Interactions with Healthcare Professionals*. Available at: http://www.phrma.org/publications/policy/2004–01–19.391.pdf [Accessed November 16, 2005].

6 Industry perspectives on equity, access, and corporate social responsibility: a view from the inside

Robert A. Freeman

The global pharmaceutical industry is comprised of a number of privately held or publicly traded firms that must deliver sustained and increasing value to shareholders. The global industry is highly profitable, yet it operates in an environment of stringent regulations dealing with the safety and efficacy of the products it develops. It is also an industry that is subject to price controls and reimbursement limits in all major geographic markets with the exception of the U.S., although there are limits (as discussed below) with certain public programs such as Medicaid.

In general, the industry is multinational in its operations, closely regulated by national governments, capital-intensive, driven by high levels of R&D spend, and reliance on the U.S. market for its profitability. It is also an industrial sector that is in transition – its reliance on the U.S., Japan, and the EU is challenged by marginal growth opportunities in these markets, and some industry observers (IMS 2005) have formed the opinion that future expansion is now shifting toward the emerging markets of China, India, and specific South American country markets where a growing middle class are demanding early access to newly developed medicines and are willing to pay for increased access.

The pharmaceutical industry has been much more effective in producing strong financial returns for investors than it has in discharging its obligations to society. The industry would argue that it meets its social responsibilities by producing innovative products that meet society's needs for improved health outcomes. There is merit in its argument, but pharmaceutical R&D is by its very nature cyclical. Cycles of high output from research alternate with cycles that are not as demonstrably productive.

We are now in a cycle characterized by incremental innovation, not therapeutic breakthroughs, and it is reasonable for industry critics to question the industry on the value of its innovations. A wave of patent expiries, high failure rates of developmental products, pressure to reduce or contain healthcare inflation (prices and expenditures), and access to essential medicines in developing countries have resulted in a global environment of increasing hostility. At this point it is difficult to predict the direction in which the environment will move over the next three to five years.

In effect, a growing imbalance between shareholder expectations for continued short-term financial performance and the longer-term needs of the industry to change its operating model to deliver new product innovations is resulting in increased tension.

Limits on monopoly power – the realities of pharmaceutical pricing

Patents are essential to provide a long-term incentive to innovate. During the period of the patent's term, a pharmaceutical company can, within limits, exact a premium price or at least a parity price with comparable single-source products. In countries other than the U.S., prices and/or reimbursement levels are set directly or indirectly by governments. Consequently, prices in the U.S. are generally higher than the rest of the world. Additionally, the American market is the only one in which the industry can raise prices over the products' life-cycles. In other markets, once a price or reimbursement is set, that price will be at its maximum and further price increases are unattainable.

Although commercial success in the American market is vital to multinational pharmaceutical companies, firms generally cannot charge monopoly prices for extended periods because its customers, managed care plans, hospital buying cooperatives and the states' Medicaid programs, use restrictive drug formularies, prior authorization programs, consumer cost-sharing (tiered co-payments), and contracting mechanisms with pharmaceutical companies to exact price concessions. It is estimated, for example, that perhaps three-quarters of the sales of a single prescription drug are subject to contracted prices. Due to the consolidation in the managed care industry and increased market penetration in geographic markets, third-party payers have been able to use their power to influence the market share of patented drugs, thereby securing substantial rebates from pharmaceutical companies.

Also, federal law requires companies participating in Medicaid to pay rebates of at least 15 per cent off list price. All of these price concessions and reimbursement limits are largely unknown by consumers and government policymakers because these contracting practices are highly protected trade secrets. Consequently, this lack of understanding of how pharmaceutical markets operate has led to a number of misconceptions about the industry and, in turn, to distrust if not outrage about its practices: "profits before people" and "charging what the market will bear"; e.g., at present the industry has very high negatives in the U.S. and EU, a position that severely limits the industry's ability to influence public policy.

Another criticism of the pharmaceutical industry is its "excessive" expenditures for marketing and sales. It is true that abuses have occurred and that expenditures are high; however, new drugs will not be adopted by physicians in the absence of constant, repetitive communications from some source. While we would like to believe that physicians make drug prescribing information on the latest scientific information they have obtained from clinical and other scholarly, independent sources, they do not. (Yes, there are exceptions to this generalization, but physicians as a group tend to behave in this way.) Communication about new innovations to physicians requires ongoing and major financial support to affect behavior, and this is not a role that governments and other information dissemination organizations are funded sufficiently to perform. Pharmaceutical marketing creates social value, but this is neither an accepted nor a well-established perception.

Reduced sales and marketing expenditures for companies are likely in the U.S. The highest expense item within the sales and marketing category is the sales force, followed by the cost of providing drug samples. About US$200,000 is spent per year for a sale representative's compensation and field support expenses. Sales productivity has been falling for years and supporting sales forces of upwards of 10,000 employees per company (U.S.) is no longer justified. As noted elsewhere, the operating models of pharmaceutical companies are undergoing rapid evolution and reductions beyond the margin will continue to occur.

The relationship between prices and innovation

The industry must innovate and bring therapeutic value for patients with acute and chronic illnesses and demonstrate that value to other stakeholders, including patients, medical providers, payers, and governments. The explicit objective of the firm is realized through the development and marketing of a portfolio of drug products that will deliver an uninterrupted stream of free cash flows and operating profits sufficient to fund current and future R&D. The stream must be supported by adequate pricing levels globally and by IPR (patents) and trade secrets related to patents and the clinical trials used to document safety and efficacy, formulation and basic chemistry.

Pharmaceutical R&D is expensive to undertake and subject to an extraordinarily high risk of failure. Most recently, we have noted that even successfully marketed products such as Cox-2 inhibitors can be withdrawn from the market because of the occurrence of serious side-effects that were not observed during clinical trial programs submitted for regulatory approval. It is difficult, at best, to justify to corporate boards and major institutional investors that a company intends to pursue research platforms that have an inherently high risk of developmental failure or that have limited commercial prospects.

In the recent past, the industry's operating model has been based on the discovery and launch of blockbusters or mega-brands, products with annual global sales of US$1 billion. This model requires extraordinary high levels of sales and marketing expenses, levels that are acknowledged as no longer sustainable because the mega-brands are delivering only incremental therapeutic value.

Accordingly, the industry is rapidly changing its operating model to focus on breakthrough innovation for targeted illnesses, not for the general population whose therapeutic needs are relatively satisfied with existing therapies. The R&D environment is now categorized by a high level of risk-aversion, collaborative arrangements with niche pharmaceutical and biotechnology companies, and outsourcing of R&D and manufacturing to countries such as China, India, and Singapore.

Even with the switch to more targeted research, the industry is almost universally criticized for neglecting the diseases of developing countries and diseases that affect very small patient numbers. Again, it is a case of "profits before people" that industry critics use to call for reform of the industry and its practices. In reality, profits are essential to the industry's research programs across the portfolio, and both profit and revenue targets must be met, if not exceeded, if the companies are to engage in any research platform.

Profit levels

Industry profits are indeed high related to those found in other sectors, notably service (retail and wholesaler) industries. This is due in part to the fact that the pharmaceutical industry is asset-intensive rather than labor-intensive, which leads to a low asset-to-sales turnover ratio, which in turn leads to a high rate of return on equity. Conversely, sectors with low asset-to-sales turnover ratios will have low rates of return on equity.

Additionally, the firms within the industry report R&D expenditures as a current expense not a capital expense. Not amortizing the cost streams associated with R&D means that profits are somewhat overstated by not having an ongoing cost stream to charge against the revenue stream that result from launching new products.

Grabowski, Vernon, and DiMasi (2002) have reported that only 30 per cent of marketed products will reach breakeven and only 10 per cent will return a profit. Whether one agrees with their estimates of the cost of R&D, the key point is this: regulatory approval does not guarantee profitability; rather, it is the market environment into which the product is launched and the intrinsic value of the product as perceived in the marketplace that *ceteris paribus* determines profitability.

Guell and Fischbaum (1995), among others, have observed that the industry uses Ramsey pricing to segment markets according to their willingness and ability to pay. Differential pricing is indeed the pricing policy the industry prefers to use as the mechanism to make drugs available to poorer countries. This means, of course, that wealthier countries like the U.S. subsidize drug utilization and research for much of the rest of the world, a practice that has led to intense criticism in the U.S. However, alternatives, such as a single global price, or at least regional pricing bands, do not produce the social welfare gain that Ramsey (or differential) pricing produces. In effect, a single global price would likely be too high for poor countries and too low for countries that demand sustained innovation and are willing to underwrite its development and early access.

Non-price issues related to R&D

While it is fair to criticize the industry for not devoting resources to major diseases of the developing world, criticism based on the lack of profitability is something of an oversimplification and requires additional context. Developing countries often lack the core infrastructures to deliver essential medicines to their populations. The lack of transportation, clinics, and health personnel are often overwhelming challenges. In effect, developing medicines without a country having a secure channel of distribution is a major concern of pharmaceutical companies because the company pursuing research in disease areas representing a public health crisis will also have to address infrastructure issues, areas in which a single company has either limited or no expertise. In effect, both the lack of price levels to justify the product's development and the lack of a basic market structure are contributing factors.

The way most major companies enter new markets is through establishing joint ventures with existing leading companies in the national market. Alternatively, the multinational firm may elect to acquire a smaller company within the country of interest. The problem in Africa and much of Asia is that firms capable of R&D or marketing do not exist. Accordingly, market entry is at a high cost given the commercial opportunities that are present or attainable in the near term. This difficulty is often compounded by the lack of research capabilities in academic institutions and medical centers. Even in India and China, drug discovery expertise is only in the emerging stages. Certainly, India and China have excellent scientists and research-intensive institutions, but their focus has largely been directed towards chemical synthesis and other applied scientific areas, not on basic research that will lead to novel drug therapies.

Technical factors in infectious disease research

Moreover, the discovery of effective agents to treat infectious diseases such as malaria and tuberculosis is inherently difficult – bacterial resistance and viral mutations are common, so that therapies have very limited efficacy, and a discovery platform in infectious disease is a multi-year commitment of financial and other research resources. Again, developmental failures are expensive and R&D expenditures are what economists call "sunk costs," meaning that the costs are not recoverable in the future.

Compounding the difficulty in undertaking basic scientific research is that the margin between efficacy and toxicity is typically very small – the dosage that is safe to administer to humans is often very close to the dose that results in dangerous adverse drug reactions. Also, the formulations, or dosage forms, require special handling, adding to the difficulties in delivering a new drug when basic transportation and storage facilities are lacking.

Finally, parallel trade, the fear of compulsory licensing, and counterfeiting are major risks for pharmaceutical companies entering emerging and underdeveloped markets. Government enforcement of patent laws is uneven at best, and the industry's fear of loss of intellectual property rights has resulted in the industry's adopting patent protection strategies that appear unreasonable to many policymakers. The most recent WTO round has highlighted the industry's fear that developing countries can capriciously define diseases found primarily in industrialized countries (e.g., diabetes) as "public health crises" and seize patents through compulsory licensing.

Consensus (or its lack)

There is no industry consensus on pricing strategies other than that free markets are preferable to government-regulated markets. Free markets work relatively efficiently in developed countries because by definition they are self-correcting and imperfections can be remedied either by mild governmental intervention or by pharmaceutical companies changing their marketing practices. For instance, increased access to affordable medicines can, within limits, be addressed in part by the distribution of free goods (drug samples) and programs that offer drugs at reduced prices for indigent patients. (The previous statement will be viewed as heretical by some, but the key point is that wealthy nations have the ability to solve their access problems if they are part of the collective political will.)

It is becoming apparent to some companies that market solutions will not work in developing countries. Aid for these least developed countries will not be met sufficiently through the World Bank; the OECD member states will remain insufficient. This recognition begs the question of how to fund R&D in emerging and underdeveloped markets in the absence of a price system for allocating resources. Past models of direct government and foundation grants for drug development and guaranteed purchase agreements for vaccines have not proved effective due to lack of long-term financial commitment.

There are encouraging signs of novel government–industry partnerships in malaria, avian influenza and AIDS, but it is too early to predict if these ventures will be successful. The key determinant will be the sustainability of the commitment and the level of financial commitment from all vested parties.

Corporate social responsibility

As noted elsewhere in this volume, pharmaceutical companies have slowly come to recognize that they have social responsibilities that must be addressed beyond those associated with R&D output. Multinational pharmaceutical corporations have a genuine desire to serve public health needs but are constrained by their obligation to shareholders and other factors. All companies aspire to be good corporate citizens in the communities and countries in which they operate and with the populations in which their products are used.

The decisions involving CSR reside with the board of directors. The operating units within the firm (R&D, Commercial Operations, Manufacturing, Country and Regional Managers, etc.) are concerned with meeting expense and profit goals set by the board. CSR targets are set by the board and, in turn, delegated to the divisions to implement.

Perceptions of their role in meeting societal and public policy needs are also significantly influenced by the firms' recognition that widespread public health problems are beyond the firms' individual and the industry's collective abilities to impact positively. Product and monetary donations in response to natural and environmental disasters are substantial, but tension often results between the donor company and the recipient organization or country over lack of evidence that funds or product donations were used for the intended purpose.

As profit-making corporations that operate under stringent regulations and laws, distrust of governments is profound and colored by the industry's prior contentious, negative experiences with national price controls, international trade agreements, regulatory approvals, and patent protection. As a consequence, many of the ventures that pharmaceutical companies undertake are in partnerships with NGOs, including international relief organizations (e.g., the Red Cross, Red Crescent), international organizations (e.g., the World Bank, WHO), charities (e.g., Oxfam), and public foundations. A number of major firms have established their own foundations, but the level of funding, with some exceptions (such as the Robert Wood Johnson Foundation and the Lilly Endowment), is relatively small.

The current status of global relationships between governments and the pharmaceutical industry can be described as clearly strained and in a state of disequilibrium. At this point it is difficult to forecast the precise timing at which a new equilibrium will emerge, but the implications on the future of the industry are profound. Two bipolar scenarios for the nature of the disequilibrium's resolution include a government-directed R&D agenda with price controls vs. a patient-centric scenario characterized by patients, providers, and/or governments demanding proof of value for money and treatment guidelines based on evidence-based medicine. It is largely concern about the former scenario that underlies the industry's desire to implement CSR initiatives.

The industry and its trade associations have been late to realize that they must address social needs in order to prevent the balance of power shifting to governmental control. As a result, the industry is expanding its scope of CSR beyond the traditional environment and employee health and safety areas. The majority of firms have a long history of product donations through patient assistance programs. Notably, PhRMA reports that the value of free medications was US$10.5 billion in the U.S. in 2003.

This shift to formal CSR programs and their associated investments must be justified by and subjected to performance measures that are typically not found in NGOs and not-for-profit corporations. Pharmaceutical companies view programs that constitute their global social responsibility as cost centers, which in turn must be managed in concert with the programs' impact on both short-term and longer-term financial objectives. Accordingly, public access and other programs are designed, implemented, and evaluated under stringent management control processes.

As noted, the industry has relied on patent protection and differential pricing to address access and affordability issues. As stated elsewhere, Ramsey pricing is used rather than a single global price (or regional pricing bands) under the assumption that Ramsey pricing is a more efficient mechanism to meet the needs of poor nations while generating sufficient operating margins in wealthier nations to sustain R&D. In other words, social welfare is improved for many countries but not for the poorest. Some companies do pursue a single global price strategy, but this strategy is difficult to sustain because of factors such as parallel trade, currency fluctuations, internal price control schemes, and international political pressure on the industry to reduce prices to developing nations, or as an alternative, to require compulsory licenses to be granted.

Operationalizing corporate social responsibility

Although variation among definitions and scope are to be expected, many companies will include some of the following elements:

- Environmental:
  - Energy conservation (greenhouse gases)
  - Water purification and conservation
  - Waste management
- Social:
  - Workforce diversity
  - Safety and health
    - Accident reduction among employees
  - Animal research (ethical issues)
  - Bioethics and clinical research
    - Clinical trial registries and transparency
    - Human rights
    - Capital investment in developing countries
- Compliance and controls:
  - Site audits
  - External benchmarking
  - Governance controls
  - Regulatory infringement reporting
- Community support
- Programs for patient assistance:
  - Product donations
  - Charitable donations

Implementation of CSR programs

One of the more recent organizational changes within pharmaceutical companies is the formal incorporation of CSR activities into the culture and managerial structures and processes of the firm. This formalization involves consolidating disparate activities into both corporate and affiliate management structures that will be objective-driven, transparent to employees, and complied with consistently across the corporations divisions. Operationalization is a deliberate, multi-year plan, and progress is measured according to achievements of specific objectives.

CSR operationalization is not a simple task: a global pharmaceutical company may employ over 50,000 people in as many as 100 countries. To move this workforce spread across operating units of the firm throughout many diverse geographic markets requires a multi-year commitment of the corporate board to implement it. It is partially for this research that the industry's efforts to act more responsibly are largely unknown outside the firm. Added to this problem of visibility is that individual companies have little identity *per se* – their products may be known but very little corporate visibility exists with patients and other stakeholders.

Summary

It is critical for all stakeholders that the pharmaceutical industry better manage health and shareholder needs. Society benefits from a viable, financially stable, and productive global pharmaceutical industry. An equilibrium that recognizes the interdependence of all stakeholders is a desirable but challenging goal, which will not be attained unless progress is made in operationalizing this recognition. Clearly, the first step is for the industry to demonstrate that its contributions are based on R&D, not sales and marketing of incremental innovations and product-line extension. Also, governments and NGOs must recognize that the industry must have a favorable environment for innovation to flourish. This translates into maintaining strong intellectual property rights, a stable regulatory, pricing, and reimbursement environment, and the recognition that pharmaceutical innovation is a major contributor to the health of nations.

References

Grabowski H., J. Vernon, and J. A. DiMasi. 2002. Returns on Research and Development for 1990s New Drug Introductions. *PharmacoEconomics* 20, no. 3: 11–29.
Guell, R. and M. Fischbaum. 1995. Toward Allocative Efficiency in the Prescription Drug Industry. *Milbank Quarterly* 73: 213–229.
IMS. 2005. *World Markets: Looking to China and Cancer as Cost Containment Slows Sales Growth*. Plymouth Meeting, PA. IMS Health. Available at: http://www.imshealth.com/web/content/0,3148,64576068_63872702_70260998_73052844,00.html [Accessed January 12, 2006].

Part II

Justice – medicines as global public goods

7 Pharmaceuticals, public health, and the law: a public health perspective

Wendy E. Parmet

In 1721, after many years of absence, smallpox came to colonial Boston. Traveling aboard ship from the West Indies, the "destroying angel" threatened to devastate the unexposed population (Winslow 1974). Faced with potential calamity, many residents turned to prayer, others to escape. Still others braved Dr Zabdiel Boylston's new and fearful practice of variolation, also known as inoculation, which injected pus from a smallpox patient into the skin of a healthy person. Following the inoculation, the patient generally contracted a mild case of smallpox, which provided protection, what today we would call "immunity," from the severe, life-threatening form of the disease (Carrell 2003).

Unfortunately, inoculation not only prevented virulent cases of smallpox, it also caused them. The mild cases of smallpox triggered by inoculation were contagious and could spread the natural, deadly, form of the disease. As a result, the entire community could be affected by inoculation. Practiced under conditions of strict isolation and quarantine, it could reduce the number of people who would become sick and thereby infectious; without such precautions, it could trigger an epidemic.

Given the novelty and risks associated with variolation, it is not surprising that it was initially greeted with skepticism and anger (Blake 1959). According to Boylston's chief supporter, Reverend Cotton Mather, the people "rave, they rail, they blaspheme; they talk not only like Ideots, but also like *Fanaticks* ..." (Winslow 1974). Over the years, however, the benefits of inoculation became clear and the public increasingly clamored for it, at least when smallpox threatened. The question was how to use the practice in a way that reduced its dangers.

Although the select men of colonial Boston were untrained in immunology or epidemiology, they understood that inoculation was not a matter to be left to individuals. Neither the colonial medical marketplace nor the good judgement of physicians such as Dr Boylston could be trusted to determine the use of such a powerful but dangerous innovation. Hence, after several failed attempts to stop the practice, town leaders eventually regulated it, insisting that it be administered under conditions of quarantine. They also provided support for the establishment of inoculation hospitals and, ultimately, during the epidemic of 1764, for the mass inoculation of residents, to be provided free of charge to the poor. With these legal interventions in place, almost all residents of Boston became immune to the disease (Blake 1959).

I begin with this story because it highlights three important points that remain salient to a contemporary discussion of the "power of pills." First, pharmaceuticals – a term I will use broadly and interchangeably with the terms "medicine" and "drugs" to include all foreign substances including biologics administered to prevent or ameliorate disease – are often at least partial public goods with significant implications for the health of populations. Second, many diseases and many of the pharmaceuticals we use to combat them are global in their development and impact; hence drugs are not simply public goods, they also share many characteristics of what Richard Smith and colleagues term "global public goods," in that they exhibit a "significant degree of publicness (i.e. non-excludability and non-rivalry) across national boundaries ..." (Woodward and Smith 2003). Third, given the global public attributes of pharmaceuticals, there is a strong role for law to play in regulating the conditions under which medications are developed, administered, and allocated.

Pharmaceuticals as public goods

Over the last 25 years, teachings in bioethics and law have highlighted the private and individual aspects of health and healthcare (Illingworth and Parmet 2005). We have come to recognize that health plays an important role in shaping an individual's life and identity, and that respect for an individual's dignity and worth demands that at least a competent individual should have a significant, if not determinative, say about decisions affecting her health. These decisions clearly encompass whether to take a particular medical treatment, including medication. Thus the question of whether a patient should accept chemotherapy for cancer or anti-depressants for seasonal affective disorder are, in the first instance, private and properly left to the individual. From this perspective, medications would appear to be private goods that should be left largely to individual determination.

Pharmaceuticals are private in another, important way. In contrast to classic public goods, such as national defense, they can be privately consumed (Cornes and Sandler 1996). Once intellectual property protections are in place, granting manufacturers monopolies over their products (and the degree they should be is much mooted), manufacturers can prevent those who do not pay from accessing their product. Hence, from the perspective of welfare economics, drugs, especially those protected by patents, are not "non-excludable." In addition, they do not satisfy another traditional criterion for public goods: non-rivalry, or the inability of the use of a good to limit its use by others. Generally, the consumption of a medication by one person reduces its availability to others, at least in the short term, a phenomenon especially evident when vaccines are in short supply and must be rationed, as was the case with the influenza vaccine in the fall of 2004 (Wahlberg 2004). Non-rivalry is but one of the reasons there can be a highly profitable private market for many pharmaceuticals (Angell 2004).

Yet, at least some medications have the capacity to significantly impact the health and well-being not only of the individuals who take them, but also of others. In essence, these medications have positive externalities, benefits that are not captured by the individuals who consume the drugs. Medications may also impose risks, or negative externalities, on the community. In either case, they can affect public health significantly and while they themselves may not be classic public goods from the perspective of welfare economics (because they are neither non-excludable or subject to non-rivalry), they may be thought of, both from the perspective of welfare economics and from the perspective of public health, as partial public goods (Woodward and Smith 2003).

Variolation clearly demonstrated the potential negative externalities of pharmaceuticals. As noted above, the practice conferred immunity on those who were inoculated by giving them a mild form of smallpox. The mild disease, however, could be transmitted to someone lacking immunity, who could then spread it to others. Variolation could therefore start an epidemic. Hence an individual's decision to be inoculated could pose a health risk to others in the town. Only by imposing a public, legal solution, such as enforcing isolation and quarantine, could this public danger be averted.

Today's vaccines pose far less of a risk to public health than did variolation. Yet, even with extensive regulation, modern vaccines continue to have negative externalities. For example, the Sabin oral polio vaccine (OPV) can cause polio in an unvaccinated individual (it can also confer immunity in such individuals) and the contemporary smallpox vaccination (which, in contrast to variolation, uses the vaccina virus) can spread disease to immune-suppressed individuals who come into contact with someone recently vaccinated (American Academy of Pediatrics 1997; Johnson 2003; Cherkasova et al. 2005). As a result, during the recent campaign by the U.S. government to vaccinate first, or emergency, responders against smallpox, hospitals and healthcare institutions had to consider the possibility that vaccinated workers would spread vaccina to AIDS or chemotherapy patients (Gursky and Parikh 2005). Moreover, as that campaign illustrates, the public good achieved by the eradication of smallpox came at a public cost: it left a non-immune population highly vulnerable to a bioterrorist's use of smallpox (Johnson 2003).

Vaccinations can also confer enormous benefits to populations. When vaccination rates are sufficiently high they can create "herd immunity," a condition that occurs when the rate of susceptibility within a population is so low it interrupts the chain of transmission of a disease within a community (Board of Health Care Services 2004). "Herd immunity" is a classic public good; it benefits all individuals within a population.

In the case of smallpox, a worldwide campaign to vaccinate led eventually to the complete eradication of the disease in its natural state (Gursky and Parikh 2005). As R. Bruce Aylward and colleagues note, the eradication of a disease is a prime example of a public good: "Once a disease is eradicated, no one person's receipt of this protection will diminish the protection everyone else enjoys, and every newborn entering the global community is also protected" (Aylward et al. 2003). On the other hand, as discussed above, this public good may leave the world's population even more vulnerable to the disease's reemergence.

Because of their significant public benefits, vaccines are subject to significant collective action problems (Olson 1965). Individual and collective risks and benefits do not align. As a result, choices that are left to individuals might not be optimal from a population perspective. For example, when parents in developed countries with high vaccination rates decide whether their child should be vaccinated, they often do so in an environment in which the disease the vaccine protects against is relatively rare. Knowing that the risk that their child will come down with the disease is minuscule, the parent may well decide to let their child be a free rider and benefit from everyone else's vaccination while avoiding the small, but individualized, risk of a vaccine-related reaction (Fredrickson et al. 2004). Of course, if many parents make just such a choice, vaccination rates will decline and herd immunity will suffer. Hence as a result of individually rational choices, a community may face the risk of an outbreak. This is one reason why modern governments institute myriad programs to enhance vaccination rates (Parmet 2005). Nevertheless, the fact that individual preferences for vaccines do not match the public good they confer is one among many complex factors that helps to explain why the demand for and price of vaccines are insufficiently low to induce manufacturers to regularly produce a supply adequate to protect public health (Board of Health Care Services 2004). Hence, there is today an insufficient supply of influenza vaccine to meet the needs of a global pandemic (Gostin 2004).

It may appear that vaccines are *sui generis* and that other pharmaceuticals do not exhibit the same mix of public benefits and costs. That is not so. Antibiotics and antiviral medications raise many of the same issues as vaccines. Like vaccines, they can provide protection for individuals other than the patient. For example, numerous studies have shown that the transmission of HIV from mother to fetus can be dramatically reduced if the mother is treated with an antiviral near the time of delivery (American Academy of Pediatrics 2004). Likewise, studies have suggested that the reduction of viral load that can result from effective antiviral treatment for HIV can reduce the infectiousness of an HIV positive individual (Scheer et al. 2001).

The same phenomenon arises when antibiotics are administered to children with infectious diseases, such as strep throat. Every parent understands that if a child in a congregate setting, such as daycare, is left untreated, others may become sick. The use of an antibiotic in such a setting may not only treat the child, but help break the chain of transmission, thereby reducing the chance that other children will become ill. Thus antibiotics, like vaccinations, can confer public benefits.

Like vaccines, antibiotics and antivirals also have negative externalities. When bacteria and viruses are exposed to such drugs, they evolve to develop resistance (Smith and Coast 2003). As a result, the more often antibiotics are prescribed, the less effective they are apt to be in the future. Hence a decision that is rational from an individual perspective, perhaps to take an antibiotic for an ear infection, can be harmful from a social perspective, as it may breed resistant bacteria that can undermine the efficacy of the antibiotic for future users.

The phenomenon of antibiotic resistance gives the public a significant stake in whether an individual completes or complies with therapy. For example, in the case of tuberculosis, an individual's failure to comply with the lengthy therapeutic regime can give rise to the development of multi-drug resistant strains (MDR-TB) of the disease, which are difficult and expensive to treat (Kim 2003). MDR-TB can spread and cause a primary infection in previously uninfected patients (Villarino, Geiter, and Simone 1992). Because of this risk, public health officials have instituted the practice of directly observed therapy, in which healthcare workers or community members observe when a patient takes her medication. This highly social intervention has been widely credited with reducing overall TB morbidity and mortality (Villarino, Geiter, and Simone 1992).

Although the public nature of drugs is most evident with respect to medicines for infectious diseases, other drugs also confer public benefits and costs. Most obviously, medications can benefit a society by decreasing the impact of serious, chronic diseases. Thus insulin lowers the healthcare costs associated with diabetes and keeps people with the disease active and productive, sparing society from having to bear the costs of unemployed workers or orphaned children. Conversely, the rapidly rising costs of prescription drugs, due to a variety of factors including the marketing strategies of pharmaceutical companies, have created burdens for public and private payers (Kaiser Family Foundation 2004). Less obviously, a medication such as Ritalin may create a public benefit by making it easier for teachers to control a classroom. Indeed, there have been at least anecdotal accounts of schools trying to force parents to medicate their children (Barlas 2005). In contrast, other drugs, including many that are legal, can impose costs on the public. For example, painkillers that help control an individual's pain can make that individual a more dangerous driver, risking the health of others on the road. And of course addictive drugs, such as the analgesic OxyContin, may offer great benefits to individual patients but harm society by leading to addiction and criminal behavior (Inciardi and Good 2003).

More subtly, drugs can affect a society by altering its perception of what is normal and what is pathological. For example, prior to the discovery of the selective serotonin reuptake inhibitors (SSRIs) fewer people were diagnosed with the mental illnesses for which they are prescribed (Healy 2005). Perhaps there were then fewer undiagnosed cases. More likely, society's expectations for behavioral differences changed once the medication became widely available. In effect, because SSRIs are so widely prescribed in our society, they have the potential of changing what constitutes normal. Likewise, Viagra and the other drugs in its category have a significant potential to alter social understandings of what constitutes normal sexual functioning. And, if any proof was needed of how pharmaceuticals can affect culture, recall the "revolution" brought about by the development of the birth control pill in the 1960s. No one who studies that social phenomenon can believe that the decision whether or not to take the oral contraceptive solely impacted the individual women who made it. Rather, the "pill" was a drug that changed society.

To note the public nature of drugs is not to argue for the total socialization of their production, a policy option that might well reduce the availability of medications and hence the public good they can confer. Nor is it to disregard the private nature of individual choices. The question of whether any individual patient takes a specific medication is usually an intensely private affair in which the individual's interest will greatly outweigh the public's. Thus although society is affected by the use of medications such as SSRIs and the birth control pill, in both instances, the private impacts are so great as to counsel that individuals be granted a choice as to whether or not to take the medication. Moreover, even in the case of vaccinations, the medications with the most direct public benefit, there are strong reasons to permit individuals in most instances to choose whether or not to be vaccinated (Parmet 2005). The significant public impact of individual decisions as well as the collective problem, however, suggests that governments refrain from a neutral or *laissez-faire* posture with respect to those decisions. To the contrary, as in colonial Massachusetts, governments can intervene to align private choices with the public good by instituting a variety of policies that fall far short of mandating or prohibiting that particular individuals take or refrain from particular medications. For example, governments can regulate the quality of the medications that come to market; they can create incentives to develop medications with strong public benefits; and they can make drugs available to those who would otherwise be unable or less willing to take them. They can also influence the informational environment from which patients and physicians decide what medication to use and under what circumstances to use them. The question today, as in 1621, is not whether to regulate but how to devise the optimal mix, to respect individual health autonomy as well as public health.

The global nature of drugs

It is common to think that globalization is a relatively new phenomenon. No doubt in many ways this is true, but not with respect to either disease or pharmaceuticals.

In 1621 smallpox came to North America from a ship sailing from the West Indies. This importation of smallpox was not, of course, the first or even the most lethal transmission of the disease to the continent. When the indigenous peoples of the New World initially encountered this Old World disease, the impact was far more horrific (McNeil 1976). Smallpox, like other diseases, has the potential to wipe out civilizations.

Smallpox, however, was not the only disease that wreaked havoc as it traversed the globe. In the Middle Ages, bubonic plague reduced the population of Europe by a third after arriving there from the steppes of Eurasia (McNeil 1976). In the nineteenth century, cholera spread around the globe (McNeil 1976). In the twentieth century, diseases such as influenza, HIV, and SARS have traveled with the speed of jet planes.

Although people in the developed world are apt to think, like the colonial Bostonians, that diseases come from somewhere "out there," the developed world is not only a receiver in the global microbial intercourse. The 1918 pandemic of influenza, which probably was the single most lethal disease event in recorded history, is thought to have originated in Kansas, from where it traveled with American troops to the four corners of the globe (Barry 2004). And pathogens such as HIV and Ebola, which have their biological genesis in Africa, pose a global threat in part due to complex social and economic developments, including urbanization, deforestation, and climate change which have their roots beyond the borders of that continent (Institute of Medicine 1992). Thus, even diseases that may in one sense emerge from the Third World do so in part due to the contributions of highly industrialized nations and the global economy they foster.

Since the terrorist attack on New York's World Trade Center, discussions about the global exchange of disease have often focused on bioterrorism. In response to a possible bioterrorist release of smallpox, the U.S. government has stockpiled vaccine and implemented a largely unsuccessful program to vaccinate first responders (Gursky and Parikh 2005). Yet, if smallpox reappears, it will likely do so from the laboratories in the world's most scientifically developed nations. When it comes to infectious diseases, each part of the world threatens and is a threat to its neighbors.

The same holds true with respect to non-infectious diseases. Since the twentieth century, tobacco has been one of the leading causes of death in the U.S. and the developed world. Tobacco, of course, is not caused by a microbe. Indeed, it contains a drug, nicotine. In the last few years, as the rates of cigarette smoking have fallen in the West, they have risen in Third World and developing countries as cigarette manufacturers have targeted those new markets (Sugarman 2001). Tobacco-related illnesses have thus traveled the globe, like an infectious epidemic.

A very similar pattern appears to be occurring with respect to obesity and obesity-related illnesses. While obesity was initially associated with wealthier countries, where people had virtually unlimited access to calories and lived relatively sedentary lifestyles, numerous studies have shown that obesity is increasing in prevalence in many parts of the world. Although many factors are likely implicated, researchers have pointed to the adoption of Western cultural norms, including the fast-food habit (Rigby, Humanykika, and James 2004). If this is true, then obesity, like smoking, has spread like an infection from one part of the globe to another. As cultural and economic ties have increased around the world, social and environmental determinants of health in one quarter of the planet have begun to affect health in faraway quarters. Thus despite the many significant remaining (and in some ways increasing) differences in health status and health threats around the world, all humanity is increasingly acting as a single population immersed in a single environment when it comes to a multitude of health threats.

The recognition that we are one global population facing a single microbial, and even social, environment is pertinent to a discussion of drug policy because it helps to establish that the public nature of drugs is global. Thus, access to appropriate treatment for tuberculosis in one section of the globe helps to prevent the spread of MDR-TB in another. Likewise, microbial resistance that breeds due to over-prescription on one continent may undermine the treatment of patients on another. Moreover, because the health effects of social and economic activity are both public and global in their reach, the need for pharmaceuticals such as cholesterol-lowering drugs that help to mitigate those effects are global. Hence as a normative matter, those sectors of the globe (that is, all) that help create the conditions of ill health around the world owe it to the global community to share the medications that can help to reduce those ill effects. As the Puritans seemed to grasp, ethics and self-interest can offer the same advice.

Thus far, the discussion has focused on globalization's impact on the spread of disease. The story of Boylston's inoculation efforts in Boston reveals an additional aspect of the globalization of pharmaceuticals: the global exchange that goes into the development of the medicines that save lives. In Boylston's day, the knowledge about inoculation came to Boston from three continents: from Africa via slaves who remembered the practice; from Asia, where the practice was witnessed by a visiting British physician; and from Europe, where that physician published what he saw in Turkey in an account that it made its way to Boston (Blake 1959).

Today, too, the development of pharmaceuticals often spans the globe. While highly developed countries conduct the lion's share of the R&D that goes into producing a new pharmaceutical, assets from the developing world, including products from the rainforest and medicinal knowledge of other cultures, are also critical to the expansion of our pharmacopoeia. People from around the world also contribute to the development of pharmaceuticals in numerous ways: local residents share their knowledge of native plants and medicines with researchers; students from developing countries work in the laboratories and become the leading scientists in American universities; and more problematically, residents of developing countries serve as human subjects in clinical trials, sometimes for medications that they may themselves be unable to afford. Thus as in 1621, the pathways for the creation of new therapeutics remain global and reciprocal. As a result, the global community that has participated in the development of new therapies has a strong claim to access them. Moreover, from a public health perspective, because global public health depends on the development and distribution of new medications, it is in the interest of each nation to enact and endorse policies and laws that serve to keep the global pipeline open.

Conclusion

The global interdependence with respect to pharmaceuticals provides powerful reasons for international, legal responses. Because both the risks of disease and the benefits of pharmaceuticals raise global externalities, individuals anywhere have an interest in the appropriate use and allocation of pharmaceuticals everywhere. Both the common good and enlightened self-interest preclude us from concluding that control over and access to pharmaceuticals should be considered as entirely private matters.

Today there remains a widely shared consensus that public health and pharmaceuticals are not simply a matter of individual concern. Throughout the world, pharmaceuticals are heavily regulated, for example, to ensure their safety and efficacy. Numerous public programs also exist worldwide (as in colonial days) to help make essential pharmaceuticals available to the poor. In addition, important programs from the WHO's plan to eradicate polio to the establishment of the Global Fund to Fight AIDS, TB, and Malaria are evidence of a recognition of the global nature of the need. There are, however, significant reasons to worry that the international community will not undertake the interventions necessary to protect global public health.

First, the increasing dominance of individualism and free market ideology in the West has eroded the appreciation of the public nature of pharmaceuticals. Although space precludes a full examination of this issue, a few brief examples from the U.S. may suffice. During the 1980s, patient rights advocates, including especially AIDS advocates, who viewed access to risky or potentially ineffective drugs as a question of individual rights, pressured the FDA to expedite the approval of new drugs. The result has been an easing of the regulatory climate, which many believe has led to the approval of drugs with significant population risks (Harris 2004).

At the same time, the FDA's approval in the 1990s of direct-to-consumer (DTC) advertising of prescription drugs both reflects and reinforces the perception that the decision to take powerful medications is a private choice, which an "informed" consumer should make (Illingworth and Parmet 2005). Amidst seductive advertisements showing blooming fields and romantic couples, little mention is made of the public costs and benefits of drugs. Under the power of image advertising, the question of whether or not to take a medication is presented as one that an individual who wants to look young and be energetic should make, presumably with the advice or approval of a physician, but certainly with little regard to the public consequences. The advent of Internet sales of pharmaceuticals exacerbates this problem, providing a global marketplace in which individuals can purchase drugs on their own, often beyond the jurisdiction of regulators and without much more than the pretense of physician involvement (Fentiman 2003).

Not surprisingly, the increasing privatization of drugs has had public consequences. For example, ready access to Viagra has been implicated in the spread of HIV among gay men (*Alcoholism and Drug Abuse Weekly* 2004). Moreover, the increasing profitability of lifestyle and image drugs has spurred drug companies to invest in those products and away from the development of drugs necessary to save lives around the world (Angell 2004). Thus the global collective action problem is magnified by the increasing privatization of drug choices.

There are no quick or simple answers to the global collective action problem. In colonial Boston, a highly regulated, semi-theocratic community, the lure of individualism was weak, and even so it took decades to develop an effective public response. Today, we have a better understanding of epidemiology but we are also (rightly) more respectful of individual decisions. Moreover, increased globalization has added to the complexity of the problem. As we struggle against the forces of privatization to maintain and develop domestic responses to the public nature of drugs, we need also to develop and implement international ones.

The task is not easy. This is not 1721. The issues before us are neither as simple nor as stark as those faced by the young colony. Still, as was true then, the planet faces both enormous public health threats and great opportunities. These challenges cannot be faced by individuals, individual firms, or even individual nation-states alone. Only by recognizing the public international dimensions of the challenge as well as the necessity for global, legal interventions can we use the power of pills to benefit the world's well-being.

References

Alcoholism and Drug Abuse Weekly. 2004. Meth and Other Factors Contribute to Increase in STDS. 16(14): 8.

American Academy of Pediatrics. 1997. Poliomyletis Prevention: Recommendations for the Use of Inactivated Polio Virus Vaccine and Live and Live Poliovirus Vaccine. *Pediatrics* 99: 300–305.

American Academy of Pediatrics Committee on Pediatric AIDS, 2002–2003. 2004 Evaluation and Treatment of the Human Immunodeficiency-Virus 1-Exposed Infant. *Pediatrics* 114: 497–505.

Angell, M. 2004. *The Truth about Drug Companies: How They Deceive Us and What to Do About It.* New York: Random House.

Aylward, Bruce R. et al. 2003. Polio Eradication. In *Global Public Goods for Health: Health Economic and Public Health Perspectives*, edited by Richard Smith et al., note at 33. New York: University Press.

Barlas, Stephen. 2005. Special Education Bill Limits Use of Stimulants. *Psychiatric Times* February 1.

Barry, John M. 2004. *The Great Influenza: The Epic Story of the Deadliest Plague in History.* New York: Viking Press.

Blake, John B. 1959. *Public Health in the Town of Boston: 1630–1822.* Cambridge, MA: Harvard University Press.

Board of Health Care Services. 2004. Committee On the Evaluation of Vaccine Purchase Financing in the U.S. *Financing Vaccines in the 21st Century: Assuring Access and Availability.* Report prepared by the Institute of the National Academies.

Carrell, Jennifer Lee. 2003. *The Speckled Monster: A Historical Tale of Battling Smallpox.* New York: Dutton Press.

Cherkasova, E. A. et al. 2005. Spread of Vaccine-Derived Poliovirus from a Paralytic Case in An Immunodeficient Child: An Insight into the Natural Evolution of Poliovirus. *Journal of Virology* 79(2): 1062–1070.

Cornes, Richard and Todd Sandler. 1996. *The Theory of Externalities, Public Goods and Club Goods*, 2nd edn. Cambridge and New York: Cambridge University Press.

Fentiman, Linda C. 2003. Internet Pharmacies and the Need for a New Federalism: Protecting Consumers while Increasing Access to Prescription Drugs. *Rutgers Law Review* 56: 119–179.

Fredrickson, Doren D. et al. 2004. Childhood Immunization Refusal: Provider and Parent Perceptions. *Family Medicine* 36: 431.

Gostin, Lawrence O. 2004. Pandemic Influenza: Public Health Preparedness for the Next Global Health Emergency. *American Journal of Law, Medicine & Ethics* Winter: 565–573.

Gursky, Elin and Avani Parikh. 2005. Some Right Jabs and Back in the Ring: Lessons Learned from the Phase I Civilian Smallpox Program. *Journal of Health Care Law & Policy* 8(1): 162.

Harris, Gardiner. 2004. At FDA, Strong Drug Ties and Less Monitoring. *New York Times*, December 6: A-1.

Healy, David. 2005. Good Science or Good Business. In *Ethical Health Care*, edited by Patricia Illingworth and Wendy E. Parmet. Upper Saddle Ridge, NJ: Prentice-Hall.

Illingworth, Patricia and Wendy E. Parmet. 2005. *Ethical Health Care.* Upper Saddle Ridge, NJ: Prentice-Hall.

Inciardi, James A. and Jennifer L. Good. 2003. OxyContin and Prescription Drug Abuse: Miracle Medicine or Problem Drug? *Consumer's Research Magazine* 86(7): 17.

Institute of Medicine. 1992. Committee on Emerging Microbial Threats to Health. *Emerging Infections: Microbial Threats to Health in the United States*, eds. Joshua Lederberg, Robert E. Sharpe, and Stanley C. Oaks Jr. Washington, DC: National Academy Press.

Johnson, Judith A. 2003. Report for Congress. *Smallpox Vaccine Stockpile and Vaccination Policy.* Congressional Research Service, Library of Congress, January 9, 2003.

Kaiser Family Foundation. 2004. *Prescription Drug Trends.* Available at: http://www.kff.org/rxdrugs/loader.cfm?url=//commonspot/security/getfile.dfm§PageID=48305 [Accessed May 24, 2005].

Kim, Jim Yong. 2003. Tuberculosis Control. In *Global Public Goods for Health: Health Economic and Public Health Perspectives*, edited by Richard Smith et al., 54–72. New York: University Press.

McNeil, William H. 1976. *Plagues and Peoples.* Garden City, NY: Anchor Books. ,

Olson, Mancur. 1965. *The Logic of Collective Action.* Cambridge, MA: Harvard University Press.

Parmet, Wendy E. 2005. Informed Consent and Public Health: Are They Compatible When it Comes to Vaccines? *Journal of Health Care Law & Policy* 8(1): 71–110.

Rigby, Neville J., Shiriki Humanykika, and Philip T. W. James. 2004. Confronting the Epidemic: The Need for Global Solutions. *Journal of Public Health Policy* 25(3/4): 418–434.

Scheer, Susan et al. 2001. Effect of Highly Active Antiretroviral Therapy on Diagnoses of Sexually Transmitted Diseases in People with AIDS. *Lancet* 357(9254): 432.

Smith, Richard D. and Joanna Coast. 2003. Antimicrobal Drug Resistance. In *Global Public Goods for Health: Health Economic and Public Health Perspectives*, edited by Richard Smith et al., 73–93. New York: University Press.

Sugarman, Stephen D. 2001. International Aspects of Tobacco Control and the Proposed WHO Treaty. In *Regulating Tobacco*, edited by Robert L. Rabin and Stephen D. Sugarman, 246–249. Oxford and New York: Oxford University Press.

Villarino, Margarita E., Lawrence J. Geiter, and Patricia M. Simone. 1992. The Multi-Drug Resistant TB Challenge to Public Health Efforts to Control Tuberculosis. *Public Health Reports* 107: 616–625.

Wahlberg, David. 2004. U.S. Scrambles to Find Flu Shots: Ration Supply. *Atlanta Journal-Constitution*, October 7, A-1.

Winslow, Ola Elizabeth. 1974. *A Destroying Angel: The Conquest of Smallpox in Colonial Boston*. Boston, MA: Houghton Mifflin.

Woodward, David and Richard D. Smith. 2003. Global Public Goods and Health: Concepts and Issues. In *Global Public Goods for Health: Health Economic and Public Health Perspectives*, edited by Richard Smith et al., 8. New York: University Press.

8   Access to medications and global justice

David B. Resnik

Developing nations continue to struggle under the burden of HIV/AIDS, malaria, tuberculosis, diarrhea, pneumonia, measles, and other infectious diseases. Sixty per cent of all deaths in developing nations are due to infectious diseases, as compared to only 10 per cent in developed nations (IOWH 2005). In the developing world, each year diarrhea kills two million children, measles kills about 700,000 children, malaria takes about two million lives, and HIV/AIDS claims about 2.3 million lives (IOWH 2005). In sub-Saharan Africa, 25.4 million people are infected with HIV/AIDS, and there are 3.1 million new cases reported every year. In all, 7.4 per cent of the adult population in sub-Saharan Africa has the virus. In some countries, the infection rate among adults is greater than 20 per cent (UNAIDS 2004). Infectious diseases also have an economic and social impact. Infectious diseases restrict productivity, erode economic growth, discourage foreign investment, disrupt families, undermine education, and expend valuable resources on healthcare. The impact of malaria alone reduces Africa's GDP by US$100 billion a year (IOWH 2005). In sub-Saharan Africa, there are 12.3 million children orphaned by HIV/AIDS (AVERT.ORG 2005). Many developing nations have little hope of breaking out of the cycle of poverty and disease.

Access to medications can play an important role in helping developing nations to deal with infectious diseases. However, many essential drugs are simply too expensive for people in developing nations. Per capita income in 2003 was US$90 in Ethiopia, US$100 in the Congo, US$150 in Sierra Leone, US$170 in Malawi, US$200 in Niger, US$220 in Rwanda, and US$240 in Uganda (FinFacts 2005). Even with drug discounts and foreign aid programs, the cost of ART for treating HIV/AIDS ranges from US$300 to US$1,200 in the developing world (WHO 2005a). UNAIDS had a goal of providing ART to three million people in the developing world infected with HIV/AIDS by 2005. Currently, it is believed, fewer than one million people in the developing world have access to it (UNAIDS 2005).

The high cost of medications is not the only reason why many people in the developing world are not receiving ART. Most developing nations lack an adequate healthcare infrastructure to provide the testing, counseling, education, and monitoring that is required for the administration of the drug (WHO 2005b). Also, many people with HIV/AIDS in the developing world rely on traditional healers and accept traditional beliefs about the causes of disease. Many people in Africa believe that HIV/AIDS is caused by evil spirits and they reject Western solutions, such as medications and practicing safe sex (Kalichman and Simbayi 2004).

Lack of sufficient research on treatments for medical diseases is another reason why developing nations do not have access to medications. Only about 10 per cent of the world's biomedical R&D funds are spent on the problems responsible for 90 per cent of the world's burden of disease (Resnik 2004a). Although drug companies have developed medications to treat and prevent HIV/AIDS, they have sponsored little research on vaccines or treatments for malaria, diarrhea, Chagas disease, leishmaniasis, and other infectious diseases with a disproportionate affect on the developing world. Most drug companies would rather invest their R&D money in diseases with a sizeable market in the developed world, such as heart disease, arthritis, high blood pressure, sexual dysfunction, and depression. While government agencies that sponsor biomedical research devote significant sums to health problems of the developing world, they are under considerable political pressure to allocate their funds to address problems of the developed world. Private charities that have taken an interest in the problems of the developed world, such as the Bill and Melinda Gates Foundation, do not provide nearly enough to sustain the level of R&D funding needed to address the problems of the developing world (Resnik 2004a).

Infectious diseases are largely responsible for the health inequalities between developing nations and developed nations. More than 70 per cent of the world's HIV/AIDS cases and 90 per cent of the world's malaria infections occur in Africa. Ninety per cent of the deaths from TB and diarrhea each year occur in the developing world (IOWH 2005). The average HALE at birth was 38.7 in Chad, 33.2 in Ethiopia, 29.8 in Malawi, 33.2 in Niger, 26.5 in Sierra Leone, 28.7 in Uganda, and 30.9 in Zambia, as compared to 71.6 in Australia, 69.9 in Canada, 70.1 in Denmark, 71.3 in France, 73.6 in Japan, 69.6 in the United Kingdom, and 67.6 in the United States (WHO 2005b).

The differences in health between the developing and developed nations are an important problem for theories of international justice. Are these differences just or unjust? If they are unjust, how should they be addressed? What moral obligations do developed nations have toward developing nations? Do developing nations have an obligation to take steps to reduce global health inequalities? This chapter will examine these and other questions related to global justice and access to medications.

International justice

Political philosophers have traditionally conceived of justice as a relationship among people living within the same nation or state. Plato (1974), for example, held that a just state is rationally ordered. Hobbes (1982) held that principles of justice are rules that people adopt in order to attain the benefits of social cooperation and avoid the dangers of the state of nature. Conceptual problems arise when one extends this standard account of justice to the international domain, because people around the globe are not living in the same nation. The world's five billion people live in more than 150 nations. How can there be justice among people in different nations?

Skeptics argue that there cannot be anything like international justice because this is a relationship among different states. Since states are not moral agents, and cannot agree on any legal or moral principles, justice among nations is a delusion (Beitz 1999).

According to the skeptic, global health inequalities do not raise any concerns from the perspective of international justice, because there is no such thing.

There are two responses to the skeptic. Realism accepts the claim that justice is a relationship among states, but it holds that states can make choices and obey rules (Beitz 1999). While states do not make conscious choices, they can make collective decisions and be held responsible for those decisions in the same way that corporations and organizations can be held responsible for their collective decisions (DeGeorge 1995). States have a moral status and are moral actors. States can also agree on moral and legal principles of international law and conduct. Many nations have adopted treaties and declarations concerning different issues, such as human rights, human research, arms control, warfare, diplomacy, commerce, and intellectual property. Even though some nations have not accepted these agreements and others do not comply with them, the existence of these treaties and declarations proves that agreement among nations is possible. Perfect adherence and consensus are not necessary for general agreement.

Cosmopolitanism rejects the claim that justice is a relationship among states, and holds that it is a relationship among people who happen to live under different governments. According to this approach, states do not have an independent, moral status; they derive their legitimacy from how they represent the rights and interests of the people who live in their territory (Beitz 1999). Control of a geographic territory is not the same as legitimacy (i.e., political sovereignty). Legitimate states can and should help implement international justice by participating in negotiations and agreements with other legitimate states.

I reject the skeptical approach to international justice because I think it makes sense to treat some, but not all, nations as moral agents. States that demonstrate a capacity to negotiate and adhere to international rules should be regarded as moral agents. States that do not exhibit this capacity – states that are outside the bounds of international law and ethics – should be regarded as amoral (or renegade) nations. Although I am sympathetic to cosmopolitanism's idea that justice is a relationship among people in different nations, and not a relationship among nations, I believe international justice should be based on the participation of nations, because nations, not people, have the most significant impact on international justice. Nations have the power to wage war, negotiate treaties, provide foreign aid, and engage in other activities with significant consequences for international justice. Nations are moral actors on the international stage. Corporations and other organizations can also have a significant impact on international justice, but their impact is not nearly as large as the impact of nations. People living in different nations clearly have moral duties to benefit people in other nations, but these duties are a matter of personal morality, not international justice. My failure to provide aid to people who have suffered a natural disaster is very different from the United States' failure to do so. In discussing international justice, I will therefore focus on justice among nations, not on justice among the world's people.

Since international justice is possible, nations should be concerned about global health inequalities and how best to respond to them. The decision on how to respond to health inequalities depends on the approach adopted to international justice. There are three basic approaches, which mirror approaches to national justice: libertarianism, egalitarianism, and utilitarianism. Libertarians hold that individuals have a right to life, liberty, and property. An individual is free to act as he or she pleases, provided that he or she does not interfere with another's rights. Libertarians take a "minimalist" approach to justice in that they hold that individuals do not have any duties to benefit each other, unless they have made agreements to do so. Libertarians place no restrictions on social or economic inequalities, as long as these differences among people result from fair procedures of acquiring and transferring property. Libertarians hold that the sole function of the state is to protect the life, liberty, and property of individuals (Nozick 1974). If one applies this framework to international justice, it implies that states have rights to make their own decisions, to enter into relationships with other states, and to defend and govern their own territory. States do not have any obligations to benefit other states, unless they have made agreements to do so. There should be no restrictions on social or economic differences among nations, as long as these differences result from fair procedures for acquiring and transferring property. Additionally, the sole function of international law and diplomacy should be to protect the interests and property of states. A libertarian account of international justice would have very little concern for global health inequalities, provided that these differences do not result from unfair transactions among nations, such as theft, fraud, or corruption.

One of the main critiques of libertarianism is that it is a heartless and cruel philosophy, one that provides no social safety net to care for the least advantaged members of society, such as the poor, uneducated, diseased, or disabled. I accept this critique and will not rehearse it in detail here (Rawls 1971). A theory of justice should address the interests of the least advantaged members of society. A just state should do more than protect the rights and interests of its most powerful members; it should protect its least powerful members. A theory of international justice should also address the interests of the least advantaged nations, and a just system of international agreements should provide economic, diplomatic, or military aid to nations in dire need.

Egalitarianism is a theory of justice that addresses the needs of the least advantaged members of society. There are many different types of egalitarianism, ranging from Marxism to Kantianism to Christian ethics. The main idea uniting these different strands of thought is that people should be treated equally. But in what way should people be treated equally? Should they have equal rights, wealth, or opportunities? Different forms of egalitarianism have different answers to these questions (Arneson 2002). Rawls developed one of the most influential egalitarian theories. He (1971) defended two principles of justice: (1) all people should have equal rights and liberties (the equality principle); and (2) social and economic differences among people are permissible only if they benefit everyone, especially the least advantaged members in society, and there is equality of opportunity (the difference principle). Daniels (1984) has extended Rawls' theory to healthcare. He argues that diseases undermine equality of opportunity by limiting a person's range of life plans (or normal opportunity range). Healthcare institutions should promote equality of opportunity by meeting people's healthcare needs.

How might Rawls' egalitarianism apply to international justice? A straightforward way of extending the theory would be to apply his two principles to relationships among nations. Thus, all nations should have equal rights and liberties, and social and economic differences among nations would be permissible only if they benefit the least advantaged nations and there is equality of opportunity among nations. This application of Rawls' theory of justice to the international setting would imply that global health inequalities are a significant problem, since poor health can undermine equality of opportunity. Nations that are struggling with infectious diseases and other public health crises have limited opportunities for economic, social, and political development. Developed nations, according to this view, have an obligation to help developing nations break out of the cycle of disease and poverty, so that they can participate economically, socially, and politically in the community of nations. (It is important to note, however, that Rawls (1999) did not think that his two principles of justice could be applied internationally, and that he developed different principles to deal with international justice.)

Utilitarianism also addresses the interest of the least advantaged members of society, but not directly. According to a utilitarian approach to justice, principles of justice should promote the greatest good for the greatest number of people, or society's aggregate good (Mill 2002). Social and economic inequalities among people are acceptable to the extent that they help to maximize the good (utility); they are unacceptable to the extent that they have the opposite effect. For utilitarianism, helping the least advantaged members of society is not important for its own sake; it is important only as a means of promoting utility. If it turns out that utility can be better achieved by ignoring the interests of the least advantaged members, then utilitarianism would recommend this strategy. Utilitarians would also accept health inequalities among people to the extent that these differences promote utility (Häyry 2002). Although taking care of the least advantaged members of society might not promote utility, it often does, because poverty, disease, illiteracy, and other problems of the least advantaged members of society have a detrimental affect on the whole society as they lead to crime, disease epidemics, social unrest, and economic malaise. Society benefits from measures to improve the welfare of the least advantaged members, including measures to fight disease.

A utilitarian approach to international justice would hold that rules of international justice should promote the greatest good for the greatest number of nations. Social and economic differences among nations are acceptable, in this view, to the extent that they help to maximize the overall good of nations; they are unacceptable if they have the opposite effect. Utilitarianism is not concerned with helping the least advantaged nations *per se*; it advocates helping those nations only if this promotes the overall good of all nations. If the overall good of all nations can be better achieved by not helping the least advantaged nations, then utilitarianism would recommend that course of action. However, taking care of the least advantaged nations (that is, developing nations) often promotes the utility of all nations, because poverty, famine, epidemics, illiteracy, and other problems of developing nations can have a negative impact on all the nations in the world by leading to crime, war, terrorism, global epidemics, trade barriers, and other economic troubles. All the nations of the world usually benefit from efforts to improve the welfare of the least advantaged nations, including efforts to reduce the burden of disease on those nations. Thus, a utilitarian approach to international justice would hold that the world's nations should take steps that tend to reduce global health inequalities. The utilitarian would be concerned about reducing health inequalities not for the sake of narrowing the gap between developing and developed nations, but so that all the world's nations can benefit from the effect of reducing the disease burden of developing nations.

To summarize, two different approaches to international justice, Rawls' egalitarian theory and utilitarianism, would both recommend that the world's nations take steps to reduce global health inequalities, but for different reasons. A Rawlsian would hold that the world's nations should provide aid to the least advantaged nations so that these nations can have an opportunity to develop and participate in the community of nations. A utilitarian would hold that world's nations should help to reduce the disease burden of the least advantaged nations to prevent these countries from causing harm to other countries, and to help these countries participate in economic activities that can benefit other countries.

Access to medications

Since international justice requires developed nations to help reduce global health inequalities, and one of the best ways of reducing health inequalities is to promote access to medications for developing nations, it follows that international justice requires developed nations to help developing nations attain access to medications, especially those used to treat or prevent infectious diseases. There are two different access issues that need to be addressed: availability and cost.

Medications do not appear out of thin air: they become available to the world only after extensive R&D. There are two primary sponsors of biomedical R&D: private industry, which sponsors about 60 per cent of R&D, and the government, which sponsors about 35 per cent. Private foundations and universities sponsor the remaining 5 per cent. Seventy per cent of clinical trials are industry-sponsored (Resnik 2004a). According to industry estimates, it costs, on average, US$800 million to discover and test a new drug and bring it to market (PhRMA 2005). While some authors have argued that this cost is inflated and that the real cost is closer to US$100 million, even US$100 million is well beyond the budgets of most developing nations (Angell 2004). Since most developing nations simply cannot afford to spend hundred of millions of dollars on developing a single drug, they must rely on R&D sponsored by corporations or governments from developed nations.

Most pharmaceutical companies consider profitability of the new potential products when deciding how to allocate their R&D funds. Factors that affect profitability include: (1) the size of the potential market; (2) competing products; (3) consumer demand; (4) time from the laboratory to the market; and (5) intellectual property protection (Resnik 2004a). Private companies have invested relatively little in medications used to prevent or treat disease with a disproportionate impact on developing nations, and have focused instead on chronic diseases that are of great concern to developed nations. These include hypertension, heart disease, arthritis, depression, diabetes, and sexual dysfunction. In 2004, the two drugs that generated the highest global sales both lower blood cholesterol: Lipitor, made by Pfizer, with sales of US$10.6 billion; and Zocor, made by Merck, with sales of US$6.1 billion. Other top sellers included Zoprexa, an anti-psychotic, made by Eli Lilly, with sales of US$4.8 billion; and Norvasc, an anti-hypersensitive, made by Pfizer, with sales of US$4.5 billion (Herper 2004). Drugs used to prevent or treat infectious diseases were not among the sales leaders.

One could argue that pharmaceutical companies have a social responsibility to conduct research on diseases that have a disproportionate impact on developing nations. Pharmaceutical companies have social responsibilities because they are moral agents with obligations to the countries in which they do business. Companies that conduct business in developing nations have a moral duty to help those nations, which they can discharge by offering drug discounts, enhancing the healthcare infrastructure, or sponsoring research on diseases that affect developing nations (Resnik 2001).

Although there are strong moral arguments for pharmaceutical companies to sponsor R&D on diseases that have a disproportionate effect on developing nations, it is unrealistic to expect private industry to shoulder this burden, because a great deal of money is needed to develop the medications for the developing world and many (if not most) pharmaceutical companies are not interested in helping to solve the developing world's problems. Private charities are playing an increasingly important role in sponsoring biomedical research for the developing world, but they do not have enough money to make a significant impact on global health inequalities. Governments from developed nations, however, do have enough to make an impact. Therefore, governments from developed nations should lead the way in sponsoring R&D to meet the health needs of developing nations. To facilitate this effort, the UN should establish a trust fund and countries from around the world should contribute to it. New medications developed via this funding mechanism should be made available to developing nations as cheaply as is feasible (Resnik 2004a).

Intellectual property laws help to keep medications prices high by allowing companies to limit the supply. When a company obtains a patent on a new drug in a particular country, it has the legal right to exclude other companies from making, using, or marketing that drug in that country until the patent expires, usually about 20 years after the patent application. Patents, in effect, give the patent holder a monopoly on a particular invention. By preventing other companies from selling a patented drug, a pharmaceutical company can charge whatever the market will bear. When the patent expires, the price of the drug usually drops dramatically, as other companies start selling generic versions (Resnik 2004b). Pharmaceutical companies often use a variety of maneuvers to keep generic drugs off the market and extend their patent protection, such as filing patents that do not meet the conditions of patentability, attempting to patent the same invention twice, or suing generic companies for patent infringement (Angell 2004). Since patent rights represent a delicate balance between public and private interests, governments should take steps to prevent private companies from abusing those rights, such as tightening up the enforcement of patent laws and using anti-trust laws to deter anti-competitive practices. In addition to patent protection, companies gain exclusive market rights in the U.S. from the FDA, a period that may last from three to seven years after the drug goes on the market.

There are strong utilitarian justifications for the patent system. First, patents reward inventors and businesses for innovation. Without the economic reward of a patent, many inventors and businesses would refrain from pursuing inventions or would use trade secrecy to protect them. Since a business can protect its trade secrets for an indefinite period, the secret information might never become available to the public. When a government agency awards a patent to an inventor, the information provided on the patent application becomes part of the public domain, and the public can make, use, or market the invention when the patent expires. Second, patents encourage investment in R&D. As noted earlier, it costs hundreds of millions of dollars, on average, to develop a new drug. No company will spend this much unless it is assured that it will be able to protect its intellectual property. Innovation and investment in R&D lead to many important benefits for society, such as scientific, medical, and technological progress, the improvement of human health and well-being, and economic development. Although the benefits of patenting may not outweigh the harms in particular instances, there is substantial evidence for the economic and social utility of the patent system on the whole (Jaffe and Lerner 2004).

Developed and developing nations have negotiated a variety of international treaties to protect intellectual property rights. One of the most important of these is TRIPS, which has been adopted by members of the WTO (WTO 1994). There are 148 members of the WTO and many more nations that are planning to become members. WTO members first negotiated TRIPS during the Uruguay Round in 1994, and they have renegotiated the Agreement several times since then, most recently in 2003. The TRIPS Agreement requires that patents last at least 20 years and are available in all fields of technology. Governments may refuse to grant a patent if commercial exploitation of the invention would be regarded as immoral or against the public order. Governments may also refuse to grant patents on "diagnostic, therapeutic and surgical methods, plants and animals (other than microorganisms), and biological processes for the production of plants or animals (other than microbiological processes)" (WTO 1994: 331). The Agreement allows governments to issue compulsory licenses, which allow competitors to market or use an invention, without obtaining permission from the patent holder. Compulsory licenses may be issued only if the patent holder is abusing his patent rights. TRIPS also allows nations to take measures, such as compulsory licensing or importation from other WTO member countries, to respond to national emergencies or other situations of extreme urgency. This last measure was adopted to help developing nations to protect public health and promote access to medications needed to prevent or treat infectious diseases (WTO 2005). The Doha Declaration (WTO 2001) sets out the rationale for these exceptions to the TRIPS Agreement.

The TRIPS Agreement is consistent with the requirements of international justice discussed here. While the Agreement recognizes and reinforces intellectual property rights, it also includes important exceptions to allow nations to deal with public health or other national emergencies. The Agreement allows developing nations to take measures to help bring down drug prices if they have difficulty obtaining access to medications. However, it would still be prudent for nations to use the emergency powers under TRIPS with great discretion and care, since these exceptions could soon become the rule if countries apply them to every medication that they need. To avoid undermining the Agreement, nations should articulate a clear definition of a "national emergency" and should use the emergency exception only after failing to achieve reasonable access to medications through good faith negotiations with pharmaceutical companies. Developing nations should cooperate with pharmaceutical companies (and developed nations) to promote access to medications. They should resort to more drastic measures only when cooperation fails (Resnik and DeVille 2002).

Conclusion

International justice requires developed nations to help developing nations attain access to medications, especially drugs to prevent or treat infectious diseases. Promoting access to medications is part of a more general obligation to address global health inequalities. Developed nations should work to reduce global health inequalities so that developing nations can break out of the cycle of poverty and disease and participate economically, politically, and socially in the community of nations. It is also important to address global health inequalities in order to prevent global epidemics, crime, terrorism, and other harmful effects of poverty and disease. There is a variety of measures that developed nations can take to promote access to medications, including funding R&D on diseases that have a disproportionate affect on developing nations, preventing abuses of the intellectual property system, working with developing nations on implementing the TRIPS Agreement judiciously, supporting the WHO GRRF, and collaborating with pharmaceutical companies in socially responsible activities, such as price reductions for developing nations, drug giveaways, and R&D for the developing world.

Acknowledgements

I am grateful to Gerard Roman and Adil Shamoo for helpful comments. This work was supported by the intramural research program of the NIEHS/NIH. The ideas and opinions expressed in this chapter do not represent the views of the NIEHS or NIH.

References

Angell, M. 2004. *The Truth about Drug Companies*. New York: Random House.

Arneson, R. 2002. Egalitarianism. In *The Stanford Encyclopedia of Philosophy*, edited by E. Zalta. Available at: http://plato.stanford.edu/archives/fall2002/entries/egalitarianism/ [Accessed April 7, 2005].

AVERT.ORG. 2005. *HIV/AIDS Orphan Statistics*. Available at: http://www.avert.org/aidsorphans. htm [Accessed April 5, 2005].

Beitz, C. 1999. *Political Theory and International Relations*. 2nd edn. Princeton, NJ: Princeton University Press.

Daniels, N. 1984. *Just Health Care*. Cambridge: Cambridge University Press.

DeGeorge, R. 1995. *Business Ethics*. 4th edn. Englewood Cliffs, NJ: Prentice-Hall.

FinFacts. 2005. *Global/World Income Per Capita/Head 2005*. Dublin: FinFacts. Available at: http://www.finfacts.com/biz10/globalworldincomepercapita.htm [Accessed April 5, 2005].

Häyry, M. 2002. Utilitarian Approaches to Justice in Health Care. In *Medicine and Social Justice*, edited by R. Rhodes, M. Battin, and A. Silvers, 53–64. New York: Oxford University Press.

Herper, M. 2004. The World's Best Selling Drugs. In *Forbes.com*. Available at: http://www.forbes.com/technology/2004/03/16/cx_mh_0316bestselling.html [Accessed April 10, 2005].

Hobbes, T. [1660] 1982. *Leviathan*. Reprint, New York: Penguin.

Institute for One World Health (IOWH). 2005. *The Burden of Infectious Disease*. Available at: http://www.oneworldhealth.org/global/global_burden.php [Accessed April 5, 2005].

Jaffe, A. and J. Lerner. 2004. *Innovation and its Discontents*, Princeton, NJ: Princeton University Press.

Kalichman, S and L. Simbayi. 2004. Traditional Beliefs about the Cause of AIDS and AIDS-Related Stigma in South Africa. *AIDS Care* 16: 572–580.

Mill, J. [1863] 2002. *Utilitarianism*. 2nd edn. Reprint, Indianapolis: Hackett.

Nozick, R. 1974. *Anarchy, State, and Utopia*. New York: Basic Books.

Pharmaceutical Research and Manufacturing Association (PhRMA). 2005. *Intellectual Property: Overview*. Available at: http://www.phrma.org/issues/intprop/ [Accessed April 10, 2005].

Plato. [*circa* 400 BC] 1974. *The Republic*, translated by G. Grube. Indianapolis: Hackett.

Rawls, J. 1971. *A Theory of Justice*. Cambridge, MA: Harvard University Press.

——. 1999. *The Law of Peoples*. Cambridge, MA: Harvard University Press.

Resnik, D. 2001. Developing Drugs for the Developing World: an Economic, Legal, Moral, and Political Dilemma. *Developing World Bioethics* 1: 11–32.

——. 2004a. The Distribution of Biomedical Research Resources and International Justice. *Developing World Bioethics* 4: 42–57.

——. 2004b. Fair Drug Prices and the Patent System. *Health Care Analysis* 12: 91–115.

Resnik, D. and K. DeVille. 2002. Bioterrorism and Patent Rights: Compulsory Licensure and the Case of CIPRO. *American Journal of Bioethics* 2, no. 3:29–39.

UNAIDS. 2004. *AIDS Epidemic Update 2004*. Geneva: UNAIDS. Available at: http://www.unaids.org/wad2004/EPIupdate2004_html_en/epi04_00_en.htm [Accessed April 5, 2005].

——. 2005. *3 by 5 Initiative*. Geneva: UNAIDS. Available at: http://www.unaids.org/Unaids/EN/Treat+3+million+by+2005+Initiative.asp [Accessed April 5, 2005].

World Health Organization (WHO). 2005a. *Anti-retroviral Therapy*. Available at: http://www.who.int/hiv/topics/arv/en/#cost [Accessed April 5, 2005].

——. 2005b. *Health Adjusted Life Expectancy*. Geneva: WHO. Available at: http://www3.who.int/whosis/hale/hale.cfm?path=whosis,burden_statistics,hale&language=english [Accessed April 5, 2005].

World Trade Organization (WTO). 1994. *Agreement on Trade-Related Aspects of Intellectual Property Rights*. Geneva: WTO. Available at: http://www.wto.org/english/docs_e/legal_e/27-trips.pdf [Accessed January 15, 2006].

——. 2001. *Doha WTO Ministerial 2001: Ministerial Declaration*. Geneva: WTO. Available at: http://www.wto.org/english/thewto_e/minist_e/min01_e/mindecl_e.htm [Accessed November 15, 2005].

——. 2005. *Decision Removes Final Patent Obstacle to Cheap Drug Imports*. Geneva: WTO. Available at: http://www.wto.org/english/new_e/pres03_e/pr350_e.htm [Accessed April 11, 2005].

——. 2005c. *Declaration on the TRIPS Agreement and Public Health*. Geneva: WTO. Available at: http://www.wto.org/english/thewto_e/minist_e/min01_e/mindecl_trips_e.htm [Accessed April 11, 2005].

9 Pharmacogenetics and global (in)justice

Søren Holm

The aim of this chapter is to analyze how pharmacogenetics is likely to influence the possibility of resource-poor countries gaining access to reasonably priced drugs that the pharmaceutical industry is going to develop in the future. This is not the first paper to consider this issue (Wertz 2003), but I hope to be able to deepen the analysis. A substantial literature is already developing on the link between pharmacogenetics and race, and although there is clearly a link between race and poverty, I will in the main not engage with the race debate here (McLeod 2001; Lee 2003; Lillquist and Sullivan 2004; Tate and Goldstein 2004; Duster 2005).

In the heated debate about access to drugs and the influence of the international intellectual property protection regime, most notably the TRIPS Agreement, on this access (Holm 2000; Oliveira et al. 2004; Sterckx 2004), it has usually been assumed that when a drug is finally out of patent it will be produced by generic producers at much lower prices than when it was still under patent protection, and it will thereby become available to patients in resource-poor countries. (I do believe that the current international patent regime concerning drugs and other healthcare products is fundamentally unjust and should be scrapped, but most of the problems discussed below will occur whether or not drugs are protected by patent.) The benefits of pharmaceutical developments will thus eventually, and with considerable delay, "trickle down" to the poor. It has long been clear that the trickle-down theory is not true for those who are very poor or who live in very poor countries, since even the price of generics is beyond their reach, but certain likely developments in the way drugs are developed and registered in the era of pharmacogenetics may mean that the likelihood of trickle-down will decrease or completely disappear for certain new drugs.

What is pharmacogenetics?

Pharmacogenetics is essentially:

> the discipline which takes the patient's genetic information of drug transporters, drug metabolizing enzymes and drug receptors into account to allow for an individualized drug therapy leading to optimal choice and dose of the drugs in question. (Ingelman-Sundberg 2001: 186)

There is a large number of well-documented examples of clinically significant pharmacogenetic interactions, some concerning very well-known drugs like the analgesic codeine and the anticoagulant warfarin (Ingelman-Sundberg 2001; NCB 2003), and the first major pharmacogenetic test-kit has just received regulatory approval from the USFDA one year after being marketed in Europe at a price of €400 (Roche Diagnostics 2005). (This does not include the capital investment in the machine needed to read and interpret the DNA chip, or the cost of preparing the blood sample for testing.) In its press release about this product Roche Diagnostics describes it thus:

This new test allows physicians access to information that could help to prevent harmful drug interactions and to assure drugs are used optimally. Adverse drug reactions cause a huge number of hospitalizations in the US. Our new test also will, in some cases, enable patients to avoid suboptimal or even harmful treatment choices. For patients it is extremely important to know whether painkillers or anesthetics might work differently or not at all for them. Poor or slow metabolizers may experience much longer-lasting effects of the treatment. The knowledge of the reasons behind this will empower people to ask for different and better-to-tolerate medicines. The use of this test is an important step forward in making personalized medicine a reality and has the potential to help physicians improve patient outcomes.

Two key genetic regions encoding the enzymes of the cytochrome P450 complex are established as the "gold standard" of molecular diagnostics worldwide. The knowledge Roche Diagnostics has acquired in the past 18 years is protected by several hundred patents.

CYP2D6 and CYP2C19 genes. The multiple variations in the CYP2D6 gene can result in poor, intermediate, extensive ("normal"), or ultra-rapid metabolism of CYP2D6-dependent drugs from a variety of classes, including anti-depressants, anti-psychotics, anti-arrhythmics, beta-blockers, pain medications, anti-emetics, and some anti-cancer drugs. Variations in the CYP2C19 gene result in either normal or poor metabolism of CYP2C19-dependent drugs from a variety of classes, including anti-convulsants, proton pump inhibitors, benzodiazepines, and anti-malarials.

Poor metabolizers treated with drugs that are dependent on "normal" enzyme activity are at increased risk for excessive or prolonged levels of the drug in their blood (excessive or prolonged therapeutic effect or toxicity), while ultra-rapid metabolizers may not achieve sufficient therapeutic levels in their blood with standard dosing. In the case of pro-drugs (that is, drugs that require enzymatic action before they become the therapeutic compound in the body), the opposite phenomenon occurs. (Roche Diagnostics 2005: 1–2)

In the future pharmacogenetics is undoubtedly going to influence the way in which NMEs are taken through the clinical trial phase by the pharmaceutical industry and eventually registered as marketable drugs (NCB 2003). The industry has economic incentives to perform pharmacogenetic studies and regulators in resource-rich countries have legitimate incentives to require that pharmacogenetic studies are performed in order to protect future patients from preventable side effects and ensure that drugs are used in the most cost-effective manner.

Although developments in pharmacogenetics may lead to a situation where extremely lucrative blockbuster drugs become rarer, it will also lead to a situation where drugs that would previously have been terminated in the late stages of clinical development because of toxicity can be rescued and marketed, and where drugs can be shown to be (much) more effective than competitors for certain defined groups (Rioux 2000; Wolf et al. 2000). Because of the peculiarities of the patent system and the American market exclusivity system, finding a pharmacogenetic marker for enhanced effect may also allow a firm to gain further patent extensions or further periods of market exclusivity (Sullivan 2004). Whereas the molecular structure of NMEs are made public in patent applications and submission to the regulatory authorities, a pharmaceutical firm can rely on a proprietary pharmacogenetic test in its submission to the regulatory authority concerning an NME, and the eventual license and labeling can rely on that proprietary test (USFDA 2005). This means that even if generic producers can produce the NME, they can market it linked only to the specific proprietary test, unless they themselves conduct new clinical trials where patients are chosen based on a generic version of the pharmacogenetic test. Using a proprietary test will thus increase the development costs for generic producers very significantly, and will in most circumstances mean that no generic alternative is developed.

Two future scenarios

In order to focus the ethical analysis it will be useful to outline two possible future scenarios for the use of pharmacogenetics in drug development, a "business-as-usual" scenario and a "fundamental change" scenario.

Business as usual

In the business-as-usual scenario current drug development procedures continue with pharmacogenetics as an add-on in clinical phase II–IV trials. The main aim of pharmacogenetics is to develop knowledge useful at the individual level to predict toxicity or effectiveness. The populations in the trials are not selected by pharmacogenetic testing and the NME is eventually registered for general use, but a pharmacogenetic test is developed for use with the drug to identify people at high risk of side-effects or people with better chances of effect, or to ensure more accurate dosing.

In this scenario knowledge about the effects and side-effects of the drug in a general population of patients will still be developed, and trickle-down can still occur. Patients in resource-poor countries will probably not benefit from the extra information that pharmacogenetic testing will give the treating physician, but they can still benefit from the use of the drug.

Fundamental change

In the fundamental change scenario current drug development procedures are fundamentally reconfigured and pharmacogenetic testing is used to restrict the group of patients enrolled in clinical phase III and IV trials, either to those where the drug is likely to be effective or to those where it is likely that there will be no toxicity. The drug is trialed in genetically defined sub-populations only, and not across the whole population of people with a certain disease, and the NME is eventually registered only for use in persons with a specific genotype (or in persons who do not have a specific genotype).

In this scenario, knowledge generated about the effects and side-effects of the drug will refer only to a selected population. This means that, unless the pharmacogenetic test is used, the drug cannot be used or cannot be used safely. Since very little will be known about the effects and side-effects outside the selected groups, this also entails that it will be impossible to calculate a population estimate of these effects, even if the distribution of the pharmacogenetic marker in question is known in a given population.

The ethics of pharmacogenomic regulation in a context of global injustice

If the business-as-usual scenario continues to be dominant, it will not affect the possibility of generic producers producing and marketing the NME for a general population, whether or not this is before or after the patent has expired, and it will therefore not affect the possibility of resource-poor nations benefiting from the drug in question. Patients in resource-poor nations will not get the added benefits that pharmacogenetic testing can provide, but they will have access to a drug with known and quantified benefits and risks. This clearly raises issues about the just distribution of pharmacogenetic testing itself, but I will leave these aside for the moment.

If the fundamental change scenario becomes dominant, it will significantly affect the possibility of the drugs developed in this way ever becoming available in resource-poor countries.

If pharmacogenetic testing became very cheap, there would initially seem to be no problem, since resource-poor countries that could afford the drug would probably also be able to afford the test. It is well known that the cost of new technologies tends to fall, and why should this not be true of pharmacogenetic testing? It is probably true that pharmacogenetic testing will become considerably cheaper, but there are nevertheless reasons to believe that the very low-cost scenario is not going to arise, and that even if it did, it would not solve the problem. First, as mentioned above, pharmacogenetic tests can be proprietary and most tests are likely to be proprietary, since this is a convenient way for the industry to extend its control over the sale of the drug. There will thus be no generic competitors to drive the price down. Second, it is not only price that matters, but also whether the test can practically be carried out in the local circumstances. The industry has no general incentive to develop tests that can be carried out without electricity or without the possibility of keeping the test-kits reliably refrigerated. There may be special circumstances where simplified test-kits are developed, for instance if the test is intended to be carried out in a general practitioner's surgery, but this is not likely to be a general feature.

If pharmacogenetic tests continue to be outside the price or practicality range of resource-poor countries, it means that patients in these countries cannot get access to those drugs that can only be used with testing, and if the drug development process moves down the fundamental change route, this will become the case for more and more drugs.

It might be suggested that regulators in resource-poor countries could perform their own regulatory assessments of the use of the NMEs without pharmacogenetic testing, and rely less on the regulatory assessments made by the USFDA or the EMA. While an interesting idea in principle (but who should pay for the upskilling and running costs needed for this expanded role?), it runs into the very practical problem that if testing of a NME has been restricted to a specific, pharmacogenetically defined population early in the development process, there will simply be no reliable data available on the risks and benefits outside this population, and there will be no way to perform a risk assessment of the unlimited use of the drug.

This creates a fundamental problem of justice. I take it as axiomatic that no morally acceptable justification can be given for the current distribution of global resources, and that we therefore live in an unjust world. One of the often heard defenses of global injustice and/or justification of why it is not so bad after all is that, although we (the rich) benefit from technological and economic developments first, they eventually benefit everyone. But as shown above one of the likely scenarios for the future development of pharmacogenetics will have as a consequence that no trickle-down will occur. It is important to note that this is not a necessary consequence of pharmacogenetics, but it is a consequence of a combination of economic and regulatory incentives. If regulators did not allow registration of NMEs unless they had been trialed in the general target population, the problem would not occur. But can the regulator act in this way? There is an ethical argument that seems to show that regulators cannot and should not prevent the restrictive scenario from happening, but that they should in certain circumstances actively require it. The argument is basically an argument from non-maleficence, the duty not to harm, or perhaps in the case of regulatory agencies the more comprehensive duty actively to protect.

According to this argument: 1) regulatory agencies have a duty to protect the population of patients and research subjects; 2) if animal work or phase I–II trials provide evidence that a pharmacogenetic test can select a population of patients who are not at risk of a major side-effect, or who will have increased benefit it therefore follows; 3) the regulatory agency should require the developer of the drug to restrict further trials to the population of patients who are not at risk, or who are likely to benefit, in order to prevent harm and maximize benefit.

This argument seems unassailable, but does contain an important ambiguity. In summarizing the duty of the regulatory agency it is described as extending to "the population of patients and research subjects," but this is inherently ambiguous. In legal terms it is clear that a given national regulatory agency primarily has a responsibility to protect the national population of patients and research subjects (here I am considering neither what general wider obligations might be derivable in international law, nor the obligations to research subjects in third countries participating in trials approved by the regulatory agency; on this latter point see the excellent and exhaustive analysis by Macklin 2004), but it is much more questionable whether such a restriction can be justified in ethical terms. If a regulatory agency promulgates rules or makes decisions that have a major impact on the life and health of people abroad, it becomes difficult to maintain that it does not have some form of obligation to take their interests into account.

This sets up an ethical dilemma. On the one hand the regulator promotes restrictive pharmacogenetics and thereby ensures that as few persons in the protected national population are harmed as possible, while creating potentially very significant harm elsewhere; and on the other hand the regulator rejects restrictive pharmacogenetics and thereby ensures that the total amount of harm is limited, while knowing that more than the minimal number of persons possible is harmed in the protected national population (e.g., because some people in the clinical trials who could have been screened out by pharmacogenetics develop serious side-effects).

At the moment all pharmaceutical regulators choose the first horn of the dilemma and prioritize their own national populations. However, it is very difficult to find a principled justification for this.

The regulator might argue that the rules of informed consent mean that it would be impossible to pursue any other policy. If there is a known method prior to phase III trials of selecting a population that will either have serious side-effects or have no benefit from the trial intervention, the potential research participants have to be informed in order for them to be fully informed, and no one will consent to participate in a trial without the pharmacogenetic test. The weak point in this argument is that we do allow persons to consent to studies that entail some risk, and that we know that people do actually consent to such studies. If the risk inherent in a trial without pharmacogenetic screening is not higher than the risk we deem acceptable in other trials, the mere existence of risk does not make the trial ethically illegitimate. It is obvious that if people can choose between a low-risk and a high-risk trial of the same drug, they will probably choose the low-risk trial. But this is not the situation we are contemplating here. What we are contemplating is a situation where the choice is between participation and non-participation in the only trial on offer, a trial which, because of ethically based regulations taking into account the interests of all future patients, will contain a slightly higher risk than a trial taking into account only the interests of the trial participants and rich future patients. There could be no ethically based objection to taking part in such a trial. There are many types of research where we ask people to give up rights or take risks simply because of regulatory requirements. In standard clinical drug trials, participants, for instance, give permission to regulatory agencies to look into their files, and they take on the risk of the treating doctor not knowing what drug they are receiving.

Conclusion

Pharmacogenetics is undoubtedly here to stay. The technology offers such large economic advantages that it will become a standard element in the drug development process. As we have seen, the standard use of pharmacogenetics in drug development may, however, further decrease the access to drugs of people in resource-poor countries. This is not an inevitable but a likely consequence as long as the use of pharmacogenetics is primarily driven by the interests of firms, patients, and regulators in resource-rich countries. The ethical challenge raised by pharmacogenetics in drug development is therefore very similar to the challenge raised by the current intellectual property regime: whose interests should count? If all interests in life, health, and well-being were counted equally, irrespective of nationality or wealth, we would regulate pharmacogenetics in a way that ensures that all the benefits of pharmaceutical development become realistically available to everyone who need them whether they live in a rich or a poor country.

This is not the place to rehearse Peter Singer's or Peter Unger's well-known arguments for a radical redistribution of wealth (although they are rather convincing) (Singer 1972; Unger 1996), or to provide a fully worked-out scheme for remuneration of intellectual property rights in pharmacogenetic tests (like the one developed by Thomas Pogge 2005, for pharmaceuticals). However convincing Singer and Unger are, a radical redistribution is probably not going to happen soon, and I do not have the space here to develop a Poggean scheme fully. Instead, I want to put forward a more circumscribed and moderate argument that does not target the status quo, but only looks to the future. Rawls' difference principle, that changes in resource distribution should take place only if they benefit the least well-off, is well known, as are the critiques of its application at the margins where the least well-off receive no benefit, but a huge benefit can be secured for others (see, for instance, Temkin 1993). Despite these critiques I think that the idea or intuition behind the difference principle is sound. When we consider a move from one social distribution of wealth to another we should always pay special attention to how this move affects the least well-off, and if it actually worsens their situation that is a strong argument against the move. Likewise, when we consider new regulations with international implications we should pay special attention to how they will affect the least well-off (that is, in general the poorest citizens in the poorest countries), and should not implement regulations that will immediately or in the long run lead to a worsening of their situation or to a significant widening of the gap between them and us (I am assuming as a matter of empirical generalization here that the rich countries exert most control over the formulation of regulations). Otherwise we will not only not have taken the interests of the poor into account, we will have affected these interests negatively. If we see the introduction of pharmacogenetics, and especially of regulatory requirements for pharmacogenetic testing in the drug development process as a stepwise move in regulations, we will realize that even applying the moderated difference principle described here there is no way in which the stepwise change can be described as promoting justice. It may make the well-off even better off, but it does so at the price of making the least well-off worse off in the long run than they would have been if these regulations had not been implemented. My modest suggestion is therefore that no regulatory requirements should be implemented that will make future use of a NME absolutely dependent on pharmacogenetic testing (except if the NME only works, or has very severe and frequent side-effects, in one genetically defined group), unless the pharmacogenetic test in question is non-proprietary, not protected by patent, and suitable for use in resource-poor countries. I fear, however, that the poor count for so little in the world of international regulation that even this proposal will not be taken seriously.

Acknowledgement

I gratefully acknowledge the expert research assistance provided by David William Jarmain.

References

Duster, T. 2005. Medicine – Race and Reification in Science. *Science* 307: 1050-1051.

Holm, S. 2000. Three Reasons why a Global Market in Pharmaceutical Products is Inherently Unjust. *Journal of Social Philosophy* 31: 391–400.

Ingelman-Sundberg, M. 2001. Pharmacogenetics: An Opportunity for a Safer and More Efficient Pharmacotherapy. *Journal of Internal Medicine* 250: 186–200.

Lee, S. S. 2000. Race, Distributive Justice and the Promise of Pharmacogenomics: Ethical Considerations. *American Journal of Pharmacogenomics* 3: 385–392.

Lillquist, E. and C. A. Sullivan. 2004. The Law and Genetics of Racial Profiling in Medicine. *Harvard Civil Rights – Civil Liberties Law Review* 39: 391–483.

Macklin, R. 2004. *Double Standards in Medical Research in Developing Countries*. Cambridge: Cambridge University Press.

McLeod, H. L. 2001. Pharmacogenetics: More than Skin Deep. *Nature Genetics* 29: 247–248.

Nuffield Council on Bioethics (NCB). 2003. *Pharmacogenetics: Ethical Issues*. London: NCB.

Oliveira, M. A., J. A. Bermudez, G. C. Chaves, and G. Velasquez. 2004. Has the Implementation of the TRIPS Agreement in Latin America and the Caribbean Produced Intellectual Property Legislation that Favours Public Health? *Bulletin of the World Health Organization* 82: 815–821.

Pogge, T. W. 2005. Human Rights and Global Health: A Research Program. *Metaphilosophy* 36: 182–209.

Rioux, P. P. 2000. Clinical Trials in Pharmacogenetics and Pharmacogenomics: Methods and Applications. *American Journal of Health-System Pharmacy* 57: 887–901.

Roche Diagnostics. 2005. *Roche's Amplichip Cyp450 Test Receives FDA Clearance*. Basel: Roche Diagnostics. Press release, January 12.

Singer, P. 1972. Famine, Affluence and Morality. *Philosophy and Public Affairs* 1: 229–243.

Sterckx, S. 2004. Patents and Access to Drugs in Developing Countries: An Ethical Analysis. *Developing World Bioethics* 4: 58–75.

Sullivan, C. G. 2004. How Personalized Medicine is Changing the Rules of Drug Life Exclusivity. *Pharmacogenomics* 5: 429–432.

Tate, S. K. and D. B. Goldstein. 2004. Will Tomorrow's Medicines Work for Everyone? *Nature Genetics* 36: S34-S42.

Temkin, L.S. 1993. *Inequality*. Oxford: Oxford University Press.

Unger, P. 1996. *Living High & Letting Die*. Oxford: Oxford University Press.

US Food and Drug Administration (USFDA). 2005. *Guidance for Industry – Pharmacogenomic Data Submissions (with attachments)*. Rockville: USFDA.

Wertz, D. C. 2003. Ethical, Social and Legal Issues in Pharmacogenomics. *The Pharmacogenomics Journal* 3: 194–196.

Wolf, C. R., G. Smith, and R. L. Smith. 2000. Pharmacogenetics. *British Medical Journal* 320: 987–990.

Part III

The social, ethical, and political challenge: neglected diseases

10 The enduring crisis in neglected diseases

Nathan Ford

Communicable diseases continue to kill around 14 million people each year, mostly in the developing world. Infectious and parasitic diseases account for a quarter of the disease burden in low- and middle-income countries, compared to only 3 per cent in high-income countries (WHO 1999). According to the World Bank, eliminating communicable diseases would almost completely level the mortality gap between the richest 20 per cent of the world population and the poorest 20 per cent (Gwatkin and Guillot 2000).

The inadequacy or nonexistence of health tools to combat tropical diseases is a key factor preventing effective control efforts. This was not always the case. During the first part of the twentieth century, tropical diseases were a concern of European colonial administrators because of their impact on territorial expansion: diseases such as river blindness, sleeping sickness, and malaria incapacitated workers and limited exploitation of natural resources. This led to the establishment of the study of tropical medicine and the development of the European drug industry. But, as western interests withdrew, so did concern for tropical disease control (Janssens, Kivits, and Vuylsteke 1992).

Today, many gaps exist. New medicines are needed to control the reemergence of human African trypanosomiasis, to replace the ineffective and toxic drugs for Chagas disease, to overcome resistance to anti-leishmanial and anti-malarial drugs, and to simplify treatment for TB. Other diseases, such as dengue fever, Ebola hemorrhagic fever, and Buruli ulcer, remain completely untreatable. This chapter gives a brief overview of the neglected disease crisis.

Little innovation in the last 25 years for neglected disease

Drug development for tropical diseases has ground to a virtual standstill as noted elsewhere in this book. The reason these treatment needs persist is not a lack of money. Global spending on health research increased from US$30 billion in 1990 to US$105.9 billion in 2001, but over 90 per cent of this is spent on the health problems of less than 10 per cent of the world's population (GFHR 2004). Nor is it a problem of lack of knowledge. The last few decades have seen substantial advances in molecular biology and physiopathology of infectious diseases, including the recently completed genome sequencing of a number of tropical disease parasites including malaria, leishmaniasis, and African sleeping sickness (Torreele, Usdin, and Chirac 2004).

The overriding explanation is that over 90 per cent of the worldwide pharmaceutical development and production activity is done by the private sector in developed countries, where profit prospects, not health needs, drive the R&D agenda.

Money, not mortality, drives the drug development agenda

The heavy reliance on an increasingly consolidated and highly competitive multinational drug industry to generate new medicines has left the development of medicines subject to market forces. As a result the developing world, which accounts for 80 per cent of the world's population, represents barely 20 per cent of drug sales (Trouiller et al. 2001).

Drug development outcomes closely follow profit prospects. A study published in 2002 showed that drugs for cardiovascular and central nervous system diseases account for 35 per cent of worldwide pharmaceutical sales, and represent 28 per cent of new drugs developed, compared to less than 1 per cent for all tropical diseases combined. Profitability dictates that there is a 13-fold greater chance of a drug being brought to market for central nervous system disorders or cancer than for a neglected disease (Trouiller et al. 2002).

Globally, five disease groups account for 70 per cent of the total burden of disease. Infectious diseases come first, representing 31.01 per cent of the burden, followed by mental conditions, injuries, cardiovascular disease, and obstetric conditions (12.85 per cent, 12.24 per cent, 9.25 per cent, and 8.64 per cent, respectively) (Kaplan 2004). These conditions afflict both the developed and developing world. There is, therefore, a commonality of interest for some diseases, including HIV/AIDS and TB, which are increasingly prevalent in the developed world.

This overlap leads to some diseases being more neglected than others (see Figure 10.1). A degree of R&D activity exists for TB and malaria for example, as there is a market for these medicines in wealthy countries, even if the need is by far the greater in the developing world. Tropical diseases such as African sleeping sickness and visceral leismaniasis, on the other hand, afflict the developing world only and so represent little financial interest: these are the most neglected disease (see Figure 10.2).

Neglect can also exist within a single disease. HIV/AIDS, for example, represents on the one hand a major success story in terms of drug R&D, with over 20 new medicines produced in as many years, generating sales in excess of US$5.3 billion. Yet there are still gaps in AIDS-related R&D, especially for patients in poor countries. For instance, some important medicines need to be refrigerated, which limits their usefulness in many settings. The dwindling number of pediatric cases in wealthy countries has also led to a dearth of pediatric formulations, and tools to diagnose infants and monitor their treatment are maladapted to use in many developing country settings. New tools are needed for other patient groups that predominate in the developing world, such as people co-infected with tuberculosis and HIV, and pregnant women (Calmy et al. 2004).

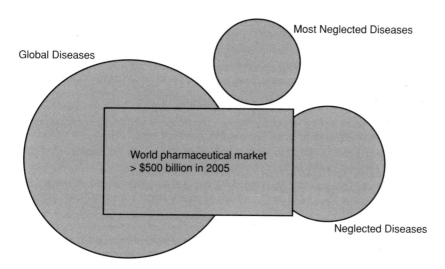

Figure 10.1: What are "neglected diseases"?

Patent-driven R&D is failing to deliver

Rather than focusing on priority health needs, companies guide drug development according to opportunities for increased market share – whatever sells, in other words. Studies show that between two-thirds (NIHCM 2002; Trouiller et al. 2002) and nine-tenths (UNDP 1999; USFDA 2004) of all medicines are copies or "me-too" drugs – variants of existing medicines that offer little, if anything, in the way of therapeutic advance. In fact, the situation appears to be getting worse: one study, which looked at a twelve-year period up to the year 2000, found that the rate of true innovation is declining (NIHCM 2002).

While the pharmaceutical industry continues to claim that patents are at the heart of the innovation process, there is increasing evidence that the patent system fails to stimulate innovation in the field of neglected diseases. The expert analysis of the UK CIPR (whose board includes the vice-president of the largest pharmaceutical company, Pfizer) concluded that:

All the evidence we have examined suggests IP [intellectual property] hardly plays any role in stimulating R&D on diseases prevalent in developing countries, except for those diseases where there is a large market in the developed world (e.g. diabetes or heart disease). (CIPR 2002)

Responding to these concerns, the WHO established the CIPIH in 2003 to:

[P]roduce an analysis of intellectual property rights, innovation, and public health, including the question of appropriate funding and incentive mechanisms for the creation of new medicines and other products against diseases that disproportionately affect developing countries. (CIPIH 2003)

Human African trypanosomiasis (African sleeping sickness): around 60 million people at risk in sub-Saharan Africa, resulting annually in around 500,000 cases and 50,000 deaths. Fatal if not treated. Most drugs are old and difficult to administer. Until recently the only treatment available for the second-stage of the disease was Melarsoprol, an arsenic-based drug that kills 5 per cent of patients.

Chagas disease: prevalent in South and Central America, affecting 16–18 million people in 21 countries. Causes 13,000 deaths per year. Infection is often asymptomatic for years but can eventually cause fatal heart damage. Two drugs are available for treatment, but can have serious and frequent side-effects.

Dengue fever: more than one-third of the world's population are under threat from this mosquito-borne disease. Responsible for 21,000 deaths per year. No specific treatment exists.

Leishmaniasis: affects 88 countries, putting 350 million people at risk and killing 59,000 people each year. Transmitted by sandflies. Drugs are either toxic or unaffordable.

Leprosy: although eradicated in most parts of the world, 650,000 cases are still reported; each year, 4,000 people die from leprosy. Effective drugs have been available since the 1940s but an extended course is needed.

Lymphatic filariasis (Elephantiasis): mosquito-borne infection causing massive swelling of the limbs and genital area. Of the 120 million people infected, around one-third are seriously incapacitated or disfigured. Two-thirds of cases occur in India and Africa. Drugs can be effective if given early enough.

Malaria: results in at least one million deaths a year, mostly children in Africa. Extensive resistance to some drugs has now prompted the WHO to recommend protocol switches to artemisinin-based combination therapies in recent years, but these are the last line of effective treatment and the ability of the parasite to develop resistance to anti-malarial drugs means a pipeline of new medicines needs to be assured.

Onchocerciasis (River blindness): a parasitic disease causing blindness. Some 18 million people in tropical Africa are infected. Of these 800,000 have vision impairment and another 270,000 are blind. A single dose of ivermectin, taken annually, is effective but does not completely clear the infection.

Schistosomiasis: affects 200 million people living in 74 developing countries. Causes damage to the bladder and kidneys. Kills around 15,000 people each year; children are especially vulnerable. Two effective drugs are available (praziquantel and oxamniquine).

Tuberculosis: kills around 1.6 million people a year. Existing treatment is long for simple treatment and even more complicated for drug-resistant cases. Diagnosis is a significant challenge.

Figure 10.2: Examples of neglected diseases*

* Diseases listed are those targeted by the WHO, UNICEF, UNDP special program for research and training in tropical disease (www.who.int/tdr)

The setting up of this Commission clearly reflects awareness that the current system for driving innovation requires serious examination and that new proposals for national and international action are urgently needed.

Drug development is a government responsibility

Awareness of the lack of effective treatments for neglected diseases has grown in recent years. In 2000, the G8 committed itself to "increasing our support at the global level for the R&D of international public goods such as AIDS vaccines; treatment drugs for AIDS, TB and malaria; microbicides and other health commodities" (G8 2000) and to "increasing incentives for the development of international public goods according to the priorities for vaccines, drugs and diagnostics set out in the Chairman's Summary" (G8 2000). G8 members also expressed strong commitment to the principle that new tools for diseases affecting developing countries should be considered international public goods (listing vaccines, drugs, methods of treatment, and health commodities as examples) (G8 2000). But since then, R&D has progressively dropped off the G8 agenda (Moran and Ford 2003).

Several recent examples demonstrate that when there is sufficient political concern, money and innovation will flow. The SARS outbreak in 2003 led to unprecedented international cooperation and a tremendous marshaling of resources to cope with this new threat. In a matter of weeks, scientists had sequenced the virus, and through successful public and private cooperation, a diagnostic kit was rapidly developed and deployed. Similarly, the anthrax scare in the U.S. in 2001 led biodefense research spending at the U.S. NIH to increase from US$53 million in 2001 to US$1.6 billion in 2004.

Lack of political will, it can be concluded, is the most important reason why neglected diseases remain just that.

Philanthropy is not enough

Significant hope is placed in the relatively new model of PPPs, which bring together R&D for neglected diseases by matching existing capacity, expertise, and resources in both the public and private sectors on specific projects or diseases. Typically, these initiatives play a coordinating role in setting a disease-specific R&D agenda, raising funds, and managing R&D projects. Examples of PPPs include the GATB, the MMV, the IAVI, and the IOWH. The recently established not-for-profit DNDI aims to research and develop new drugs for neglected diseases, with an initial focus on sleeping sickness, Chagas disease, and leishmaniasis. The DNDI model places responsibility for public health on governments, and is based on leadership from the public sector with contributions and support for the R&D process from the private sector.

A recent study showed increases in activity due to PPPs, identifying over 60 neglected disease drug development projects in progress at the end of 2004, for seven neglected diseases. The projects addressed the following diseases: malaria (33), TB (16), human African trypanosomiasis (5), Chagas (2), onchoceriasis (1), dengue (3), and visceral leishmaniasis (3). Three-quarters of these projects were conducted by PPPs (Moran et al. 2005). Factoring in usual attrition rates, the study concluded that only 8–9 drugs could be expected to come out of these projects within five years.

While governments are highly supportive of the PPPs model, they receive very little public funding and are largely dependent on philanthropic grants. For example, in 2004 the Bill and Melinda Gates Foundation provided around US$159 million to support PPPs, ten times more than the U.S. government (US$16 million). OECD governments collectively provide only 16 per cent of PPPs' total budgets, with a further 3 per cent coming from UN agencies. It is estimated that the existing PPPs will need around US$85 million in 2005 as projects go into human trials; however only US$50 million in public and private funds have been pledged to date (around a 40 per cent shortfall) (see Table 10.1; Moran et al. 2005).

Table 10.1: Philanthropic and public funding (as of April 2005, including funding committed)

Donor	Total Funding ($US)	Per cent of total
Philanthropic		
Bill and Melinda Gates Foundation	158,757,717	58.9
Médecins Sans Frontières	29,738,133	11.0
Rockefeller Foundation	20,300,000	7.5
The Wellcome Trust	2,827,504	1.1
Sub-total	211,623,354	78.5
Public		
US government	16,000,000	5.9
UK government	10,909,468	4.1
Netherlands government	10,489,255	3.9
Swiss government	4,422,285	1.6
European Commission	1,554,150	0.6
Sub-total	43,585,077	16.2

Source: Moran et al. 2005.

An international framework for neglected diseases?

There is a lot of talk about neglected diseases at the moment, but this has yet to translate into clear political action. More of the same appears to be the favored solution, as evidenced by the CfA Report that stated that the solution to the crisis was "giving large pharmaceutical firms incentives to investigate the diseases that affect Africa" (CfA 2005). This is a highly questionable policy approach. The pharmaceutical industry is already among the most profitable and privileged in the world, benefiting enormously from publicly funded research, government-granted patents, and significant tax breaks (Ford 2003). Pharmaceutical patent life has increased in the past 20 years, but the rate of innovation has not (Trouiller et al. 2002). There is little evidence that more incentives will shift the direction of drug development.

The mushrooming of PPPs has altered the neglected disease landscape, leading to a growing number of promising development projects, but funding is insecure. These efforts need to be situated within a larger framework that guarantees sustainable health R&D according to global needs and priorities. The 2001 DMD on TRIPS and Public Health acknowledged the need to address intellectual property barriers to accessing drugs, but there has been no similar movement in international policy to address the crisis in pharmaceutical innovation (Dentico and Ford 2005).

Stimulating R&D for neglected diseases will not be possible without genuine involvement of developing countries themselves. They are best placed to evaluate needs and priorities, and often also to implement R&D. Sharing knowledge and transferring technology will enable developing countries to build on their existing expertise and capacity in R&D and lead the process of redressing the imbalance in today's status quo.

Acknowledgements

This chapter draws on the work of many people who have dedicated their time to confronting the issue of neglected diseases over the past five years. In particular, I would like to thank all members of the Neglected Diseases Group (www.accessmed-msf.org).

Note

The opinions expressed in this piece are those of the author and do not necessarily represent those of Médecins Sans Frontières.

References

Calmy, A., E. Klement, R. Teck, D. Berman, B. Pecoul, L. Ferradini, and N. Ford. 2004. Simplifying and Adapting Antiretroviral Treatment in Resource-poor Settings: a Necessary Step to Scaling-up. *AIDS* 18: 2353–2360.

Commission for Africa (CfA) (2005) *Final Report: "Our Common Interest"*. March 2005. London: CfA. Available at: http://www.commissionforafrica.org/english/report/thereport/english/11–03–05_cr_report.pdf [Accessed November 11, 2005].

Commission on Intellectual Property Rights (CIPR). 2002. *Integrating Intellectual Property Rights and Development Policy. Report of the Commission on Intellectual Property Rights*. London: CIPR. Available at: http://www.iprcommission.org/ [Accessed November 11, 2005].

Commission on Intellectual Property Rights, Innovation and Public Health (CIPIH). 2003. *Commission on Intellectual Property Rights, Innovation and Public Health*. Geneva: CIPIH. Available at: http://www.who.int/intellectualproperty/en/ [Accessed November 11, 2005].

Dentico, N. and N. Ford. 2005. The Courage to Change the Rules: A Proposal for an Essential Health R&D Treaty. *PLoS Medicine* 2: 96–99. Available at: http://medicine.plosjournals.org/archive/1549–1676/2/2/pdf/10.1371_journal.pmed.0020014-L.pdf [Accessed November 11, 2005].

Ford, N. 2003. Public Health and Company Wealth. *British Medical Journal* 326: 1296.

G8. 2000. *Communiqué Okinawa. 23 July 2000*. Okinawa: G8. Available at: http://www.g8.fr/evian/english/navigation/g8_documents/archives_from_previous_summits/okinawa_summit_-_2000/g8_communique_okinawa_2000.html [Accessed December 14, 2005].

Global Forum for Health Research (GFHR). 2004. *10/90 Report on Health Research 2003–2004*. Geneva: GFHR. Available at: http://www.globalforumhealth.org [Accessed November 11, 2005].

Gwatkin, D. and M. Guillot. 2000. *The Burden of Disease among the Global Poor: Current Situation, Future Trends and Implications for Strategy*. Washington, DC: World Bank.

Janssens, P. G., M. Kivits, and J. Vuylsteke. 1992. *Médecine et Hygiène en Afrique Centrale de 1885 à nos Jours*. Brussels: Fondation Roi Baudoin.

Kaplan, W. 2004. *Priority Medicines for Europe and the World A Public Health Approach to Innovation: Priority Setting*. Geneva: WHO. Available at: http://mednet3.who.int/prioritymeds/report/background/3_chap.doc [Accessed November 11, 2005].

Moran, M. and N. Ford. 2003. The G8 and Access to Medicines: No More Broken Promises. *Lancet* 361: 9369.

Moran, M., A-L. Ropars, J. Guzman, and C Garrison. 2005. *The New Landscape of Neglected Disease Drug Development*. London: LSE/Wellcome Trust. Available at: http://www.lse.ac.uk/

collections/pressAndInformationOffice/PDF/Neglected_Diseases_05.pdf [Accessed November 11, 2005].

National Institute for Health Care Management (NIHCM). 2002. *Changing Patterns of Pharmaceutical Innovation.* Washington, DC. Available at: http://www.nihcm.org/innovations. pdf [Accessed November 11, 2005].

Torreele, E., M. Usdin, and P. Chirac. 2004. *Priority Medicines for Europe and the World A Public Health Approach to Innovation: A Needs-Based Pharmaceutical R&D Agenda for Neglected Diseases.* Geneva: WHO. Available at: http://mednet3.who.int/prioritymeds/report/background/n_ diseases.doc [Accessed November 9, 2005].

Trouiller, P., E. Torreele, P. Olliaro, N. White, S. Foster. D. Wirth, and B. Pécoul. 2001. Drugs for Neglected Diseases: a Failure of the Market and a Public Health Failure? *TMIH* 6: 945–951.

Trouiller, P., P. Olliaro, E. Torreele, J. Orbinski, R. Laing, and N. Ford. 2002. Drug Development for Neglected Diseases: a Deficient Market and a Public-health Policy Failure. *Lancet* 359: 2188–2194.

United Nations Development Programme (UNDP). 1999. *Human Development Report.* Geneva: UNDP. Available at: http://hdr.undp.org/reports/global/1999/en/ [Accessed December 14, 2005].

US Food and Drug Administration (USFDA). 2004. NDAs Approved in Calendar Years 1990–2003 by Therapeutic Potentials and Chemical Types. Rockville, MD: USFDA. Available at: http:// www.fda.gov/cder/rdmt/pstable.htm [Accessed November 11, 2005].

World Health Organization (WHO). 2000. *The World Health Report 1999, Estimates for 1998, Burden of Disease by Cause, Sex and Mortality Stratum in WHO Regions.* Geneva: WHO.

11 Moving beyond charity for R&D for neglected diseases

James Orbinski and Barry Burciul

Over the last several decades, unprecedented gains have been made in global health. Between 1960 and 2003, child mortality for under-five year olds fell from 198 per 1,000 births, to 80 (UNICEF 2005). Smallpox has been eradicated, and polio is on the verge of annihilation. However, people living in developing countries have not benefited equally from this revolution. Millions continue to die from preventable and treatable diseases, such as HIV/AIDS, malaria, and TB, and one category of diseases has been all but forgotten by drug developers. Tropical diseases such as leishmaniasis, lymphatic filariasis, Chagas and schistosomiasis continue to cause significant morbidity and mortality. The same is true for the particular treatment needs in the developing world, for example, chloroquine-resistant malaria and the need for a fixed-dose combination pediatric formulation of ARV therapy for HIV/AIDS. Other diseases such as dengue fever and human African trypanosomiasis are reemerging. In the absence of new treatments, physicians are forced to continue using old medicines that are becoming less and less effective due to the inevitable development of drug resistance. At the same time, the handful of new medicines relevant to tropical diseases tend to be unaffordable and poorly adapted to the living conditions of those who need them. Together with TB, these disabling and/or life-threatening diseases represent an enduring and unmet medical need. Collectively, they can be called "neglected diseases," and they represent a risk to the lives of some 350 million people worldwide (Pécoul 2004).

In 1999, MSF, the WHO, and the Rockefeller Foundation brought together a team of international experts to study the crisis in drug R&D for neglected diseases. These are diseases for which treatment options are either inadequate or do not exist, mainly because they affect patients with little or no purchasing power. This group of approximately 30 experts, the DND-WG, focused on identifying the causes of the crisis and finding innovative strategies to promote the development and accessibility of medicines for neglected diseases. The mission statement of the DND-WG held that:

> [I]t is the responsibility of society to address this public health failure, and seek new and creative strategies to solve this problem … Solutions and recommendations need to be sustainable, affordable, need-driven and involve input and active engagement of developing countries. (MSF 2001: 4)

In 2001, the working group proposed the development of a new kind of initiative: an independent, not-for-profit entity that would focus on developing new drugs or new formulations of existing drugs for patients suffering from neglected diseases. This initiative – DNDI – was created in July 2003. DNDI has built regional networks of scientists actively involved in the research of new drugs for neglected diseases in Asia, Africa, and Latin America. As well as priority setting, funding, and conducting scientific R&D itself within its new networks, DNDI seeks to strengthen, catalyze, and provide direction to existing, fragmented R&D capacity from around the world. In keeping with the "virtual" nature of the organization, these networks gather information on available regional expertise, capacity, and patients' needs. They also advocate for DNDI nationally and internationally, encourage scientists to submit proposals to DNDI's calls for letters, and organize regional scientific meetings that target specific neglected disease research needs (DNDI 2005).

This chapter outlines the political analysis that led to the creation of DNDI. We begin by describing the crisis in R&D for neglected diseases, and how the twin dynamics of market failure and public policy failure bear principal responsibility for this crisis. We then outline the DND-WG's analysis of existing attempts to ameliorate the crisis, focusing on aspects of the political environment that made these attempts insufficient. The chapter concludes with a discussion of the challenges DNDI poses to the existing global public health order.

Defining the crisis

It is important to draw a distinction between "neglected diseases" and "most-neglected diseases." The former category includes illnesses such as malaria and tuberculosis, in which the R&D-based pharmaceutical industry has only a marginal interest. Although people in wealthy countries are sometimes afflicted with these illnesses, they primarily affect people in developing countries. Most-neglected diseases, on the other hand, almost exclusively affect people in developing countries. Because they are often too poor to pay for any sort of treatment, these patients do not represent an attractive market for pharmaceutical R&D investment. Most-neglected diseases include, for example, human African trypanosomiasis (sleeping sickness), South American trypanosomiasis (Chagas disease), Buruli ulcer, dengue fever, leishmaniasis, leprosy, lymphatic filariasis, and schistosomiasis.

An analysis of drug development over the past 25 years shows that only 15 new drugs were indicated for tropical diseases (Trouiller et al. 2001). These diseases primarily affect poor populations, and they account for 12 per cent of the global disease burden. By contrast, 179 new drugs were developed for cardiovascular diseases alone, which represent 11 per cent of the global disease burden. Of the 1,393 total new drugs approved between 1975 and 1999, only 1 per cent (13 drugs) was specifically indicated for a tropical disease (Trouiller et al. 2001). It is well known that just 10 per cent of the world's health research expenditures is spent on diseases that account for 90 per cent of global disease burden. And yet, of this US$60–70 billion, less than 0.001 per cent was earmarked for research into neglected diseases (DNDI 2004).

An examination of the drug development pipeline of the R&D-based pharmaceutical industry gives little cause for optimism. In 2001, the DND-WG and the HSPH sent written questionnaires to the top 20 pharmaceutical companies globally to assess their levels of R&D activity with regard to sleeping sickness, leishmaniasis, Chagas disease, malaria, and TB. Eleven companies responded fully (among them, six of the top ten largest pharmaceutical companies). The report revealed:

Eight out of the eleven companies spent nothing at all over the last fiscal year on R&D for the most neglected diseases included in the survey (sleeping sickness, leishmaniaisis and Chagas disease); one company did not answer this question. Only two companies reported spending on malaria. Five companies reported spending on tuberculosis … [S]even companies reported spending less than 1 per cent on any of the five diseases included in the survey or failed to respond to that question. (MSF 2001: 12)

As Bernard Pécoul, Executive Director of DNDI notes:

What makes the lack of drugs more difficult to accept is that scientists know an enormous amount about kinetoplastids, the organisms responsible for sleeping sickness, Chagas disease, and leishmaniasis. The wealth of knowledge generated in this field could easily be used for drug development if the treatment of neglected diseases were perceived as financially attractive. (Pécoul 2004: 19)

This observation points to one of three crucial gaps in the drug development process: the failure to exploit published basic research that is apparently relevant only to neglected diseases. Although some publicly funded researchers are engaged in basic science that could eventually bear fruit in the form of treatments for these illnesses, the vast bulk of the costly work of drug development is not conducted by public institutions; rather, it is carried out by corporations which make their investment decisions primarily (if not solely) according to concerns of profitability. In this context, it is sobering to note that "While the public sector has traditionally been the major funder of health research, the private sector has recently taken the lead. Global health research priorities are changing accordingly" (MSF 2001: 16).

The second gap in the drug development process occurs when pre-clinically validated candidate drugs fail to enter the clinical study phase because of profit-minded choices made by pharmaceutical companies. While it is not as expensive to develop drugs as the pharmaceutical lobby claims, it is still a costly and risky business (MSF 2001: 17). Where a substantial reward at the end of the development process is clearly absent, corporate decision-makers are ill disposed to incur this risk.

Finally, there are instances in which drugs that pass clinical trials fail to reach patients for a variety of reasons: lack of production, high prices, poor adaptation to local conditions (particularly in developing countries), and regulatory obstacles. Again, the profit motive looms large with regard to these factors. However, corporate executives in pharmaceutical companies are not making R&D and production decisions in a social vacuum: they are responding, in part, to circumstances created by politicians, bureaucrats, stockholders, universities, scientists, and other corporations. All of these actors make numerous active and passive moral choices that have, in effect, conspired to create and sustain the present impasse in R&D for neglected diseases. Stockholders, of course, bear much of the responsibility for demanding that pharmaceutical corporations engage in a race toward ever greater profitability – a race that is won all too frequently through enormously costly marketing battles and through the relatively quick and cheap formulation of "me-too" drugs.

Governments in the industrialized world are quick to respond to pressure from pharmaceutical corporations aimed at putting public funds to work in the service of private wealth. Some of the instruments deployed toward this end include the patent system, tax credits, R&D grants, and subsidies from national healthcare systems. This is not to argue that such incentives are bad *per se*; rather, they must be called into question when they are offered without regard to their ultimate social utility.

Nor are the research agendas of universities and individual scientists immune to influence in the form of research subsidies from pharmaceutical companies. It has also become routine for state agencies such as the U.S. NIH and the Canadian IHR to offer grants specifically aimed at promoting collaboration between university research scientists and pharmaceutical corporations.

In short, the mechanisms of the market have performed admirably in serving the needs of corporations and health consumers in wealthy countries. These same mechanisms have proven all but useless for citizens of poor countries – particularly those who are suffering from diseases that do not occur in the developed world. This dynamic is referred to as "market failure." It has been compounded by the failure of governments to implement robust public policy measures aimed at supporting public health where the market leaves off.

Existing measures

This is not to say that there have not been attempts and proposals aimed at addressing the crisis. These have taken several forms: market interventions, PPPs, multilateral initiatives by states, and private philanthropy.

Market interventions

Some states (e.g., the U.S. with its Orphan Drug Act 1983) have implemented economic and legal incentives to encourage the development and marketing of drugs for rare diseases. "Push" mechanisms such as R&D grants, tax write-offs, and access to public resources, are intended to make it more attractive to engage in certain forms of R&D. "Pull" mechanisms, such as market exclusivity arrangements, patent extensions, and the promise of bulk purchases by the state, act as a "pot of gold at the end of the R&D rainbow," intended to lure pharmaceutical companies to research and bring to market otherwise neglected treatments. However, these have only proven effective in a small number of cases where patients in wealthy countries are suffering from a rare disease.

PPPs attempt to bring together R&D capacity, skills, and resources from the public and private sectors. Their roles are typically focused on a particular disease or form of medical intervention (e.g., vaccination). PPPs engage in the coordination of R&D activities and management of projects. To varying degrees some conduct research, and all engage in awareness-raising and lobbying, and fund-raising. Examples include the MMV, the GATB, and the IAVI. Although they tend to be multilateral and global or regional in focus, PPPs largely rely on market push-and-pull incentives that are similar to those employed in individual countries. Not surprisingly, then, they often focus on diseases that also affect people in wealthy countries. Where there is no Northern market, however, there tends to be an absence of financial, political, and public relations incentives for pharmaceutical companies to "take the bait." Hence, PPPs have not made a significant impact with regard to the most neglected diseases.

The UNICEF/UNDP/World Bank/WHO Special Program for Research and Training in Tropical Diseases (TDR) was established in 1975 in response to appeals from countries where neglected diseases are endemic. TDR addresses ten tropical diseases: African trypanosomiasis, dengue, leishmaniasis, schistosomiasis, tuberculosis, Chagas disease, leprosy, lymphatic filariasis, and onchocerciasis. Its mission is:

> to improve existing and develop new approaches for preventing, diagnosing, treating, and controlling neglected infectious diseases which are applicable, acceptable and affordable by developing endemic countries, which can be readily integrated into the health services of these countries, and which focus on the health problems of the poor. (TDR 2005a)

It also intends to strengthen the capacity of disease-endemic countries to undertake the research required to develop and implement the treatment and disease control approaches arrived at via R&D.

TDR played a significant and leading role in establishing the GATB and MMV, and has helped to support the development of several new treatments for tropical diseases. It has also been highly effective in that 6 of the 13 drugs developed for tropical diseases between 1975 and 1999 were developed with TDR support, and the program has also raised awareness of tropical diseases and helped set the agenda for research (Trouiller et al. 2001).

However, TDR has been woefully underfunded, with a budget that has remained around US$35 million for many years. ("The total budget of about $100 million for the [2004–2005] biennium is shown with two income scenarios, i.e. one with full funding, including undesignated income of $54 million; and one, in which there is a resource gap of $18 million," see TDR 2005b.) TDR is also limited in its action given that its funding is too often piecemeal and project-specific, and is staffed by international civil servants who are bound by a somewhat conservative set of norms, and it must remain conscious of the policies of its constituent organizations as well as those of UN member states. This is salient for two main reasons. First, given the rapid pace of scientific development and of IP decision-making in the pharmaceutical industry, the bureaucratic and consensus-seeking nature of TDR is a drawback. Second, many UN member states – particularly some of the biggest potential funders of TDR – are loath to accept actions by UN bodies that might push the envelope of IP practices. Given the degree to which IP laws and norms shape decisions around pharmaceutical practices and priority setting, this political fact further limits TDR's ability to act autonomously.

Private philanthropy occupies an important place in the past and present of global health. For example, the Rockefeller Foundation has made significant contributions to public health, and the Bill and Melinda Gates Foundation has made major investments in this regard over the past 15 years. While these contributions are welcome, they cannot and will not form the basis of concerted global public sector action to control an entire class of infectious diseases. Private philanthropy is, by definition, not accountable to the public in the way that action undertaken by the public sector is. It is neither fully transparent nor predictable, nor is it subject to the checks and balances that come from engaging in multilateral cooperation involving national health authorities that are accountable to their citizens.

Private philanthropy also raises (or should raise) profound questions about the type of society we wish to build and inhabit. What principles – and who – should govern the distribution of social goods pertaining to health? Should we allow health priorities to be set increasingly by wealthy individuals and corporations? Does a country's membership in the community of nations not entitle it to make certain demands of the rest of humanity when it comes to the health of its people? For those of us who believe that health is a human right and a public good, the enhanced role of private philanthropy raises concerns that governments will use it as a fig leaf as they cede their responsibility to provide public goods in a fair and just manner. The widespread retrenchment of the welfare state and the privatization and outsourcing of social services gives little reason to believe otherwise.

DNDI: global health dissident?

DNDI was established because it was necessary to respond to the shortcomings of the initiatives outlined above. It stands not in opposition to these efforts, but alongside them. And yet, it does pose several challenges – variously explicit and implicit – to the existing social order surrounding public health.

First, and most fundamentally, DNDI vigorously promotes the idea that health is a public good, and that public goods must be provided by the public sector. This concept is omnipresent in DNDI's advocacy activities, its emphasis on multilateral cooperation with the governments of industrialized and developing countries, and its long-term funding strategy. DNDI challenges states to expand their operational sense of responsibility beyond narrow, politically and economically utilitarian boundaries. It also poses a challenge to the tendency of Northern states to address only the largest and "most global" health issues, as if somehow there is not enough money to engage more distant pathogens. Scarcity of resources is an excuse only to the extent that states shirk their obligation to secure the right of all humans to health.

At the same time, by providing coordination, networking, expertise, and a lean decision-making structure, DNDI seeks to reduce the costs that states would incur by acting responsibly. Mindful of the ossification that can afflict international organizations, DNDI facilitates what might be termed "opt-in" multilateralism: a system in which states and other entities cooperate voluntarily through the auspices of a non-state actor. Furthermore, from its inception, DNDI has challenged the prevailing wisdom that technologically advanced solutions to health challenges must flow from the North to the South. This is indicated by the roster of its founding members: five public sector institutions – the OCF from Brazil, the ICMR, the KMRI, the MoH of Malaysia and France's PI; one humanitarian organization, MSF; and one international research organisation, TDR, which acts as a permanent observer to the initiative. DNDI facilitates South–South as well as North–South collaboration. Over time, these collaborations will enhance Southern pharmaceutical R&D and production capacity.

Hand in hand with the concept of health as a public good is the concept of research that is driven by an analysis of needs and capacities, rather than an analysis of the market. Just as DNDI rejects the idea that political parochialism should govern investment in R&D, so it rejects the idea that concerns of profitability should do so. A needs-based framework for making R&D decisions involves public input and advice from physicians and scientists. DNDI also hopes to show that important drugs can be developed and produced for a fraction of the costs claimed by the R&D-based pharmaceutical industry. The ability of DNDI to eschew marketing activities will provide the world with a more realistic sense of what drug R&D actually costs.

Issues of IPR have loomed large in recent debates concerning global health. More and more, the concept of health as a public good has gained legitimacy: it is now widely accepted that states may legitimately issue compulsory licenses for essential medicines in response to grave public health threats. DNDI engages with questions of IP on several levels. A key founding principle is that drugs must be affordable to those who need them. For this reason, among others cited above, DNDI will develop drugs as public goods whenever possible.

One of the most promising sources of potential drugs for neglected diseases is embodied in the "compound libraries" of pharmaceutical companies. These are collections of potentially useful chemicals that have been developed, but not yet validated by clinical or pre-clinical testing. DNDI is actively seeking access to this knowledge (and is getting it), and will negotiate royalty-free rights to resulting drugs whenever possible. Because it does not seek to produce highly marketable products, DNDI should have modest success in navigating the "patent thickets" that make it unprofitable (or impossible) for one company to license the discoveries of another. However, the rampant trend toward patenting even basic compounds will remain a significant obstacle to drug development.

The key challenge

The goal of DNDI is not to singularly take on the dearth in public capacity for R&D around neglected diseases. Rather it is to demonstrate through targeted neglected disease-specific drug R&D achievements that alternatives to a purely market-driven system of drug R&D are possible. DNDI seeks to move beyond notions of charity in establishing R&D for neglected diseases as both a public responsibility and a public good. Its governance is purely by national and international public sector actors, and MSF as a civil society organization, and it is working closely with the private sector to achieve results.

The key challenge at this time for DNDI is long-term sustainable funding. Such funding is the best measure of endorsement for new approaches. Initial funding has been established with five years of start-up financial support from MSF, and with substantial in-kind support from board member organizations and network members. As is the case for the many PPPs, international public sector financial support for DNDI is not yet firmly established. Whether it will be remains to be seen.

References

Drugs for Neglected Diseases Initiative (DNDI). 2004. *An Innovative Solution*. Geneva: DNDI. Available at: http://www.dndi.org/cms/public_html/images/article/268/An per cent20Innovative per cent20Solution.pdf [Accessed December 14, 2005].

——. 2005. *About DNDI*. Geneva: DNDI. Available at: http://www.dndi.org/cms/public_html/insidearticleListing.asp?CategoryId=87&ArticleId=288&TemplateId=1 [Accessed December 14, 2005].

Médecins Sans Frontières (MSF). 2001. *Fatal Imbalance: The Crisis in Research and Development for Drugs for Neglected Diseases*. Geneva: MSF. Available at: http://www.accessmed-msf.org/documents/fatal_imbalance_2001.pdf [Accessed December 14, 2005].

Pécoul, B. 2004. New Drugs for Neglected Diseases: From Pipeline to Patients. *PLoS Medicine* 1: 19–22. Available at: http://www.dndi.org/pdf_files/new_drugs.pdf [Accessed December 14, 2005].

The Special Programme for Research and Training in Tropical Diseases (TDR). 2005a. *Mission*. Geneva: TDR. Available at: http://www.who.int/tdr/about/mission.htm [Accessed December 14, 2005].

——. 2005b. *Approved Programme Budget 2004–2005*. Geneva: TDR. Available at: http://www.who.int/tdr/publications/publications/budget_04.htm [Accessed December 14, 2005].

Trouiller, P., E. Torreele, P. Olliaro, N. White, S. Foster, D. Wirth, and B. Pécoul. 2001. Drugs for Neglected Diseases: A Failure of the Market and a Public Health Failure? *Tropical Medicine and International Health* 6: 945–951.

United Nations International Children's Emergency Fund (UNICEF). 2005. *The State of the World's Children*. Statistical table 10: The Rate of Progress. Geneva: UNICEF. Available at: http://www.unicef.org/sowc05/english/statistics.html [Accessed December 14, 2005].

12   Neglected disease research: health needs and new models for R&D

Aidan Hollis

While pharmaceuticals are of tremendous importance in treating many diseases and conditions, pharmaceutical research has tended to focus on products that can be profitably marketed in wealthy countries. Not surprisingly, drug firms have eschewed investing in drugs for which the principal markets are found in poor countries, where consumers cannot afford to pay high prices. This has led to the problem of so-called "neglected diseases," diseases for which drug firms are not investing significant sums in research even though the therapeutic benefits might be great. Such benefits do not translate into profits if potential consumers are too poor to pay.

Poverty has the very important effect of reducing the purchasing power of consumers, so that, even if drugs are very effective from a therapeutic perspective, buyers are unable to pay for them. To see how important this is from a research investment perspective, consider the case of Chagas disease, which afflicts approximately 20 million people worldwide. A commonly cited estimate of drug development expense is over US$800 million (DiMasi, Hansen, and Grabowski 2003). This figure includes the risk of failure and the cost of capital, up to the time the drug is approved. For a firm to be willing to develop a drug for Chagas disease, it has to expect earnings to cover its development costs. If expected development costs are US$800 million, the firm has to earn at least US$40 over the cost of production and distribution per person taking the drug if 20 million people follow the therapy during the life of the patent. If manufacturing and distribution costs were, say, US$50 per course of therapy, and retail mark-ups another US$30, US$120 would be the minimum price just for the firm to cover its production and development costs. Sadly, US$120 is quite a lot of money for people with Chagas disease, particularly since their ability to earn is compromised by their illness. Not everyone with the disease would be able to purchase the drug at this price, which implies that a higher price would be necessary to cover the costs, and of course, as the price increases, the number of afflicted consumers who can pay for the drug decreases. Put in these terms, it is apparent that while there may be a market for drugs for diseases like Chagas, unless development costs are lower than expected, or unless there is an external reward for developing such drugs, they do not offer a tempting target for drug firms motivated by profit. Certainly, there is no chance that a drug for Chagas disease could ever be a "blockbuster."

Poor countries typically have a host of other problems that make it difficult for drug developers to make a profit. Typically, they lack ancillary health inputs such as doctors, nurses, clinics, hospitals, and equipment. Without enough doctors and other health professionals, patients may not be diagnosed and treated. As an extreme example, Angola has only one doctor for every 13,000 people, and most of them practice in Luanda (see Eisenstein 2004). Similarly, diagnostic equipment is often not available for widespread use. For example, the standard test for CD4 counts used in diagnosis of HIV/AIDS status is typically available only in major clinics in developing countries because the equipment required for the test is bulky and expensive. Patients in rural areas and small towns may be distant from such diagnostic equipment. As a result, less than 15 per cent of HIV-positive individuals worldwide receive the regular CD4 monitoring required for appropriate diagnosis (see EI Spectra 2005). The shortage of health professionals and diagnostic equipment not only undermines the health of people in poor countries, it also reduces demand for drugs, which consequently are not prescribed. In addition, retail drug markets are often uncompetitive in developing countries, leading to high retail markups, which reduce sales and profits for patentees. Many countries impose taxes and import tariffs on pharmaceutical products (see Miller 2005). In South Africa, problems of access due to poverty were aggravated by politics: during the late 1990s, President Thabo Mbeki argued that HIV and AIDS are not connected, and refused to distribute anti-retrovirals (see *New York Times* April 23, 2000).

Finally, intellectual property protection is weak in many countries. Pharmaceutical markets in many developing countries are plagued by counterfeit medicines that harm consumers and decrease the rewards for drug innovators. High prices for genuine products and low production costs for counterfeits make counterfeiting very profitable. And given the tacit approval of governments in some places – or at least slack enforcement of intellectual property laws – the usual penalties for counterfeiting may be absent. While there are no reliable statistics on the extent of pharmaceutical counterfeiting, estimates of the proportion of medicines that are counterfeit range from 20 per cent to 60 per cent in various developing countries (Lybecker 2003). In addition, under WTO rules, countries can issue a "compulsory license" permitting production of generic medicines, so that even when a successful drug is developed, the innovator may not be able to make many sales. This is not to say that the use of compulsory licenses is never justified – they may in some circumstances be very important to enhance access to existing medicines – but to the extent that they reduce the potential profits of patentees, they will lead to fewer incentives for innovation in drugs.

The result of these problems – which are themselves largely the outcome of poverty – is that drug companies, small or large, lack strong incentives to develop new medicines for diseases which primarily affect people in developing countries.

It is useful to contrast the problem of neglected diseases with the problem of access to new medicines for global diseases. A global disease is one such as cancer, which has universal incidence. The patent system operating in wealthy countries offers strong incentives to develop drugs for global diseases. While under patent, new drugs are priced very high and for that reason may be largely inaccessible to people in developing countries. However, in this case, upon patent expiry, which typically takes approximately ten years from approval, drugs become available for generic imitation, driving down prices to around average production cost. Thus, for global diseases, access to the newest (and possibly most effective) medicines is delayed by a few years because of the patent. Sometimes a delay in access means that people who need specific drugs will never get them, as they may die before the drugs become available, so even a short delay is not unimportant. In contrast, for diseases which principally affect the poor in developing countries, access can be delayed indefinitely, since no innovation occurs at all!

The result of the neglected disease problem has been an increasing range of initiatives designed to promote research into finding solutions for neglected diseases, with billions of dollars potentially available if the right approach can be developed. The question then is, what is the best way of using this funding to address the neglected disease problem? There are two margins on which money can make a difference. It can increase *access* to existing medicines, which is valuable since many very effective medicines are currently priced too high for consumers to afford. The second is to increase *incentives* to develop new drugs for neglected diseases. These two margins are complementary, of course: new drugs priced so high that few people can benefit appear to offer little value to society and access to cheap drugs offers little value when the drugs are not effective. So it is important that progress be made on both fronts. The following discussion offers a very brief evaluation of some of the models that are in use or have been proposed.

Any mechanisms for stimulating research into neglected diseases can be classified into two types: push and pull. Push mechanisms encourage research to go in a particular direction through reducing the cost to the private company of undertaking research. Pull mechanisms provide enhanced rewards when the research is successful. Mechanisms can be used simultaneously, though using more than one at a time requires care to ensure that the combination of incentives does not lead to perverse outcomes.

Push mechanisms

Push mechanisms induce firms to undertake research in specific areas by reducing the firm's private cost of research. There are two widely used types of push mechanisms: direct funding incentives and tax incentives. Tax incentives reduce the firm's cost of research by allowing tax credits for relevant research and may be useful in some situations.

Direct funding initiatives include a wide variety of forms, but most involve technology transfer from a public institution to a private firm, which the firm is able to exploit – in which case there is a so-called "public–private partnership" (PPP). Direct funding reduces the firm's cost of research in a specific area. For example, a public institution may pay for early testing of compounds, with information on the most valuable compounds being transferred to a drug firm for later development and clinical testing. The largest and most important PPP is the relationship that the National Institutes of Health (NIH) has with drug companies: the NIH invests about US$30 billion annually in basic health research, with many valuable insights transferred to drug companies for commercial development (NIH 2004). PPPs sometimes involve restrictions on how much the firm is able to charge for any drugs derived from the partnership, though such restrictions inevitably reduce the incentives of the firm to continue development of the drug.

There are a number of concerns about PPPs. First, even where drugs are successfully developed, prices may be very high, as the firm, which is responsible to its shareholders, tries to maximize its profits. Second, firms will naturally try to steer research subsidies from public institutions into therapies that are likely to be most profitable. The firm has private information on its costs of later-stage development and it can use this strategically. To the extent that a firm can use subsidies to pay for drugs that would be profitable anyway, the subsidies simply reduce the firm's costs without increasing innovation, essentially crowding out private funding. Finally, PPPs impose significant risks on public institutions: they may provide substantial funding and yet have no results.

A reverse version of the standard PPP is for the public institution to develop drugs that have been identified as of potential interest in early testing, but which were shelved because market considerations limited the profitability even if development was successful. The IOWH offers a leading example of such an approach, and is currently in the final stages of clinical testing of a drug for visceral leishmaniasis. An important advantage of this approach is that the public institution can increase access to the drug by offering a license to manufacture the product to multiple generic companies. This approach also minimizes the strategic behavior on the part of the private drug companies: the drug company has no particular interest in the drug after it has handed over a promising compound to the IOWH. The risks of late-stage drug development, of course, fall entirely on the public institution in this case.

Pull mechanisms

Pull mechanisms reward innovation through enhanced profits. In general, their main advantage over push mechanisms is that firms are rewarded for success in innovating. This is an attractive property since it aligns the interests of the innovator (profits) with the interests of society (new and improved products). In addition, there is no payment made under pull mechanisms for failed innovation.

The patent system

The standard pull mechanism is the patent system, which offers the reward of exclusive use of the innovation. The patent system is designed so that innovators with products that are highly valued relative to the cost of manufacture will be able to earn large profits, since the patentee is granted exclusive use of the innovation disclosed in the patent for a period of 20 years.

The patent system suffers from two important problems with respect to so-called neglected diseases. First, as noted above, drugs addressing neglected diseases may have great therapeutic value and yet be unable to command high market prices because of the poverty of consumers and their governments. In this case, the market value of the innovation is low, resulting in small profits for the patentee. There may be other institutions that would be willing to pay for appropriate use of medicines for neglected diseases, but there is no mechanism within the patent system to harness this support; instead, the system depends on market value, where the market is created by private valuations of consumers. This raises the possibility that such institutions could either subsidize or buy medicines. However, unless the institutions can commit to this in advance of product development, their purchases do not increase the incentives for innovation, although they may increase access. The AMC proposal discussed below is an attempt to design a commitment mechanism for this kind of subsidy.

Second, WTO rules authorize governments to use compulsory licenses for pharmaceutical products. Thus, the expected benefits of the patent right to the patentee are reduced, and this may be of particular importance in the case of neglected diseases. This does not mean that the use of compulsory licenses is inappropriate, but there can be no question that it may reduce the potential profits of patentees, and hence harms their incentives to undertake research on neglected diseases.

Advanced market commitments

An important and very promising proposal is the use of AMCs for certain types of pharmaceutical products – principally vaccines – to stimulate research by promising a subsidy of a fixed value per unit for a given number of units. The most attractive candidate product for such a commitment is a malaria vaccine, since the health (and economic) benefits from an effective malaria vaccine could be huge.

An AMC system would include the following key points, as described in Kremer and Glennerster (2004) and CGD (2005). First, a technical committee would identify the desired feasible technical characteristics of a vaccine. Second, a donor institution (sponsor) would offer a minimum price to any firm that could develop a vaccine meeting the technical characteristics. The minimum price would be higher than the market can currently sustain, and could be achieved by the donor offering co-payments to the manufacturer to make up the difference between the market price and the minimum price. The donor would be committed to meeting this minimum price only for a fixed number of units (e.g., 200 million doses). Third, any firm which had received this subsidy would be required to set a low price on any additional units, on the basis that the producer would already have received a suitable reward. In order to make the proposal effective, it would be necessary to have a legally binding commitment on the part of sponsors to make the agreed payments, with a suitable arbitration mechanism.

AMC thus offers a way to make development of vaccines profitable, but is a pull mechanism since the sponsor pays only if the product meets the technical requirements and sells lots of units. Thus, the incentives are made similar to those of drugs for global diseases, in which innovators receive healthy profits only if their drug is approved and is purchased at a high price by many consumers. In addition, the sponsor has to make disbursements only if vaccine development leads to a product that consumers value: it bears no unwanted risks.

Despite these important advantages, the AMC scheme has some important limitations. First, it requires that the technical specifications of the vaccine be described comprehensively in advance, since it must be possible for firms to be able to know whether their vaccine is acceptable. But it is not clear that it is possible to do this for many types of products: even vaccines, which are relatively straightforward, have many different important characteristics. For example, some of the technical characteristics, which might require specification, include: (1) the probability that a properly administered, vaccination will protect against the various strains of malaria; (2) the extent of side-effects, including death; (3) the duration of protection; (4) the ease of administration and number of doses required for vaccination; and possibly (5) the production cost. The technical requirements would have to specify minimally acceptable levels for each characteristic, and it would be important that the required standards could not be changed later to make them more difficult to achieve. While in principle requirements might be relaxed, this would have to be discretionary on the part of the sponsor or the arbitration committee, leaving firms in considerable doubt as to whether they would be able to benefit from the contract. For a product whose technical characteristics can be well described in advance, this may not be a major obstacle. So it seems that for specific vaccines, or perhaps for drugs that have passed through stage II clinical trials, AMCs should be effective. However, for drugs in early stages of development, or for vaccines with greater uncertainty about achievable technical characteristics, AMCs appear unlikely to be productive in stimulating additional research. So while AMCs may be useful for some particular pharmaceutical preparations whose characteristics can be fully described in advance, or which have already been developed and undergone extensive clinical testing, there is also a need for other ways of creating incentives directed towards neglected disease drug development.

Rewards based on therapeutic impact

I have proposed elsewhere a broad-based optional reward system for drugs for neglected diseases, where the rewards are to be based on the therapeutic impact of a drug in developing countries (Hollis 2005). The proposal requires any firm wishing to take up the rewards to offer an open license for manufacture and sale of the drug in developing countries. Innovators are to be rewarded through payments from reward sponsors. Since entering the reward system is optional, it increases incentives for drug firms to engage in research on neglected diseases. The way that rewards are to be allocated is that the incremental therapeutic impact of each drug in the reward system is measured in QALYs or a similar measure, with each drug obtaining a share of the total available rewards in proportion to its therapeutic impact during the period of the patent (or alternatively for up to ten years following approval and first marketing). Total rewards paid out annually would be fixed, and firms could choose to try to make money through the standard patent monopoly or by entering the reward system.

The optional nature of the system creates the helpful characteristic that rewards are automatically adjusted at an appropriate level with respect to the therapeutic impact of a given drug. The reason for this is that, if rewards are too low, firms will not opt in to the system, but will prefer to use the patent system, leaving a greater share of the fixed reward fund available for others. Firms that do opt in to the reward system are obviously receiving higher profits than they would through the patent system. Thus rewards are higher for therapeutically valuable drugs than under the patent system, but not too high – if excessive, more firms would choose to switch their drugs over from the patent system.

To ensure the widest access to drugs, the proposal requires open licensing of all relevant patents, thus enabling generic competition from the outset. The innovating firm, however, retains an interest in the product for some years, since its reward is based on the number of units sold. This provides incentives for promotion of the drug as well as oversight of quality control.

The most problematic aspect of the proposal is that it requires the reward sponsor to make estimates of the incremental therapeutic effectiveness of the drugs in the system, certainly not a trivial requirement, in order to determine the rewards. Estimating therapeutic impact would be expensive and subject to some gamesmanship by drug companies. As Morris, Stevens, and van Gelder (2005: 15) observe, "As with all prize mechanisms, the potential for political rent-seeking is great, as the prize-awarding authority may be tempted to favour political or commercial allies. Senior individuals within the authority might even accept bribes." It seems that rent-seeking and other abuses are inevitable under such a reward system, and would likely be worse even than under the patent system, where political favors also determine, to a large extent, the profits of drug companies. An important question, then, is whether the greater rent-seeking, fraud, and manipulation under an optional reward system would be too large for it to function better than alternatives.

Transferable intellectual property rights

Jean-Paul Garnier, CEO of Glaxo, has been promoting a system of TRIPS that would consist of extensions of patent rights on drugs in wealthy countries in exchange for successful development of drugs for neglected diseases (Foley 2004). This is a pull scheme that offers additional reward to promote innovation, but does not address the problem of access. The principal merit of the proposal appears to be that it can, in theory, increase innovation at no cost to governments. Instead, the cost falls on hapless consumers of pharmaceuticals in wealthy countries. It is hard to see why this allocation of costs would be efficient or desirable. In addition, the mechanism for deciding which drugs would be rewarded in this way, and which patents would be extended, is unclear. If there is a coherent methodology, it has not yet been explained.

Accelerated approval process

Moran (2005) suggests auctioning "fast-track" rights for approval, with the proceeds used to support neglected disease research. Such funding could be used in a variety of ways, including providing direct funding for neglected disease research or as rewards through a scheme such as Advanced Market Commitments. Ridley, Grabowski, and Moe (2004) have proposed a pure pull incentive in which a firm that successfully developed a neglected disease drug would be given a voucher for priority review for a selected rich country drug. This is, in effect, the pull version of the Moran proposal, since firms are given a reward for neglected disease research success. In both cases, an important issue is that there is no clear connection between the fast-track approval or priority review and the support for neglected disease research. On the contrary, it appears from the papers that speedier approval may be desirable in any case.

Conclusions

This chapter has discussed some of the ways that research into drugs for neglected diseases is being, or could be, funded, and how to create incentives for relevant research. It seems likely that no single method is going to be adequate or ideal. In the long run, it should be recognized that extreme poverty is at the heart of the neglected disease problem: if everyone were richer, many important neglected diseases would be eliminated. The importance of poverty in this debate leads to the temptation to simply argue that creating wealth is the only realistic solution. However, while one can hope that in the long term improving technology and governance will lift all the world's peoples out of poverty, the long term is a long way off. In the meantime, we need to use the available instruments to reduce the burden of disease in developing countries, which will in turn help to increase wealth. There is a virtuous circle available here, and one of the ways to get started is to improve healthcare outcomes through judicious investment in research on therapies for neglected diseases.

References

Center for Global Development (CGD). 2005. *Making Markets for Vaccines: Ideas to Action.* Washington, DC: CGD. Available at: http://www.cgdev.org/Publications/vaccine/_files/MakingMarkets-complete.pdf [Accessed April 28, 2005].

DiMasi, J., R. Hansen, and H. Grabowski. 2003. The Price of Innovation: New Estimates of Drug Development Costs. *Journal of Health Economics* 22: 151–185.

Eisenstein, Z. 2004. *Angola Health System in Tatters*, February 26. Reuters Alertnet. Available at: http://www.alertnet.org/thefacts/reliefresources/10778091zq65.htm [Accessed April 28, 2005].

El Spectra. Available at: http://www.elspectra.com [Accessed April 28, 2005].

Foley, S. 2004. Glaxo Tells Blair to Press G8 for Patents Reform. *Independent*, November 29.

Hollis, A. 2005. *An Optional Reward System for Neglected Disease Drugs* (unpublished manuscript). Available at: http://econ.ucalgary.ca/fac-files/ah/optionalrewards.pdf [Accessed December 7, 2005]

Kremer, M. and R. Glennerster. 2004. *Strong Medicine: Creating Incentives for Pharmaceutical Research on Neglected Diseases.* Princeton, NJ: Princeton University Press.

Lybecker, K. 2003. *Product Piracy: The Sale of Counterfeit Pharmaceuticals in Developing Countries.* Mimeo: Drexel University (unpublished manuscript). Available at: http://emertech.wharton.upenn.edu/WhartonMiniConfPapers/Lybecker%20-%20Product%20Piracy.pdf [Accessed December 7, 2005].

Miller, S. 2005. Taxes Raise Drug Costs for Poor, Report Says. *Wall Street Journal*, April 21, A14.

Moran, M. 2005. *Fast Track Options as a Fundraising Mechanism to Support R&D into Neglected Diseases.* Mimeo: London School of Economics (unpublished manuscript). Available at: http://www.who.int/entity/intellectualproperty/submissions/Mary.Moran2.pdf [Accessed December 7, 2005].

Morris J., P. Stevens, and A. van Gelder. 2005. *Incentivizing Research and Development for the Diseases of Poverty.* London: International Policy Press.

National Institutes of Health (NIH). Summary of the 2004 President's budget. Available at: http://www.nih.gov/news/budgetfy2004/fy2004presidentsbudget.pdf [Accessed April 30, 2005].

Ridley, D., H. Grabowski, and J. Moe. 2004. *Developing Drugs for Developing Countries.* Mimeo: Duke University (unpublished manuscript).

13 Advanced purchase commitments: moral and practical problems

Donald W. Light

In recent years, under large-scale pressure from the public and international organizations like Oxfam and Médecins Sans Frontières, the leaders of the wealthiest nations, and especially the Bill and Melinda Gates Foundation, have committed themselves to eradicating malaria, HIV/AIDS, and tuberculosis. The U.S., UK, Italy, France, and others have each pledged to donate US$3 billion or more to this goal. The new, favored way to achieve this goal is with advanced purchase commitments (APCs). For example, the Finance Ministers of the G8 wrote in June 2005, "We recognise also that APCs are potentially a powerful mechanism to incentivise research, development and the production of vaccines for HIV, malaria and other diseases." They then asked for concrete proposals to be developed by December 2005 (HM Treasury 2005).

What is an APC, and why is it morally troubling? How did it acquire such enthusiastic support? Why is such a high-profile concept unlikely to work as it is proposed, and how could a different version of APCs overcome their moral and practical problems? These are the questions that will be addressed here.

In its original form, which underlies current modifications, an APC is designed to simultaneously overcome the inability of poor nations to afford essential medicines and stimulate basic research to discover them by wealthy nations or other large donors committing several billions of dollars to buying a large quantity when a new, effective medicine is discovered and proven to be effective in populations of low-income countries (Kremer and Glennerster 2004; Center for Global Development 2005). The principal focus has been on vaccines for these three major causes of death and the much larger burden of disease that hold back the economic growth of poor nations. APCs "make markets" where none has ever existed in a way that will unleash the research talent of the private sector.

APCs are sometimes called "advanced market commitments" (AMCs), based on the claim that an AMC creates a market and on the fact that the amount committed is for all qualifying and competing vaccines (or drugs) that effectively address the target disease. But they are a single, monopsonistic purchase that does not resemble a market, and the fact that qualifying vaccines compete for the purchase dilutes its main goal of matching the total revenues that a company can earn from the average new drug sold in affluent markets.

Morally troubling

Public policies often acquire the status of a moral imperative through a sociological process of moral entrepreneurs (often NGOs) who are committed to a given cause (Conrad 1992).The moral problem with APCs is that the deaths of an equal number of infants and children can be averted now from diseases for which vaccines already exist but are not affordable to low-income countries. According to WHO estimates, the total number of deaths in 2001 preventable by existing vaccines was about 4.45 million (WHO 2005). If the utilitarian goal is to relieve poor countries of the greatest amount of disease, suffering, medical costs, and death, then committing the same amount of money to possibly achieving the same outcome 10–15 years from now is indefensible. For example, using a discount rate of 5 per cent, the net present value of eliminating an equal amount of disease, suffering, cost, and death 15 years from now is about half the value of doing so now. Thus if one leader of a wealthy nation used the same amount of money (say, US$3 billion) to eradicate the diseases now that have effective vaccines, he would be doing twice as much good as another leader who committed US$3 billion to an APC to discover a vaccine for malaria or HIV/AIDS. Indeed a report to the Gates Foundation emphasizes that immunizing infants and children now will reduce poverty and foster economic growth in poor nations (Abt Associates nd). Skipping over this present moral imperative because malaria or HIV/AIDS are the high-profile diseases of the day is morally unacceptable.This moral imperative is made greater by four other contrasts between committing US$3 billion or more to them now versus an equivalent achievement in 2020. First, the promise of an equally effective vaccine in the future is not certain whereas effective vaccines are. This uncertainty is due not only to doubts about how effectively APCs induce basic research (discussed below), but also to good scientific reasons why the many efforts to develop an effective vaccine for malaria or HIV/AIDS have failed so far. Malaria is a whole parasite and does not provide a specific target for a vaccine. HIV/AIDS presents several, ever-changing targets. Even if a promising vaccine were to be discovered, it would have to meet several other requirements to be used in many low-income countries.

Second, it is a moral imperative to treat infants and children who are diseased and dying now, before treating infants and children who are not or not yet born. Third, paying off the patent holders of current, effective vaccines or arranging licenses to have the vaccines manufactured by qualified, low-cost companies in India and elsewhere is likely to cost much less and leave large sums for other benefits, such as strengthening the delivery systems in poor countries to administer the vaccines. The delay before most vaccines become cheap and widely distributed to developing countries is more like 15–20 years. If a million infants and children are dying in each of those years, and ten times that many become seriously ill, then we are talking about 15–20 million who die unnecessarily and 150–200 million preventable deaths and serious illnesses that are skipped over because effective vaccines are not being purchased now. The breakthrough report by the research team headed by Mary Moran (Wellcome Trust and London School of Economics and Political Science 2005) on all the research projects for discovering new drugs for neglected diseases in recent times estimates that the companies or venture capitalists involved have spent much less than the research costs reported on drugs by the large firms and much prefer a quick profit in the vicinity of US$100 million than the prospect of possibly more profits later.

Fourth, committing the funds needed to make current vaccines available to all who need them at a profit for the patent holders is a much more persuasive way to show venture capitalists, biotech firms, and multinational corporations that a market for diseases of the poor exists, than promising to buy a future vaccine without paying researchers or developers a dime until they have taken all the risks of failure and fully tested a yet-to-be-discovered vaccine many years from now.

Finally, the current APC model draws uncritically on estimates of costs and profits that the large multinational corporations claim they need to structure the terms in their favor, when the goal should be to develop R&D capacity in the major regions of need, such as Latin America, Africa, and Asia (Light 2005). Only a handful of large corporations have the funds to pay for R&D over many years with no milestone payments. Early sign-up works in favor of the multinationals and cuts out new firms that only start up later or small firms that find out later that they have discovered a promising vaccine. Legal terms and managements of contracts by a law firm that has represented the major firms for many years may make other firms wary of participating.

Why, then, is the current APC model so appealing to leaders of the G8? One possibility is that it favors the giant multinationals that spend millions on lobbying the G8 governments and pressuring them to provide favorable terms for their growth. Another is that an APC for a future, undiscovered vaccine does not require any money be spent now or even during the tenure of the current leaders. It is a promise to buy, let us say, 200 million courses (the number of doses for complete vaccination) at US$15 each for US$3 billion in the distant future when an effective vaccine has been fully tested. Even if the promise is legally binding, a future regime might decide it cannot afford it and renege on the promise. Given that the promised amount would increase at the compounded rate built into the current model, reneging is even more likely (Center for Global Development 2005). Ten years from now, a US$3 billion promise would be more than US$8 billion, and 15 years from now it would be more than US$12 billion. One has to wonder if any investor or corporation would take seriously an APC that does not set aside in escrow the promised amount.

Impractical

The current APC model that the Finance Ministers of wealthy countries are using to guide how they will spend their donations of several billion dollars each is based on the conviction that the key to discovering effective vaccines (or drugs) for neglected diseases is to involve researchers in the private sector. They will succeed, advocates claim (Kremer and Glennerster 2004), where research teams from universities and government laboratories have failed. Further, this innovative, advanced commitment approach will induce investors to fund private teams in hopes of developing a successful product and walking away with some or all of the big prize. The evidence that this strategy will work is based primarily on two studies which actually provide evidence that the strategy will not work.

Basic research unlikely

Finkelstein (2004) provides a systematic analysis of how APC-like funding for an expanded market for vaccines affects R&D. Using a large sample over many years, she finds that "for every $1 of permanent increase in expected annual market revenue from vaccines against a particular disease, the pharmaceutical industry will spend an additional 6 cents annually in present discounted value on R&D for vaccines against that disease." This result indicates that using APCs to induce R&D, which require investing in a search that will take more than a decade, is very inefficient, uncertain, and costly compared to funding promising research proposals and strategies directly. In fact, the principal report on which the current APC campaign is based (Center for Global Development 2005) contains evidence to that effect. Finkelstein's empirical analysis leads her to conclude that in most cases "induced innovation is entirely socially wasteful business stealing, although the magnitude of the dynamic social costs is small" (Finkelstein 2004).

Finkelstein's empirical study of actual vaccines markets has some other key findings that testify to the impracticality of the current APC model to purchase a vaccine not yet discovered. The main effect of enlarging the market for vaccines (as one might suppose) is that only the large firms react in the first six years, and they do so by pulling an already discovered and partially developed vaccine candidate off the shelf and developing it further. GlaxoSmithKline's phase II malaria vaccine is an example, especially given that the Gates Foundation is helping to pay for clinical trials and thus further reducing the company's risk and cost. It was sitting on the shelf for 15 years until the Gates Foundation offered to help develop it. Even more dramatic "evidence" for the practicality of making an advanced purchase for a vaccine or drug that has not yet been discovered is presented in the principal report from the study by Acemoglu and Linn (2004), which claims that just a 1 per cent increase in market size leads to a 4–6 per cent increase in new drugs. A close reading of their article found that this conclusion is based on a highly artificial econometric model. For example, the authors assume that all individuals live infinitely, that there is only one firm at any one time with the best-practice technology, that anticipated (not actual) future market size prompts more innovation over long periods, and that "new drugs" include all generics (which by definition are not new) and all newly approved FDA drugs, even though only 15 per cent or less of newly approved drugs are therapeutically superior to existing drugs (NIHCM 2002; Prescrire International 2003). The authors also went through several alterations of what a drug category is, from the 159 identified by the FDA (with 20 major categories), to 34 and then lumped into just five categories. Since generics are about half of the new drugs, the ratio of market size increase to superior new drugs would be 0.075×4–6 or a 0.3–0.45 per cent increase in better new drugs. Thus, under this artificial model one would need a 222–333 per cent increase in market size to generate one new better drug. The authors note that "pharmaceutical companies may respond more to profit incentives at the later stages of the research process than at the earlier stages" (Acemoglu and Linn 2004). This conclusion reflects the realistic approach of multinational firms, but undermines the claim that APCs will induce basic research to discover new vaccines.

Inaccurate pricing

The prevailing APC requires that the company or companies that successfully develop a new vaccine must promise that, after they receive their high-priced contract, they will produce it at a price close to manufacturing cost (Love 2003). In other words, an APC is a buy-out or pay-off to get to this point where the new vaccine will be available forever at a very low price. This means an APC must get two prices right: the buy-out price and the post-buy-out price. For example, the principal APC report sets the buy-out price at US$15 a course for 200 million courses and the post-buy-out price at US$1 (Center for Global Development 2005). In order to arrive at the buy-out price, the APC report draws on industry-supported research that claims R&D costs are US$800 million or higher, without citing or discussing critical doubts about this estimate (Relman and Angell 2002; DeMasi et al. 2003; Goozner 2004). It then uses sales estimates from other industry-supported research to conclude that an APC would have to offer US$3 billion or more to match revenues from other projects and thus attract the major pharmaceutical firms to invest in discovering a new vaccine (Grabowski, Vernon, and DiMasi 2002). This appears to be much more than the sales from successful vaccines. This total led to suggesting the model APC purchase 200 million courses for US$15 each in 2005. The amount would have to be several times larger by 2015 or 2020, as pointed out before. But why were the costs and revenues for previous vaccines not used? R&D costs for new drugs for neglected diseases have been much lower (Wellcome Trust and London School of Economics and Political Science 2005). Moran's study reported that 40 R&D projects had cost only US$112 million, including ten clinical trials, four of them in phase III. On the other hand, the R&D costs for an effective vaccine for malaria or HIV/AIDS might be much greater. If governments or foundations (as is likely) paid for much of the R&D, including the risk of failures, the net costs to a company are only a fraction of the overall costs. Or some companies might have no outside help while others do. Thus, one cannot with any certainty set the pre-buy-out price accurately, though econometricians will model predicted prices based on a number of untested assumptions.

Note that there are ways a global company could win US$3 billion without incurring much cost at all: 1) take the most promising candidates off the shelf, get development costs covered by R&D funding foundations, governments, or public–private partnerships (PPPs); 2) subcontract trials to much less costly vendors in developing countries, where recruitment costs are very low, retention rates are much higher, and trials can be shorter; and 3) subcontract manufacturing to a low-cost but high-quality producer in a developing country. In short, a great deal of donated money could be wastefully spent giving windfall profits to a clever company, rather than using it to prevent millions of deaths.

The ability to get the post-buy-out price right is equally difficult. Most vaccines cost very little to manufacture in large volume – well under a dollar. Further, many poor countries have decided again and again that they cannot afford to buy vaccines, even at less than one dollar each. And since one does not know what kind of vaccine will be discovered, setting a price of one dollar for one requiring a complex technology would guarantee that no vaccines would be produced at all.

These impracticalities of pricing are largely avoided, however, if an APC is directed at existing, effective vaccines. One knows their research history and how much risk and net cost the patent-holding firms bore. It could range from great risk and cost to practically nothing (Government Accounting Office 2003). One would also know the technology of the vaccine and its manufacturing costs so that the post-buy-out price can be realistically set. One could negotiate for a buy-out price, using a variety of purchasing strategies with real people in real time, rather than speculating on what terms would work a decade from now or more.

Pay-off uncertain

Although the reward for years of R&D is equal to the revenues that the large firms earn from new drugs sold in affluent markets, their legal advisers will quickly realize that the pay-off may be much lower. This may amplify the effects of getting the prices wrong. The current APC model makes room for a second and third effective vaccine (or drug if applied to them), and it requires that poor countries both come up with a co-payment of one dollar per course and meet other criteria for qualifying. Further, the qualifying recipient countries can choose which vaccine among those approved (if there is more than one) they prefer. Many poor countries have great difficulties raising a dollar per course. Or, to put it another way, they give greater priority to developing potable water, better sewerage systems, or better nutrition (or perhaps fighting a war) than to purchasing vaccines. Put these together and the portion of the total a given pharmaceutical company will receive depends on how many competing alternatives there are, how many countries raise their co-payment and qualify, and how many of those choose their vaccine.

Keeps all IP rights with the seller

The current APC is regarded as an inspired way to leapfrog the well-known time-lag between when a vaccine is available and purchased in affluent countries and when it becomes available at an affordable price in poor countries (Birdsall 2005). Yet it keeps new vaccines as fully protected private goods, even though IPRs are primarily responsible for the time-lag. Further, if a given company controls when and how it meets its obligation, and with which partners, a competitive market for the lowest price would be prevented, even though it would benefit poor countries the most. For a few billion dollars one would think that the buyer would at least acquire the IPRs to the vaccine and the technical know-how that is so vital to vaccine production and to leaping the 10–15-year time-lag. But this pro-industry APC leaves all IPRs in the hands of the seller. Given that vaccines are viewed as a public good, it is unclear why they would be protected as a private good. And why is there no demand for an accounting of how rapidly the company's costs are recovered for this public good? When asked, reasons given include the belief that major firms would not participate. However, most of them shut down their vaccine operations and capacities years ago, and most of the innovation comes from public–private partnerships and small biotech companies (Wellcome Trust and London School of Economics and Political Science 2005). A third reason given is that the problem of not buying out rights is solved by requiring that companies receiving a contract must promise to produce and sell their vaccine thereafter at a very low cost. Logically, this means that keeping their IPRs does not matter. Or does it matter because there are many ways in which companies can and have impeded the availability of vaccines at low cost?

Promotes secrecy

All participating competitors for the APC prize will be strongly motivated to keep secret their discoveries, techniques, lessons from unsuccessful strategies, and other valuable insights. This effect runs counter to one of the main efforts and benefits of the recent flourishing of research on neglected diseases – sharing techniques, new leads, and lessons in order to generate synergy in pursuit of effective solutions to global challenges. Moreover, an effective inoculation for malaria or HIV/AIDS is likely to require cooperation to develop a vaccine cluster – precisely what an APC discourages.

In sum, the appeal of advanced purchase (or market) commitments seems based on its focus on future benefits that cost national leaders nothing to promise, its design that favors the multinational drug companies, and its strong promotion by an elite group of advocates. Yet if a modified APC were applied to existing vaccines for diseases of the poor, it could rapidly begin to eradicate many of these diseases.

References

Abt Associates. nd. *Poverty Reduction and Immunizations*. Seattle: Gates Foundation, Children's Vaccines Program.

Acemoglu, D. and J. Linn. 2004. Market Size in Innovation: Theory and Evidence from the Pharmaceutical Industry. *Quarterly Journal of Economics* 119: 1049–90.

Birdsall, N. 2005. *Making Markets for Vaccines: Ideas to Action*. Washington, DC: Center for Global Development.

Center for Global Development. 2000. *Making Markets for Vaccines: Ideas into Action*. Washington, DC: Center for Global Development.

——. 2005. *Making Markets for Vaccines: Ideas into Action*. Washington, DC: Center for Global Development.

Conrad, P. 1992. *Deviance and Medicalization: From Badness to Sickness*. Philadelphia: Temple University Press.

DiMasi, J.A., Hansen, R.W., and Grabowski, H. 2003. The Price of Innovation: New Estimates of Drug Development Costs. *Journal of Health Economics* 22: 151–185.

Finkelstein, A. 2004. Static and Dynamic Effects of Health Policy: Evidence from the Vaccine Industry. *Quarterly Journal of Economics* 119: 527–564.

Goozner, M. 2004. *The $800 Million Pill: The Truth Behind the Cost of New Drugs*. Berkeley, CA: University of California Press.

Government Accounting Office. 2003. *NIH–Private Sector Partnership in the Development of Taxol*. Washington, DC: Government Accounting Office.

Grabowski, H. G., J. Vernon, and J. A. DiMasi. 2002. Returns on Research and Development for 1990s New Drug Introductions. *Pharmcoeconomics* 20 (suppl. 3): 11–29.

HM Treasury. 2005. *G8 Finance Ministers' Conclusions on Development*. London: HM Treasury.

Kremer, M. and R. Glennerster. 2004. *Strong Medicine: Creating Incentives for Pharmaceutical Research on Neglected Diseases*. Princeton, NJ: Princeton University Press.

Light, D. W. 2005. Making Practical Markets for Vaccines. *Public Library of Science – Medicine* 2(10): 101–105.

Love, J. 2003. *Evidence Regarding Research and Development Investments in Innovative and Non-Innovative Medicines*. Washington, DC: Consumer Project on Technology.

National Institute for Health Care Management (NIHCM), Research and Education Foundation. 2002. *Changing Patterns of Pharmaceutical Innovation*. Washington, DC: National Institute for Health Care Management, Research and Education.

Prescrire International. 2003. A Review of New Drugs and Indications in 2002: Financial Speculation or Better Patient Care? *Prescrire International* 12(64): 74–77.

Relman, A. and M. Angell. 2002. America's Other Drug Problem: How the Drug Industry Distorts Medicine and Politics. *The New Republic* 4, 587: 27–36.

Wellcome Trust and London School of Economics and Political Science. 2005. *The New Landscape of Neglected Disease Drug Development*. Pharmaceutical R&D Policy Project. London: Wellcome Trust and London School of Economics and Political Science.

World Health Organization (WHO). 2005. *State of the Art of New Vaccines: Research and Development*. Geneva: WHO.

14 Harnessing the power of pharmaceutical innovation

Thomas Pogge

One-third of all human deaths are readily avoidable. Every year, some 18 million people (50,000 each day) die prematurely from treatable medical conditions including (with 2002 death tolls in thousands) respiratory infections (3,963 – mainly pneumonia), HIV/AIDS (2,777), perinatal conditions (2,462), diarrhea (1,798), TB (1,566), malaria (1,272), childhood diseases (1,124 – mainly measles), obstetric conditions (510), malnutrition (485), sexually transmitted diseases (180), meningitis (173), hepatitis (157), and tropical diseases (129) (WHO 2004). Hundreds of millions more suffer grievously from these conditions or from other treatable diseases such as dengue fever, leprosy, trypanosomiasis (sleeping sickness and Chagas disease), onchocerciasis (River blindness), leishmaniasis, Buruli ulcer, lymphatic filariasis, and schistosomiasis (bilharzia) (Gwatkin and Guillot 1999). The lives of even more are shattered by severe illnesses or premature deaths in their family. And these medical problems also put a great strain on the economies of many poor countries, thereby perpetuating their poverty, which in turn contributes to the ill-health of their populations.

This huge incidence of mortality and morbidity is not randomly distributed. For a variety of social reasons, females are significantly over-represented among those suffering severe ill-health (UNDP 2003; Social Watch 2005; UNRISD 2005). Being especially vulnerable and helpless, children under five are also over-represented, accounting for nearly 60 per cent of the death toll (UNICEF 2005). But the most significant causal determinant is poverty: nearly all the avoidable mortality and morbidity occur in the poor countries (WHO 2004) and especially among their poorer inhabitants who lack access to the things that help the rest of us ward off ill-health – including adequate nutrition, medicines, safe drinking water, adequate clothing and shelter, basic sanitation, and mosquito nets in malaria-infested regions. Among the global poor, some 850 million are undernourished, 1,037 million lack access to safe water, 2,600 million lack access to improved sanitation (UNDP 2005); about 2,000 million lack access to essential drugs (www.fic.nih.gov/about/summary.html); approximately 1,000 million have no adequate shelter and 2,000 million no electricity (UNDP 1998).

These huge mortality and morbidity rates can be dramatically reduced by reforming the way we offer incentives to and reward the development of new medical treatments – preventive (vaccines) or remedial. Here I sketch a concrete, feasible, and politically realistic reform plan that would give medical innovators stable and reliable financial incentives to address the medical conditions of the poor. Adopting this plan would not add much to the overall cost of global healthcare spending. In fact, on any plausible accounting, which would take note of the huge economic losses caused by the present global disease burden, the reform would actually save money. Moreover, it would distribute the cost of global healthcare spending more equitably across countries, across generations, and among those lucky enough to enjoy good health and the unlucky ones suffering from serious medical conditions.

The existing rules for encouraging pharmaceutical research are morally deeply problematic. Long recognized among international health experts, this fact has become more widely understood in the wake of the AIDS crisis, especially in Africa, where the vital needs of poor patients are pitted against the need of pharmaceutical companies to recoup their investments in R&D (Barnard 2002). Still, this wider recognition does not easily translate into political reform. Some believe that the present regime is the lesser evil in comparison to its alternatives that have any chance of implementation. Others, more friendly to reform, disagree about what the flaws of the present system are exactly and have put forward a wide range of alternatives.

We need a concrete and specific reform plan that is fully informed by the relevant facts and insights from science, statistics, medicine, economics, law, and (moral and political) philosophy. This plan must be fully worked out to the point where it is ready for implementation and can serve as a clear focal point for advocacy, media discussions, and for the general public. And it must be politically feasible and realistic. To be *feasible* it must, once implemented, generate its own support from governments, pharmaceutical companies, and the general public (taking these three key constituencies as they would be under the reformed regime). To be *realistic*, the plan must possess moral and prudential appeal for governments, pharmaceutical companies, and the general public (taking these three constituencies as they are now, under the existing regime). A reform plan that is not incentive-compatible in these ways is destined to remain a philosopher's pipe-dream.

Bringing new, safe, and effective life-saving medications to market is hugely expensive, as inventor firms must pay for R&D of new drugs as well as for elaborate testing and the subsequent approval process. (Some might contest this statement. It has been asserted that pharmaceutical companies wildly overstate their financial and intellectual contributions to drug development, that most basic research is funded by governments and universities and then made available to the pharmaceutical industry free of charge (Angell 2004; Consumer Project on Technology, UNDP 2005.) In addition, newly developed medical treatments often turn out to be unsafe or not effective enough, to have bad side-effects, or fail to win government approval for some other reason, which may lead to the loss of the entire investment.

Given such large investment costs and risks, very little innovative pharmaceutical research would take place in a free market system. The reason is that an innovator would bear the full cost of its failures, but would be unable to profit from its successes because competitors would copy or retro-engineer its invention (effectively free-riding on its effort) and then drive down the price close to the marginal cost of production. This is a classic instance of market failure leading to a collectively irrational (Pareto-suboptimal) outcome in which medical innovation is undersupplied by the market.

The classic solution, also enshrined in the TRIPS Agreement (adopted under WTO auspices during the Uruguay Round), corrects this market failure through patent rules that grant inventor firms a temporary monopoly on their inventions, typically for 20 years from the time of filing a patent application. With competitors barred from copying and selling any newly invented drug during this period, the inventor firm (or its licensees) can sell it at the profit-maximizing monopoly price, typically very far above (up to 400 times greater than) its marginal cost of production. In this way, the inventor firm can recoup its research and overhead expenses plus some of the cost of its other research efforts that failed to bear fruit.

This solution corrects one market failure (the undersupply of medical innovation), but its monopoly feature creates another. During the patent's duration, the profit-maximizing sale price of the invented medicine will be far above its marginal cost of production. This large differential is collectively irrational by impeding many sales to potential buyers who are unwilling or unable to pay the monopoly price but are willing and able to pay substantially more than the marginal cost of production. If modified rules could facilitate these potential transactions, then many patients would benefit – and so would the drug companies as they would book additional profitable sales and typically also, through economies of scale, reduce their marginal cost of production.

One idea for avoiding this second market failure (associated with monopoly pricing powers) involves a *differential-pricing strategy*. One variant would have inventor firms themselves offer their proprietary drugs to different customers at different prices, thereby realizing a large profit margin from sales to the more affluent without renouncing sales to poorer buyers at a lower margin. Another variant is the right of governments, recognized under TRIPs rules, to issue compulsory licenses for inventions that are urgently needed in a public emergency. Exercising this right, a government can force down the price of a patented invention by compelling the patent holder to license it to other producers for a set percentage (typically below 10 per cent) of the latter's sales revenues. It is often suggested that poor countries should assert their compulsory licensing rights to cope with their public health crises, and with the AIDS pandemic in particular.

Differential pricing solutions are generally unworkable unless the different categories of buyers can be prevented from knowing about, or trading with, one another. In the real world, if the drug were sold at a lower price to some, then many buyers who would otherwise be willing and able to pay the higher price would find a way to buy at the lower price. Selling expensive drugs more cheaply in poor countries, for example, would create strong incentives to smuggle this drug back into the more affluent countries, leading to relative losses in the latter markets that outweigh the gains in the former. Anticipating such net losses through diversion, inventor firms typically do not themselves try to overcome the second market failure through differential pricing, resist pressures to do so, and fight attempts to impose compulsory licensing upon them. As a result, differential pricing has not gained much of a foothold, and many poor patients who would be willing and able to purchase the drug at a price well above the marginal cost of production are excluded from this drug because they cannot afford the much higher monopoly price (Kanavos et al. 2004). While such exclusion may be acceptable for other categories of intellectual property (software, films, and music), it is morally highly problematic in the case of essential medicines.

Insofar as a government does succeed, against heavy pressure from pharmaceutical companies and often their governments, in exercising its right to issue compulsory licenses, any net losses due to diversion are simply forced upon the patent holders. But, were this to become more common, it would engender the first market failure of undersupply: pharmaceutical companies will tend to spend less on the quest for essential drugs when the uncertainty of success is compounded by the additional unpredictability of whether and to what extent they will be allowed to recoup their investments through undisturbed use of monopoly pricing powers.

Doubtful that the differential-pricing strategy can yield a plan for reform that would constitute a substantial improvement over the present regime, I assume that the *public good strategy* is more likely to yield a reform plan that would avoid the main defects of the present monopoly-patent regime while preserving most of its important benefits.

Let me sketch three components of such a reform plan. First, the results of any successful effort to develop (research, test, and obtain regulatory approval for) a new essential drug are to be provided as a public good, which all pharmaceutical companies may use free of charge. This reform would eliminate the second market failure (associated with monopoly pricing powers) by allowing competition to bring the prices of new essential drugs down close to their marginal cost of production. Implemented in only one or a few countries, this reform would engender problems like those attending differential-pricing solutions: cheaper drugs produced in countries where drug development is treated as a public good would seep back into countries adhering to the monopoly patent regime, undermining research incentives in the latter. The reform should therefore be global in scope, just like the rules of the current TRIPs regime are.

Implemented in isolation, this first reform component would destroy incentives for pharmaceutical research. This effect is avoided by the second component which is that, similar to the current regime, inventor firms should be entitled to take out a multi-year patent on any essential medicines they invent, but, during the life of the patent, should be rewarded, out of public funds, in proportion to the impact of their invention on the global disease burden. This reform component would reorient the incentives of such firms in highly desirable ways. Any inventor firm would have incentives to sell its innovative treatments cheaply (even below their marginal cost of production) in order to help get its drugs to even very poor people who need them. Such a firm would have incentives to prioritize prevention over treatment. (The conventional patent system has the opposite effect, with new treatments offering much greater profit opportunities than new vaccines.) It would have incentives also to ensure that patients are fully instructed in the proper use of its drugs (dosage, compliance, etc.), so that, through wide and effective deployment, they have as great an impact on the global disease burden as possible (the absence of such incentives under the present rules gravely undermines the effectiveness even of donated drugs delivered into poor regions) (UNDP 2001). Rather than ignore poor countries as unprofitable markets, inventor firms would moreover have incentives to work together toward improving the heath systems of these countries to enhance the impact of their inventions there. Any inventor firm would have reason to encourage and support efforts by cheap generic producers to copy its drugs, as such copying would further increase the number of users and hence the invention's favorable impact on the global disease burden. In all these ways, the reform would align and harmonize the interests of inventor firms with those of patients and the generic drug producers – interests that currently are diametrically opposed. (This opposition was dramatically displayed when a coalition of 31 pharmaceutical companies went to court in South Africa to prevent their inventions from being reproduced by local generic producers and sold cheaply to desperate patients whose life depended on affordable access to these anti-retroviral drugs. In April 2001, their attempted lawsuit collapsed under a barrage of worldwide public criticism; Barnard 2002.) The reform would also align the moral and prudential interests of the inventor firms which, under the present regime, are forced to choose between recouping their investments in the search for essential drugs and preventing avoidable suffering and deaths.

This second component of the envisioned public good strategy has yet another tremendous advantage. Under the current regime, inventor firms have incentives to try to develop a new medical treatment only if the expected value of the temporary monopoly pricing power they might gain, discounted by the probability of failure, is greater than the full development and patenting costs. They have no incentives, then, to address diseases mainly affecting the poor, for which treatments priced far above the marginal cost of production could be sold only in small quantities. As a result, very few treatments are developed for medical conditions that cause most of the premature deaths and suffering in the world today. Even if common talk of the 10/90 gap ("only 10 percent of global health research is devoted to conditions that account for 90 percent of the global disease burden," DND-WG 2001) is now an overstatement, the problem is certainly real: malaria, pneumonia, diarrhea, and TB, which together account for 21 per cent of the global disease burden, receive 0.31 per cent of all public and private funds devoted to health research (GFHR 2004). And diseases confined to the tropics tend to be the most neglected. Of the 1,393 new drugs approved between 1975 and 1999, only 13 were specifically indicated for tropical diseases and five out of these 13 actually emerged from veterinary research (DND-WG 2001; Trouiller et al. 2001).

Rewarding pharmaceutical research in proportion to its impact on the global disease burden would attract inventor firms to medical conditions whose adverse effects on humankind can be reduced most cost-effectively. This reorientation would greatly mitigate the problem of neglected diseases that overwhelmingly affect the poor and would afford new profitable research opportunities for pharmaceutical companies.

One may worry that the second component of the reform would also *reduce* incentives to develop treatments for medical conditions that, though they add little to the global disease burden, affluent patients are willing to pay a lot to avoid. This worry can be addressed by limiting the application of the reform plan to *essential* drugs, that is, to medicines for diseases that destroy human lives. Drugs for other medical conditions, such as hair loss, acne, and impotence, for example, can remain under the existing regime with no loss in incentives or rewards.

Incorporating this distinction between essential and non-essential drugs into the reform plan raises the specter of political battles over how this distinction is to be defined and of legal battles over how a particular invention should be classified. These dangers could be averted by allowing inventor firms to classify their inventions as they wish and then designing the rewards in such a way that these firms will themselves choose to register under the reform rules any inventions that stand to make a substantial difference to the global disease burden. Such freedom of choice would also greatly facilitate a smooth and rapid phasing-in of the new rules, as there would be no disappointment of the legitimate expectations of firms that have undertaken research for the sake of gaining a conventional patent. The reform plan should be *attractive* for pharmaceutical companies by winning them lucrative new opportunities for research into currently neglected diseases without significant losses in the research opportunities they now enjoy – and by restoring their moral stature as benefactors of humankind.

This second reform component requires a way of funding the planned incentives for developing new essential medicines, which might cost some US$45–90 billion annually on a global scale. (This is my extrapolation from recent spending on pharmaceutical research (GFHR 2004), scaled up to take account of the fact that the rewards offered under the reformed rules must not merely match, but substantially exceed, projected research expenditures, because pharmaceutical companies will brave the risks and uncertainties of an expensive and protracted research effort only if its expected return substantially exceeds its cost. A more precise estimate is impossible because the cost each year would depend on how successful innovative treatments would be in reducing the global disease burden. The reform would cost billions of dollars only if and insofar as it would save millions of lives.) The third component of the reform plan is then to develop a fair, feasible, and politically realistic allocation of these costs, as well as compelling arguments in support of this allocation.

While the general approach as outlined may seem plausible enough, the intellectual challenge is to specify it concretely in a way that shows it to be both feasible and politically realistic. Here one main task concerns the design of the planned incentives. This requires a suitable measure of the global disease burden and ways of assessing the contributions that various new medical treatments are making to reduce it. When several medicines are alternative treatments for the same disease, then the reward corresponding to their aggregate impact must be allocated among their respective inventors on the basis of each medicine's market share and effectiveness. More complex is the case (exemplified in the fight against HIV/AIDS, TB, and malaria) of "drug cocktails" that combine several drugs, often developed by different companies. Here the reform plan must formulate clear and transparent rules for distributing the reward, proportional to the impact of the drug cocktail, among the inventors of the drugs it contains. And it must also include specific rules for the phase-in period so as not to discourage ongoing research efforts motivated by the existing patent rules. It is of crucial importance that all these rules be clear and transparent, lest they add to the inevitable risks and uncertainties that sometimes discourage inventor firms from important research efforts.

Another main task, associated with the third component, concerns the design of rules for allocating the cost of the incentives as well as the formulation of good arguments in favor of this allocation. Effective implementation of the reform requires that much of its cost be borne by the developed countries which, with 16 per cent of the world's population, control about 81 per cent of the global social product. This is feasible even if these countries, after retargeting existing subsidies to the pharmaceutical industry in accordance with the reformed rules, still had to shoulder around US$70 billion in new expenditures. This amount, after all, is only 0.22 per cent of the aggregate gross national incomes of the high-income countries, or US$70 for each of their residents. (The high-income countries had aggregate gross national income of US$32,064 billion and aggregate population of 1,000.8 million in 2004; World Bank 2005.)

This expense can be supported by prudential considerations. The taxpayers of the wealthier countries gain a substantial benefit for themselves in the form of lower drug prices and/or insurance premiums. Shifting costs within affluent countries from patients to taxpayers would benefit less healthy citizens at the expense of healthier ones. But such a mild mitigation of the effects of luck is actually morally appealing – not least because even those fortunate persons who never or rarely need to take advantage of recent medical advances, still benefit from pharmaceutical research, which affords them the peace of mind derived from knowing that, should they ever become seriously ill, they would have access to superb medical knowledge and treatments.

A second prudential reason is that, by making pharmaceutical research sensitive to the interests of poor populations, we are building goodwill in the developing countries by demonstrating in a tangible way our concern for their horrendous public health problems. This argument has a moral twin: in light of the extent of avoidable mortality and morbidity in the developing world, the case for including the interests of the poor is morally compelling.

There are three further prudential reasons. The reform would create top-flight medical research jobs in the developed countries. It would enable us to respond more effectively to public health emergencies and problems in the future by earning us more rapidly increasing medical knowledge combined with a stronger and more diversified arsenal of medical interventions. And better human health worldwide would reduce the threat we face from invasive diseases. The SARS outbreak and the avian flu scare illustrate the last two points: dangerous diseases can rapidly transit from poor country settings into cities in the industrialized world; and the current neglect of the medical needs of poor populations leaves us unprepared to deal with such problems when we are suddenly confronted with them.

Bringing enormous reductions in avoidable suffering and deaths worldwide, the reform would furthermore be vastly more cost-effective and also be vastly better received in the poor countries than similarly expensive humanitarian interventions we have undertaken in recent years and the huge, unrepayable loans our governments and their international financial institutions tend to extended to (often corrupt and oppressive) rulers and elites in the developing countries. Last, not least, there is the important moral and social benefit of working with others, nationally and internationally, toward overcoming the morally pre-eminent problem of our age, which is the poverty-induced and largely avoidable morbidity and mortality in the developing world.

References

Angell, M. 2004. *The Truth about the Drug Companies: How They Deceive Us and What to Do About It*. New York: Random House.

Barnard, D. 2002. In the High Court of South Africa, Case No. 4138/98: The Global Politics of Access to Low-Cost AIDS Drugs in Poor Countries. *Kennedy Institute of Ethics Journal* 12(2):159–174.

DND-WG (Drugs for Neglected Diseases Working Group). 2001. *Fatal Imbalance: The Crisis in Research and Development for Drugs for Neglected Diseases*. Geneva: MSF and DND-WG. Available at: http://www.msf.org/source/access/2001/fatal/fatal.pdf [Accessed May 26, 2006].

GFHR (Global Forum for Health Research). 2004. *The 10/90 Report on Health Research 2003–2004*. Geneva: GFHR. Available at: http://www.globalforumhealth.org [Accessed May 26, 2006].

Gwatkin, D. R. and M. Guillot. 1999. *The Burden of Disease Among the Global Poor: Current Situation, Future Trends, and Implications for Strategy*. Washington and Geneva: The World Bank and the Global Forum for Health Research.

Kanavos, P., J. Costa-i-Font, S. Merkur, and M. Gemmill. 2004. The Economic Impact of Pharmaceutical Parallel Trade in European Union Member States. LSE Working Paper. Available at: http://www.lse.ac.uk/collections/LSEHealthAndSocialCare/pdf/Workingpapers/Paper.pdf [Accessed May 26, 2006].

Pogge, T. 2002. *World Poverty and Human Rights: Cosmopolitan Responsibilities and Reforms*. Cambridge: Polity Press.

——. 2005. The First UN Millennium Development Goal: A Cause for Celebration? in Andreas Follesdal and Thomas Pogge (eds) *Real World Justice*. Berlin: Springer.

——. 2005. Human Rights and Global Health: A Research Program, in Christian Barry and Thomas Pogge (eds), *Global Institutions and Responsibilities*. Oxford: Blackwell.

Social Watch (Advance Social Watch Report). 2005. *Unkept Promises What the Numbers Say about Poverty and Gender*. Montevideo Social Watch. Available at: http://www.mdgender.net/resources/monograph_detail.php?MonographID=38 [Accessed May 30, 2006].

Trouiller, P., E. Torreele, P. Olliaro, N. White, S. Foster, D. Wirth, and B. Pécoul. 2001. Drugs for Neglected Diseases: A Failure of the Market and a Public Health Failure? *Tropical Medicine and International Health* 6(11): 945–951.

UNDP (United Nations Development Programme). 1998. *Human Development Report 1998*. New York: Oxford University Press.

——. 2001. *Human Development Report 2001*. New York: Oxford University Press.

——. 2003. *Human Development Report 2003*. New York: Oxford University Press.

——. 2005. *Human Development Report 2005*. New York: Oxford University Press.

UNICEF (United Nations Children's Fund). 2005. *The State of the World's Children 2005*. New York: UNICEF.

UNRISD (United Nations Research Institute for Social Development). 2005. *Gender Equality: Striving for Justice in an Unequal World*. Geneva: UNRISD/UN Publications.

WHO. 2004. *The World Health Report 2004*. Geneva: WHO Publications. Available at: http://www.who.int/whr/2004.

World Bank. 2005. *World Development Report 2006*. New York: Oxford University Press.

Part IV

Patents and access to medicines

15 Patents, profits, and the price of pills: implications for access and availability

Michael J. Selgelid and Eline M. Sepers

When examining the problem of lack of adequate healthcare, one should distinguish between *availability* – the existence of needed pharmaceuticals and diagnostics – on the one hand, and *accessibility* – the extent to which patients can obtain already existing products – on the other. Regarding the former, there are different reasons why needed treatments, vaccines, and diagnostic technologies are not (yet) offered on the market. First, the development of new medicines is scientifically challenging. The process from investigating a disease to the launch of a successful drug takes many years. This is exemplified by AIDS for which, despite intensive ongoing research efforts, there is still no effective cure. Second, it is commonly the case that very little, or no, relevant R&D is done in the first place. This holds true for many poverty-related diseases (Pécoul et al. 1999). A patient population lacking purchasing power is not an attractive target for industry, and hence the diseases that predominantly affect the poor are typically neglected. Third, when a market is not lucrative the production of existing medicines is sometimes stopped. This happened with chloramphenicol, a drug used to treat a type of bacterial meningitis common in sub-Saharan Africa. Although the oily suspension of chloramphenicol was both cost-effective and easy to use in developing countries, its "production and availability … are no longer guaranteed" (Pécoul et al. 1999).

There is also a variety of explanations why poor people in developing countries commonly fail to have *access* to drugs that *are* available in the market. Access problems are partly due to the poverty and/or remoteness of the communities where they live. Transportation to distant hospitals can be prohibitively expensive or difficult; local healthcare infrastructures are weak; and drug stockouts are frequent (Farmer 1999). Social and cultural factors also prevent many from obtaining the medical care they need. Because of their diminished status, the healthcare needs of women and children are often overlooked, and the social stigma attached to AIDS prevents many potentially HIV-infected people from seeking help. The major barrier to healthcare access, however, is poverty: for the billions of people living on US$2 or a less a day, healthcare, no matter how cheap by Western standards, is too often simply unaffordable. This is the case with both malaria and TB, where extreme poverty prevents many from obtaining inexpensive cures and preventative items.

For these and other complex reasons "nearly all the avoidable mortality and morbidity occurs in the poor countries" (Pogge 2005). As Kremer and Glennerster have noted,

"Infectious and parasitic diseases account for one-third of the disease burden in low-income countries – in fact for over half of Africa's disease burden. In contrast, infectious and parasitic diseases account for only 2.5 per cent of the burden of disease in high-income countries" (Kremer and Glennerster 2004). Given the relationships between poverty and disease, fighting poverty is a key to improving health in the developing world. However, poverty and disease are two sides of the same coin: while poverty promotes disease, disease itself devastates the economies of entire communities.

Big killers

In terms of illness and death, AIDS, TB, and malaria have the largest global impact: combined, they kill some six million people every year. In 2004, the WHO reported that "AIDS is now the leading cause of death and lost years of productive life for adults aged 15–59 years worldwide" (WHO 2004a). During each of the past few years, three million people have died from AIDS and five million have been newly infected. Of the 34–46 million people currently living with HIV/AIDS, two-thirds reside in Africa, where one in twelve adults are infected, and 95 per cent reside in developing countries. AIDS has killed over 20 million people during the past 25 years; 14 million children (mostly in Africa) have lost one or both parent(s) to AIDS, and "the projected number will nearly double to 25 million by 2010" (WHO 2004a).

In 1999, only 5 per cent of those infected could afford life-saving anti-retroviral therapy (Garrett 2000). By 2003, 6.7 per cent (but only 2 per cent in Africa) (WHO 2004a) of those in need received treatment. In 2003, "WHO, the Joint United Nations Programme on HIV/AIDS (UNAIDS) and the Global Fund declared lack of access to AIDS treatment with anti-retroviral medicines a global health emergency" and (with additional partners) launched the 3 by 5 initiative – "an effort to provide 3 million people in developing countries with anti-retroviral therapy by the end of 2005 ... one of the most ambitious public health projects ever conceived" (WHO 2004a). Though the situation has since improved significantly, with 11.6 per cent of those in need receiving anti-retroviral therapy at the end of 2004 (the number of people receiving treatment increasing from 440,000 to 700,000 over the course of six months), there is a long way to go before the goal of 3 by 5, let alone universal coverage, is achieved.

Though the cost of anti-retroviral therapy has dropped dramatically from over US$10,000 to as low as US$140 per year, the cost is still far out of reach for the world's 2.7 billion people living on less than US$2 a day (including one billion living on US$1 a day or less) (Pogge 2005). This problem is exacerbated by the fact that governmental health spending is low in developing countries. "Low income sub-Saharan African nations", for example, "spen[d] only 6 per cent of their average US$300 per capita GDP on health – around US$18 per person" (Kremer and Glennerster 2004). As a consequence, people living in developing countries usually have to pay for treatment themselves, which means that AIDS treatment is usually only available to the few who can afford it out of their pocket.

Though usually entirely curable with relatively inexpensive medications, TB kills almost as many as AIDS does each year. Declared a global health emergency by the

WHO in 1993, TB currently claims two to three million lives each year – more than ever before (Reichman and Tanne 2002; see also Farmer 1999). A third of the world population – two billion people – are infected with latent TB, and 5–10 per cent of these are expected to develop active illness. WHO estimates "that between 2002 and 2020, approximately 1,000 million people will be newly infected, over 150 million people will get sick, and 36 million will die of TB – if control is not further strengthened" (WHO 2002).

In the case of infectious diseases such as TB, incomplete access to drugs can have additional sinister consequences. When patients fail to complete their treatment – because they cannot afford to do so, for example – this can lead to the emergence of drug resistance. In 2003, "400,000 of the 9 million reported cases of tuberculosis were multi-drug resistant" (Kremer and Glennerster 2004). Drug resistance, and by implication poor people's lack of (complete) access to medication, threatens rich and poor countries alike. In the late 1980s and early 1990s, New York City spent over US$1 billion fighting an epidemic of multi-drug-resistant TB. Ordinary TB can be treated with a six-month course of treatment costing US$10. While drug-resistant TB treatment takes two years and costs 100 times as much, "[e]ven then a cure is not guaranteed". It is thus widely acknowledged that new TB drugs (and diagnostics) are needed. In the meantime it is tragic that, according to the WHO, there has been "a 40 year standstill in TB drug development" (WHO 2004b).

The scale of malaria is harder to assess, but it is estimated to kill at least one million (and perhaps as many as three million) people each year. Virtually all cases occur in low-income countries, and 90 per cent occur in Africa (Kremer and Glennerster 2004). Children are especially vulnerable: 90 per cent of deaths occur in those under the age of five. An African child dies of malaria every 30 seconds (WHO 2003). Those who survive may suffer brain damage, learning disorders, and incapacitating weakness and lethargy later in life. It is difficult to estimate the proportion of people in need who lack access to malaria medication; the matter is complicated by the large number of patients who are children and the fact that the disease is usually treated at home, so that many maltreated or untreated cases go undetected. (For an explanation of why the causes of death are harder to establish for young children, see UNICEF, Integrated Management of Childhood Diseases. An initiative for effective case management. Available at http://www.childinfo.org/eddb/imci/.) In any case, the scale of malaria morbidity and mortality demonstrates that effective malaria drugs, despite the fact that they are relatively inexpensive, fail to reach millions of people who need them.

Cost constraints also prevent many from obtaining simple preventative items such as mosquito nets and sprays: "tens of millions of families in Africa simply have no access to affordable bed nets or insecticide" (UNICEF 2000) and "only two per cent of children in Africa sleep under a bednet treated with insecticide" (GFATM 2004). As in the case with TB, deficient diagnosis drives drug resistance. Though it is widely acknowledged that new malaria drugs and diagnostics – and a vaccine if scientifically feasible – are needed, very little in the way of R&D resources have been directed toward such efforts.

Because tropical diseases, probably more than any other medical condition, are so confined to the poor, development of appropriate drugs is severely lacking. An oft-quoted study found that "[o]f the 1,393 new chemical entities that were approved between 1975 and 1999, only thirteen were specially indicated for tropical diseases" (Trouiller et al. 2001, cited in Pogge 2005). Moreover, even these 13 products were generally *not* the result of research efforts focused on tropical diseases as "[t]wo of these 13 drugs are actually updated versions of previous products ... 2 are the result of military research ... 5 come from veterinary research ... and only 4 (0.3 per cent) may be considered direct results of R&D activities of the pharmaceutical industry" (Pécoul et al. 1999, based on the same study). Pharmaceutical research into these conditions is almost nonexistent, reflecting a market too weak to spur necessary innovation. For most tropical diseases the available drugs are ineffective, complicated to use, and/or outdated.

Additional diseases making substantial contributions to the global disease burden are respiratory infections, measles, perinatal and maternal conditions, and diarrheal diseases (WHO 2000). Tetanus and syphilis, causing 308,662 and 196,533 deaths a year respectively, are also relatively common in the developing world (Kremer and Glennerster 2004). Though all these conditions can be averted or easily cured, they are responsible for millions of deaths every year. Again, children are particularly hard-hit: "[e]very year, over 10 million children under the age of five die from readily preventable and treatable illnesses such as diarrhoeal dehydration, acute respiratory infection, measles, and malaria" (UNICEF 2005). Together, diarrhea, respiratory infections and measles are responsible for about a quarter of all deaths among children and young adults in Africa and Southeast Asia (WHO 2000). Prevention and treatment of these diseases is easy, but poverty – in almost all cases the child is malnourished (UNICEF 2005) – continues to drive up the death toll.

The problem of patents

While the avoidable mortality from HIV/AIDS, TB, malaria, and other infectious diseases is due to a multitude of factors, much controversy has surrounded the strengthening of intellectual property right protection via the TRIPS Agreement of 1995. Objectors claim that the monopoly pricing enabled by patents makes drugs unaffordable to those who need them most. Two recent studies by Amir Attaran (and co-author Lee Gillespie-White in the earlier study) have in the meantime thrown a twist into this debate (Attaran and Gillespie-White 2001; Attaran 2004). Simply speaking, according to Attaran, because so few AIDS drugs are patented in African countries, and because so few "essential medicines," in general, are patented in developing countries – and because access to care does not vary inversely with the frequency of drug patents – intellectual property rights are not in reality a serious barrier to care. Poverty rather than patents is the main problem, according to Attaran, and activists should focus their energy on poverty alleviation rather than IPR protection.

In the earlier of the two studies, published in *JAMA* in 2001, Attaran and Gillespie-White examined the extent to which 15 AIDS medications were patented in 53 African countries. They found that most AIDS medications were patented in only a few African countries (mean = 3) and that in most African countries only a few AIDS medications were patented (mean = 4 for those countries where patents exist; while there were no patents on the studied drugs in 13 of the 53 countries). With the exception of South Africa, where 13 of the 15 medications were patented, the upshot is that pharmaceutical companies for the most part had not bothered to apply for patents on AIDS medications in Africa. "[O]f a theoretically possible 795 instances of patenting that [might have been identified] only 172 (21%) actually exist[ed]" (Attaran and Gillespie-White 2001).

Because "geographic patent coverage [did] not appear to correlate with anti-retroviral treatment access in Africa," they concluded, "patents and patent law are not a major barrier to treatment access in and of themselves" (Attaran and Gillespie-White 2001). Their point here was simply that access to anti-retrovirals in Africa was low across the continent; it was not the case that populations in countries with fewer, or no, patents had better access to anti-retrovirals than those with more patents. Because patent application deadlines had already passed for (the majority of) the drugs in question, they furthermore claimed that this situation could be expected to remain the same (even as TRIPS comes into full effect): in the case of already existing AIDS medication, anyway, patents have not been and will not be a serious barrier to care – because the unpatented drugs are at this stage (for the most part anyway) unpatentable.

In a second, more recent study, published in *Health Affairs* in 2004, Attaran examines the extent to which "essential medications" are patented in low-income and middle-income countries more generally. The findings are once again surprising:

in sixty-five low- and middle-income countries, where four billion people live, patenting is rare for [the] 319 products on the World Health Organization's Model List of Essential Medicines. Only seventeen essential medicines are patentable, although usually not actually patented, so that overall patent incidence is low (1.4 per cent) and concentrated in larger markets ... I find that patents for essential medicines are uncommon in poor countries and cannot readily explain why access to those medicines is often lacking, suggesting that poverty, not patents, imposes the greater limitation on access. (Attaran 2004)

Findings from the study of patents on AIDS medications in Africa were thus shown to be generalizable for "essential medications" worldwide. Essential medicines are hardly (even less so than AIDS medications in Africa) patented – especially in the poorest countries.

Each of these studies has been criticized on numerous grounds. The earlier study fails to acknowledge that not all existing AIDS drugs are equally important in treating the disease. Some have argued that the quantitative approach taken by Attaran and Gillespie-White is misleading because the most effective combinations of anti-retroviral medication are in fact blocked in a large number of African countries (CPT 2001; Boelaert et al. 2002; Goemaere et al. 2002). A second criticism is that Attaran and Gillespie-White fail to acknowledge the extent to which patents in one country have implications for others. In addition to being the country with the largest number of HIV-positive persons worldwide, SA is also the wealthiest African nation and would have been best able to produce and supply generic drugs to its neighbors (Selgelid and Schüklenk 2002). That this country, where 13 out of the 15 drugs are patented, is the exception to their rule demands further explanation.

That the first study suffered fundamental scientific flaws, furthermore, was verified by the second study. Given that critics (Selgelid and Schüklenk 2002) of the first study took pains to point out that the data revealed that patent frequency varied with the wealth of the African country in question – insofar as wealthy nations generally had more patents on AIDS medications than poorer neighbors – it is ironic that Attaran explicitly acknowledges that such a relationship was demonstrated by the second study insofar as essential medications were found to be more frequently patented in wealthier countries/bigger markets. The critical point here is that confounding variables – level of wealth and/or size of market – undermine any inference from the fact that "geographic patent coverage [did] not appear to correlate with anti-retroviral treatment access in Africa" to the conclusion that "patents and patent law are not a major barrier to treatment access" (Attaran and Gillespie-White 2001).

Mere correlation is notoriously insufficient for demonstrating causal connections, and this is why *controlled* studies are important from a scientific perspective. To test a claim that "patents cause lack of access to medicine" one would need to compare countries that were the same in other relevant respects (i.e., equally wealthy, or with equally big markets). The real question is whether or not SA and other wealthier African countries where more drugs are patented *would have* better access to AIDS medications were it not for the number of drugs patented there. Attaran and Gillespie-White's finding – that *poorer* nations (with fewer patents) have no better access to medicine – tells us nothing about this. Attaran and Gillespie-White's correlation-based inference is undermined by the obvious confounding variables of national wealth/market size – the relevance of which is explicitly demonstrated by Attaran's second study. If it were found that drug access did not vary with patent frequency *in equally wealthy countries* (which were also similar in other obviously relevant respects), then things would be different. Nothing like this was shown, however, by either of the studies.

The second study suffers fundamental flaws of its own. Attaran here stacks the deck by using the WHO's EML when deciding which drugs to study (the patenting frequency of). Because the WHO intentionally takes cost into account when making this list – explicitly favoring inexpensive medications – it should be less of a surprise to discover that so few "essential medicines" are patented (Goemaere et al. 2004). If patents increase prices and thus make medicines less likely to appear on the list, then it should be no surprise that few drugs on the list turn out to be patented. Attaran is right that the WHO has no explicit policy of automatically rejecting patented drugs as potential EML candidates, but the fact that its expert committee considers cost when constructing the list and the fact that patented drugs generally cost more than non-patented ones – that, after all, is the purpose of patents – deflates the significance of the finding that so few "essential" drugs are patented.

Even if, for the sake of argument, Attaran had succeeded in showing that patents pose no serious barriers of *access* to existing medications, his final conclusion that activists should divert attention away from the issue of IPR is misplaced. Attaran (and

Gillespie-White) here simply fails to acknowledge that another central reason for being concerned about patents is that they apparently "fail to provide the kind of incentive they are supposed to provide, in so far as patents have not led to – and are not likely to lead to – the development of medicines, which are most important from a global perspective. Patents offer little incentive to develop medical technologies specifically needed by the poor. Patents enable price increases, but this does not translate into profits if those in need are unable to pay high prices to begin with.

Alternative incentive schemes

One way to correct the current shortage of safe and effective drugs for poverty-related disease is to make relevant research more financially attractive to the pharmaceutical industry. We thus favor alternative incentive schemes along the lines of those recommended by Michael Kremer and Rachel Glennerster (2004) and Thomas Pogge (2005). The basic idea behind both these programs is that wealthy donor organizations or countries should offer advance guarantees to pharmaceutical companies that they will be financially rewarded for developing and delivering the kinds of technologies most needed from a global health perspective.

The central idea of Kremer and Glennerster's "pull program" is that donor organizations or national governments should (legally, via public offering) commit in advance to purchasing specified numbers of things like malarial vaccines (meeting predetermined specifications) at specified prices from the companies that develop them. If such advance commitments were sufficiently attractive, reflecting the true social value of the technologies in question, then pharmaceutical companies would have an (otherwise lacking) incentive to develop medical technologies most needed in developing countries. Because the purchase and provision of the vaccine, drug, or other technology would be assured in advance, and because stipulations would be made about price (i.e., that after X doses are sold at price Y, the company must provide additional doses at reduced price Z) concerns about *availability* as well as *access* to essential medicines are accounted for: *availability* because more drugs will be developed and brought to the market, and *access* because they will be sold at more affordable prices. This elegant scheme uses market mechanisms to correct market failure.

Pogge's reform program is more comprehensive. The first component of his scheme is that it should be possible for any drug manufacturer to use any products coming from the successful research efforts of other firms (including manufacturing details, results of clinical testing, and regulatory approval data) "free of charge". The resultant increase in competition would bring down prices close to their manufacturing cost, thereby making the drugs as affordable as possible. To ensure future pharmaceutical research, drug companies will need to be rewarded for engaging in innovative research. This matter is addressed by the second central component of Pogge's plan: that innovating *firms should be paid as a function of the extent to which their drugs contribute to the reduction in the global burden of disease*. The idea here is that the more successful a drug is in reducing the global mortality and morbidity caused by a particular disease, the higher will be the financial reward – and thus incentive – for the inventor. Pogge's point is that essential drugs should be seen as global public goods and their development should thus be paid for out of public funds in proportion to their true public value – that is, the extent to which they reduce morbidity and mortality.

It is important to highlight that Pogge's scheme is meant to complement rather than replace the current patent regime. Drug development firms would be able to choose which regime to register their inventions under. The new scheme will be attractive for life-saving drugs targeted at diseases that have a larger global impact, while the old regime will be more appealing for life-style products demanded by the rich. A strength of Pogge's proposal is that, by coupling the reward to global disease reduction, both the *availability* of drugs and their *accessibility* would be prime concerns of industry.

It should be noted that neither Pogge's nor Kremer and Glennerster's proposals provide (explicit) mechanisms for improving access to already existing, non-patented, and cheap drugs (such as first-line TB treatment). Kremer and Glennerster's pull programs are predominantly concerned with enhancing the development and dissemination of *new* drugs, and the issue of improving access to existing drugs is presumably outside their research focus. Pogge's program, however, could straightforwardly be extended to improve access to existing medications by rewarding *manufacturers and distributors* of already existing, off-patent drugs as a function of the extent to which the drugs they manufacture and/or distribute reduce morbidity and mortality.

A third alternative consists in the call, by the CPT and others, for a new global MRDT, the signatories of which would take on obligations to fund a minimal amount of basic biomedical research as well as priority research for neglected diseases, pharmaceuticals, vaccine development, diagnostic tools, and so on (CPT 2005a). The extent of funding to which each nation would be committed would depend on national wealth, and the wealthiest nations would pay more. Provisions would be made whereby "research supported by the public sector [is] made available to the public through open access archives or repositories"; and, importantly, members would agree "to forgo dispute resolution over intellectual property or pricing issues relating to the products covered by the agreement" (CPT 2005b).

Relevant medical R&D would thus be treated as a public good, and the proposed treaty aims (like the proposals of Kremer and Pogge) to address problems of both access and availability. In comparison with Kremer's and Pogge's plans, however, financing would be more wide-ranging. Funding would include public sector support for relevant research, tax expenditures and credits, philanthropic expenditures on relevant research, research financing by businesses and non-profit organizations, national expenditures on medical products, and the awarding of innovation awards. In contrast to Kremer's and Pogge's plans, there would be more direct (push) spending on relevant R&D; but, like Kremer's and Pogge's plans, (pull) incentives would also be offered to industry (via national expenditures on medical products and the awarding of innovation prizes).

Conclusion

Rather than choosing between such schemes, we emphasize the fact that each of these alternatives would require things already recognized as crucial to the solution of the healthcare situation in developing countries: that is, political will and a substantial influx of funding from wealthy developed nations. On each of these schemes the funds for pharmaceutical innovation would need to be assured up-front, and the vast majority of funds would need to come from NGOs, charities, and national governments. Pogge has estimated that his plan would cost US$45–90 billion globally, an expense that would have to be carried by high-income countries. This is a substantial amount, but Pogge argues that it is feasible.

What would be "compelling reasons" to support Pogge's plan or one of the others (assuming that they would in fact be effective)? Obviously, there are strong moral arguments: if an alternative scheme prevented millions of deaths, that alone is a valid reason to adopt it. From an egalitarian perspective, such alternatives would be desirable because they would help to correct the vast differences, in health and well-being, between the rich and poor. Utilitarians would argue that an alternative scheme would offer the best use of resources, as the same financial resources would lead to a larger reduction in global disease and hence an increase in global well-being. Libertarians should recognize that the healthcare situation in developing countries is largely a product of past injustices – warranting reparation (Selgelid 2004; 2005). Finally, it should be noted that health is not just another commodity, but is declared a basic human right by article 25 of the UDHR, and for that reason should be pursued. If countries such as the U.S. wish to avoid the impression that they are hypocritical to spend enormous sums of money fighting wars in the name of human rights while neglecting the healthcare situation in developing countries, this point should not be taken lightly.

Not only may the adoption of such schemes reflect the moral values of affluent countries and their citizens, but there are also valid self-interested reasons to support them. In the first place, the incentive schemes are attractive from a financial viewpoint. Such proposals would be beneficial for the pharmaceutical industry as they correct the "patent tradeoff" and open up a part of the market that is now lost by monopoly pricing strategies (Kremer and Glennerster 2004; Pogge 2005). More generally, the increase in research would increase high-skilled employment opportunities in developed countries (Pogge 2005). The status quo, in the meantime, is that wealthy developed nations can expect to bear costs as disease-ravaged economies collapse in developing countries where they do – or would like to do – business.

Second, by enhancing research into infectious diseases, the schemes will contribute to global and national safety. As noted in a report by the CIA:

New and reemerging infectious diseases will pose a rising global health threat and will complicate US and global security over the next 20 years. These diseases will endanger US citizens at home and abroad, threaten US armed forces deployed overseas, and exacerbate social and political instability in key countries and regions in which the United States has significant interests. (NIC 2000: 5)

We deny that Attaran has shown that patents are not significant barriers of *access* to existing medications; even if he were correct, however, he is wrong to conclude that activists should shift attention away from the issue of IPR. Alternative schemes to the current patent regime could plausibly improve both *availability* of and *access* to new drugs for poverty-related diseases. The development and implementation of such schemes, however, will inevitably require goodwill and substantial funding from developed countries. More resources will also be needed to address other issues (such as improving sanitation, education, social equality, etc.) and to promote access to preventative items (condoms, needles, mosquito nets, and so on). To a limited extent, these matters can be and are being addressed by organizations such as the GFATM and WHO. However, there is still much more to be done. The role for academics in this respect should be to further develop, compare, and analyze strategies (such as the alternatives we have considered) that would be effective in enhancing global health. They should also more forcefully demonstrate why it is important to address such issues now. Hopefully, it will not take long before politicians, policymakers, the public, industry, and donor organizations realize that fighting global diseases should be a higher global priority, that intellectual property rights have failed to provide promised incentives, that other live options are on the table, and that powerful cumulative – including self-interested – reasons support the case for change. As the WHO has noted, "our window of opportunity is closing" (WHO 2000).

References

Attaran, A. 2004. How Do Patents and Economic Policies Affect Access to Essential Medicines in Developing Countries? *Health Affairs* 23: 155–166.

Attaran, A. and L. Gillespie-White. 2001. Do Patents for Antiretroviral Drugs Constrain Access to AIDS Treatment in Africa? *JAMA* 286: 1886–1892.

Barton, J. H. 2004. TRIPS and the Global Pharmaceutical Market. *Health Affairs* 23: 146–154.

Boelaert, M., L. Lynen, W. Van Damme, and R. Colebunders. 2002. Letter to the Editor: Do Patents Prevent Access to Drugs for HIV in Developing Countries? *JAMA* 287: 840–841.

Consumer Project on Technology (CPT). 2001. *Comment on Attaran/Gillespie-White and PhRMA Surveys of Patents on Antiretroviral Drugs in Africa.* Washington, DC: CPT. Available at: http://www.cptech.org/ip/health/africa/dopatentsmatterinafrica.html [Accessed December 17, 2005].

——. 2005a. *Medical Research and Development Treaty. Discussion Draft 4.* Washington, DC: CPT. Available at: http://www.cptech.org/workingdrafts/rndtreaty4.pdf [Accessed November 11, 2005].

—— 2005b. *Request to Evaluate Proposal for New Global Medical R&D Treaty. Letter to World Health Assembly Executive Board and World Health Organization Commission on Intellectual Property, Innovation and Health.* Washington, DC: CPT. Available at: http://www.cptech.org/workingdrafts/24feb05WHOen.pdf [Accessed November 11, 2005].

Farmer, P. 1999. *Infections and Inequalities: The Modern Plagues.* Berkeley, CA: University of California Press.

Garrett, L. 2000. *Betrayal of Trust: The Collapse of Global Public Health.* New York: Hyperion.

Global Fund to Fight AIDS, Tuberculosis and Malaria (GFATM). 2004. *Fighting Malaria.* Geneva: GFATM. Available at: http://www.theglobalfund.org/en/about/malaria/default.asp [Accessed April 29, 2005].

Goemaere, E., A. Kaninda, L. Ciaffi, M. Mulemba, E. 't Hoen, and B. Pécoul. 2002. Letter to the Editor: Do Patents Prevent Access to Drugs for HIV in Developing Countries? *JAMA* 287: 841–842.

Goemaere, E., M. Lotrofska, Y. Marchandy, and E. 't Hoen. 2004. Patent Status Matters. *Health Affairs* 23: 279–280.

Joint United Nations Programme on HIV/AIDS (UNAIDS). 2004. *2004 Report on the Global AIDS Epidemic.* Geneva: UNAIDS. Available at: http://www.unaids.org/bangkok2004/report.html [Accessed April 12, 2005].

Kremer, M. and R. Glennerster. 2004. *Strong Medicine.* Princeton, NJ: Princeton University Press.

Lee, M. B. and H. M. Gilbert. 1999. Current Approaches to Leishmaniasis. *Infections in Medicine* 16 (34): 37–45.

National Intelligence Council (NIC). 2000. *The Global Infectious Disease Threat and its Implications for the United States.* Washington, DC: NIC. Available at: http://www.odci.gov/nic/PDF_GIF_otherprod/infectiousdisease/infectiousdiseases.pdf [Accessed May 10, 2005].

Pécoul, B., P. Chirac, P. Trouiller, and J. Pinel. 1999. Access to Essential Drugs in Poor Countries: A Lost Battle? *JAMA* 281: 361–367.

Pogge, T. W. 2005. Human Rights and Global Health: A Research Program. *Metaphilosophy* 36: 182–209.

Reichman, L. B. and J. H. Tanne. 2002. *Timebomb: The Global Epidemic of Multi-Drug-Resistant Tuberculosis.* New York. McGraw-Hill.

Selgelid, M. J. 2004. Ethics, Economics and AIDS in Africa. *Developing World Bioethics* 4: 96–105.

——. 2005. Ethics and Infectious Disease. *Bioethics* 19: 272–289.

Selgelid, M. J. and U. Schüklenk. 2002. Letter to the Editor: Do Patents Prevent Access to Drugs for HIV in Developing Countries? *JAMA* 287: 842–843.

United Nations (UN). 1999. *Declaration of Human Rights.* First adopted and proclaimed in 1948. New York: UN. Available at: http://www.un.org/Overview/rights.html [Accessed May 10, 2005].

United Nations International Children's Emergency Fund (UNICEF). 2000. *To the African Summit on Roll Back Malaria.* New York: UNICEF. Available at: http://www.UNICEF.org/media/media_11948.html [Accessed April 29, 2005].

——. 2005. *Integrated Management of Childhood Diseases. An Initiative for Effective Case Management.* New York: UNICEF. Available at: http://www.childinfo.org/eddb/imci/ [Accessed April 27, 2005].

World Health Organization (WHO). 2000. *Report on Infectious Diseases 2000. Preface.* Geneva: WHO. Available at: http://www.who.int/infectious-disease-report/2000/preface.htm [Accessed April 27, 2005].

——. 2002. *Fact Sheet No 104. Tuberculosis.* Geneva: WHO. Available at: http://www.who.int/mediacentre/factsheets/fs104/en/print.html [Accessed March 13, 2005].

——. 2003. *Basic Facts on Malaria.* Geneva: WHO. Available at: http://www.who.int/malaria/docs/Basicfacts.pdf [Accessed April 29, 2005].

——. 2004a. *The World Health Report 2004.* Geneva: WHO. Available at: www.who.org [Accessed March 15, 2005].

——. 2004b. *Drug-Resistant Tuberculosis Levels Ten Times Higher in Eastern Europe and Central Asia.* Press Release. Geneva: WHO. Available at: http://www.who.int/mediacentre/releases/2004/prl17/en/print.html [Accessed March 20, 2005].

16 Fair followers: expanding access to generic pharmaceuticals for low- and middle-income populations

Kevin Outterson

From free riders and pirates to fair followers

U.S. trade officials frequently employ the rhetoric of free riding and piracy when discussing intellectual property (IP) rights for medicines (Drahos with Braithwaite 2002; Benson 2005). The gentler term *free rider* is applied when developed country governments (OECD) use monopsony power to negotiate price discounts on patented pharmaceuticals (Outterson 2004, 2005b; U.S. Department of Commerce 2004; PhRMA 2005). Poorer governments usually lack sufficient market power as a purchaser to negotiate discounts for their low- and middle-income populations. In these cases, governments and patients may resort to unlicensed generic drugs and compulsory licensing. In response, U.S. trade officials and IP owners inflame the rhetoric and label such activity *piracy*.

Free riders use something they haven't paid for. The term itself calls to mind someone riding on a bus without paying the fare. But free riding is not limited to tangible goods and services. With intangible property, free riding is not only possible, but in many ways easier. Downloading music from the Internet is the new paradigm case.

Piracy is a crime against humanity. Pirates steal and destroy wantonly. They rape and kill with abandon. Piracy is an inappropriate term for providing essential medicines to the world's poorest people. Médecins Sans Frontières (MSF) broke the law when it began offering anti-retroviral therapy (ART) in Khayelitsha Township in South Africa in 2001. The crime against humanity would have been a studied failure to act in the face of the AIDS crisis.

The rhetoric of IP law should consider the economic structure of pharmaceutical knowledge. Unlike tangible property, pharmaceutical knowledge does not suffer from exhaustion or congestion. In economic terms, it is generally *non-rivalrous*. This chapter explores the powerful implications of that feature, and concludes that low- and middle-income populations should be encouraged to use pharmaceutical knowledge as *fair followers*. In particular, fair followers should use low-cost generic versions of essential patented medicines to maximize access, so long as incentives for innovation are not harmed thereby.

Property rights are designed to resolve the problems of rivalry and appropriation

The dominant system of property rights makes eminent sense for traditional categories of tangible goods. Physical things are subject to at least two problems which are addressed by property rules: rivalry and appropriation.

Rivalry

Any item that can suffer exhaustion or congestion is rivalrous. Congestion occurs when too many people attempt simultaneous use: if everyone has equal claims to my car, then I may not find it available when I want it. Ten thousand people cannot simultaneously sleep in the same bed, or farm the same small field, or eat my fig. Exhaustion occurs when multiple users degrade the resource. Classic examples include overgrazed fields and depleted fisheries (Hardin 1968).

The OECD market-based economy relies on property rights as the primary solution to rivalry. Ownership is entrusted to one person, and that person is given control of the property's use, including the right to exclude others. The owner takes the decisions regarding use of their property, including issues of congestion and exhaustion. But ownership is not absolute. Property owners are also subject to duties, particularly when their actions negatively impact others. Property may also be taken for a public use with compensation through the sovereign power of eminent domain.

Globalized legal and moral cultures generally respect private property. If someone takes property without permission, we call them a thief. Moral norms cover similar ground, but an exception might be made for a starving child taking a loaf of bread from a wealthy family. In such a case the need is great and the loss is small, so perhaps taking the property is morally justified. Similar moral sentiments have propelled MSF and their Access to Essential Medicines Campaign. MSF campaigns for significantly lower drug prices for the poor, even when the drugs are unauthorized generics or produced under a compulsory license (MSF 2005a). The medical need is great and the damage from the taking is minuscule. Action is not only appropriate, but may be a moral necessity. MSF were not arrested as a pirate or a thief; instead they are celebrated for their service to humanity.

Appropriation

The second problem addressed by property rules involves appropriation, or more precisely, the inability to appropriate returns on common pool resources. Absent an appropriation tool, no single individual retains an economic incentive to invest in common pool resources. Few would purchase or maintain an automobile if they could not control its subsequent use. The market gardener cares for her trees in the spring in anticipation of a harvest in the autumn. Property rules permit a person (the "owner") to appropriate the fruits of their investment. It is thought that society generally benefits when owners invest in their property, particularly if duties are imposed to account for negative externalities like pollution.

Intangibles

Now consider the case of property rights for intangibles such as patents, copyrights, trade secrets, and the like. Intangibles are even more exposed to appropriation by strangers. Stealing my car requires physical theft; taking my land will lead to adverse physical occupation. Both are relatively easy to identify. Using a patent or trade secret without permission may be harder to discover and easier to accomplish. Music and video files can be copied anonymously over the Internet. Such copying can happen in many locations simultaneously, all over the world. The artist and the distributor may never know. Copying is also possible with pharmaceutical knowledge. For many years, India produced unlicensed generic versions of drugs which were still under patent outside India. In many cases, these drugs were the best or only low-cost source for humanitarian programs in Africa and elsewhere.

This type of activity might well reduce innovation incentives. Appropriation on IP investments would be more difficult if many potential customers did not pay. IP laws hinder misappropriation (or free riding) by creating temporary legal barriers such as patents and copyrights. But the analogy between tangible and intangible property breaks down on the question of rivalry. Tangible goods are rivalrous. They suffer from exhaustion and congestion. But most intangibles are non-rivalrous, including the biomedical knowledge which forms the basis of the pharmaceutical industry. Most pharmaceutical knowledge is non-rivalrous, and this fact enables a transformation from free riding and piracy to fair following.

Reconsidering moral and property rights in non-rivalrous pharmaceutical knowledge

Different property rules might be appropriate for non-rivalrous knowledge. Bread is consumed when eaten, but knowledge may be shared by an infinite number of persons without exhaustion or congestion. Rivalry still afflicts the physical expressions of knowledge, such as books and pills, but the underlying knowledge itself remains non-rivalrous. Knowledge may be widely disseminated without creating shortages, a potential boon for humanity.

Non-rivalrous goods may result in different moral rules concerning theft. Let us return to the example of the starving child. Assume that a loaf of bread was a non-rivalrous good. The biblical example is Jesus feeding the crowds with miraculous bread and fish: as the contents of the baskets were distributed by the disciples, more food appeared. Although they began with only five loaves and two small fish, thousands were fed and the leftover food filled twelve baskets (Matthew 14: 13–21). In a world of non-rivalrous goods, the moral imperative would require sharing. If the bus ride is truly free, let everyone ride.

Property laws must also be reconsidered. By definition, additional users can be added without exhaustion, congestion, or other costs. If the appropriation (investment) problem can be resolved, then the hegemony of absolutist property rules would crumble. If the appropriation (investment) issue is resolved, there is no reason to strengthen IP rights further to deny access to additional users, particularly when the users are low- and medium-income populations faced with inadequate access to essential medicines.

For example, Lipitor (atorvastatin calcium) is an important lipid-reducing drug, patented by Pfizer. The global medical need for reducing cholesterol is great, in both rich and poor countries (WHO 2004). Generic drug companies could sell much cheaper dosages without congestion or exhaustion, but doing so might diminish appropriation by Pfizer. To be successful, *fair following* must simultaneously improve access to generic Lipitor, without undermining optimal innovation incentives for Pfizer.

The pharmaceutical industry frames the issue as intellectual property *rights*, with little regard for potential IP *duties*. The industry assumes that maximizing IP laws and therefore pharmaceutical appropriation is the best course of action (PhRMA 2006). But the creation of property rights sometimes creates associated negative externalities, and those negative externalities imply duties. With real property, the negative externality could be pollution, and a possible duty is abatement. With pharmaceutical IP, one prominent negative externality is inadequate access: millions (indeed, billions) of people lack access to patented drugs which would improve health (Outterson 2005d). The duty could be to permit fair following. Put another way, if appropriation (investment) issues are resolved and the goods are non-rivalrous, then no reason remains to deny access to additional users, especially for low- and medium-income populations facing inadequate access to essential patented drugs.

The concept of an IP duty might seem radical, but it is already a prominent feature of U.S. food and drug law. The current U.S. practice of permitting generic drug entry after patent expiration is an imperfect application of this policy, embodied in the Hatch–Waxman Act. Mindless maximization of pharmaceutical IP rights is bad public policy. Taken to its logical conclusion, generic drugs would be abolished entirely. Consumers would pay higher prices and many would suffer adverse health effects from inadequate access. The more reasonable public policy option is to optimize pharmaceutical innovation incentives, balancing access and innovation (Outterson 2005a).

Whatever one thinks of the balance struck for the U.S. market, we have every reason to suppose that optimization would result in different outcomes in other countries, particularly amongst low-income populations. In such groups, their poverty will limit the effectiveness of appropriation, permitting the relaxation of pharmaceutical IP laws. Poverty also magnifies the damage that high drug prices inflict, strengthening the case for earlier generic entry. But current U.S. policy exports Hatch-Waxman to other countries without appropriate modifications (Outterson 2005c). This fair followers proposal is an attempt to reverse that policy.

The following section describes how pharmaceutical knowledge may be shared with low- and medium-income populations without damaging optimal innovation incentives. The foundations for the global pharmaceutical IP system crumble if this appropriation question is resolved.

Pharmaceutical rent extraction from low- and medium-income populations should be limited

When it comes to the world's low-income populations, pharmaceutical appropriation is nearly irrelevant. Low-income populations cannot contribute much to global pharmaceutical rents in any case. They should be exempt from IP property rules based upon appropriation. The economist F. M. Scherer (2004) described a similar proposal, giving economic language to the human rights appeals by essential medicines advocates like MSF. Scherer's point is that any pharmaceutical patent rent extraction from low-income populations is likely to be very damaging to people and not very helpful to innovation. In a similar vein, Lanjouw and Jack (2004) suggest that poor countries really shouldn't be expected to contribute much toward global pharmaceutical R&D, with the possible exception of locally endemic diseases. Their proposal would effectively exempt low- and medium-income countries from most pharmaceutical patent laws, permitting instantaneous generic entry for global pharmaceutical innovation in these markets.

Pharmaceutical rent extraction amongst low-income populations is both cruel and unnecessary: cruel because people will die when a life-extending treatment is possible, but unaffordable; unnecessary because low-income populations would never have contributed much towards global pharmaceutical rent extraction in any case. Low-income populations have dramatically higher demand elasticities. Pricing AIDS drugs at US$10,000 per year might be optimal in the U.S. market (or not), but at that price virtually no one in sub-Saharan Africa can afford them. Moreover, we know that the marginal cost of production of these drugs is less than US$240 per year (MSF 2005b). Given these facts, the very poorest cannot be expected to pay thousands of dollars for AIDS drugs. Indeed, the poorest should not pay any patent appropriation rent for these drugs: the extremely modest contribution from low-income populations is much more valuable to them than it is to the global pharmaceutical industry. Middle-income populations present a transitional case: some patent rent extraction might be appropriate, but full OECD pricing would deny needed access.

These factors are not limited to AIDS drugs, but are present in many other chronic and infectious conditions. Much of the global burden of disease is from conditions which are truly global in nature: AIDS, cancer, cardiovascular disease, infections, and depression (WHO 2004; Outterson 2005a). Global diseases afflict both rich and poor. For global diseases, innovation is assured by demand in wealthy OECD countries. Appropriation from low-income populations is not important for global disease innovation. These drugs could be provided generically to the poorest without undermining optimal innovation.

The same cannot be said for neglected diseases. The fair follower proposal neither improves nor harms the prospects for neglected disease innovation. Fair following is primarily geared to global diseases such as cancer, cardiovascular disease, diabetes, depression, and AIDS. Neglected diseases are endemic primarily in poor regions of the world. Innovation has lagged because of the poverty of the afflicted. The very poorest are not a good market, particularly when the wealthy countries have no need for the drug. Several recent proposals attempt to correct this market failure by creating mechanisms such as purchase commitments and prize funds (Hollis 2004; Kremer and Glennerster 2004). Many public–private partnerships have accelerated neglected disease research (Moran et al. 2005). Others look to non-market incentives such as grants and government-sponsored research (Love 2003a and b; Hubbard 2003; but see DiMasi and Grabowski 2004). Occasionally proposals are coupled with an expansion of IP rights in poor countries (Sykes 2002), but expanded IP rights are an unnecessary and unwelcome addition. Expansion of IP rights will not create incentives in the absence of money to buy the product. These diseases are neglected due to the poverty of the afflicted, not the lack of IP rights (Outterson 2005a).

Pharmaceutical rent extraction is best accomplished in high-income populations, amongst people who can afford expensive patented drugs. The burden of supporting innovation should rest upon those with the ability to afford expensive medicines. This principle has been embraced by pharmaceutical companies and major Western governments. Price discrimination based upon ability to pay underlies all voluntary differential pricing programs, as well as the recent Canadian legislation to permit export of compulsory licensed pharmaceuticals for low-income populations. In the Canadian program, the royalty varies with the poverty of the target country (The Jean Chrétien Pledge to Africa Act 2004). The U.S. Department of Commerce followed suit in December 2004 when it calculated pharmaceutical free-riding by various OECD countries, with adjustments for per capita GDP (U.S. Department of Commerce 2004). High-income individuals typically have low demand elasticities for patented pharmaceuticals, permitting both high prices and relatively modest access externalities. In such situations, both clinical needs and innovation goals can be met simultaneously.

Fair following in practice

Several models of fair following are possible. Each may potentially reach the same end – providing low- and medium-income populations with affordable access to essential drugs without harming optimal innovation incentives – but the legal forms differ widely. They also differ wherein the authority lies to make a decision on granting access. The four models discussed here are: (1) compulsory licensing; (2) voluntary differential pricing; (3) patent buy-outs; and (4) the proposed Global R&D Treaty.

Streamline and expand compulsory licensing

Compulsory licensing is the sovereign power to use a patent absent permission from the patent owner. Compulsory licensing is often mischaracterized as "breaking a patent." Compulsory licensing is analogous to the power of eminent domain over real property, with one important caveat: while eminent domain often takes the property completely, compulsory licensing is only a partial taking. The owner retains all rights against all other persons. Under U.S. law, compensation must be paid to the patent owner. Compulsory licensing is fully consistent with the WTO TRIPS Agreement. WTO members may compel licensing to protect public health, without limitation concerning the disease or drug at issue (WTO TRIPS Agreement 1994; WTO Doha Declaration 2001; 't Hoen 2002; Love 2005).

Royalty rates for compulsory licenses should be modest when the intended recipients are very poor. Canada has proposed royalty rates ranging from 4 per cent down to 0.02 per cent depending upon the importing country's level of poverty. While Canada's law raises many questions (Outterson 2005a), it is clearly a step in the direction of fair following. Canada recognizes that pharmaceutical patent rent extraction is largely inappropriate from low-income populations.

Sovereign threats of compulsory licensing have led to much lower prices. Prominent examples include Brazil's highly successful anti-retroviral program for AIDS (Bermudez 2002; Reichman with Hasenzahl 2003; Benson 2005) and the October 2001 threat by the U.S. government to issue a compulsory license for Bayer's Cipro (ciprofloxacin) during the anthrax scare (Carroll and Winslow 2001, see also Reichman with Hasenzahl 2003). Most of the affordable AIDS drugs listed in the MSF pricing guide were produced by Indian companies as generics prior to the phase-out of the TRIPS flexibilities afforded to India as a developing country (MSF 2005b). Even nominally voluntary licenses, such as Merck's grant to the South African-Indian company Thembalami Pharmaceuticals (Merck & Co., Inc. 2004), are frequently a response to litigation and the threat of compulsory licensing (Outterson 2005a). Roche's experience with Tamiflu (oseltamivir phosphate) is quite similar: Roche reluctantly agreed to discuss voluntary licenses only when governments began to threaten compulsory licensing. The pressing need to build stockpiles against an influenza epidemic goaded both governments and Roche into action.

The U.S. has consistently opposed compulsory licensing by other countries. In January 2001, the U.S. requested a WTO panel against Brazil to prevent Brazilian "local manufacture" of AIDS drugs (WTO 2001). Under international pressure, the U.S. withdrew the panel request in the months leading up to the Fourth WTO Ministerial Conference in Doha (Thomas 2001; 't Hoen 2002). More recently, U.S. groups attacked Brazil in July 2005 over a proposed compulsory license of Kaletra (lopinavir and ritonavir), an AIDS fixed-dose combination drug. The patent owner, Abbott Laboratories, reached a voluntary price reduction agreement with Brazil which made the formal compulsory license unnecessary, another demonstration of the power of compulsory licenses to improve access (Benson 2005).

Compulsory licenses, like any good thing, can become dangerous if used to excess. The power to issue compulsory licenses rests with the government where the patent resides (in the case of an export under special WTO rules, a compulsory license must also be issued by the exporting country). If this decision may be made unilaterally, a collective action problem may result. Each country could resort to compulsory licensing excessively, depressing global drug sales and retarding optimal innovation. This is unlikely for at least three reasons. First, pressure from the United States Trade Representative's (USTR) Office has coerced countries to abandon flexibilities inherent in the WTO TRIPS Agreement, including compulsory licensing (Thorpe 2004). As a result, the empirical use of compulsory licenses has been modest, other than the examples discussed above. Second, prior to the avian influenza scare, the U.S. has been the only OECD country to recently display an appetite for compulsory licensing of a patented drug (Carroll and Winslow 2001). OECD countries would in any case pay royalties to compensate the patent holder for the non-exclusive use. If compulsory licensing is limited to low- and medium-income populations, then the damage to optimal innovation incentives will be negligible. Finally, most OECD countries do not need to resort to compulsory licensing at all, but may effectively control costs through the mechanism of government pharmaceutical reimbursement (U.S. Department of Commerce 2004; PhRMA 2005). The TRIPS Agreement does nothing to prevent OECD countries from effectively holding down drug prices (and pharmaceutical rents) through these reimbursement mechanisms (U.S. Department of Commerce 2004; Outterson 2005b). This wealthy country free riding is many orders of magnitude larger than any potential abuse by low-income populations through compulsory licensing (Outterson 2005b, 2005c).

In short, if compulsory licensing for low-income populations was streamlined and greatly expanded, it would do little or no damage to global pharmaceutical innovation, while greatly improving global access to life-saving medicines.

Voluntary differential pricing

A second model is voluntary differential pricing. Drug companies suggest that greatly improved generic access is not required because they can engage in voluntary differential pricing programs. The drug companies retain exclusive ownership of the IP, but agree to make the product available at reduced prices for some low-income populations. Voluntary differential pricing could facilitate fair following if adopted for all essential drugs and expanded to guarantee marginal cost pricing for all low- and medium-income populations. It is highly unlikely to substantially achieve these goals. Millions have died in Africa while waiting for AIDS drugs to reach them under publicly announced voluntary differential pricing programs. For other drugs and conditions not in the media spotlight, the record of voluntary differential pricing programs is equally dismal.

These programs are generally limited to particular diseases, drugs or countries. Voluntary differential prices are not nearly low enough, and are not generally priced at the marginal cost of production. Voluntary differential pricing programs allow the drug companies to retain full control. Countries are not able to act unilaterally, so the collective action problem does not appear, but inadequate access remains. Establishing a few programs may respond to a particularly compelling crisis or a public relations problem, but pharmaceutical companies have no internalized economic incentive to systematically address inadequate access. The empirical track record of voluntary differential pricing programs has proven to be very disappointing as a comprehensive solution (Outterson 2005a). As discussed above, many notable programs have appeared only as responses to threatened compulsory licensing.

To some extent, fear of pharmaceutical arbitrage from low-income markets to high-income markets has stifled drug company support for voluntary differential pricing. Similar fears could also be raised against expanded use of compulsory licensing. Empirically, such arbitrage is rarely observed, and need not be a significant threat to optimal pharmaceutical innovation when proper tools are utilized to minimize leakage (Outterson 2005a). For innovation purposes, the most important price discrimination barrier is between OECD markets and the rest of the world. This is exactly the same divide that fair follower models will utilize. Even within a single country, Pharmaceutical Research and Manufacturers of America (PhRMA) has been able to deploy a myriad of legal, contractual, and unilateral mechanisms to successfully price discriminate. Drug prices within the U.S. vary dramatically between Medicaid, Medicare, 340b, Federal Supply Schedule, insurance carriers, institutions (hospitals and nursing homes) and free clinics (Outterson 2005b). The alleged dangers of pharmaceutical arbitrage may well be overstated (Outterson 2005a).

Purchase patents for generic production for low- and medium-income populations

A third fair follower model is to leave IP laws undisturbed, but to simply purchase the pharmaceutical patent rights for low- and medium-income populations. The purchased patents would then be donated to the public domain, permitting marginal cost production for the world's poorest people. For example, patents could be purchased for the non-OECD world, and left in place for the wealthy OECD countries. The great majority of pharmaceutical appropriation would still flow through the OECD market system; the buy-out would cover only low- and medium-income populations and would be a relatively modest part of global pharmaceutical sales. Appropriation would be supported by the combination of the continuing rent extraction (patent laws) in high-income markets and the buy-out prices for other markets. This is the patent buy-out model (Guell and Fischbaum 1995; Guell 1997; Kremer 1998; Ganslandt, Maskus, and Wong 2001; Stein and Valery 2004).

Existing buy-out proposals

The common feature of patent buy-out proposals is to separate the market for innovation from the market for drugs, particularly for the poor. (This feature is also shared by the Global R&D Treaty, discussed below.) If patents are purchased and then donated to the public domain, competition will permit the widest possible distribution at the lowest possible market price, freed from the distortions, rent-seeking and inefficiencies inherent in monopolistic pricing through patents. Guell and Fischbaum (1995) make this case plainly, although their focus is primarily buy-outs for the U.S. market. The access improvements they describe would be even greater amongst low-income populations with higher demand elasticities. Kremer's (1998) proposal is primarily an incentive for neglected disease innovation. Kremer would create a market for a neglected disease innovation by making a credible promise to purchase the patent at an attractive price. Purchasing the patent enables generic production, but Kremer's focus is on the innovation side of the problem. Kremer has also proposed a commitment to purchase large quantities of the item (such as a drug or vaccine), leaving the patent in place (Kremer and Glennerster 2004). Stein and Valery (2004) reject patent buy-outs as a solution for the U.S. market, and make the case for the Federal government entering the drug business as a full competitor. Their only proffered reason for rejecting patent buy-outs is the failure to reduce overall patent rents, completely ignoring the access and allocative efficiency gains described by Guell and Fischbaum (1995). Patent buy-outs need not alter patent rents (for that would affect innovation), but merely separate innovation from production and permit the widest possible access to pharmaceutical innovation at generic prices.

Patent buy-outs for low- and medium-income populations

Three existing proposals could be considered fair following because they focus on low- and medium-income populations: the DEFEND proposal by Ganslandt, Maskus, and Wong (2004); the patent option proposal by Lanjouw and Jack (2004); and Scherer's article (2004) encouraging poor countries to free ride on pharmaceutical patents. Ganslandt, Maskus, and Wong (2004) suggest a buy-out of exclusive pharmaceutical licenses for poor countries. Their DEFEND proposal and Scherer's article are generally consistent with my own views, with some caveats (described below). Lanjouw and Jack (2004) do not utilize buy-outs at all, but force pharmaceutical companies to choose between patenting the drug in rich countries or poor countries, but not both. For global diseases, drug companies will always choose to patent in rich countries. In effect, Lanjouw and Jack permit generic production of any global disease drug for poor countries without the expense of a buy-out. This proposal enjoys the virtues of simplicity and economy, but to the extent we are concerned about maintaining optimal innovation incentives, some payment should be considered for market rights, at least in middle-income countries. Lanjouw and Jack also ignore the political realities of PhRMA and USTR's joint campaign over the past 15 years to establish a single global standard for pharmaceutical IP.

Patent buy-outs have great potential to improve access to life-saving medicines. In 2004 the global R&D cost recovery from non-OECD markets for all anti-retroviral (ARV) drugs was less than US$110 million per year. In all of Francophone West Africa, commercial sales of ARVs were only US$33,000 in 2004, according to IMS data (IMS Health 2005a). Retail sales of branded NRTI AIDS drugs in Peru have never exceeded US$19,000 per year (IMS Health 2005b). In short, the indicated buy-out price for ARVs for these regions of the world is quite modest, cutting the Gordian knot of the global AIDS patent battles. Anything that lowers treatment costs for effective AIDS drugs should be deployed in the face of this global health catastrophe.

Patent buy-outs are controlled by the wealthy donor (a foundation or government) rather than the country wherein the potential patient resides. One collective action problem is avoided, but the target country lacks control over one important element of the health and safety of its citizens. Unless a global mechanism is created to buy out all global pharmaceutical IP for low- and medium-income populations, then the target countries will be dependent upon continued foreign charity.

Setting the buy-out price

The buy-out price must be set high enough to optimize global pharmaceutical innovation and low enough to be affordable as a routine finance mechanism. Lanjouw and Jack (2004) effectively set the price at zero by requiring drug companies to choose between patents in rich countries or poor countries. If global pharmaceutical appropriation is already supra-optimal, then zero (or a negative value) is the correct price (Outterson 2005a). Policymakers should have transparent access to reliable data on global pharmaceutical innovation in order to answer that question. Drug company surveys based upon unverifiable data should not be relied upon for this important question.

If the goal of the buy-out price is to mimic what would have happened under best-case competitive market conditions, then the price should be based on expected profits rather than sales or costs. Ganslandt, Maskus, and Wong (2001) used cost data to calculate the buy-out, which rewards effort rather than success. Gross sales are certainly an element of pharmaceutical appropriation, but the relevant market metrics are the net present value (NPV) of the cash flow or the NPV of the profit stream. The purpose of the buy-out price should be to restore the expected profits , and more particularly, the lost R&D cost recovery.

Expected future profits will of course be difficult to estimate. The following formula relies to the greatest extent possible on externally generated data, to avoid data manipulation and methodological squabbles, with retrospective experience adjustments:

$$BOP = NPV_{t\,d}\,(U_t * MCP)\,\boldsymbol{p}$$

where BOP is the buy-out price; NPV is the net present value over the patent period t at discount rate d; U is the number of generic units sold in the target markets by all sellers during t; and MCP is the marginal cost of production per unit, estimated as 90 per cent of the lowest sustained ex-factory actual price per unit during t; $\boldsymbol{p}$ is a profit adjustor, reflecting the percentage of revenues allocated to R&D cost recovery (14–17 per cent are the estimates from drug companies). Estimated payments could be made at buy-out, subject to periodic and retrospective adjustment as actual data developed on U and MCP, and perhaps for changes in d. The formula avoids any need to know actual costs, profits, or average sales prices. The only data required are aggregate generic unit sales and the lowest sustained ex-factory price by any generic seller in the target markets. Both are relatively easy to collect and difficult for the patent holder (or anyone else) to manipulate.

This formula aligns incentives against rent-seeking and allocative inefficiency in helpful ways. The buy-out permits any pharmaceutical company to manufacture and sell the drug generically in all target markets. Competition will drive the unit price down towards the actual marginal cost of production. In a competitive market with multiple entrants, no single company controls either U or MCP, but they each have strong market incentives to maximize U and to minimize MCP, which translates into the greatest access for a market-determined optimal price.

The proposed global R&D Treaty

The fourth model is both simple and powerful: a global treaty on medical innovation. James Love, Tim Hubbard and a growing chorus of other commentators have discussed a Global R&D Treaty to separate the global market for innovation from the market for drug sales (Hubbard 2003; Love 2003a and b; Baker 2004; Hollis 2004; but see DiMasi and Grabowski 2004). In January 2006, Kenya and Brazil introduced a resolution to the WHO Executive Board calling for a serious evaluation of the proposal (WHO 2006a). In May 2006, the World Health Assembly established an intergovernmental working group based on this resolution and the work of the WHO Commission on Intellectual Property Rights, Innovation and Public Health (WHO 2006b, 2000c). The R&D Treaty would serve as a global coordination mechanism to prevent free riding by high-income countries, while clearly specifying the fair following obligations of poorer countries. The Treaty does not commit any country to a particular method of meeting its R&D obligations. Each country retains considerable flexibility. A country could keep (or expand) pharmaceutical patent rent appropriation if it desired, but it could also meet Treaty obligations through government financed R&D, purchase commitments, patent buy-outs, prize funds, or some other mechanism.

One advantage of the Treaty is that many countries could choose to abandon the patent system as the appropriation tool for pharmaceutical innovation. Problems of inadequate access, inefficiency of allocations, counterfeiting and rent-seeking behavior by drug firms could be reduced if innovation was not dependent on the high retail sales price of patented drugs. Every drug could be a generic, with innovation incentives addressed through the Treaty.

If the Global R&D Treaty were adopted, one could expect quite different drug price levels in various countries, depending on the Treaty mechanisms chosen for innovation. If so, cross-border pharmaceutical arbitrage would need to be blocked from entering those countries which attempted to support innovation through high retail drug prices. As stated above, empirically, this type of arbitrage has been more limited than often supposed and is susceptible to effective legal interdiction and control (Outterson 2005a).

Conclusion

The world is facing a pharmaceutical access crisis. For rivalrous goods like food and cell phones, rationing scarce resources is a necessity. For non-rivalrous intangibles like pharmaceutical knowledge, a different world is possible. We must demand to know why rationing separates most of humanity from effective access to life-saving drugs. The primary answer offered by pharmaceutical companies is innovation. The discussion then descends into name-calling: anyone who challenges the dominant IP system is at best a free rider and at worst a pirate. The purpose of this chapter is to transcend this impasse, and to offer fair follower alternatives which preserve innovation whilst greatly expanding access.

Acknowledgements

Many thanks to Dan Rosan at the Interfaith Center on Corporate Responsibility and Professors John Duffy, Valorie Vojdik, and Peter Yu, as well as the participants in the November 2004 WHO Global Forum for Health Research (Forum 8) in Mexico City for their comments and suggestions. I believe Professor Jerome Reichman first connected "free riders" with "fair followers," although I modify the context and meaning of the phrase. His project was to encourage significant use of flexibilities available under the World Trade Organization TRIPS Agreement (Reichman 1996). The U.S. government has labored to deny this option to many countries in the past decade ('t Hoen 2002; Outterson 2005c; Thorpe 2004). David Davis provided excellent research assistance. This work was supported by an unrestricted grant from the West Virginia University College of Law.

References

Baker, D. 2004. *Financing Drug Research: What are the Issues?* Available at: http://www.cepr.net/ [Accessed February 5, 2006].

Benson, T. 2005. Brazil and U.S. Maker Reach Deal on AIDS Drug. *New York Times*, July 9.

Bermudez, J. 2002. Expanding Access to Essential Medicines in Brazil: Recent Economic Regulation, Policy-Making and Lessons Learnt. In *Economics of Essential Medicines*, edited by Brigitte Granville, 178, 193.

Carroll, J. and R. Winslow. 2001. Bayer Agrees to Slash Prices for Cipro Drug. *Wall Street Journal*, October 25, A3.

DiMasi, J. and H. G. Grabowski. 2004. *Patents and R&D Incentives: Comments on the Hubbard and Love Trade Framework for Financing Pharmaceutical R&D 2*. Available at: http://www.who. int/intellectualproperty/news/en/Submission3.pdf [Accessed February 5, 2006].

Drahos, P. with J. Braithwaite. 2002. *Information Feudalism: Who Owns the Knowledge Economy?* New York: New Press.

Ganslandt, M., K. E. Maskus, and E. V. Wong. 2001. Developing and Distributing Essential Medicines to Poor Countries: The DEFEND Proposal. *The World Economy* 24: 779–795.

Guell, R. C. 1997. Haggling for a Patent: What a Government Would have to Pay for Prescription Drug Patents. *Health Economics* 6: 179–185.

Guell, R. C. and M. Fischbaum. 1995. Toward Allocative Efficiency in the Prescription Drug Industry. *Milbank Quarterly* 73: 213–230.

Hardin, G. 1968. The Tragedy of the Commons. *Science*. December 13, pp. 1243–1248.

Hollis, A. 2004. An Efficient Reward System for Pharmaceutical Innovation. July 2 (unpublished manuscript, on file with author).

Hubbard, T. 2003. Alternatives to the Price System. Available at: http://www.earthinstitute. columbia.edu/cgsd/accesstomedicines_papers.html [Accessed February 5, 2006].

IMS Health. 2005a. (Francophone West Africa, US$ sales of J5C1 (NRTIs), J5C2 (PIs), and J5C3 (NNRTIs) (data on file with author).

——. 2005b. Peru retail, US$ sales of J5C1 (NRTIs) (data on file with author).

The Jean Chrétien Pledge to Africa Act. 2004. House of Commons, 3rd Sess., 37th Parliament, 52–53 Eliz. II, 2004 (Bill C-9) (received Royal Assent May 14, 2004).

Kremer, M. 1998. Patent Buy-Outs: A Mechanism for Encouraging Innovation. *Quarterly Journal of Economics* November: 1137–1167.

Kremer, M. and R. Glennerster. 2004. *Strong Medicine: Creating Incentives for Pharmaceutical Research on Neglected Diseases*. Princeton, NJ: Princeton University Press.

Landes, W. M. and R. A. Posner. 2003. Indefinitely Renewable Copyright. *University of Chicago Law Review* 70: 471, 484–486.

Lanjouw, J. O. and W. Jack. 2004. Trading Up: How Much Should Poor Countries Pay to Support Pharmaceutical Innovation? *Center for Global Development Brief* 4(3): 1–8. Available at: http://www.cgdev.org/docs/CGDbrief%20pharmaceutical.pdf [Accessed February 5, 2006].

Love, J. 2003a. *From TRIPS to RIPS: A Better Trade Framework to Support Innovation in Medical Technologies.* (Workshop on Economic Issues Related to Access to HIV/AIDS Care in Developing Countries).

——. 2003b. *A New Trade Framework for Global Healthcare R&D.* Available at: http://www.earthinstitute.columbia.edu/cgsd/accesstomedicines_papers.html [Accessed February 5, 2006].

——. 2005. *Remuneration Guidelines for Non-Voluntary Use of a Patent on Medical Technologies.* World Health Organization, Health Economics and Drugs, TCM Series No. 18, WHO/TCM/2005.1. Available at: www.who.int [Accessed February 5, 2006].

Médecins Sans Frontières. 2005a. *Access to Essential Medicines.* Available at: http://www.accessmed-msf.org [Accessed February 5, 2006].

——. 2005b. *Untangling the Web: MSF ARV Pricing Guide*, 6th edn. New York: MSF.

Merck & Co., Inc. 2004. *Merck & Co., Inc. Grants License for HIV/AIDS Drug Efavirenz to South African Company, Thembalami Pharmaceuticals in Effort to Accelerate Access to Life-Saving Treatment* (Press Release) July 14. Available at: http://www.pressmethod.com/releasestorage/5003645.htm [Accessed February 5, 2006].

Moran, M., A.-L. Ropars, J. Guzman, J. Diaz, and C. Garrison. 2005. The New Landscape of Neglected Disease Drug Development. Available at: http://www.wellcome.ac.uk/assets/wtx026592.pdf [Accessed February 5, 2006].

Outterson, K. 2005a. Pharmaceutical Arbitrage: Balancing Access and Innovation in International Prescription Drug Markets. *Yale Journal of Health Policy, Law & Ethics* 5(1): 193–286. Available at: www.ssrn.com [Accessed February 5, 2006].

——. 2005b. Drug Importation: Would the Price Be Right? In *Hearing Before the Committee on Health, Education, Labor, & Pensions.* 109th Cong., February 17. Available at: http://www.help.senate.gov/bills/hlh_63_bill.html and at www.ssrn.com [Accessed February 5, 2006].

——. 2005c. Agony in the Antipodes: The Generic Drug Provisions of the Australia-US Free Trade Agreement. *Journal of Generic Medicines* 2: 316–326. Available at: www.ssrn.com [Accessed February 5, 2006].

——. 2005d. The Vanishing Public Domain: Antibiotic Resistance, Pharmaceutical Innovation & Global Public Health. *University of Pittsburgh Law Review* 67: 67–123. Available at: www.ssrn.com [Accessed February 5, 2006].

——. 2004. Free Trade Against Free Riders? *Pharma Pricing & Reimbursement* 9(9): 254–255. Available at: www.ssrn.com [Accessed February 5, 2006].

Pharmaceutical Research and Manufacturers of America (PhRMA). 2005. Special 301 Submission to USTR. Available at: http://www.phrma.org/international/Appendix_C_Market_Access.pdf [Accessed February 5, 2006].

——. 2006. PhRMA Website. Available at: http://www.phrma.org/issues/researchdev/ [Accessed February 5, 2006].

Reichman, J. H. 1996. From Free Riders to Fair Followers: Global Competition Under the TRIPS Agreement. *New York University Journal of International Law & Politics* 29: 11.

Reichman, J. H. with C. Hasenzahl. 2003. *UNCTAD, Non-Voluntary Licensing of Patented Inventions: Historical Perspective, Legal Framework Under TRIPS, and an Overview of the Practice in Canada and the USA.* (Project on IPRs and Sustainable Development, Issue Paper No. 5, 2003).

Scherer, F. M. 2004. A Note on Global Welfare in Pharmaceutical Patenting. *The World Economy* 27: 1127, 1141.

Stein, P. and E. Valery. 2004. Competition: An Antidote to the High Price of Prescription Drugs. *Health Affairs* 23(4): 151–158.

Sykes, A. O. 2002. TRIPS, Pharmaceuticals, Developing Countries, and the Doha "Solution." *Chicago Journal of International Law* 3: 47, 56.

't Hoen, E. 2002. TRIPS, Pharmaceutical Patents, and Access to Essential Medicines: A Long Way from Seattle to Doha. *Chicago Journal of International Law* 3: 27.

Thomas, J. R. 2001. *HIV/AIDS Drugs, Patents, and the TRIPS Agreement: Issues and Options.* Congressional Research Service.

Thorpe, P. 2004. *Study on the Implementation of the TRIPS Agreement by Developing Countries.* (Comm. on Intellectual Prop. Rights, Study Paper 7, circa 2004). Available at: www.who.int [Accessed February 5, 2006].

US Department of Commerce. 2004. *Pharmaceutical Price Controls in OECD Countries: Implications for U.S. Consumers, Pricing, Research and Development, and Innovation.* Available at: http://www.ita.doc.gov/drugpricingstudy [Accessed February 5, 2006].

World Health Organization (WHO). 2006a. Resolution EB117/Conf. Paper No. 3. Available at: www.who.int [Accessed February 5, 2006].

——. 2006b. *Global Framework on Essential Health Research and Development.* A59/17. May 27. Available at: www.who.int.

——. 2006c. *Public Health Innovation, Essential Health Research and Intellectual Property Rights: Towards a Global Strategy and Plan of Action.* A59/A/Conf. Paper No. 8. May 26. Available at: www.who.int.

——. 2004. The 10/90 Report on Health Research. Geneva: WHO.

World Trade Organization (WTO). 2001. *Permanent Mission of the United States, Brazil Measures Affecting Patent Protection, Request for the Establishment of a Panel by the United States.* WT/DS199/3. Available at: www.wto.int [Accessed February 5, 2006].

WTO Doha Declaration. 2001. *Declaration on the TRIPS Agreement and Public Health, Doha WTO Ministerial 2001.* WT/MIN(01)/DEC/2, para 7. Available at: www.wto.int [Accessed February 5, 2006].

WTO TRIPS Agreement. 1994. *Agreement on Trade-Related Aspects of Intellectual Property Rights, Apr. 15, 1994, Marrakesh Agreement Establishing the World Trade Organization*, at Annex 1C, art. 27.1.

17 Abolishing the product patent: a step forward for global access to drugs

Adam Mannan and Alan Story

A tale of two conditions

Dengue fever is one of the ten leading causes of child death and hospitalization in at least eight Asian countries (WHO 1997). Dengue causes leukopenia, muscle aches, joint pains, headaches, rashes, nausea, and vomiting; in 20 per cent of children suffering their second dengue infection, acute hemorrhagic phenomena and hypovolemic shock will result in death unless the child is rapidly hospitalized and intensively treated (WHO 1997). Endemic to more than 100 countries in Africa, Southeast Asia, the Americas, the eastern Mediterranean, and the Western Pacific, dengue is a risk to two-fifths of the world's population (WHO 2006). Though first identified in the Philippines in 1953 (WHO 1997), little was done about dengue for decades. Only the U.S. military invested in vaccine development when its troops were exposed to the virus while on tour in endemic regions (BUMED 2002). Recently the CIGB in Cuba has been doing promising work on a possible vaccine. Furthermore, because of the likelihood that a dengue vaccine will be realized in the near future and that it might become a profitable commodity, others are beginning to register patents and property rights in the likely components of such a vaccine. However, 50 years after dengue was first identified as a serious epidemic and after millions have died unnecessarily, the key questions about a possible vaccine remain unanswered: When and where will it be distributed? To how many children? And, at what cost?

By comparison, erectile dsyfunction (ED) is an example of how social dissatisfaction can be transformed into medical dysfunction and then remedied by a pill. On the one hand, it is certainly true that, in some cases, ED is the consequence of organic causes, including peripheral vascular diseases, hypertension, drug-side effects, hormonal imbalance, and diabetes. The MMAS suggests, for example, that 10 per cent of American males have complete inability to achieve erection of the penis (Feldman et al. 1994). But ED is primarily a socially constructed condition based on a socially constructed male "problem." As one commentator has explained, "[T]he more anxiety a corporation can produce, the larger its market. In other words, worrying about ED may in fact cause ED" (Loe 2004).

In the early 1990s, British employees of Pfizer discovered that certain pyrazolopyrimidinone compounds had the effect of enhancing trial patients' erections.

By 1996, Pfizer held patents on both sides of the Atlantic for this property of the sildenafil citrate compound. USFDA approval to market the drug in the U.S. as a treatment for ED followed in March 1998 and the drug hit the market soon afterwards. Viagra's launch more than doubled Pfizer's stock price. In its first month of sales, Viagra generated over US$100 million and quickly became the fastest selling patented drug in history; between 1999 and 2001 annual sales of Viagra in the U.S. were in excess of US$1 billion. Direct advertising and clever marketing had facilitated Viagra's affirmation as *the* treatment for impotence, but more importantly, as a "necessary" component of healthy masculinity.

Other pharmaceutical multinationals have joined the ED and erection enhancement markets: GlaxoSmithKline produces Vardenafil, Bayer has Levitra, and Eli Lilly has joined in with Cialis. The marketing cost of any one of these drugs exceeds the total investment across the world for the development of a dengue fever vaccine. More importantly, this contrast between the dengue and ED stories is not atypical of drug research investment in the current conjuncture. Dengue fever, however horrible its symptoms and prognosis in children, is not on the list of "lucrative diseases" and is, in fact, only one of many diseases for which vaccines are not accessible. HIV/AIDS is another, as are leishmaniasis, malaria, and sleeping sickness. Also missing from the shelves of doctors and chemists are new generation antibiotics due, in great measure, to their supposedly low profitability. (This is surprising considering the potential demand exhibited by the growing number of deaths caused by methicillin-resistant *Staphylococcus aureus*.) Perhaps pharmaceutical patents are not sufficient incentive for innovation. And if they are sufficient incentive for innovation, then patents prevent access to medicines for a growing majority of the world's population who cannot afford the immense prices that patents allow companies to charge. Succinctly, the patent is the wrong incentive in the wrong direction; obtaining and distributing cures to diseases ought to come before pecuniary profit. In a civilized world ought we or should we let people die so that the pharmaceutical industry can charge the rest of us a few more dollars for a few more years on their 600 per cent mark-up?

The principal bars to medicine access are not found in a deficit of manufacturing capacity or the lack of distribution infrastructure; rather they subsist in high drug prices or a dearth of medicine development. At the root of this barrier lies the patent system. An organic analogy is fitting, for the regime of pharmaceutical patents has sustained considerable growth through lobbying, subdolous use of the "Scare Card" (Public Citizen 2001), and artful use of realist legal machinery. The access to medicine's crisis is the consequence of the inaccessibility of medicines to a growing proportion of the world's population. Strengthening barriers to access can never solve this crisis.

This paper asks why we continue to strengthen an ill-functioning institution. Let us cut back the barriers to access and reassess how medicines, new and old, can be delivered effectively. There are two pharmaceutical patent types: the product patent, that is, the chemical itself; and process patents, that is, the ways a medicine can be manufactured or administered. The difference between the two is that whilst the process patent only makes market entry more difficult, the product patent is an absolute bar to market entry and product competition. Simply, where there is a product patent the chemical that comprises the medicine is owned, and no one else can use it without permission. Where there is a process patent the chemical is owned, but only for a particular purpose, or only if obtained in a specific way. Thus, where there is a product patent the patent owner can charge what they like for the chemical. Where there is only a process patent there is some leeway for competitive medicines to be made available. The first step in reforming the systems of innovation and distribution is clear. Abolish the product patent: it is pernicious to world health. Medicines were invented long before the product patent existed and abolishing it will save billions of lives.

The patent: an invention

The patent, a form of IP, "confers the right to secure the enforcement power of the state in excluding unauthorized persons, for a specified number of years, from making commercial use of a clearly identified invention" (Machlup 1958). As with all forms of IP, patents exist only because government says they do. Unlike real property, a house, a chair, a book, IP is non-rivalrous. There is no natural limit to the number of users of IP and no natural economic value except the production cost of the physical support. Thus, patents do "not arise out of the scarcity of the objects which become appropriated" (Plant 1934).

The idea of patents is not about the allocation of resources, it is rather about the adjustive function of property; that is, individuals can use property law either to gain advantages for themselves or to shift burdens to others. Patents are limited to a very small group who are able to bear the costs of excluding others from its enclosure. This has led some eminent practitioners to note that the patent is not "so much a monopoly in the working of ... [an] invention as a licence to compel ... competitors to join ... [the patent holder] in spending large sums in litigation" (Blanco White 1974). Filing a patent and policing it require considerable expense: a cost unnecessary to pharmaceutical innovation and one that is inevitably added to a medicine's price.

The patent is a product of outdated trade economics and national protectionism that have grown into a highly profitable exercise of the adjustive function of property. The artificial creation of scarcity is an ancient practice (Gaius 2.14; see Gordon and Robertson 2001), but the patent for inventions apparently began in the fifteenth century. This was a period when the Italian city-states, flush with the wealth of revived merchantry, used patent grants to attract skilled workers. This scheme was gradually adopted throughout Europe and foreign workers migrating to countries where conditions were favorable distributed the superior technological achievements from the advanced civilizations of the East (Prager and Scaglia 1970). In the seventeenth century, a landmark change in the grant of patents occurred. England, through the Statute of Monopolies 1624, established the principle that only a 'true and first inventor" should receive a patent. For countries seeking the growth of national industries the patent was a strong form of infant industry protection. Despite the patent system's limitations, expense and the uncertainty of its acquisition, its function in protecting national interest during the severe depression of the late nineteenth century ensured its adoption in industrialized nations (Machlup and Penrose 1950). The patent system was not the result of creating necessary conditions for innovation; it was the creation of national market protectionism during a great depression. In Switzerland and the Netherlands, where industries had flourished in the absence of a patent system, the patent system was introduced as a result of threatened trade sanctions by patent granting states. For some nations outside Western Europe and the U.S., the patent system was imposed by colonial powers. This was not to promote innovation in these countries. The transplant of patent acts was to extend the markets of the colonial powers. The South African, Irish, Pakistan, Australia, New Zealand, and Indian Patent Acts are good examples.

The TRIPS Agreement as discussed elsewhere in this volume brought IP into the fold of trade issues. Developing countries were compelled to agree to TRIPS given their interests in other economic gains as part of the trade agreement. TRIPS (WTO 1994) sets a minimum standard (Article 1) for patent and other IP protection. Further, it obliges ratifying parties to adopt the principle of "most favoured nation treatment" (Article 4) and most importantly the principle of "national treatment" (Article 3). The principle of most favored nation requires that a nation does not discriminate between WTO trade partners by obliging states to make the same trade relations – for example, the same customs duties – available to all WTO members. The principle of national treatment prevents a nation from discriminating against the rights of nationals from other states by awarding foreign nationals the same IPR as home nationals. TRIPS includes a large number of Articles from the Berne and Paris Conventions – two nineteenth-century agreements between European powers concerning artistic and industrial property respectively. All of which are important to the world's present IP status quo.

An arbitrary invention

With the advantages and theoretical freedom from sanctions conveyed by WTO membership, the majority of the world's nations have now joined, and thus agreed to TRIPS and all that it entails. Ideally, assuming the efficient function of the patent system in providing an incentive for innovation, then those inventions a society considers useful, but requiring incentive, will be embodied in the legislation. The reasoning is that without scarcity "usefulness to society and economic value have nothing in common" (Penrose 1951). Thus, by creating scarcity in those things useful to society those entities obtain an economic value and because they are only available through the channels authorized by the patent holder, the patent holder receives an economic reward. Patent law assumes that ownership vests in the inventor, or where the inventor is an employee, in the employer. Thus, people or corporations are given incentives to invent by the economic reward that they will receive from the control the state permits them over their invention.

There is great diversity amongst the cultures and traditions of the world that can constitute irreconcilable difficulties. What one state considers worthy of protection another may consider part of its commons. What is to the economic advantage of one nation may be to the economic detriment of another. IP, however, is seed sown in the design of the Washington Consensus (Chang 2002). That seed, TRIPS, in Article 27(1), sets out the mandatory minimal standard for the scope of patent protection. It states, "patents shall be available for any inventions, whether products or processes, in all fields of technology, provided that they are new, involve an inventive step and are capable of industrial application" (WTO 1994), which is clearly a very extensive starting point for a minimum standard and a strictly hermeneutical interpretation is unable to reveal the domain of its encompassment. On two levels TRIPS is a one-size-fits-all standard for patent protection. First, it is the starting point for patent protection in all WTO member states. Second, it makes no distinction between a microorganism, software, business, mechanical, chemical, or pharmaceutical patent. TRIPS makes no exceptions; a signatory has to grant patents for pharmaceuticals regardless of specific economic and health conditions, even if this creates a barrier to medicine access.

According to Article 27 of TRIPS an invention can be either a "product" or a "process". Product refers to a substance claim. For a pharmaceutical product patent, or product *per se* patent, this would be the chemical structure defining the chemical compound. Process refers to a method or use claim. Thus, in the case of a pharmaceutical process patent, or product by-process patent, this might be either the means of making the product or the method of using the product to treat a disease. In practice the strategic advantage between the two patent types is great. Where only a process patent is held competitors can find alternative processes or uses for the chemical compound. If a product patent is held, then there is no opportunity to work around the patent. The product *per se* is firmly under the control of the patent holder, regardless of new ways of obtaining it or for a similar purpose using it. Thus, the product *per se* patent holder can charge any price they desire without fearing competition by rivals. Contrary, if the price of a process-patented pharmaceutical is too high, then eventually a competitor will be able to enter the market and the price of the medicine will fall.

The product patent is in fact a license to charge unrestricted prices for pharmaceuticals. It is unsurprising that until very recently few countries recognized pharmaceutical product patents. Pharmaceutical product patents are a recent introduction in many countries, including France (1968), Germany (1968), the Nordic countries (1968), Japan (1976), Switzerland (1978), Italy (1978), Canada (1987), Spain (1992), Thailand (1992), Argentina (2000), and India (2005).

There are two principal reasons for the slow adoption of pharmaceutical patents, with respect to other patent forms. First, there were national concerns over public health; it was feared that the grant of patents for pharmaceuticals would dramatically raise the price of medicines. Second, where there was a competitive weakness of national chemical industries, an absence of pharmaceutical patents allowed for the rapid growth of a strong and competitive national industry.

These two considerations have not declined in importance with time. As medicines inexorably climb in price over the rate of inflation and less westernized countries develop pharmaceutical industries, admittedly small compared to the financial magnitude of major western companies, western governments are caught between two conflicting interests. The interest of the citizen who cannot access the medicines they need and the western pharmaceutical companies' fear that competition will prevent annual record profits. To relinquish the pharmaceutical product patent will reduce barriers to market entry, facilitating competition and leading to lower drug prices at home and abroad.

A tale of two consequents

The Indian Patent Act 1970 came into force in April 1972. It replaced the nation's first Patent Act of 1911, a copy of the British Act, which had been imposed under colonial rule. Ripe with the national fervor to attain self-sufficiency in pharmaceutical chemical production, the 1970 regime for the protection of pharmaceutical patents was a discontinuity with the old patent regime. Product patents for pharmaceuticals, food and agrochemicals became unavailable. The patent term for pharmaceutical processes was shortened to five years from the date of sealing of the patent, or seven years from the date of the patent (section 53(1)(a); see OCGPDT 2005).

Additional measures were also adopted, including restrictions on the import of finished pharmaceutical formulations, high tariffs, and equity limitations on foreign participation. Further the DPCO 1970, limiting prices, reduced the profitability of marketing drugs in India.

The multinational pharmaceutical companies, even those with lucrative markets elsewhere, remained but the stage was set for competition. Where there had previously been product *per se* patents, there were now only process patents. Through developing expertise in reverse engineering and highly efficient organizing of pharmaceutical manufacturing chemical compounds could be synthesized expediently. Some of the drugs that were patented, product *per se*, in the West had processes that were obvious and thus were not eligible for a patent in India. Furthermore, with the 5–7-year process patent duration even firms without reverse engineering capabilities could make generic medicines available within a short period, "[t]he idea between the product/process distinction was that Indian pharmaceutical manufacturers would have an incentive to find cheaper and cheaper processes for the production of drugs" (Drahos 2002). The effect on the market was staggering. Drug prices fell to 1/10th–1/60th of their U.S. prices, and 1/5th–1/25th of their UK prices. An HIV/AIDS anti-retroviral that cost more than US$10,000 a year in the U.S. became available for less than US$200 a year in India (MSF 2005).

The demand in the market that had hitherto been unmet in order to maintain price levels was now taken up by Indian start-up companies willing to supply the whole market, even where it could barely break even. High quality, comparably very low-cost generics lowered the price bar to medicine access. Thus, when the HIV/AIDS crisis came to India there was an industry able to prevent the travesty that occurred in Africa.

In 1971, there were only two Indian companies in the top ten by pharmaceutical sales in India. By 1996 there were six (Lanjouw 1997). Today, India has about 20,000 pharmaceutical firms and employs over two and a half million people directly or in related work. It produces high-quality drugs with prices that are amongst the lowest in the world. India has become the prime source of generic medicines and supplies over 27 developing nations with desperately needed pharmaceuticals, including generic anti-retroviral drugs at prices that have lowered immensely the price bar for those nationals.

The Indian pharmaceutical story is not finished and great changes are on the horizon. As the Uruguay Round came to a close, India was one of the developing countries that foresaw some of the TRIPS Agreement's negative impact on national development. It was a leading developing nation in the opposition of TRIPS, but nevertheless joined the WTO in 1995, thereby pledging to become TRIPS-compliant by January 1 2005. An Indian presidential decree in December 2004 made product *per se* patents available and implemented a 20-year term for all pharmaceutical patents. On March 22–23 2005 both Houses of Parliament passed the Patents (Amendment) Bill (see MLJ 2005). Generic medicines can be available through compulsory licensing, though this will require compensation payments to the patent holder. PhRMA has already expressed concern over the legislative provisions, but although the provisions may not satisfy the TRIPS plus agenda of the Washington Consensus, they appear to satisfy the requirements of TRIPS.

Adherence to TRIPS, however, particularly the institution of product patents, by the least developed nations' prime source of generic medicines spells an end for access to medicines for many people. Some nations, such as those in Africa, in the grip of terrible mortality and suffering protested their need for essential medicines. Backed by emphatic support from the citizens of the developed and developing world, a conference was called to resolve the issue. The Ministerial Conference in Doha, after much difficult negotiation, resulted in the Doha Declaration of August 30 2003 (WTO 2003). The Doha Declaration appeared to contain two very useful provisions regarding the access to medicines by developing countries. For the least developed nations, that is, those with insufficient economic and technical capacity to produce their own generic medicines or have any likelihood of doing so in the near future, pharmaceutical patents would not be obligatory until 2016 (WTO 2003: paragraph 7). Less naïve than in 1994, even the least westernized world was aware that this concession by the Washington Consensus alone was insufficient to maintain even current levels of medicine access. Thus, it was also agreed that countries with insufficient manufacturing capacity could after issuing a compulsory license import medicines from another country (WTO 2003: paragraph 6).

However, the advantages of paragraph 6 (WTO 2003) begin to wane when it is remembered that India, the prime source of generic medicines, will soon have in effect, as well as legislatively, the same patent restrictions as the western world. A product patent and a 20-year patent term for pharmaceuticals will effectively bar access to medicines at any but western prices for a 20-year period. In order to create generic medicines within these 20 years India will have to issue compulsory licenses on the drugs. Under TRIPS, compulsory licenses can only be issued to predominantly supply a domestic market (TRIPS 31(f)) after attempts to establish reasonable terms of authorization from the patent holder fail (TRIPS 31(b)) and for adequate remuneration that is legal and subject to judicial review (TRIPS 31(h, i, j)) (see WTO 1994).

Furthermore, a condition of importing generic medicines, manufactured in another country, under paragraph 6 (WTO 2003) requires that the importing country issue a compulsory license for that medicine. A compulsory license can only, in effect, be issued by a nation that grants patents on that medicine. There are two problems inherent in this. First, many of the poorest countries cannot afford a patent system and thus cannot grant pharmaceutical patents. Second, many companies do not expend resources in patenting pharmaceuticals in nations where there is insufficient economic and technical capacity to produce generic medicines, even if these nations do have patent systems. In terms of the access to medicines in the poorest countries Doha now seems to be of little assistance.

Within India the consequences of the new Patent Act will be revealed over the next few years. It is expected, following the introduction of the product patent, that drug prices will increase by a mean of 200 per cent (Sherer and Watal 2001). Moreover, as the structure of the pharmaceutical companies in India changes, through merger or returning western company dominance, it is expected that prices will rise far more. For some medicines the prices in India may become comparable with the West. From the perspective of social welfare imposing a product patent on India is a death knell for a significant number of people in at least India and Africa.

A useful invention

What is immediately falsifiable is the commonly held assumption that without a patent system there would be little or no innovation in pharmaceuticals. History is replete with evidence that the invention of medicines occurs regardless of the existence of a patent system. Modern biomedical research has for the most part been conducted in environments with patent systems, but modern biomedical research is expensive and the only countries with the technical and financial reserves for the undertaking had process patents. Nevertheless, modern examples of pharmaceutical innovation conducted outside the patent incentive abound. Examples include the world's first safe malaria vaccine developed by Manuel Patarroyo, who donated the vaccine rights to the WHO because he felt that the vaccine ought to benefit all of humankind; Howard Florey and his team, who were able to design a method of penicillin mass production; Jonas Salk, who devoted nearly a decade to developing a vaccine against polio, but claimed if there was a patent that it belonged to the people; Albert Sabin revolutionized the polio vaccine both by developing an oral version and insisting that the vaccine be administered free of charge (Story 2000). There is also a substantial number of pharmaceutical innovations developed by publicly funded research at institutions like the NIH in the U.S. In the light of these examples the necessity of the pharmaceutical patent for pharmaceutical innovation to occur is highly questionable. However, whether there is an industrial dependence on a patent system for obtaining financial and technical resources is another matter, but one that might have proceeded very differently if there had been a TRIPS Agreement before the westernized nations had their industrial revolutions (Chang 2002). In the absence of the protectionism TRIPS affords western pharmaceutical companies there would be a radical redistribution of the medicine market. Rivalry between competing firms would require medicine providers to innovate and produce efficiently and with smaller profit margins. Those firms unwilling to lower prices to competitive levels would be undercut and ousted from their market share. Furthermore, it is also disputable whether all modern biomedical research is the product of the westernized nations, the patenting of so-called refined agents of traditional medicines, herbal treatments in India and Africa for example, has become ever more popular over the last two decades. Perhaps if there were fewer barriers to supply less westernized nations would be able to explore their pharmaceutical knowledge and manufacture useful medicines yet unknown in the West.

Considering this use of traditional knowledge as a basis in creating "new" drugs it might be true to say that "individuals merely make explicit what was already implicit in the technological organism which conditions their thought and effort within which they must work" (Khan 1940).

Furthermore, trends in the number of biomedical patents filed suggest biomedical research is discovery-led and a natural evolution of the environmental conditions of our biological and medical knowledge, rather than a consequence of the patent system's existence. The correlation between knowledge breakthroughs in science, or new scientific hypotheses, and the development of breakthrough medicines is of tremendous importance in decisions relating to the allocation of resources for pharmaceutical research. The trend is apparent from Agostino Bassi (*c.* 1835) onwards, though medical historians may be able to assert an earlier beginning for the relationship.

New scientific knowledge, in medicine, chemistry, molecular biology, and other fields important to pharmaceutical research, is not the product of massive private investment. Instead it arises from the "work of creative academic or government researchers" that can manipulate the science, and have the intellectual curiosity and dedication to expand and falsify knowledge hypotheses (Love 2004).

The individual inventor may often work under a sense of illusion, which an institution with its accountants, market researchers and informed scientists and technologists would never do; but blind pushing has not infrequently brought returns under conditions where cataloguing the obstacles would have been tantamount to failure (Jewkes et al. 1969).

Even according to the US pharmaceutical industry association, only 43 per cent of pharmaceutical R&D is funded by the industry itself, while 29 per cent is funded by the NIH (Chang 2002).

Two conclusions

To profit from an invention is a privilege that has a correlative no right in the use of the invention for everyone else. For the medicine patent holder's right to control access to a drug, there is a reciprocal duty on everyone else, including the ill, to respect that control by not infringing it. TRIPS makes no provision for moral value attribution to human life. There is no internality of patent norms that permit illation when the chance of life is of greater consequence than economic gain. In the western legal world, which TRIPS imposes, law and morality are taken as distinct. As the HIV/AIDS crisis, another western legal Holocaust, has shown us, there are times when morality is more important than what is posited as law. The starting point for resolving the access to medicines problem is not the law, it is a pragmatic assessment of natural, as opposed to artificial, resources and the effective deployment of these resources so that the problem itself is redressed.

References

Ayta, I. A., J. B. Mckinlay, and R. J. Krane. 1999. The Likely Worldwide Increase in Erectile Dysfunction Between 1995 and 2025 and Some Possible Policy Consequences. *BJU International* 84: 50–56.

Baker, Dean. 2004. *Financing Drug Research: What Are the Issues?* Washington, DC: Center for Economic and Policy Research. Available at: www.who.int/entity/intellectualproperty/news/en/Submission-Baker.pdf [Accessed January 15, 2006].

Blanco White, T. A. 1974. *Patents for Inventions*. London: Stevens and Sons.

Bureau of Medicine and Surgery (BUMED). 2002. *Navy Medicine Awarded Patent*, Press release 26 September. Available at: http://www.dcmilitary.com/navy/journal/7_38/national_news/19433–1.html [Accessed January 16, 2006].

Chang, H-J. 2002. *Kicking away the Ladder*. London: Anthem Press.

Drahos, P. 2002. *Information Feudalism*. London: Earthscan Publications.

Feldman, H. A., I. Goldstein, D. G. Hatzichristou, R. J. Krane, and J. B. McKinlay. 1994. Impotence and its Medical and Psychosocial Correlates: Results of the Massachusetts Male Aging Study. *Journal of Urology* 151: 54–61.

Gordon, W. M. and O. F. Robinson. 2001. *The Institutes of Gaius*. London: Gerald Duckworth & Co.

Jewkes, J., D. Sawers, and R. Stillerman. 1969. *The Sources of Invention*. New York: W.W. Norton.

Khan, A. E. 1940. Fundamental Deficiencies in the American Patent Law. *American Economic Review* 30: 478.

Lanjouw, J. O. 1997. The Introduction of Pharmaceutical Product Patents in India: Heartless Exploitation of the Poor and Suffering. *National Bureau of Economic Research Working Paper*, No. 6366.

Loe, M. 2004. *The Rise of Viagra: How the Little Blue Pill Changed Sex in America*. New York: New York University Press.

Love, J. 2004. Monopoly Medicine: The Built-in Inefficiencies of a Patent-Based Pharmaceutical R&D System. *Multinational Monitor* 25, nos. 7 & 8. Available at: http://multinationalmonitor.org/mm2004/07012004/july-aug04corp1.html [Accessed January 16, 2006].

Machlup, F. 1958. *An Economic Review of the Patent System: Study of the Subcommittee on Patents, Trademarks and Copyrights of the Committee of the Judiciary*, US Senate, 85th Congress, 2nd Session, Study Number 15, Washington, DC: US Government Printing Office.

Médecins Sans Frontières (MSF). 2005. *Will the Lifeline of Affordable Medicines for Poor Countries be Cut? Consequences of Medicines Patenting in India*. External Briefing Document. Available at: http://www.msf.fr/documents/base/2005-02-01-msf.pdf.

Machlup, F. and E. T. Penrose. 1950. The Patent Controversy in the Nineteenth Century. *Journal of Economic History* 10: 1–29.

Ministry of Law and Justice (MLJ). 2005. *The Patents (Ammendment) Act, 2005*. New Delhi, India: MLJ. Available at: http://www.patentoffice.nic.in/ipr/patent/patent_2005.pdf [Accessed January 15, 2006].

Office of the Controller General of Patents, Designs and Trademarks (OCGPDT). 2005. *Tne Patents Act 1970*. Kolkata, India: OCGPDT. Available at: http://ipindia.nic.in/ipr/patent/patAct1970-3–99.html [Accessed January 15, 2006].

Plant, A. 1934. The Economic Theory Concerning Patents for Inventions. *Economica*, new series 1: 30–51.

Penrose, E.T. 1951. *The Economics of the International Patent System*. Baltimore, MD: Johns Hopkins Press.

Prager, F. D. and G. Scaglia. 1970. *Brunelleschi: Studies of his Technology and Inventions*. Cambridge, MA: MIT Press.

Public Citizen. 2001. *Rx R&D Myths: The Case against the Drug Industry's R&D "Scare Card"*. Washington, DC: Public Citizen. Available at: http://www.citizen.org/documents/ACFDC. PDF [Accessed January 16, 2006].

Sherer, F. M. and J. Watal. 2001. Post TRIPS Options for Access to Patented Medicines in Developing Countries. *Commission on Macroeconomics and Health Working Paper Series*, No. WG 4:1: 15–16.

Story, A. 2000. *The Oxfam "Access to Essential Medicines" Project: Some Patent and Research and Development Issues*. Expanded version. Canterbury: Kent Law School.

World Health Organization (WHO). 1997. *Dengue Haemorrhagic Fever: Diagnosis, Treatment, Prevention and Control*. Geneva: WHO.

——. 2006. DengueNet: Improving Global Surveillance. Geneva: WHO. Available at: http://www.who.int/csr/disease/dengue/denguenet/en/ [Accessed January 14, 2006].

World Trade Organization (WTO). 1994. *Agreement on Trade-Related Aspects of Intelectual Property Rights*. Geneva: WTO. Available at: http://www.wto.org/english/docs_e/legal_e/27-trips.pdf [Accessed January 15, 2006].

——. 2003. *Implementation of Paragraph 6 of the Doha Declaration on the TRIPS Agreement and Public Health*. Geneva: WTO. Available at: http://www.wto.org/english/tratop_e/trips_e/implem_para6_e.htm [Accessed January 15, 2006].

18 Trading health for profit: the impact of bilateral and regional free trade agreements on domestic intellectual property rules on pharmaceuticals

Lisa Forman

By introducing mandatory global patent rules for WTO members, the TRIPS Agreement (1994) has significantly restricted members' domestic policy options on medicines. Yet, while TRIPS provides unprecedented global protection to pharmaceutical patents, its text includes a range of provisions to enable member countries to ease patent rules where social welfare and public health needs so demand. Mechanisms such as compulsory licensing and parallel importing enable countries not simply to procure or manufacture lower-cost medicines, but to facilitate the generic competition so crucial to lowering medicine costs. (Compulsory licensing enables a government, or authorized third parties, to use patented medicines without authorization, and can be used to manufacture or import generic versions of patented medicines. Parallel importing enables countries to seek the lowest priced patented products from other countries without the authorization of the patent holder; WHO 2000.)

In 2001, the WTO's Ministerial Conference produced the Doha Declaration on Public Health (WTO 2001), which, in affirming the right of WTO members to protect public health, confirmed the indisputable TRIPS legality of measures like compulsory licensing and parallel imports. Yet the lawful use of these mechanisms is being dramatically eroded by bilateral and regional FTAs in which governments, including developing countries with shocking disease burdens, are being persuaded and strong-armed into contracting out of TRIPS' flexibilities and exceptions. The U.S. in particular has coupled unilateral "big stick" strategies using trade sanctions with bilateral and regional "carrot-and-stick" trade strategies (Drahos 2002) to ensure that developing countries adopt stringent "TRIPS-plus" IP standards in FTAs, as well as IP legislative reform as a precondition for eligibility for increased trade and investment.

There are already serious questions about the relevance and suitability of TRIPS' *minimum* IP standards for developing countries (CIPR 2002; UNDP 2003). The gross inflation of these standards in "free trade" agreements severely limit national strategies to provide affordable medicines and limits market access for generic medicines, irrespective of the country's level of development or disease burden. These practices not only raise serious ethical concerns, but also sharply curtail country capacity to realize the right to health for all.

A fine balance in TRIPS

TRIPS introduces global minimum standards for the protection of patents, trademarks, copyrights and other IP rights, and makes extensive provision for their domestic and multilateral enforcement. While the protection and enforcement of IP rights is its primary purpose, TRIPS also seeks to ensure that IP protection is neither abused by rights-holders nor abusive of public policy goals, including public health. As such, members are authorized to adopt TRIPS-compliant measures necessary to protect public health, promote the public interest and prevent the abuse of IP rights by rights holders, which include compulsory licensing in Article 31 and parallel importing in Article 6 (WTO 1994). Compulsory licenses can be issued on any ground, but must comply with several conditions, including the requirement that production must be predominantly for the supply of the domestic market, and that efforts to obtain a voluntary license must have been unsuccessful. However, there is no need to seek a voluntary license in a national emergency, for public non-commercial use, or to remedy a practice determined to be anti-competitive. Compulsory licensing has long been recognized as a critical tool for addressing the adverse effects of the patent grant on public welfare (Penrose 1951), and as Canadian experience demonstrates, compulsory licenses can reduce drug costs both through generic manufacture and by posing a credible threat in negotiations with drug manufacturers (Hollis 2002).

TRIPS excludes parallel importation of patented goods from dispute settlement under the agreement, leaving countries free to make provision for such measures in domestic legislation. Since patented drugs are often differentially priced in different countries, importing drugs may be a relatively easier means of accessing lower-priced medicines than manufacturing them.

The impact of TRIPS on medicines access

TRIPS' global IP standards create extended barriers to market entry for generic medicines, enabling proprietary manufacturers to maintain monopolistic prices for the duration of patent terms, and limiting the sharp price-reducing effects of generic competition (Scherer 2000). Indeed a U.S. study suggests that patents are significant in sustaining high drug prices with generic competition driving drug prices much closer to marginal production costs (Caves et al. 1991). Similarly, MSF has reported that its experience in anti-retroviral procurement in ten countries has shown that the ability to use generics has been a critical factor in allowing competition and guaranteeing a continuous supply of medicines (MSF 2003a).

TRIPS is, therefore, mostly affecting countries with strong domestic generic industries, and those without domestic production who use generic substitutes from countries with export-oriented generic suppliers (Scherer and Watal 2001). After 2005, when developing countries such as India must implement TRIPS-compliant patent protection, current supplies of generic substitutes for patented drugs will disappear (CIPR 2002). Compulsory licensing and parallel imports will become increasingly vital policy options (and negotiating tools) for developing countries seeking to address essential drug gaps primarily attributable to price and a lack of competition (Cohen et al. 2004).

The Doha Declaration on the TRIPS Agreement and Public Health and August 2003 decision

Despite TRIPS' allowance for compulsory licensing and parallel imports, pharmaceutical companies and developed countries, particularly the U.S., have fiercely contested their use. In response to these obstacles (and not because of a lack of clarity in the text), at the Fourth Ministerial Conference at Doha (WTO 2001), the WTO's highest decision-making body, a group of developing countries led by the African group submitted a proposal for a Declaration on TRIPS and Public Health to clarify their right to use these provisions (Correa 2002). Consequently, the Doha Declaration unequivocally promotes the use of TRIPS flexibilities to support WTO members' right to protect public health and, in particular, to promote access to medicines for all, and to use compulsory licenses and parallel importing in particular (WTO 2001). In addition, in August 2003, the WTO General Council produced a negotiated solution to enable LDC members to import medicines manufactured under compulsory licensing, albeit subject to considerable conditions and limitations.

Globalizing TRIPS-plus IP rules in bilateral and regional trade agreements

Despite this progress, very few countries have used these measures to access lower-cost medicines. This is partly the chilling effect of political, economic, and legal pressures historically imposed by the U.S., EC, and pharmaceutical corporations against developing countries and generic manufacturers who have attempted to do so, including punitive trade measures, diplomatic pressures, and litigation. Increasingly, these efforts are taking the form of "TRIPS-plus" IP protections adopted under regional or bilateral FTAs as a precondition for trade and investment. These FTAs significantly limit generic competition and accordingly affordable medicines access.

The U.S. is by far the primary initiator of bilateral and regional trade and IP agreements. Between 1986 and 2000, it signed bilateral trade agreements with 42 countries (Drahos 2002), and has negotiated several regional trade agreements affecting approximately 50 countries, such as the Andean FTA, FTAA, CAFTA, and the ongoing SACU FTA. These agreements have far-reaching implications for medicines access not only in these regions but internationally, since several developing countries with serious generic manufacturing capabilities, such as Argentina, Brazil, and Mexico, will be bound by their uniformly TRIPS-plus IP rules. Since TRIPS requires that WTO members must extend any advantage granted to another country to all other members (WTO 1994), when WTO members agree to TRIPS-plus FTA, these concessions will ultimately apply to all WTO members, "[paving] the way to a world where TRIPS-plus concessions are a rule rather than the exception" (ICTSD 2005a).

Yet the legitimacy of these terms is not simply a matter of international trade law but of international human rights law. These agreements significantly limit government ability to fulfill their population's human rights to health and life. Given the urgent need for increased access to essential patented medicines (particularly for HIV/AIDS), there is no logical or palatable way to justify trading off the instrumental value of patent protection (to provide rewards and incentives for future innovation) at the present cost of the lives of millions of people. The CIPR report states this fact simply: "there are *no* circumstances in which the most fundamental human rights should be subordinated to the requirements of [IP] protection" (CIPR 2002: 6; author's emphasis). In any event compulsory licensing and parallel importing in sub-Saharan Africa will likely have little impact on either corporate profits or incentives to innovate, since Africa accounts for just over 1 per cent of the global market (Cameron and Gupta 2002). Moreover, the disease burden in developing regions (other than HIV/AIDS) is largely ignored in the development of new drugs, as the shocking disproportion of global health R&D expenditure on wealthy country illnesses illustrates: an estimated 90 per cent is spent on conditions affecting just 10 per cent of the world's population, with priority conditional upon ability to pay (MSF 2003b).

Indeed, UN human rights bodies have cautioned countries acceding to regional trade agreements to ensure that human rights are not undermined (CESCR 2004a; CRC 2004a and b). These bodies have also promoted compulsory licensing and parallel imports to ensure greater access to generic medicines so that states can comply with their obligations under the right to health (UNCHR 2001, 2003; CESCR 2004a and b). The implication is that bilateral and regional FTAs that restrict access to generic medicines violate the right to health, and that contracting governments involved (both rich and poor) should be held to account for these violations. Given the negative health impacts, why do countries enter into these agreements? It is not surprising that countries routinely place economic growth over critical health investment, given how routinely health systems are under-financed and how access to healthcare for marginalized and poor populations is so often neglected in both rich and poor countries. Moreover, developing country trade negotiators may simply lack knowledge about the health implications of higher levels of IP protection. Certainly, the promise of increased trade and investment is attractive, yet countries are often pressured to accept these IP provisions in exchange for economically critical concessions, such as market access for agricultural products (Abbott 2004). This is evident in the fact that negotiations often take place alongside actual or threatened unilateral trade sanctions, leaving developing countries with little room to refuse bilateral agreements (Drahos 2002). These power differentials are exacerbated by the considerable secrecy of FTA negotiations (Abbott 2004; MSF 2004), with no opportunity for public input or debate. However, given the relative consistency of IP provisions in completed FTAs, civil society groups are increasingly drawing the attention of national negotiators to the health implications of probable or actual IP standards (MSF 2003b; TAC/ALP 2004). As discussed below, this has had a variable influence on the IP provision in concluded agreements.

Intellectual property provisions in free trade agreements

TRIPS-plus provisions in FTAs regularly include limits on compulsory licensing; prohibitions on parallel imports; limiting market approval for generic drugs; data exclusivity; extended patent terms and 'evergreening" provisions. Since the U.S. often uses concluded treaties as the basis for negotiations on new treaties, these agreements also suggest the content of future FTAs (Drahos 2002).

Compulsory licensing

The U.S.–Vietnam, U.S.–Jordan, U.S.–Singapore and U.S.–Australia FTAs limit the grounds on which to issue compulsory licenses to national emergencies, as anti-trust remedies and for public non-commercial use. This effectively excludes any other grounds for issuing compulsory licenses, including the denial of a voluntary license, or as a measure to protect public health under TRIPS Article 8 that fell short of a national emergency. The latter three agreements also limit the recipients of licenses to government entities or legal entities, operating under the authority of a government, whereas TRIPS makes no such restrictions, and licenses can be issued to independent private entities for commercial purposes.

These restrictions effectively exclude using compulsory licenses to promote generic competition on medicines and, as indicated above, after 2005 they will have particularly far-reaching negative consequences. Narrowing the scope for using compulsory licensing will "make governments less certain about their authority to use this critical public health tool and more worried about facing domestic lawsuits from industry if they do attempt compulsory licensing – thus inhibiting action to advance public health interests" (Weissman 2001). Compulsory licensing is also being undermined through limitations on marketing approval for generic medicines and data exclusivity, as discussed below.

Parallel importing

Agreements with Singapore, Morocco, and Australia allow patent holders to contractually prevent parallel importation, while the FTAA mandates regional exhaustion within five years of signature, effectively excluding parallel imports from outside countries. These provisions will prohibit countries from importing lower-priced patented medicines sold in other countries.

Linking intellectual property and regulatory authorities

The U.S.–Singapore, CAFTA, U.S.–Australia and U.S.–Morocco agreements prohibit a country's drug regulatory authority from approving a generic drug for marketing, while the brand-name drug is under patent, without the patent holder's permission. In these agreements, and in the U.S.–Jordan FTA, the patent owner must be notified if another party seeks marketing approval for a generic drug while it is still under patent. Since restricting marketing approval effectively limits a drug's registration, this amounts to a ban on generic versions of patented drugs (MSF 2004). It also undermines the use of compulsory licenses, since a generic company that has been issued a license would not be able to register that drug, effectively rendering the license useless (MSF 2004).

Data exclusivity

The requirement of data exclusivity is another mechanism used to block the registration of generic medicines. Concluded provisions significantly extend the TRIPS requirement that test data be protected from unfair commercial use. In the FTAA, U.S.–Singapore, U.S.–Chile, CAFTA, U.S.–Australia, and U.S.–Morocco FTAs, countries must provide five years of data exclusivity to pharmaceutical products from the date of the originator's approval. Data exclusivity prevents generic companies from using the safety information provided by the patent holder to seek registration of an equivalent generic drug, and applies even to medicines not under patent. Since compiling comparable test data is time-consuming and expensive, data exclusivity serves to extend patent terms where they exist, and poses additional obstacles to effective use of compulsory licensing (Fink and Reichenmiller 2005). Several agreements go further, and provide that foreign data exclusivity used to obtain marketing approval in other countries must be honored domestically, so that generic manufacturers could not rely on the test data submitted to a foreign regulator for seeking domestic marketing approval (Fink and Reichenmiller 2005). The U.S.–Morocco and U.S.–Bahrain FTAs provide for an additional three years of data exclusivity when patent holders seek marketing approval for previously unapproved uses of registered drugs, including older generic products for which patents have expired.

Extending patent life beyond twenty years

An increasingly standard feature in FTAs is that the 20-year patent term guaranteed under TRIPS must be extended to compensate for delays in granting patents or marketing approval, including for "unreasonable delays," as is required in the U.S.–Jordan, U.S.–Singapore, U.S.–Chile, CAFTA, U.S.–Australia, and U.S.–Morocco FTAs. The FTAA, U.S.–Singapore, U.S.–Australia, and U.S.–Morocco FTAs also provide for extensions when delays in patent grants exceed four years from filing, or two years after a request for examination of the application, whichever is later. (These periods are extended to five years and three years respectively in the U.S.–Chile FTA and CAFTA.) The FTAA extends the patent term to give a period of marketing exclusivity where the patent grant precedes the granting of marketing approval. TRIPS makes no provision for similar extensions. Since "unreasonable" is not defined in the text of concluded FTAs, it remains unclear when this provision would kick in, particularly given resource constraints for drug regulatory authorities in developing countries (MSF 2004).

New use or "evergreening" provisions

While TRIPS does not require countries to grant patents on new uses of existing medicines, the U.S.–Morocco, U.S.–Australia, and U.S.–Bahrain FTAs do, enabling companies to extend patent terms on existing products, thereby "evergreening" their monopolies (MSF 2004), and indefinitely keeping generic competitors out of the market.

SACU FTA with the U.S. and the EFTA

The impact of TRIPS-plus IP standards on medicines access will be particularly harmful in sub-Saharan African countries where approximately 25 million people are infected with HIV (UNAIDS 2004), more than 1.5 million TB cases occur each year (WHO 2002), and 90 per cent of malaria deaths occur, with approximately 3,000 deaths each day (WHO 1998a). Yet, as in other developing regions, in sub-Saharan Africa, one in three people lack access to essential medicines, a figure that rises to one in two in the most impoverished parts of Africa (WHO 1998b).

The separate efforts by the U.S. and the EFTA (Switzerland, Norway, Iceland, and Liechtenstein) to conclude similarly restrictive FTAs with the countries of SACU are, therefore, particularly troubling, given that the SACU countries of South Africa, Botswana, Lesotho, Namibia, and Swaziland have the highest HIV/AIDS rates in the world, and that HIV/AIDS medicines are largely still under patent. Promising developments indicate, however, that SACU governments are standing firm against including TRIPS-plus IP provisions in both FTAs. In early 2005, the SACU countries rejected the EFTA's proposal on TRIPS-plus IP rights, excluding these from the final agreement (ICTSD 2005b). Talks on the U.S.–SACU have similarly stalled over IP rights for AIDS drugs (Mbizwo 2005).

These developments bode well for these and future FTAs with sub-Saharan African countries, and speak to the increasing awareness of national negotiators of the health implications of IP provisions, particularly for HIV/AIDS. Yet the growth of TRIPS-plus IPR protection in this region is hardly dependent on FTAs: under the U.S. AGAO sub-Saharan African countries can become eligible for duty-free and quota-free U.S. market access for their products through political, economic, and legal reforms, including on IP rights. The result has been a flurry of legislative reform in sub-Saharan African countries. In 2002, both Kenya and Uganda introduced and amended their IP laws to restrict parallel imports and compulsory licensing (Kimani 2002; Oxfam 2002), and the USTR's 2003 and 2004 AGAO progress reports indicate that, over this period, nine African countries – Swaziland, Djibouti, Mauritius, Senegal, Ghana, Botswana, Côte D'Ivoire, Guinea, and Ethiopia – introduced or revised their IP laws (USTR 2003, 2004). In 2003 the U.S. also provided US$133 million in trade capacity-building assistance to sub-Saharan African countries, including assisting legislative reform of IP (USTR 2003, 2004). Bilateral and regional agreements are, therefore, only the most visible manifestation of an inexorable multi-strategy escalation of global IP standards.

Conclusion

Bilateral and regional FTAs extend the monopoly period for patent holders beyond 20 years, restrict the use of compulsory licensing and parallel imports, and effectively exclude generic medicines from entering the market. Their overall impact will be, "to establish potentially impenetrable obstacles to the supply of low priced medicines" (Abbott 2004), including those for devastating pandemics such as HIV/AIDS. These agreements strongly favor U.S. commercial interests at the expense of the health and lives of millions of poor people in developing countries. Imposing uniformly high standards of IP that are inappropriate to the public health and development needs of developing countries is not simply ethically questionable, but should also be viewed as a serious violation of human rights.

References

Abbott, F. M. 2004. *The Doha Declaration on the TRIPS Agreement and Public Health and the Contradictory Trend in Bilateral and Regional Free Trade Agreements*. Geneva: Quaker United Nations Office. Occasional Paper 14. Available at: http://www.geneva.quno.info/pdf/OP14Abbottfinal.pdf [Accessed February 7, 2006].

Cameron, E. and A. Gupta. 2002. Global Access to Treatment. *Canadian HIV/AIDS Policy & Law Review* 2002: 7, no. 1. Available at: http://www.aidslaw.ca/Maincontent/otherdocs/Newsletter/vol7no12002/accesstotreatment.htm [Accessed February 7, 2006].

Caves, R. E., M. D. Whinston, and M. A. Hurwitz. 1991. Patent Expiration, Entry and Competition in the U.S. Pharmaceutical Industry. *Brookings Papers on Economic Activity*; Special Issue: 1–62.

Cohen, J., L. Forman, and N. Lipkus. 2004. *Policy Barriers to Drug Access: What are the Issues? What are the Solutions?* Unpublished policy paper for Gates Foundation.

Commission on Intellectual Property Rights (CIPR). 2002. *Integrating Intellectual Property Rights and Development Policy: Report of the Commission on Intellectual Property Rights*. London: CIPR. Available at: http://www.iprcommission.org/papers/pdfs/final_report/CIPRfullfinal.pdf [Accessed February 7, 2006].

Committee on Economic, Social and Cultural Rights (CESCR). 2004a. *Concluding Observations of the Committee on Economic, Social and Cultural Rights: Ecuador*. Geneva: UN.

——. 2004b. *Concluding Observations of the Committee on Economic, Social and Cultural Rights: Chile*. Geneva: OUNHCHR.

Committee on the Rights of the Child (CRC). 2004a. *Concluding Observations of the Committee on the Rights of the Child, Botswana*. Geneva: OUNHCHR.

——. 2004b. *Concluding Observations of the Committee on the Rights of the Child, El Salvador*. Geneva: OUNHCHR.

Correa, C. M. 2002. Implications of the Doha Declaration on the TRIPS Agreement and Public Health. Geneva: WHO. Available at: http://www.who.int/medicines/areas/policy/WHO_EDM_PAR_2002.3.pdf [Accessed February 7, 2006].

Drahos, P. 2001. BITS and BIPS: Bilateralism in Intellectual Property. *Journal of World Intellectual Property* 4: 791.

——. 2002. *Developing Countries and International Intellectual Property Standard-Setting*. London: CIPR. Available at: http://www.iprcommission.org/papers/pdfs/study_papers/sp8_drahos_study.pdf [Accessed February 7, 2006].

Drahos, P. and J. Braithwaite. 2002. *Information Feudalism: Who Owns the Knowledge Economy?* London: Earthscan Publications.

Fink, C. and P. Reichenmiller. 2005. *Tightening TRIPS: The Intellectual Property Provisions of Recent US Free Trade Agreements*. Washington, DC: World Bank. Available at: http://siteresources.worldbank.org/INTRANETTRADE/Resources/Pubs/TradeNote20.pdf [Accessed February 7, 2006].

Hollis, A. 2002. The Link between Publicly Funded Health Care and Compulsory Licensing. *Canadian Medical Association Journal* 7: 167.

International Centre for Trade and Sustainable Development (ICTSD). 2005a. Intellectual Property Protection Dogs Regional Trade Deals. *Bridges Monthly Review* 2005a; 9, no. 1: 14. Available at: http://www.ictsd.org/monthly/bridges/BRIDGES9–1.pdf [Accessed February 7, 2006].

——. 2005b. Southern African Countries Reject "TRIPS-Plus" Demands in FTA Negotiation. *Bridges Weekly Trade News Digest* 2005b; 9, no. 8: Weekly Main Page. Available at: http://www.ictsd.org/weekly/05–03–09/story3.htm [Accessed February 7, 2006].

Joint United Nations Program on AIDS (UNAIDS). 2004. *2004 Report on the Global AIDS Epidemic.* Geneva: UNAIDS.

Kimani, D. 2002. New Law Blocks Import of HIV/Aids Generics into Nairobi. *The East African (Nairobi),* July 1. Available at: http://lists.essential.org/pipermail/ip-health/2002-July/003238.html [Accessed February 7, 2006].

Mbizwo, A. 2005. AIDS Drugs Dog U.S.–Southern Africa Trade Deal. *Reuters (Johannesburg) 29 April.* Available at: http://www.bilaterals.org/article.php3?id_article=1795 [Accessed February 7, 2006].

Médecins sans Frontières (MSF). 2003a. *Trading away Health: Intellectual Property and Access to Medicines in the Free Trade Area of the Americas (FTAA) Agreement.* Ferney-Voltaire: MSF. Available at: http://www.accessmed-msf.org/documents/FTAAdoc.pdf [Accessed February 7, 2006].

——. 2003b. *Doha Derailed: A Progress Report on TRIPS and Access to Medicines.* Ferney-Voltaire: MSF. Available at: http://www.accessmed-msf.org/documents/cancunbriefing.pdf [Accessed February 7, 2006].

——. 2004. *Access to Medicines at Risk Across the Globe: What to Watch out for in Free Trade Agreements with the United States.* Ferney-Voltaire: MSF. Available at: http://www.accessmed-msf.org/documents/ftabriefingenglish.pdf [Accessed February 7, 2006].

Oxfam. 2002. *Generic Competition, Price and Access to Medicines: The Case of Antiretrovirals in Uganda.* Geneva: Oxfam. Oxfam Briefing Paper 26. Available at: http://www.oxfam.org/eng/pdfs/pp020710_no26_generic_competition_briefing_paper.pdf[Accessed February 7, 2006].

Penrose, E. T. 1951. *The Economics of the International Patent System.* Baltimore, MD: Johns Hopkins University Press.

Scherer, F. M. 1998. Comments. In *Competition Policy and Intellectual Property Rights in the Knowledge-Based Economy,* edited by R. Anderson and N. Gallini, 104–110, Alberta: University of Calgary Press.

——. 2000. The Pharmaceutical Industry. In *Handbook of Health Economics. Volume 1,* edited by A. L. Culyer and J. P. Newhouse, 1297–1336, New York: Elsevier.

Scherer, F. M. and J. Watal. 2001. *Post-TRIPS Options for Access to Patented Medicines in Developing Countries.* Geneva: Commission on Macroeconomics and Health. Available at: http://www.cmhealth.org/docs/wg4_paper1.pdf [Accessed February 7, 2006].

Treatment Action Campaign and the AIDS Law Project (TAC/ALP). 2004. *Memo to the South African International Trade Negotiating Team.* Johannesburg: TAC/ALP. Available at: http://lists.essential.org/pipermail/ip-health/2004-February/005904.html [Accessed February 7, 2006].

United Nations Commission on Human Rights (UNCHR). 2001. *The Impact of the Agreement on Trade-Related Aspects of Intellectual Property Rights on Human Rights: Report of the High Commissioner.* Geneva: OUNHCHR.

——. 2003. *Note by the Secretary General: Interim Report of the Special Rapporteur of the Commission on Human Rights on the Right of Everyone to the Enjoyment of the Highest Attainable Standard of Physical and Mental Health, Mr. Paul Hunt.* Geneva: OUNHCHR.

United Nations Development Program (UNDP). 2003. *Making Global Trade Work for People.* New York: UNDP.

United States Trade Representative (USTR). 2003. *2003 Comprehensive Report on US Trade and Investment Policy Toward Sub-Saharan Africa and Implementation of the African Growth and Opportunity Act.* Washington, DC: USTR. Available at: http://www.agoa.gov/resources/annual_3.pdf [Accessed February 7, 2006].

——. 2004. *2004 Comprehensive Report on U.S. Trade and Investment Policy Toward Sub-Saharan Africa and Implementation of the African Growth and Opportunity Act.* Washington, DC: USTR. Available at: http://www.agoa.gov/resources/2004–05-agoa.pdf [Accessed February 7, 2006].

Weissman, R. 2001. Free Trade and Medicines in the Americas. *Foreign Policy in Focus Policy Brief* 2001; 6, no. 13. Washington, DC: Foreign Policy in Focus. Available at: http://www.fpif.org/pdf/vol6/13ifmeds.pdf [Accessed February 6, 2006].

——. 2002. *Essential Information on Trade Promotion Authority and Access to Medicines. Essential Action.* Washington, DC: CPTECH. Available at: http://www.cptech.org/ip/health/trade/ei-factsheet.html [Accessed February 7, 2005].

World Health Organization (WHO). 1998a. *WHO Fact Sheet on Malaria: Fact Sheet No. 94.* Geneva: WHO.

——. 1998b. *Progress of WHO Member States in Developing National Drug Policies and in Revising Essential Drugs Lists.* Geneva: WHO.

——. 2000. *WHO Medicines Strategy: Framework for Action in Essential Drugs and Medicines Policy 2002–2003.* Geneva: WHO.

——. 2002. *Global Tuberculosis Control Report.* Geneva: WHO. Available at: http://www.who.int/docstore/gtb/publications/globrep02/PDF/02-body.pdf [Accessed February 7, 2006].

World Trade Organization (WTO). 1994. *Agreement on Trade-Related Aspects of Intellectual Property Rights.* Geneva: WTO. Available at: http://www.wto.org/english/docs_e/legal_e/27-trips.pdf [Accessed November 11, 2005].

——. 2001. *Declaration on the TRIPS Agreement and Public Health. Ministerial Conference.* Geneva: WTO. Ministerial Conference. Fourth Session. Doha, November 9–14. Available at: http://www.wto.org/english/thewto_e/minist_e/min01_e/mindecl_trips_e.pdf [Accessed January 16, 2006].

Part V

Research ethics

19 Human genomic research ethics: changing the rules

Steven H. Miles

Standards for research in developing countries do not take account of how research can widen the socioeconomic gap between rich and poor nations. Research conducted in developing nations often does not target local needs or allow them to develop their own research infrastructures. This is especially so in "basic" human genomic research, which may lead to healthcare advances that poor countries cannot afford. Research ethics standards should assure that the market value of property rights from human genomic research is shared fairly and foster the development of local research infrastructures, and provide access to venture capital to capitalize on the genomic resources. The 1992 Convention on Biological Diversity (CBD) is a foundation for this effort.

Human genomic research ethics: changing the rules

Human genomic research is a form of prospecting for a precious raw material: genetic sequences. In the short term, it offers insights into the genetic basis of disease and human responses to pathogens and treatments. In the longer term, it should improve genetic screening and diagnosis. Ultimately, it may yield better ways to individualize therapies or perhaps new therapies. Genomic research produces three kinds of benefits: economic wealth, human capital (educated scientists, teachers, technicians), and social capital. Social capital is a complex national asset. It includes intentionally established, durable institutions that can set and pursue priorities and promote the formal and informal relationships to accomplish that work (Portes 1998). As social capital, a research center is more than buildings or the skills of individual professionals. It is a place where research ideas are discussed before resources are invested in them, where education and experience develop human capital in the form of scientific and managerial expertise, where funding is raised and allocated to complex interests of the national community and where research projects can be organized, performed, analyzed, and published. It is also a community of empowered middle-class persons with a stake in the social stability of the nation. Africa has the most genetically diverse population and will be the focus of human genomic research. It will also attract researchers from countries with histories of exploiting its riches and neglecting its needs.

Research ethics for poor countries

In an ideal world, medical research leads to interventions to improve health. Research also creates IP, profitable products, human capital, and social capital. Ethics standards for conducting research on humans in developing countries are based on standards designed for developed countries. They emphasize informed consent, confidentiality, and minimizing coercion or exploitation of people who are less able to protect their own interests (HUGO Ethics Committee 1995, 1998; WMA 2002). Given that much of First World research in developing countries is conducted on behalf of First World academic and industrial concerns, it is not surprising that these standards inadequately address the manner by which research reserves the value of IPR, products, and social capital to First World parties. Poorer countries will pay dearly for the products of research conducted on their own people and are unlikely to acquire the professional and institutional infrastructure to enable them to become partners in this research. This economic asymmetry reiterates colonial economics by which poor countries exported low-cost raw materials and imported expensive finished goods. Unless addressed, human genomic research will widen the economic and technological gap between rich and poor nations (Calva, Cardosa, and Gavilondo 2002; Chen 2005). Accordingly, research ethics must engage the implications of the rules of the global economy (Benatar 2002).

Developing countries contain most of the world's population, have the greatest disease burden, and have little capacity for acquiring venture capital, securing intellectual rights, or directing research to their needs. Ten per cent of global research spending goes to conditions accounting for 90 per cent of the world's disease burden (GFHR 2002). Of 1,400 drugs brought to market between 1975 and 1999, only 16 were for tropical diseases and pneumonia (Trouiller et al. 2002). Even malaria is an "orphan disease" because the 400 million persons infected each year cannot afford treatments or vaccines (Schieppati, Remuzzi, and Garattini 2001).

Charitable donation of research benefits

The U.S. NBAC, CIOMS, and WMA all say that therapeutic studies should benefit the community where the research is done in exchange for their cooperation and to avoid exploitation. Affable advice such as "Clinical trials conducted in developing countries should be limited to those studies that are responsive to the health needs of the host country" (NBAC 2001) is insufficient to redirect First World researchers to priorities, products, or benefit sharing that benefits developing countries where First World research is conducted (Kass and Hyder 2001; NBAC 2001; Kass, Dawson, and Loyo-Berrios 2003).

- The U.S. NBAC says,

    Researchers and sponsors in clinical trials should make reasonable, good faith efforts to secure continued access for all participants to needed experimental interventions that have been proven effective . . . [New] interventions [should] become available to some or all of the host country population beyond the research participants themselves. In cases in which investigators do not believe that successful interventions will become available to the host country . . . [researchers should explain] why the research is nonetheless responsive to the health needs of the country. (NBAC 2001)

Though U.S.-based researchers support the ideal of ensuring an ongoing supply of a drug to a poor country where it was tested, they are much less likely than researchers from poor countries to see this as an acceptable condition for research (Kass and Hyder 2001). As Lackey puts it, "Compassion is a good thing but . . . not something that can be commanded by moral codes. . . This is especially true in the research setting, where the goal . . . is truth, not the solution of personal health problems" (Lackey 2002).

- CIOMS (1990) say that research should respond to the health needs and priorities of the local population and assure that some research products benefit the local population or community. It also says that potential subjects and their communities must be informed of the possible commercial value of the research.
- The WMA's Declaration of Helsinki says, "Medical research is only justified if there is a reasonable likelihood that the populations in which the research is carried out stand to benefit from the results of the research" (WMA 2002: B19).

There are two fundamental problems with proposals to voluntarily share the benefits of genomic research. First, the commendation of providing immediate and modest compensation to those who cooperate with research does not address the issue of how First World genomic research in poor countries will widen the socioeconomic gap between developed and underdeveloped nations. Second, although research ethics standards commend providing local benefits to some people for some time after a successful therapeutic study, the NBAC and CIOMS are unclear about the duty to provide benefits for non-therapeutic or basic research, as is the case with human genomic data collection. Under CIOMS standards, subjects may truthfully be told that DNA samples have no significant commercial value even though secondary work may lead to commercially valuable diagnostic tools or treatments. This near-term view of the commercial value of basic research ensures that genomic data can be freely taken to ultimately return as costly secondary products.

Voluntary sharing of intellectual property rights

The HUGO Ethics Committee addresses sharing of the value of the beneficial products of genomic research. It commends building "technology transfer, local training, joint ventures, provision of health care or of information, infrastructures, or . . . royalties for humanitarian purposes" (cited in HUGO Ethics Committee 2000) into research projects. Even so, HUGO's sense of sharing is centered on the moral value of compensation and welfare and designed to protect the privileged position of First World researchers. While "researchers, institutions, and commercial entities have a right to a fair return for intellectual and financial contributions to databases" (HUGO Ethics Committee 2003: Rec. 6), they might consider donating "a percentage of the net profits [e.g., 1–3 per cent] (after taxes) to the health care infrastructure . . . or to local, national and international humanitarian efforts" (HUGO Ethics Committee 2000: Sec. D).

Two programs suggest what HUGO's proposal might look like in practice. In the GRRF, companies pay a one-time fee to a California university that manages a genomic database when product using indigenous genetic material is brought to market (ten Kate & Collis nd). The genetic source country retains the right to research the sample but must pay the GRRF if it develops a commercial application of the material from its own genomic resources. The GRRF intends to grant research fellowships for persons from the source country. There has been little corporate interest in proposed "partnerships" in which public or philanthropic funds subsidise research and product development by private firms (Trouiller et al. 2002). The private partner retains IPR and is subject to an ill-defined accountability to any of several means (e.g., multi-tier pricing) to make its products accessible to poorer nations (Buse and Walt 2000; Kasturiaratchi 2001; Macklin 2001; Mills 2001; Wheeler and Berkley 2001).

Equitably sharing intellectual property rights

Some propose a duty to equitably share intellectual rights (UNDP 2001). The KFPE says, "Research results have intellectual worth and may also have a commercial value. All partners should share equally in the benefits of both" (SCRP/KFPE 1998). Brazil says that research with human subjects "must ensure the research subjects the benefits resulting from the research project, in terms of social returns, access to procedures, products or research agents" (NBAC 2001: 57).

Several developing countries wrote:

[the] enforcement of intellectual property rights . . . should contribute to the promotion of technological innovation and to the transfer and dissemination of technology to the mutual advantage of producers and users of technological knowledge and in a manner conducive to social and economic welfare and to a balance of rights and obligations . . . [Nations] may take measures to ensure that [this] is achieved. (WTO 1994)

Harnessing research to development

The socioeconomic gap between rich and poor nations will grow unless the gap in R&D capacity is reduced. Rich countries spend 0.2 per cent of their large GDP on health research; countries like Brazil, Mexico, and India spend 0.05 per cent; the poorest nations spend an even smaller percentage of tiny economies (GFHR 2001). Rich nations have 2–4 R&D scientists per 1,000 citizens; poor countries have 0.1–0.3 per 1,000 (UNESCO 1996). Developing countries need research institutions, professionals who prioritize their needs, and the ability to focus research on local needs. These infrastructures must have stable core budgets; research and venture capital; the capacity to build partnerships between international health organizations, national Ministries of Health, institutions of higher learning, and multinational corporations; and the ability to market technologies (Ad Hoc Committee on Health Research Relating to Future Intervention Options 1996; Wolffers, Adeji, and van der Drift 1998; Mohan and Ranjith 2001; Bhutta 2002).

There is no plan to develop the R&D capacity of developing countries. International aid for training developing countries' scientists is US$300 million (Calva, Cardosa, and Gavilondo 2002). The World Bank, the largest external lender for educational development, prioritizes primary education. Only one fifth (US$480 million) of its educational lending goes to tertiary education and 7 per cent of that goes to all of sub-Saharan Africa (World Bank 2002). First World researchers take small indigenous research infrastructures away from local needs (Trostle and Simon 1992; Wolffers, Adeji, and van der Drift 1998; Benatar and Singer 2000). Efforts to foster collaborative research between wealthy and poor countries are half-hearted (GFHR 2001). The EU Framework for R&D allocates 96 per cent of its funds to EU members; 4 per cent is divided between poor countries and international organizations (De Bruycker and Hagan 1996). The PNGIMR is a showcase, but Uganda's "low-cost" model program providing limited access to a few publications, monthly meetings, and quarterly reports is more typical (Kengeya-Kayondo 1994; GFHR 2002; Alpers 2003).

First World research ethics commissions emphasize enhancing poor countries' ability to evaluate the ethics of First World sponsored research. NBAC says, "[t]he U.S. government should identify procedural criteria and a process for determining whether the human participants' protection system of a host country . . . has achieved all the substantive ethical protections" (NBAC 2001: 22). Such First World proposals are much less clear on the importance of developing local research capacity to focus on local needs or to ensure that the economic benefits or about ensuring that the social capital created by research is equitably shared (Diniz 2001; NBAC 2001; CBD 2002). For example, NBAC says, "[w]here applicable, U.S. sponsors and researchers should develop and implement strategies that assist in building local capacity for designing, reviewing, and conducting clinical trials in developing countries" (NBAC 2001). If ethics oversight is not grounded in a credible research infrastructure, it is unlikely to function well or be taken seriously (Kass and Hyder 2001). In Kenya, U.S. researchers ignored it altogether (Baraza 1998). IRBs in wealthy countries do not have the knowledge or interest in enhancing the research infrastructures of poor countries (Macklin 2001; Fitzgerald, Wasunna, and Pape 2003).

Genomic research could enhance the research, development, and technology infrastructure of developing countries as well as the economic wealth, and human and social capital of developing countries. For this progress to occur, the rules for conducting genomic research must be designed to help nations move from being technologically marginalized (Mozambique), to becoming dynamic adopters (Thailand), potential leaders (Malaysia) and on to full technological development (Trostle 1992; Trostle and Simon 1992; Tanner, Kitua, and Degremont 1994; UNDP 2001). Egypt, for example, requires intra-Egyptian research of its genomic data and built MCSRTA to turn genetic data into products. Egypt, of course, has a skilled scientific community; other mechanisms would be required for less developed countries.

A treaty for equitable human genomic research

The fight for rights to the commercial value of genomic research on plants and animals may have laid the foundation for equitable ethics for human genomic research. Agricultural, pharmaceutical, and cosmetic corporations acquired tens of thousands of specimens from developing countries. Some became valuable products: pest-resistant crops come from mass screening of the properties of exotic plants. Some corporations capitalized on the insights of indigenous cultures (WIPO nd). The new anti-obesity drug xhoba was developed from a plant that San Bushmen from the Kalahari used to suppress their appetites on long hunting trips (Carroll 2003). Monsanto's patent on the genetic sequence of chapati wheat came from sequencing a crop that was created by generations of agricultural husbandry (Guardian 2004). Developing countries' potential (and lost) royalties from such products is unknown; estimates range to tens of billions of dollars. As a Brazilian legislator put it, "Our gold, our oil is our biodiversity ... The companies [say] that the jungle's genetic riches are the 'heritage of all humanity' but when they turn a plant into a product, they want all the profits for themselves" (La Franchi 1997).

Genetic prospecting extends to humans as well. Africans are profiled to identify gene markers for increased susceptibility to diseases (Rowland-Jones et al. 1998; Corbett et al. 2002; Flanagan et al. 2001; Koch et al. 2002) or response to treatments (Babiker et al. 2001; Gower et al. 2003; Roper et al. 2003). The Coriell Institute sells DNA samples from Mayan, Karitiana, Surui, Quechua, Auca Indians and other indigenous populations (CIMR 2006). It allows commercial product development without requiring compensation to source populations. A tribal group, whose DNA is in this bank, has sued for compensation. Many centers sell DNA mapping services to Black Americans who want to learn about their African ancestry; they compare American specimens to an ethnogenetic map of Africa that was created from largely uncompensated basic research (Dula et al. 2003; Duerinck 2005 – centers selling services that purportedly trace genetic African ancestry are listed on this website).

The controversy over "genetic piracy" of commercial rights to indigenous plants and animals led to the 1992 CBD. It analogizes national ownership of natural resources to ownership of genetic diversity (CBD 1992). The Convention requires genetic researchers to provide source countries with access to the results and benefits of research. Despite hostility from developed countries, several countries enacted enabling legislation and have created royalty-sharing agreements with genetic research corporations; they have also prosecuted those who have collected specimens without providing compensation (Pollack 1999; Straus 2001). Variants on these early contracts should be explored.

The CBD was written to address expropriation of the value of indigenous plants and wild and domesticated animals, especially in South America. It may be equally valuable to genomic research in Africa, which has the greatest human genetic diversity. Though the Convention does not specify human genomic research, its language applies equally well to the human animal: humans are genetically diverse; genomic research may benefit humans; human genotypes are partly localized to particular regions and adapted to local ecologies and so on.

In 1995, the Conference on the Parties to the Convention passed a resolution that "reaffirms that human genetic resources are not included within the framework of the Convention" (CBD 1995: 68). This peculiar reaffirmation lacks foundation in a preceding affirmation. Thus, it restricted, rather than interpreted, the Convention. Furthermore, this reaffirmation does not amend the Convention; it is only an interpretive guideline. UNESCO's UDHGHR cites the Convention and is strikingly similar to the Convention in its ethical principles for human genomic research (UNESCO 1997). It says states should foster research to identify, prevent, and treat genetically based or influenced diseases, especially those that affect many people. It says that nations should disseminate scientific knowledge about the human genome especially to developing countries and enhance developing countries' capacity to carry out human research in order to equitably benefit from it.

Applying the convention on biodiversity to human genomic research

There are compelling reasons for applying the benefit-sharing framework of the Convention to human genomic research. First, the Convention has been enacted. Thus, it empowers developing countries in negotiating contracts with researchers by laying the basis for pressing claims to the commercial value or provenance of products developed from human genomic banks. Second, its framework avoids colonial economic rules by which underdeveloped countries sell cheap genetic data that they will eventually import as expensive finished products. Allowing genomic research to recapitulate colonial era economic arrangements imperils world health and retards the socioeconomics of poor countries. Finally, it would be a fitting memorial and partial compensation for the crime of taking the bodies of twelve million Africans as slaves to benefit European and U.S.'s commercial interests.

There are arguments against applying the Convention to human genomic research. Some argue that the human genome belongs to everyone and should be freely explored for the benefit of all. It seems disingenuously self-serving for economic interests in developed nations to make this argument given how the rules for allocating the benefits of this research so asymmetrically benefit their interests. Some say that sharing the commercial value of human genomic research will slow beneficial product development. Pharmaceutical companies' profits, after R&D costs, are substantially higher than other industries; there is room for a financial incentive for research and a reform of research rules. Furthermore, the equitable sharing of the economic value of this research would itself improve health and access to biomedical advances based on genomic research.

Some argue against a duty to share the commercial value of genomic research because human participants of experimental therapeutic research do not receive royalties. However, increasing interest in arrangements like the GRRF, the CBD, or contracts by which firms pay royalties for product development from genomic sources, show an emerging view that genetic information differs from experimental observations.

The Convention's assertion of national "ownership" over indigenous genotypes is a defensible if imperfect analogy (Barton 1997). In chapati wheat, tolerance to malaria, or unusual genotypes in inbred cultural groups, genotypes literally embody the folkways or experiences of local cultures.

Some argue that the social harms that may come from misusing human genomic data make this research "special" so that it merits its own, unique research ethics framework. There are legitimate concerns that human genomic research could be used to support racism, health services or insurance discrimination, eugenics, or the development of biological weapons (UNESCO 1997; Dula et al. 2003). The 2002 Bonn guidelines alluded to these risks as it asserted that the Convention did not apply to humans (see Tully 2003). Though such abuses must be addressed, it is difficult to see how the Convention increases any of them. Furthermore, human genomic research proceeds without benefit sharing to underdeveloped countries.

Many steps are required for reform. Developing countries must mobilize and pool policymaking talent to develop and harmonize legislation and commercial contracts for human genomic research. The World Bank must remedy its neglect of developing institutions for research and higher education in developing countries. Developing countries will have to invest in creating a stable research infrastructure.

Conclusion

Current research ethics do not adequately address the issue of international research on the diversity of the human genome. Under current research standards, this research will widen the gap between developed and underdeveloped countries. New ethics standards for this research should frame this research so the market value of property rights from such research fosters the development of research institutions, a scientific workforce, and access to investment and venture capital within underdeveloped countries. The 1992 CBD offers just such a foundation.

Acknowledgement

This article was prepared and presented to the Human Sciences Research Council of South Africa: Africa Genome Initiative, Genomics and African Society: The Future Health of Africa and held in Cairo, Egypt, March, 26–29 2004. The conference was organized by Genetic Engineering & Biotechnology Centre and Ain Shams University, Cairo. The author thanks the Wellcome Trust for providing his accommodation and meals during the conference.

References

Ad Hoc Committee on Health Research Relating to Future Intervention Options. 1996. *Investing in Health Research and Development.* Geneva: WHO.

Alpers, M. P. 2003. The Buttressing Coalition of the PNGIMR: An Example of International Collaborative Research. *Trends in Parasitology* 19: 278–280.

Babiker, H. A., S. J. Pringle, A. Abdel-Muhsin, M. Mackinnon, P. Hunt, and D. Walliker. 2001. High-level Chloroquine Resistance in Sudanese Isolates of Plasmodium Falciparum is

Associated with Mutations in the Chloroquine Resistance Transporter Gene Pfcrt and the Multidrug Resistance Gene pfmdr1. *Journal of Infectious Diseases* 183: 1535–1538.

Baraza, R. 1998. Ethics and International Research. *British Medical Journal* 316: 625–626.

Barton, J. H. 1997. Patents and Antitrust: A Rethinking in Light of Patent Breadth and Sequential Innovation. *Antitrust Law Journal* 65: 449–466.

Benatar, S. R. 2002. Reflections and Recommendations on Research Ethics in Developing Countries. *Social Science and Medicine* 54: 1131–1141.

Benatar, S. R. and P. A. Singer. 2000. A New Look at International Research Ethics. *British Medical Journal* 321: 824–826.

Bhutta, Z. A. 2002. Ethics in International Health Research: A Perspective from the Developing World. *Bulletin of the World Health Organization* 80: 114–120.

Bonn, D. 2002. Research Ethics Fund for Developing Countries. *Lancet Infectious Diseases* 2: 712.

Buse, K. and G. Walt. 2000. Global Public–Private Partnerships: A New Development in Health? *Bulletin of the World Health Organization* 78: 549–561, 699–709.

Calva, E., M. J. Cardosa, and J. V. Gavilondo. 2002. Avoiding the Genomics Divide. *Trends in Biotechnology* 20: 368–370.

Carroll, R. 2003. It's Green Prickly and Sour but this Plant could Cure Obesity and Save an Ancient Way of Life. *Guardian*, 4 January. Available at: http://www.guardian.co.uk/medicine/story/0,11381,868516,00.html [Accessed January 12, 2006].

Chen, L. C. 2002. *WHO Conference on Biotechnology and Genomics for Improvement of Health in Developing Countries: Concluding Reflections*. Geneva: WHO. Available at: http://www.fas.harvard.edu/~acgei/Publications/Chen/LCC_BioTech_Cuba3.25.pdf [Accessed January 12, 2006].

Convention on Biological Diversity (CBD). 1992. *Convention on Biological Diversity*. Nairobi, Kenya: UNEP. Available at: http://www.fao.org/ag/AGP/AGPS/Pgrfa/pdf/cbde.pdf [Accessed January 12, 2006].

———. 1995. *Conference of the Parties to the Convention on Biological Diversity. Report Of The Second Meeting Of The Conference Of The Parties To The Convention On Biological Diversity*. Nairobi, Kenya: UNEP. Available at: http://www.Biodiv.Org/Doc/Meetings/Cop/Cop-02/Official/Cop-02–19-En.Doc [Accessed January 12, 2006].

———. 2002. Decision II/11: ACCESS TO GENETIC RESOURCES. Nairobi, Kenya: UNEP. Available at: http://www.biodiv.org/decisions/Default.aspx?m=cop-02&d=11 [Accessed January 12, 2006].

Corbett, E. L., N. Mozzato-Chamay, A. E. Butterworth, K. M. De Cock, B. G. Williams, G. J. Churchyard, and D. J. Conway. 2002. Polymorphisms in the Tumor Necrosis Factor-Alpha Gene Promoter May Predispose to Severe Silicosis in Black South African Miners. *American Journal of Respiratory and Critical Care Medicine* 165: 690–693.

Coriell Institute for Medical Research (CIMR). 2006. Home Page. Camden, NJ: CIMR. Available at: http://coriell.umdnj.edu/ [Accessed January 12, 2006].

Council for International Organizations of Medical Sciences (CIOMS). 1990. *The Declaration of Inuyama: Human Genome Mapping, Genetic Screening and Gene Therapy*. Geneva: CIOMS. Available at: http://www.cioms.ch/index.html [Accessed January 12, 2006].

De Bruycker, M. and P. Hagan. 1996. Partnership Between Europe and Developing Countries in Health Research. *Tropical Medicine and International Health* 1: 553–557.

Diniz, D. 2001. Vulnerability, Scientific Research and AIDS. 2001. *Developing World Bioethics* 1: 153–155.

Duerinck, K. 2005. *Genetics Laboratories and Testing Sites*. Personal website. Available at: http://www.duerinck.com/dnalabs.html [Accessed January 12, 2006].

Dula, A., C. Royal, M. Secundy, and S. H. Miles. 2003. The Ethical and Social Implications of Exploring African American Genealogies. *Developing World Bioethics* 3: 133–142.

Fitzgerald, D. W., A. Wasunna, and J. W. Pape. 2003. Ten Questions Institutional Review Boards Should Ask When Reviewing International Clinical Research Protocols. *IRB* 25: 14–18.

Flanagan, K. L., E. A. Lee, M. B. Gravenor, W. H. Reece, B. C. Urban, T. Doherty, K.A. Bojang, M. Pinder, A. V. Hill, and M. Plebanski. 2001. Unique T Cell Effector Functions Elicited by

Plasmodium Falciparum Epitopes in Malaria-Exposed Africans Tested by Three T Cell Assays. *Journal of Immunology* 167: 4729–4737.

Global Forum for Health Research (GFHR). 2001. *Monitoring Financial Flows for Health Research.* Geneva: WHO. Available at: http://www.globalforumhealth.org/filesupld/monitoring_financial_flows2/MFF04chap0.pdf [Accessed January 12, 2006].

——. 2002. *The 10/90 Report on Health Research 2001–2002.* Geneva: WHO. Available at: http://www.globalforumhealth.org/filesupld/1090_report_01–02/01_02_front_matt.pdf [Accessed January 12, 2006].

Gower, B. A., J. R. Fernandez, T. M. Beasley, M. D. Shriver, and M. I. Goran. 2003. Using Genetic Admixture to Explain Racial Differences in Insulin-Related Phenotypes. *Diabetes* 52: 1047–1051.

Guardian. 2004. Monsanto Granted "Natural" Wheat Strain Patent Rights. *Guardian,* February 11: 11. Unsigned.

HUGO Ethics Committee. 1995. HUGO Ethics Committee Wishes to Reaffirm its Commitment to its Position Given Previously in its Statement on the Principled Conduct of Genetic Research. *Eubios Journal of Asian and International Bioethics* 6: 59–60.

——. 1998. Statement on DNA Sampling: Control and Access. *Eubios Journal of Asian and International Bioethics* 8: 56–57.

——. 2000. Statement on Benefit Sharing. *Eubios Journal of Asian and International Bioethics* 10: 70–72.

——. 2003. *Six Innovative Statements.* London: HUGO. Available at: http://www.genomecanada.ca/GCethique/bulletin/GE3LS_Fall03.pdf [Accessed January 12, 2006].

Kass, N., L. Dawson, and N.I. Loyo-Berrios. 2003. Ethical Oversight of Research in Developing Countries. *IRB* 25 no.2: 1–10.

Kass, N., and A. A. Hyder. 2001. Attitudes and Experiences of U.S. And Developing Country Investigators Regarding U.S. Human Subjects Regulations. In *Ethical And Policy Issues In International Research. Clinical Trials In Developing Countries Vol II,* edited by NBAC, Bethesada, MD: NBAC. Available at: http://www.georgetown.edu/research/nrcbl/nbac/clinical/Vol1.pdf [Accessed January 12, 2006].

Kasturiaratchi, N. D. 2001. Addressing Vulnerabilities in Developing Countries. *Developing World Bioethics* 1: 148–152.

Kengeya-Kayondo, J. F. 1994. Transdisciplinary Research: Research Capacity Building in Developing Countries at Low Cost. *Acta Tropica* 57: 147–152.

Koch, O., A. Awomoyi, S. Usen, M. Jallow, A. Richardson, J. Hull, M. Pinder, M. Newport, and D. Kwiatkowski. 2002. IFNGR1 Gene Promoter Polymorphisms and Susceptibility to Cerebral Malaria. *Journal of Infectious Diseases* 185: 1684–1687.

Lackey, D. P. 2002. Clinical Research in Developing Countries: Recent Moral Arguments. *Cadernos de Saude Publica* 18: 1455–1461.

La Franchi, H. 1997. Amazon Indians ask "Biopirates" to Pay for Rain Forest Riches. *Christian Science Monitor,* November 20. Available at: http://csmonitor.com/cgi-bin/durableRedirect.pl?/durable/1997/11/20/intl/intl.2.html [Accessed January 12, 2006].

Macklin, R. 2001. Four Forward-Looking Guidance Points. *Developing World Bioethics* 1: 121–134.

Mills, A. 2001. *Technology and Science as Global Public Good. Tackling Priority Diseases of Poor Countries.* Washington, DC: World Bank. Available at: http://wbln0018.worldbank.org/eurvp/web.nsf/Pages/Mills/$File/MILLS.PDF [Accessed January 12, 2006].

Mohan, R. and G. Ranjith. 2001. Research in Less-Developed Countries. *Lancet* 357: 1296.

National Bioethics Advisory Commission (NBAC). 2001. *Ethical and Policy Issues in International Research: Clinical Trials in Developing Countries.* Bethesda, MD: NBAC. Available at: http://www.georgetown.edu/research/nrcbl/nbac/clinical/Vol1.pdf [Accessed January 12, 2006].

Pollack, A. 1999. Biological Products Raise Genetic Ownership Issues. *New York Times,* November 26.

Portes, A. 1998. Social Capital: Its Origins and Applications in Modern Sociology. *Annual Review Sociology* 24: 1–24.

Roper, C., R. Pearce, B. Bredenkamp, J. Gumede, C. Drakeley, F. Mosha, D. Chandramohan, and B. Sharp. 2003. Antifolate Antimalarial Resistance in Southeast Africa: A Population-Based Analysis. *Lancet* 361: 1174–1181.

Rowland-Jones, S. L., T. Dong, K. R. Fowke, J. Kimani, P. Krausa, H. Newell, T. Blanchard, K. Ariyoshi, J. Oyugi, E. Ngugi, J. Bwayo, K. S. MacDonald, A. J. McMichael, and F. A. Plummer. 1998. Cytotoxic T Cell Responses to Multiple Conserved HIV Epitopes in HIV-Resistant Prostitutes in Nairobi. *Journal of Clinical Investigation* 102: 1758–1765.

Schieppati, A., G. Remuzzi, and S. Garattini. 2001. Modulating the Profit Motive to Meet Needs of the Less-Developed World. *Lancet* 358: 1638–1641.

Straus, J. 2001. Biodiversity and Intellectual Property. In *Rethinking International Intellectual Property*, 141–166. Seattle, WA: CASRIP. Available at: http://www.law.washington.edu/casrip/Symposium/Number6/Straus.pdf [Accessed January 12, 2006].

Swiss Commission of Research Partnership with Developing Countries (SCRP/KFPE). 1998. *Guidelines for Research in Partnership with Developing Countries*. Berne: KFPE. Available at: htpp://www.kfpe.ch/download/Guidelines_e.pdf [Accessed January 12, 2006].

Tanner, M., A. Kitua, and A. A. Degremont. 1994. Developing Health Research Capability in Tanzania: From a Swiss Tropical Institute Field Laboratory to the Ifkara Center of the Tanzanian National Institute of Medical Research. *Acta Tropica* 57: 153–173.

ten Kate, K. and A. Collis. nd. *Sharing Case Study: The Genetic Resources Recognition Fund of the University of California, Davis*. Prepared for Executive Secretary of the Convention on Biological Diversity of the Royal Botanic Gardens, Kew. Available at: http://www.biodiv.org/doc/case-studies/abs/cs-abs-ucdavis.pdf [Accessed January 12, 2006].

Trostle, J. 1992. Research Capacity Building in International Health: Definitions, Evaluations, and Strategies for Success. *Social Science and Medicine* 35: 1321–1334.

Trostle, J. and J. Simon. 1992. Building Applied Health Research Capacity in Less-Developed Countries: Problems Encountered by the ADDR Project. *Social Science and Medicine* 35: 1379–1387.

Trouiller, P., P. Olliaro, E. Torreele, J. Orbinski, R. Laing, and N. Ford. 2002. Drug Development for Neglected Diseases: A Deficient Market and a Public-Health Policy Failure. *Lancet* 359: 2188–2194.

Tully, S. 2003. The Bonn Guidelines on Access to Genetic Resources and Benefit Sharing. *Reciel* 12: 84–98.

United Nations Development Programme (UNDP). 2001. *Human Development Report 2001: Making New Technology Work for Human Development*. New York: UNDP. Available at: http://hdr.undp.org/reports/global/2001/en/ [Accessed January 12, 2006].

United Nations Educational Scientific and Cultural Organisation (UNESCO). 1996. *World Science Report 1996*, edited by H. Moore. Paris: UNESCO. Available at: http://www.unesco.org/science/publication/eng_pub/wsr96en.htm [Accessed January 12, 2006].

——. 1997. *Universal Declaration on the Human Genome and Human Rights*. Paris: UNESCO. Available at: http://portal.unesco.org/en/ev.php-URL_ID=13177&URL_DO=DO_TOPIC&URL_SECTION=201.html [Accessed January 12, 2006].

Wheeler, C. and S. Berkley. 2001. Initial Lessons from Public Private Partnerships in Drug and Vaccine Development. *Bulletin of the World Health Organization* 79: 728–734.

Wolffers, I., S. Adeji, and R. van der Drift. 1998. Health Research in the Tropics. *Lancet* 351: 1652–1654.

World Bank. 2002. *World Bank Support for Tertiary Education*. Washington, DC: World Bank. Available at http://www1.worldbank.org/education/tertiary/documents/cks/chapter5.pdf [Accessed January 12, 2006].

World Intellectual Property Organization (WIPO). Undated. *Intellectual Property and Genetic Resources, Traditional Knowledge, and Folklore*. Geneva: WIPO. Available at: http://www.wipo.int/about-ip/en/studies/publications/genetic_resources.htm [Accessed January 12, 2006].

World Medical Association (WMA). [1964] 2002. *Declaration of Helsinki: Ethical Principles for Medical Research Involving Human Subjects*, as amended by the WMA General Assembly,

Washington, DC, 2002. Ferney-Voltaire: WMA. Available at: http://www.wma.net/e/policy/ b3.htm [Accessed January 12, 2006].

World Trade Organization (WTO). 1994. *Annex 1C: Agreement on Trade-Related Aspects of Intellectual Property Rights*. Geneva: WTO. Available at: http://www.wto.org/english/docs_e/ legal_e/27-trips.pdf [Accessed January 12, 2006].

20 Assumptions in the "standard of care" debate

Florencia Luna

Over recent years a powerful debate has developed regarding standards of care in research. Why did this debate arise? In late 1997 and 1998 a fierce international polemic followed controversial placebo use in pregnant women with AIDS (Angell 1997; Lurie and Wolfe 1997; Varmus and Satcher 1997; Mbidde 1998). Studies were being conducted in sub-Saharan Africa, Thailand, and the Dominican Republic, the goal being to find a more economical and effective treatment to prevent vertical transmission of HIV. The studies provided pregnant women with short AZT treatments against placebo. The problem arose due to the fact that an effective treatment had already been available since 1994: the ACTG076. This consisted of an AZT treatment from the sixteenth week of pregnancy, intravenous administration during delivery, and oral treatment during the newborn's first six weeks of life. The original controversy focused on the use of placebo in the control group and the ethics of withholding proven treatment in clinical trials (Luna 2001a). However, the ensuing controversy centered on the standard to follow for the comparator group: a "universal" standard or one tailored to the situation of each community or country?

After these initial cases, "standards" began to permeate other discussions regarding ethics in research. For example, double standards are the backdrop in the polemic regarding a flexible use of placebo. Note the following case: In February 2001, the FDA seriously considered approving the design of a test for Surfaxin, to be conducted in Ecuador, Bolivia, Peru, and Mexico. The test proposed a control group of 325 premature babies with RDS. This potentially fatal condition was to be treated with placebo while other surfactants existed. These surfactants had FDA approval and could save their lives (Lurie and Wolfe 2001). This trial would have meant condemning 17 children to preventable deaths (Lurie and Wolfe 2001). In this case, there was a clear double standard criterion: the same laboratory was seeking approval for the drug in a European trial in which the children would not receive placebo but an FDA-approved surfactant.

The highest attainable?

The AZT trials triggered the revision and elaboration of documents such as the Declaration of Helsinki, the CIOMS-WHO Guidelines, a new report of the NBAC of the U.S. The battlefields of the standard of treatment debate were research ethical codes. The revision of the Declaration of Helsinki (WMA 2000) at the end of the 1990s is an example of this. Until then, the 1989 version of Helsinki had adopted "the best proven treatment" as the criterion for the standard of care in research. It endorsed a unique standard to be followed independently of where it was being carried out.

Contrary to that trend, one of the new proposals following the AZT cases was the introduction of standards in research. This initiative was expressed through different formulations. One of the clearest was the new "highest attainable and sustainable" criterion as a standard of care, proposed by Robert Levine (1999) in an article in the *New England Journal of Medicine*. As this bioethicist was also a member of the drafting committee of the Declaration of Helsinki, it was introduced into one of its first drafts.

What does "highest attainable" mean? (part of the following analysis is based on Luna 2001b). In Levine's words:

> The "highest attainable" therapy is the best therapy that one could reasonably provide under the conditions of the trial. The "highest sustainable" therapy refers to the level of therapy that one could reasonably expect to be continued in the host country after the trial had been completed. That is, there should be a reasonable expectation that the provision of the therapy could be sustained with the resources that would be available after the external support provided by the trial sponsors had been discontinued. (Levine 1999)

It is known that poor countries cannot sustain minimum conditions of healthcare. Some countries, for example, allocate less than US$10 per person per year (Mbidde 1998). Mbidde comments that Uganda allocates US$6 per person per year. Hence, the "sustainability" condition lowers the conditions of care and treatment. There really does not seem to be any difference between "the highest attainable" and "standard care", even if that means no care at all. (This seems contradictory, at least with the introduction of the term. The notion of "the highest attainable" originates in the WHO Constitution (WHO 1946) and in the Covenant on Economic, Social and Cultural Rights (UN 1966), where *the person has a "right" to the "highest attainable" health*. The original meaning is *the ideal goal that any country should strive for*; nearly the opposite of what is intended to mean in this context. See Lie 2000.)

Note that the "standard of care" criterion implies providing the current treatment that the country can offer. In several cases this is tantamount to nothing. Even if effective treatments exist, in resource-poor countries no treatments are given because there is no money to provide them. This signifies denying existing therapeutic treatment and letting people suffer or die from preventable diseases. For this reason, the "standard of care" criterion was unanimously rejected. The "highest attainable", this elastic criterion, implies an unacceptably low level of care given the extreme poverty in many countries. This criterion introduced a double standard in research. It established two operational modes depending on the wealth and socioeconomic structure of the country. It meant the risk of the unacceptably low. A first draft of the Declaration of Helsinki was discussed during a WMA meeting in Chile and the "highest attainable and sustainable" criterion was rejected.

Proposing this new criterion in a document like the Declaration of Helsinki implies a policy that should rule *all research being done*. Note that the Declaration of Helsinki is "the" ethical code. It morally binds all researchers and should be abided by research ethics committees when evaluating protocols and sustained as a requirement when publishing an article. Hence, changing the standard of care in such a document would have a profound impact on research. It would imply a new normative criterion for all research.

Arguments given

What is the rationale behind the proposal for a double standard and why is a double-standard proposal so appealing?

A first set of arguments points out the benefits of research *for developing countries*:

- Successful research will bring benefits and progress to that society.
- Obstacles to it may do harm in the medium and long terms.
- Since cheap and extended research will most probably offer faster results, it will in the end save more lives than research done without it. It will surely sacrifice some lives (it will let some die – for example, the case of clinical research on AIDS – it will let others go on with their illness and the handicaps it may produce) but, it will save more lives because it will find beneficial results which will be available to them.
- Maintaining a higher standard (the best proven therapy) will be more expensive. It will slow down research. It will effectively protect only those on the research protocols, just a sample compared to the thousands who might be saved or cured with the implementation of the newly tested drugs or therapies.

This kind of reasoning emphasizes the positive consequences of having a double standard – more research and faster results will be available and this will benefit these poor societies.

1. One problem this argument has to face is uncertainty and human fallibility, which is a feature of human deliberation and, in this particular case, is reinforced because of the nature of the research itself. There are no certainties in the results that might be obtained. Although this is common to all research work, it is a problem when more than minimal risks are imposed on persons. However, we have to concede that this is not a knockdown argument. It affects all research endeavors.
2. The weakest aspect of the argument is the assumption of benefit being produced by the relatively *immediate availability of the tested drug or therapy*. The double standard argument *rests* on the availability assumption.

The possibility of private access is almost nil given the extreme scarcity in many developing countries. But, availability can be proposed by previous agreements between researchers, sponsors, and the host country, or by reducing the price of the drugs in order for the government to buy them and provide them. However, it has long been evident that in a significant number of situations, the availability of the research products has not been realised.

Reconsidering the argument, if the drugs or therapies are not available, the numbers do not add up. The argument depends on two factors: *good clinical results* obtained through research and *effective access to the drugs or therapies*. Still, this not only depends on the scientific endeavor but on economic and political variables that are quite difficult to meet (see del Rio 1998; Schüklenk 1998; Tomas 1998 about the problems of infected pregnant women obtaining AZT in the case of trials in sub-Saharan Africa). If any one of these factors fail, benefits will not be provided to such communities.

Finally, let us consider the broader picture: Why should we think that lowering the standards of research will benefit developing countries? The infamous 10/90 gap shows an opposite trend: the existence of a deep imbalance in global research funding. Less than 10 per cent of the US$50–60 billion spent on health research per year is devoted to diseases that account for 90 per cent of the global disease burden. (The report reveals serious imbalances in global funding – see the editorial from the *Lancet* 2000; Vol. 355: 1706.)

Hence, if the research is of no special benefit to these countries, and instead will benefit humanity or wealthier countries that can access the new drugs and therapies, why are we burdening these already suffering populations with a lower standard treatment? Is it not preferable to provide *the same treatment for all, for the benefit of all peoples*?

A second rationale that is used excessively to justify a double standard – which implies even less than the previous argument – is the no harm argument. It does not consider the *benefit of countries or communities*, but focuses on the possible impact on the *individual subject*. An appalling example can be shown in relation to the above Surfaxin case. Robert Temple of the USFDA clearly expressed such an argument when he stated: "If they did the trial, half of the people would get surfactant and better perinatal care, and the other half would get better perinatal care. It seems to me that all the people of the trial would have been better off" (cited in Stah 2002). It would have been "rational" to "choose" to participate. Hence, for Temple, the offer is "fair." There is nothing wrong with gambling with the life or death of a newborn. The fact that the death of the newborns could easily be prevented by giving the already marketed surfactant is not relevant in Temple's estimation. Taking advantage of a desperate situation is not considered in the analysis, and the possibility of exploitation does not fit into the picture.

Finally, along a different line of argument, a third rationale defending the double standard argues for ethical imperialism. This last strategy does not consider benefits or harms but the self-determination of peoples. Refusing double standards will lead to ethical imperialism, as everything will be constrained by the high standards of the industrialized countries. The argument then points out that different countries or regions solve these problems differently. They argue that host communities themselves should decide what constitutes fair standards for research participation.

This may be true, but it is also true that many countries are not strong enough to oppose research or to negotiate better conditions for their research subjects.

Unfortunately, not all resource poor countries have the power and organization of Brazil or India. Tiny Bolivia or Zimbabwe do not appear to have the same power to negotiate. This argument relies on an idealization of the bargaining process.

Even if the previous arguments are refutable, a valid argument might still stand against a unique standard. It signals that the higher standard of treatment may be too stringent in some cases. It may create insurmountable barriers to important research, especially the one designed *for the benefit* of that community.

To this last objection we can answer that other mechanisms exist besides accepting a double standard that implies a set policy on different patterns of treatment. If we want to allow for a degree of flexibility only in exceptional cases, we can do so through existing mechanisms. For instance, the ethics committee could accept a trial that is of *fundamental and vital importance for the community or region* when no other design is viable. There might be community and expert consultation in the region. It could be evaluated by an international organization in addition to the regular ethical review. In such cases, research of vital importance to that particular community or country, which would not be feasible according to a unique standard, would be made possible. This exception model, which should clearly contain proposed prior agreements that would make the successful fruit of research available, would provide rescue treatment for the research subject, not to mention all the necessary provisions to minimize risks to participants and ensure their well-being.

The difference with the double standard model is that it does not adhere to an established policy for all research, but is flexible only for exceptional and justified cases; those that are of fundamental and vital importance to that community or region, and where successful results would become available to that community or region.

Assumptions and idealizations

Note that the above arguments defending double standards rely on the "autonomy" of the research subject or on the self-determination of the communities, possible benefits (positive consequences), and no harm. However, do these analyses suffice? Can we exhaust this discussion by signaling only pragmatic arguments? I think that at this point we should ask what the defense of a double standard implies and why the polemic regarding double standards is an ethical issue. One of the reasons is the close ties with possible exploitation, the chance of an inadequate protection of research subjects, as well as social justice concerns. Hence, if we consider the pro-double standard arguments, we can associate them, as Alex London rightly points out when discussing justice in international research, with a minimalist view of justice: justice as mutual advantage (London 2005). London is considering the case of post-trial obligations but I believe his analysis can easily be used for the double standard rationale. As London says:

> The minimalist position derives the requirements of justice from the accepted pillars of contemporary bioethics, and of research ethics in particular. A just research initiative is one that faithfully adheres to the standard values of nonmaleficence, beneficence, and respect for autonomy. … any research initiative that satisfies the conditions of

nonmaleficence, beneficence, and respect for autonomy is permissible because it offers fair terms of cooperation to the host community. (London 2005)

They leave room for host communities to bargain for the best terms of cooperation … (London 2005).

According to this minimalist view, double standards are ethical.

The pragmatic arguments presented in the previous section seem to be void of theoretical content. They appear to describe mere facts. However, as London shows, some philosophical assumptions underlie them. I think such assumptions operate at two levels: the societal, or community, and the individual.

At the societal level, they imply an anemic view of justice, as London pointed out. They rebuff any commitment to a substantive theory of justice. They only require procedures such as the approval by the community and/or the local research ethics committee. What is more, they do not commit themselves to basic conditions for such procedures to be acceptable. They naturalize the extreme and desperate situation of such communities as the baseline. Furthermore, they do not recognize the influence this baseline condition may have in the bargaining process. They force people to expose themselves in order to achieve or protect such basic goods as health or life. This fact seems to put the research subject in an unfair position or, as Ballantyne (2004) has argued, in a situation of exploitation: a mutually advantageous exploitation. This means that research (or any transaction) can be simultaneously mutually beneficial and yet also *unfair*.

In what follows, I will focus on the individual assumption operating in the "mainstream model." The individual level also presupposes a reductive and idealized view of the research subject. It reduces her to a perfect contractor and centers the ethics of research on the informed consent process. Contractors follow the pattern of businessmen striking a bargain. As long as the contract process is fair, contractors are entitled only to what they bargained for.

Can this be a fitting model? Is this conceptual scheme acceptable in the cases of English or Swedish research subjects, who can access a universal system of healthcare and who voluntarily enter a research program? In the situation of "therapeutic research," the proposal seems fair (the conclusion of this analysis will be different in the case of non-therapeutic research. In this second case, there seems to be more similarities to contractors). However, even in this case, consider the dependence of the illness or condition of the research subjects on the research product, that is, the number of therapeutic options on which to decide. If they have an ample supply of therapies, they are in a better position to choose than if they have no therapeutic alternative whatsoever. They may have the "best proven care" or they may try a new, possibly better, therapy. They can calculate risks and benefits and then decide. This might represent this position if we do not consider, amongst other variables, the severity of certain fatal illnesses and the stressful situation an ill person may be experiencing.

Regardless of the accuracy of this view of the Swedish or English research subject, this situation does not definitively reflect that of a person living in extreme poverty, without the possibility of accessing minimal healthcare. How can she bargain? This is her only chance of adequate or, at least, some treatment ("Health for all" was one of the goals of international society for the year 2000. It has not been accomplished and seems to be vanishing, even as an ideal), which in some cases may be vital. Note that these are not ideal or hypothetical contracts. These are contracts carried out in the real world. They depend on the negotiating power of each person involved and do not necessarily imply fair contracts. Onora O'Neill (1996) points out the importance and possibility of renegotiating and refusing, in order to see if consent is not just a mere formality.

It is not clear, then, whether there is a possibility to bargain in these cases, where the options are, on the one hand, death or illness, and, on the other, the hope of some treatment, even if the latter is suboptimal. *Nonetheless, it may be rational to accept any condition.* The point is that rationality is not enough; *it is not fair.*

Should we endorse the image of the research subject as one of victim? I take some of these ideas from Swazey and Glantz (1982). They present four views of research subjects: as contractors, victims, heroes, and gift-givers. They were considering injuries and the viability of compensation. We are discussing a previous step here – whether we have to give adequate treatment in order to prevent a known injury. This proposal does not seem to work accurately, either. Nowadays, research subjects cannot be used without their consent, this would be clearly unethical. However, this seems a narrow view of the concept of "victim." Being a victim might not be a matter of absent consent only. Being harmed or treated unjustly because of the unfortunate situation of having been born into extreme poverty also influences the concept of victim. People are not responsible for their social situation at birth and the "social lottery" can generate victims. There are several theories of justice that try to avoid these "circumstances," "social lottery" consequences (see Rawls 1971; Sen 1979; Cohen 1993; Dworkin 2000). In this model we have to be aware that the initial situation, prior to informed consent, is one of injustice, one where victims are also found.

Hence, even if either model does not seem to be completely accurate at conceptualizing the research subject's situation, there might be something appealing in both characterizations; as victim and as contractor. This is why I believe they should not be dismissed. What we can say is that, as a possible contractor, her autonomy and consent should be sought. And, as a possible victim, in addition to the adequacy of informed consent, she should be protected from unfair situations. We have to acknowledge both aspects of the situation. We cannot reduce the research subject to a rational contractor.

These analyses lead us back to broader issues, such as the background conditions where research is conducted, and unavoidably leads us to social justice. Therefore, we should return to a societal analysis and consider the situation of the community involved and how its socioeconomic situation impacts on the research.

Even if research ethics has ignored justice issues until recently, justice is an important aspect of any serious bioethical proposal. There are many challenges around it; but because of the difficulties of the issues, this does not indicate that we should ignore them. Mere procedural mechanisms or reducing ethics to informed consent and assuming that research subjects are perfect contractors suggest that we are avoiding the real problem. The social, economic, and cultural context of the research is fundamental. The situation of the Swedish or the Bolivian research subjects is so different that it should be acknowledged and evaluated. Considerations about justice and the possibility of exploitation are vital and point in the right direction (this is the line of authors like London 2005; Pogge 2003, 2005). A serious account of justice, redistribution, and the obligations of pharmaceuticals cannot be avoided.

Conclusion

What have we learned so far? The first issue has to do with the scope that the modification of standards would imply. The double standard as a criterion is broader than the scope that appeared to guide the initial reflections. It began by targeting AIDS but quickly pervaded all research. It has affected not only standards of treatment, but also the placebo debate. If it had been introduced into ethical codes like the Declaration of Helsinki, it would have implied a "universal policy" regulating all research.

A second issue is related to the assumptions double standards imply. Slowing down research cannot be presented as a trump card. Not harming is not enough. Costs were frequently overestimated in the most common arguments presented in this discussion. But, even if costs are an important factor in research, they cannot mandate ethics. Modifying the standards of treatment in research or introducing double standards is not merely a pragmatic decision. It is not value-free. It implies an ideal and reductive view of the research subject and the process of informed consent, and the research endeavor as a whole. Research ethics should deal with the real world and not with idealized agents or processes.

References

Angell, M. 1997. The Ethics of Clinical Research in the Third World. *New England Journal of Medicine* 337: 847–849.

Ballantyne, A. 2004. HIV International Clinical Research: Exploitation and Risk. Paper presented at the IAB Congress, November, Sydney, Australia (unpublished).

Cohen, G.A. 1993. Equality of What? On Welfare Goods and Capabilities. In *La calidad de vida*, (*The Quality of Life*), edited by M. Nusbaum and A. Sen, 27–53, Mexico: Fondo de Cultura Económica.

del Rio, C. 1998. Is Ethical Research Feasible in Developed and Developing Countries? *Bioethics* 12: 328–330.

Dworkin, R. 2000. *Sovereign Virtue*. Cambridge, MA: Harvard University Press.

Levine, R. 1999. The Need to Revise the Declaration of Helsinki. *New England Journal of Medicine* 341: 531–534.

Lie R. K. 2000. Justice and International Research. In *Biomedical Research Ethics: Updating International Guidelines. A Consultation,* edited by R. Levine and S. Gorowitz, 27–40. Geneva: CIOMS.

London, A. J. 2005. Justice and the Human Development Approach to International Research. *Hastings Center Report* 35: 24–37.

Luna, F. 2001a. *Ensayos de Bioética. Reflexiones desde el Sur.* México: Fontamara Ediciones.

——. 2001b. Is "Best Proven" a Useless Criterion? *Bioethics* 15: 273–288.

Lurie, P. and S. Wolfe. 1997. Unethical Trial Interventions to Reduce Perinatal Transmission of the Human Immunodefiency Virus in Developing Countries. *New England Journal of Medicine*, 337: 853–856.

——. 2001. Letter to Secretary Thompson, U.S. Department of Health and Human Services. *Public Citizen*, 22 February. Available at: http://www.citizen.org/publications/release.cfm?ID=6761&secID=1656&catID=126 [Accessed January 23, 2006].

Mbidde, E. 1998. Bioethics and Local Circumstances. *Science* 279: 155.

O'Neill, O. 1996, Justicia, sexo y fronteras internacionales. In *La calidad de vida* (*The Quality of Life*), edited by M. Nusbaum and A. Sen, 393–419, Mexico: Fondo de Cultura Económica.

Pogge, T. W. 2003. Probando Drogas para Países Ricos en Poblaciones Pobres de Países en Desarrollo. *Revista Perspectivas Bioéticas* 8, no.15: 11–43.

——. 2005. World Poverty and Human Rights. *Ethics and International Affairs* 19: 1–7.

Rawls, J. A. 1971. *Theory of Justice*. Cambridge, MA: Harvard University Press.

Schüklenk, U. 1998. Unethical Perinatal HIV Transmission Trials Establish Bad Precedent. *Bioethics* 12: 312–319.

Sen, A. 1979. *Equality of What?* The Tanner Lecture on Human Values. Lecture delivered at Stanford University, May 22. Salt Lake City, UT. University of Utah. Available at: http://www.tannerlectures.utah.edu/lectures/sen80.pdf [Accessed January 23, 2006].

Stah, S. 2002. Globalizing Clinical Research. *The Nation*, July 1.

Swazey, J. P. and L. Glantz. 1982. A Social Perspective on Compensation for Injured Research Subjects. In President's Commission for the Study of Ethical Problems in Medicine and Biomedical and Behavioral Research. *Compensating for Research Injuries* 2: 3–18.

Tomas, J. 1998. Ethical Challenges of HIV Clinical Trials in Developing Countries. *Bioethics* 12: 325–326.

United Nations. 1966. International Covenant on Economic, Social and Cultural Rights. New York: UN.

Varmus, H. and D. Satcher. 1997. Ethical Complexities of Conducting Research in the Third World. *New England Journal of Medicine* 337: 1003–1005.

World Health Organization (WHO). 1946. Constitution of the World health Organization. Geneva: WHO.

World Medical Association (WMA). 1964. *Declaration of Helsinki*. Ferney-Voltaire Cedex: WMA.

——. [1964] 2000. *Declaration of Helsinki*. As amended by the WMA 52nd General Assembly, Edinburgh, Scotland, 2000. Ferney-Voltaire Cedex: WMA.

Part VI

Political activism and treatment access

21 Medicines for all? Commitment and compromise in the fight for Canada's law on compulsory licensing for export

Richard Elliott

The WTO TRIPS Agreement requires all WTO member countries to adopt certain minimum standards for protecting private IPR, including with respect to pharmaceutical inventions (WTO 1994). Those rules create temporary monopolies over patented pharmaceuticals, meaning the patent holder can charge high(er) prices, a matter of particular concern in developing countries facing HIV/AIDS and other health problems along with widespread poverty and few resources to spend on expensive patented drugs.

Nonetheless, TRIPS (Article 31) also permits "compulsory licensing" – that is, authorizing someone other than the patent holder to use, make, sell, or import a patented product without the patent holder's consent. In exchange, the recipient of the compulsory license must generally pay "adequate remuneration" to the patent holder (to be defined under a WTO member's own laws). By introducing competition from generic manufacturers, compulsory licensing is one policy tool that can bring down prices. A declaration unanimously adopted by WTO members at their Fourth Ministerial Conference in Doha, Qatar in November 2001 reaffirmed that "[e]ach Member has the right to grant compulsory licences and the freedom to determine the grounds upon which such licences are granted" (WTO 2001, paragraph 5(b)). (It should be noted that, contrary to popular misconception and regularly inaccurate media reports, TRIPS does not limit WTO members to using compulsory licensing only in the event of public health "emergencies" or "crises.")

However, the "Doha Declaration" also recognized that countries "with insufficient or no manufacturing capacities in the pharmaceutical sector could face difficulties in making effective use of compulsory licensing under the TRIPS Agreement" (WTO 2001, paragraph 6). TRIPS Article 31(f) says that ordinarily compulsory licensing may only be used "predominantly" for the purpose of supplying the domestic market of the country where the license is issued. (This restriction does not apply where a compulsory license is issued to remedy a practice that a court or administrative process has found to be "anti-competitive" (WTO 1994, Article 31(k)). This limits the use of compulsory licensing to produce generic pharmaceuticals for export. This restriction on exporters means that countries lacking sufficient pharmaceutical manufacturing capacity, and hence with little or no ability to authorize domestic production of generics, find it difficult to effectively use compulsory licensing to address their population's health needs through importation. WTO members committed to finding "an expeditious solution" to this problem.

On August 30, 2003, after protracted, divisive negotiations, the WTO GC unanimously adopted a decision waiving, on an interim basis, the provision in TRIPS Article 31(f) that says compulsory licensing may only be used "predominantly" to supply the domestic market (WTO 2003). In November 2003, Canada became the first country to introduce legislation implementing the WTO decision; that law passed Parliament in May 2004 and came into force in May 2005. The legislation allows generic drug manufacturers to obtain compulsory licenses on pharmaceutical products still under patent in Canada for the purpose of producing lower-cost, equivalent products for export to eligible countries.

Canadian civil society groups, organized loosely under the aegis of GTAG, not only provided the impetus for the bill but were crucial to securing important amendments before it was enacted in its final form. In some respects, the legislation sets a number of positive precedents. But the government's unprincipled willingness to compromise its initiative to placate the multinational patented pharmaceutical industry means that the legislation falls short of being a model worth simply replicating elsewhere. Rather, activists and organizations working for access to medicines should appreciate both its merits and flaws. To that end, this paper provides an overview of civil society's campaigning for the legislation and assesses the final outcome.

Steps toward implementing the WTO Decision in Canada: Bill C-56

Canadian activists had been lobbying the government on the issue of TRIPS and access to medicines since early 2001. (For more detailed information, including copies of many of the Canadian NGO documents cited here, see the webpage of CHLN at http://www.aidslaw.ca/Maincontent/issues/cts/patent-amend.htm.) Shortly after the WTO GC's Decision in August 2003 on compulsory licensing of pharmaceuticals for export, Canadian activists redoubled their efforts. In mid-September 2003, after discussions with the CHLN, Stephen Lewis, the UN Special Envoy on HIV/AIDS in Africa, former Canadian ambassador to the UN and a highly respected figure with a long history in Canadian public life, publicly urged the government to amend the Patent Act immediately (CBC 2003). An opinion piece in the leading national newspaper by the CHLN declared 'there are no excuses left" and called for an amendment (Elliott 2003). Four national NGOs reiterated the request in a letter to the MoI (CHLN et al. 2003).

Shortly thereafter, the government responded by announcing that it would amend Canadian patent law to implement the WTO Decision (Fagan, Scoffield, and Chase 2003; Scoffield and Chase 2003). Officials from four federal government departments were tasked with drafting the legislation. On November 6, 2003, as one of the last acts of the administration of outgoing PM Jean Chrétien, the government introduced Bill C-56 (PoC 2003) in the HoC for first reading (DFAIT 2003; Dunfield 2003; NDP 2003).

As anticipated, the Bill proposed amendments to the Patent Act; it also included some related amendments to the Food and Drug Act.

Activists welcomed the fact that Bill C-56 did not contain a restricted list of diseases or health conditions for which compulsory licensing may be used to obtain pharmaceuticals, and did not limit the use of compulsory licenses to supplying countries facing an emergency or other circumstance of extreme urgency. Previous reports had revealed the government's original intention to incorporate such restrictions, a move that GTAG members had condemned as a bad faith step back from the consensus reflected in the WTO Decision (CHLN et al. 2003). In addition, they welcomed the fact that Bill C-56 specified a low royalty rate of "two percent of the value of the pharmaceutical products exported under the authorisation"(PoC 2003, section 21.08), reflecting the ultimate objective of making it possible for generic manufacturers, likely to be operating on small profit margins on contracts with developing countries, to supply products that are priced very cheaply.

However, the Bill failed to implement the full flexibility in patent rules that had been agreed at the WTO and included unnecessary privileges to patent-holding pharmaceutical companies undermining the entire initiative. Activists labeled the most egregious of these the "right of first refusal" – a provision that would have allowed the company with the patent on a medicine to block any compulsory license issuing to a generic producer by scooping the contract it had negotiated with a developing country purchaser, as long as the patent-holding company was willing to match the terms negotiated in that contract.

Activists were focused on persuading the government to fix the Bill, to avoid setting a poor "TRIPS-plus" precedent. The next day (November 7, 2003) was to be the last sitting day before the end of the parliamentary session, in anticipation of the election of a new leader of the governing LP, who would also become the new PM. The LP had secured agreement from the three opposition parties that they would support quick passage of the Bill through all three readings before the session ended the next day, rather than following the usual process of allowing committee hearings into the Bill before third and final reading. However, GTAG member groups decided to oppose immediate passage of the Bill for which they had been campaigning, given its serious flaws, and to lobby instead for the Bill to pass through its second reading only, and then to be sent to a parliamentary committee for public hearings. This would buy time for further campaigning. Furthermore, because the government had imposed confidentiality agreements on previous consultations, it would create the first real public forum for making the case for the necessary amendments.

The opposition NDP decided to trust activists' assessment both of the flaws in the Bill and that the risk of losing the entire Bill was worth running. They noted that they would withdraw their party's consent to quick passage if this were to prove necessary, even if this meant being unfairly (and implausibly) portrayed by other parties as unsympathetic to poor patients in the developing world. Activists lobbied senior Liberal advisors as well late into the night on November 6, 2003. Ultimately, the Liberal government announced in parliament the next day that it had decided to send the Bill to committee (Chase 2003; CHLN 2003).

Subsequently, representatives from MSF and the CHLN met with senior advisors and Paul Martin, the incoming PM, to discuss concerns with the legislation as drafted. When outgoing PM Jean Chrétien prorogued parliament on November 12, 2003, Bill C-56 died on the order paper. NGOs undertook further advocacy efforts – street action, media work and lobbying – in conjunction with the LP national convention confirming Martin's election as new party leader and PM. Shortly thereafter, the media reported that Martin planned to reintroduce the bill in the next session of Parliament in early 2004 and that he acknowledged "shortcomings" in Bill C-56 as tabled (Rubec 2003).

Resuming the fight: Bill C-9

The GTAG coalition resumed its advocacy efforts, intent on ensuring the Bill would be amended once reintroduced (CHLN 2004b; CHLN et al. 2004). NGO advocates met again with government officials for further discussions on the Bill, and the CHLN met with the office of the PM and of most of the ministers whose departments were involved. (The office of the MoI, the department with lead responsibility, did not respond to requests for a meeting.) On February 12, 2004, the text of what had previously been Bill C-56 was reintroduced in the HoC, now renumbered as Bill C-9 (PoC 2004a) and with the unusual name of the Jean Chrétien Pledge to Africa Act, in reference to the previous PM whose government had initially introduced the Bill. By way of parliamentary motion, the Bill was reinstated at the stage of hearings before the SCIST.

The CHLN prepared an information package on the Bill, including a brief highlighting four key flaws and proposed amendments, which was distributed to all MPs shortly before Committee hearings began. (For the transcript of hearings and deliberations of the Committee, see the entry Patent Act and Food and Drugs Act (amdt.) (Bill C-9) in the index of the Committee's proceedings at www.parl.gc.ca/InfoComDoc/37/3/INST/ Meetings/Evidence/INSTin-E.htm.) The CHLN (2004c) also submitted an extensive series of written briefs to the Committee, complete with proposed statutory language for amendments. GTAG member groups met with many of the Committee members individually, issued numerous media releases and hosted several press conferences in their campaign to secure improvements to the legislation.

Activists focused their criticism, and their advocacy efforts, principally on four key flaws in the draft Bill:

- the "right of first refusal" provisions permitting anti-competitive action by patent holders to block licenses for generic manufacturers;
- the limited list of pharmaceutical products subject to compulsory licensing for export;
- the exclusion of developing countries that do not belong to the WTO from the list of eligible importing countries; and
- the provision specifying that only contracts between a Canadian generic supplier and a government or "agent of government" could provide the basis for a compulsory license, thereby excluding NGOs as potential purchasers of lower-cost generics from Canadian manufacturers.

Some activists also flagged their concern with the proposed requirement to have any generic drug produced under compulsory license for export undergo the same regulatory review as a drug to be marketed in Canada. While not objecting in principle to ensuring proper review of any product to be exported, advocates were concerned this could make the legislation unworkable for producing generic "fixed-dose combination" products for which there were no existing originator products already approved in Canada against which the generic product could be compared as bio-equivalent (CHLN 2004c).

At the initial round of hearings, some committee members were surprised at the depth of opposition from NGOs to provisions such as the right of first refusal. The CHLN and some other NGOs stated to the committee that if this provision were not removed from the Bill, they would prefer to see the Bill die rather than set such a poor "TRIPS-plus" precedent for implementation of the WTO Decision. In response to advocates' highly public condemnation of this provision, the patented pharmaceutical industry association (Rx&D) proposed to the SC with a so-called "alternative" – namely, a provision guaranteeing to the patent holder what it called "an equal opportunity to supply" (Rx&D 2004). Under this proposal, a Canadian generic producer would be required to notify the Canadian patent holder of any negotiations with a developing country purchaser to supply a pharmaceutical product. The patent holder would be given the opportunity at that time to bid on the contract.

After further discussion with GTAG allies, the CHLN filed a supplementary submission with the Committee rejecting the supposed alternative, arguing that the Rx&D proposal would effectively preserve the "right of first refusal" and simply amount to an "early opportunity to block competition" from generic producers. Upon being notified of a generic producer's negotiations with a potential purchaser, the patent holder would have a strong incentive to undercut any price offered by the generic manufacturer in order to maintain its market monopoly. With no contract, there would be no basis on which a generic producer could seek a license to permit manufacture and export. As with the right of first refusal, such a provision would quickly frustrate the ultimate objective of enabling sustained competitive pressure on medicine prices from generic producers and was "TRIPS-plus," unnecessarily creating "rights" for patent holders exceeding WTO requirements.

On March 18, 2004, government officials held a final round of separate consultations with "stakeholders," at which civil society advocates reiterated their opposition to the Rx&D "alternative" or similar provisions. On April 20, 2004, the SC began its clause-by-clause analysis of the draft Bill and debate on all parties' proposed amendments. The SC's debates lasted two days. On April 28, 2004, the Bill, as amended by the SC, was reported back to the HoC for a final debate and vote. Civil society organizations issued press statements indicating their mixed reactions to the Bill, with particular concern expressed about the government's insistence on preserving the schedule of pharmaceutical products (CCIC et al. 2004; MSF 2004). On May 4, 2004, Bill C-9 was put to its third and final reading and adopted unanimously by the entire House and sent to the Senate. On May 13, 2004, it received its third reading and unanimous approval in the Senate. On May 14, 2004, it received Royal Assent and thereby passed into law, making Canada the first country to enact such legislation (see PoC 2004b). Regrettably, it was another year to the day before the government proclaimed the law into force. The accompanying regulations became effective two weeks later upon publication in the *Canada Gazette* on June 1, 2005.

Assessment of the Canadian legislation on compulsory licensing for export

Several aspects of the legislation, as finally enacted, warrant comment here for the benefit of treatment access activists in other jurisdictions.

Right of first refusal removed

Most importantly, the government removed the "right of first refusal" and refrained from substituting any alternative along the lines suggested by the brand-name industry, thereby avoiding setting a poor "TRIPS-plus" precedent for the implementation of the August 2003 WTO Decision. This represented a significant victory for civil society activists.

Negotiating voluntary licenses and defining the royalty payable

TRIPS Article 31(b) says that in the ordinary course of events, before a compulsory license may be issued, the party seeking authorization to use the patented invention must first make efforts to obtain authorization from the patent holder "on reasonable commercial terms and conditions" (WTO 1994). It is only if such efforts are unsuccessful "within a reasonable period of time" (WTO 1994) that a compulsory license may then issue, with "adequate remuneration" (WTO 1994) to be payable to the patent holder according to TRIPS Article 31(h). The lack of certainty as to the meaning of these terms presents a major barrier to the likely use of compulsory licensing legislation in the litigious pharmaceutical sector. However, the Canadian legislation sets a positive precedent by bringing some welcome clarity to these vague conditions.

First, the government amended the Bill to state that, if a generic manufacturer and a patent holder are unable to agree on the terms of a voluntary license within 30 days, the CoP "shall" issue a compulsory license. This provides a clear statutory definition of the term "reasonable period of time" (WTO 1994).

Second, the legislation also effectively clarifies what constitute "reasonable terms and conditions" (WTO 1994) for a voluntary license, as well as the "adequate remuneration" (WTO 1994) that must be paid to the patent holder upon compulsory licensing. The government removed from the draft Bill the flat 2 per cent royalty rate originally specified. Instead, the final legislation simply states that the calculation of the royalty in any given case would be determined by a formula to be set out in accompanying regulations. As government officials promised before the SC, those regulations, eventually promulgated in 2005, set out a formula that consists of a sliding scale, based on the ranking of the importing country on the UNDP's HDI, with an effective cap, in the case of the country with the highest HDI ranking, of 4 per cent of the value of the contract (see Use of Patented Products for International Humanitarian Purposes Regulations,

SOR 2005/143, *Canada Gazette* (Part II), Vol. 139 (No. 11), June 1, 2005. The cap of 4 per cent was suggested by the CHALN in its first submission to the SC. This had been the standard royalty rate payable in Canada during the 1960s and 1970s when compulsory licensing was a regular feature of the Canadian pharmaceutical market under earlier versions of the Patent Act). The majority of developing and "LDCs" rank well below this on the HDI, meaning significantly lower royalties. There is no discretion on the part of the CoP to vary the royalty.

If, after 30 days, the generic manufacturer and patentee have been unable to agree on the terms of a voluntary license, the CoP "shall" issue a compulsory license, assuming the other preconditions in the legislation have been satisfied. There is no discretion vested in the Commissioner and no basis on which a patent holder can delay the process by alleging, either before the Commissioner or a court, that insufficient negotiating time had passed or that the terms last offered by the generic manufacturer are unreasonable. Similarly, by virtue clearly specifying the royalty payable upon the issuance of a compulsory license, the Canadian legislation de facto defines what constitutes a "reasonable" royalty in the event of negotiating a voluntary license.

Limited list of pharmaceutical products

Regrettably, the government chose to maintain a limited list of products subject to compulsory licensing. As a result, the final law includes an initial list of 56 products to which it applies, derived principally from the WHO MLEM. In response to criticism, the government added to the list all ARVs used to treat HIV/AIDS that were approved at the time for sale in Canada (with one exception).

NGOs remain(ed) critical of the list, however, because it represents a step back from the international consensus achieved with the WTO Decision. In the negotiations leading up to the Decision, several developed countries proposed to limit its scope to addressing specific diseases or just applying to specific pharmaceutical products. These efforts were roundly condemned by civil society activists as unethical and unsound health policy, and firmly rejected by developing countries. Ultimately, all WTO members agreed that there would be no such limitations.

NGOs also argued that the bureaucratic process for expanding the list – including an advisory committee, recommendations of two ministers, and a Cabinet decision – would create further delay, as well as multiple opportunities for patent-holding pharmaceutical companies to lobby successfully to block any addition. In the days leading up to the final vote on the Bill in the HoC, these concerns proved well founded.

Members of the SC had discussed adding several medicines to the list annexed to the Bill. The opposition NDP proposed the addition of moxifloxacin and clarithromycin, both of which are used to treat pneumonia. Clarithromycin is also used prophylactically to prevent mycobacterium avium complex, a life-threatening infection in people living with HIV/AIDS. The government opposed adding these medicines, arguing that they were not on the WHO model list of essential medicines and claiming incorrectly that these medicines are not needed to treat HIV/AIDS, TB, or malaria. (For the transcript of HoC debates over Bill C-9, see the entry, Patent Act and Food and Drugs Act (amdt.) in the index to Hansard, the record of chamber business, at http://www.parl. gc.ca/37/3/parlbus/chambus/house/debates/indexE/p-37-3_-e.htm.) This was in direct contradiction to repeated assurances by government officials that incorporating a list of specific products in the Bill would not be used to limit its scope solely to products on the WHO list or medicines for treating HIV/AIDS, TB, or malaria.

Regulatory review of FDC medicines

Canadian law generally does not require that a drug manufactured solely for export undergo the regulatory approval process that applies to drugs marketed in Canada. With Bill C-9, however, the government imposed such a review on any pharmaceutical product manufactured for export under compulsory license. NGOs supported the need to ensure quality, safety, and efficacy of any product. But they were concerned that such a requirement would end up blocking use of the law to export many FDC medicines, which combine more than one drug into a single dose. FDCs of ARVs simplify HIV/AIDS treatment regimens, and are recognized by the WHO as being critical to scaling up access to ARVs in the developing world. In the case of generic medicines being reviewed for Canadian marketing approval, standard practice is to base approval on data showing bio-equivalence of the generic product to an already approved brand-name product. But in the case of FDCs for treating HIV/AIDS, there were, at the time of Bill C-9's passage, only three such products on the Canadian market, none of which is amongst those recommended by the WHO as "first-line" therapy for use in developing country settings.

Eligible importing countries

The original draft Bill defined, as countries eligible to import from Canadian generic producers, all developing countries belonging to the WTO and all countries, whether belonging to the WTO or not, recognized by the UN as LDCs. While the government, in response to activists' criticism, ultimately amended the Bill to include non-WTO, non-LDC developing countries, its approach leaves something to be desired. As a result of the government's amendments, a developing country that is neither a WTO member nor an LDC can procure cheaper medicines from Canadian generic producers *only* if it satisfies the following preconditions, which are more restrictive than those facing WTO members:

- it is eligible for "official development assistance" according to the OECD (in the result, five countries have no option to procure medicines from a Canadian generic supplier while those products remain under patent in Canada: Russian Federation, Ukraine, Belarus, Bahamas, and Libya);
- it declares a "national emergency or other circumstances of extreme urgency"; and,
- it specifies the name and quantity of a specific product needed for dealing with that emergency.

In addition, if a non-WTO developing country or LDC is added in future to the relevant schedule of countries set out in Bill C-9, it must state that it undertakes to adopt the measures set out in the WTO Decision (paragraph 4) aimed at preventing diversion of the product. Furthermore, the would-be importing country must agree the product "will not be used for commercial purposes" (CHLN 2004a: 5). Under the legislation, if the country allows such use, then it may be struck off the list as a country eligible to import medicines from a Canadian generic supplier. The term "commercial purposes" is undefined in the legislation, but is clearly aimed at limiting the possibility of commercial competition in the importing country's marketplace, hindering the longer-term benefit that competition could have in reducing medicine prices. It raises questions about the distribution of imported generics via the private sector (e.g., pharmacists) in the importing country.

NGO procurement from Canadian generic manufacturers

Responding to civil society criticisms that NGOs could not and should not be considered to fall under the category of "agent[s] of government," the government amended the Bill to authorize generic producers to sell directly to NGO purchasers for use in eligible countries. However, the Committee accepted a motion attaching the additional, unnecessary qualification that the NGO must demonstrate it has obtained "permission" from the government of the country to import the product from the Canadian generic producer.

Two-year limit on compulsory licenses

The government refused to remove the provision in the Bill stating that a compulsory license may be issued for a maximum period of two years. (The compulsory license may not authorize production of the pharmaceutical product in any quantity greater than that set out in the underlying contract between the generic manufacturer and its customer. If the full quantity has not been shipped during the two-year period of the license, the generic manufacturer may apply for the license to be "renewed" (i.e., extended) once for up to another two years. This is merely an administrative provision that does not allow for any increase in the actual quantity of product produced and exported under the license. Only one renewal of a license is permitted.) After two years, the generic company must apply for a new compulsory license, based on a new contract, if it wants to continue legally to manufacture a patented product for export. To impose this cap limits the ability of a generic producer to enter into secure supply contracts with developing country purchasers for a longer period, even though negotiating longer-term contracts would provide a greater incentive for generic manufacturers to scale up production of a particular product and would permit greater economies of scale.

Price and profit caps, an invitation to litigation

As a result of lobbying by Rx&D, the government introduced a series of new provisions inviting patent holders to harass generic manufacturers that obtain compulsory licenses under the legislation. The patent holder may allege in court that the generic producer's contract with a purchaser is "commercial" in nature, and seek a court order terminating the compulsory license or ordering a royalty higher than what is specified in the regulations. In its application to the court, the patent holder must allege that the generic producer is charging an average price for the product that exceeds 25 per cent of the patent holder's average price in Canada. In its defense, the generic producer must demonstrate through an audit that its average price is less than 15 per cent above its direct manufacturing costs, in which case no court order will issue.

Ostensibly, this provision in Bill C-9 seeks to control prices charged by generic producers to developing country purchasers. Yet that objective could have been achieved through other means (e.g., through conditions imposed in the grant of the compulsory license itself). Instead, the government's chosen approach invites vexatious litigation by patent holders, is potentially a disincentive to generic producers using the system, and is not required under TRIPS or the WTO Decision. It should be avoided by other countries enacting similar legislation. Giving further privileges to patent holders to litigate so as to interfere with the production and export of generic pharmaceuticals to developing countries is a poor way to follow through on stated commitments to increasing access to medicines for all.

W(h)ither the commitment?

The legislation represents a victory of sorts for civil society advocates, without whom the law would not have existed at all and whose efforts led to important improvements to the draft Bill. But taken in its entirety, the Bill does not fully reflect the "flexibilities" allowed under TRIPS and the WTO Decision. A parliamentary review of the law is to occur in 2007, two years after its proclamation into force; that review may provide an occasion for further amendments.

How the law will play out in practice remains to be seen. Since the passage of Bill C-9 in May 2004, some NGOs have engaged generic manufacturers in Canada to determine which companies might be willing to produce which products (if any) at a price that could be attractive and feasible for developing countries or NGOs providing treatment in such countries. At the time of writing (late 2005), activists were cautiously optimistic that at least one application, for an important triple fixed-dose combination ARV, would proceed in 2006.

The extent to which the legislation is used will depend on the political pressure that civil society can bring to bear on the generic producers to test the legislation, on the brand-name pharmaceutical industry if it attempts to frustrate use of the law, and on the government to be proactive in drawing this option for securing lower-cost medicines to the attention of developing country governments and other potential beneficiaries. It will also depend on whether the global marketplace provides sufficient financial incentives for generic manufacturers, commercial enterprises whose ultimate objective is profit, to navigate the requirements of this imperfect law. It remains to be seen whether the government's repeatedly stated commitment to ensuring access to medicines for the world's poor will ultimately be undone by the compromises it introduced into legislation. The true measure of success will be whether this law, in concert with other initiatives, ever translates into real medicines in the hands of real people.

References

Canada's Research-Based Pharmaceutical Companies (Rx&D). 2004. Providing Affordable Medicines to Patients in the Developing World. *Submission to the House of Commons Standing Committee on Industry, Science and Technology*, February 26.

Canadian Broadcasting Corporation (CBC). 2003. National News [report by M. Brosnahan], *CBC Radio*, September 13.

Canadian Council for International Cooperation (CCIC), Canadian HIV/AIDS Legal Network (CHLN), World Vision, The United Church of Canada (UCC), and Canadian Labour Congress (CLC). 2004. Canada Proceeds with Bill C-9 on Cheaper Medicine Exports: NGOs Say Initiative is Important, and Urge Other Countries Avoid the Flaws in the Canadian Model. *Press Release*, April 28.

Canadian HIV/AIDS Legal Network (CHLN). 2003. Update: Amendment to Canada's Patent Act to Authorise Export of Generic Pharmaceuticals. *Fact Sheet*, November 10.

——. 2004a. *Proposed Government Amendments to Bill C-9, An Act to amend the Patent Act and the Food and Drugs Act*. Toronto, ON: CHALN.

——. 2004b. Affordable Generic Medicines for Developing Countries: Promise in Speech from Throne, but True Commitment Requires Effective Bill. *Press Release*, February 2.

——. 2004c. *Global Access to Medicines: Will Canada Meet the Challenge? First Submission to the Standing Committee on Industry, Science and Technology Regarding Bill C-9*. Toronto, ON: CHLN.

Canadian HIV/AIDS Legal Network (CHLN), Médecins Sans Frontières (MSF) Canada, Oxfam Canada, Canadian Labour Congress and Interagency Coalition on AIDS and Development. 2003. Amending the Patent Act to Authorize Exports of Generic Medicines to Developing Countries: An Open Letter to the Government of Canada. *Open Letter*, October 16.

Canadian HIV/AIDS Legal Network (CHLN), Médecins Sans Frontières (MSF) Canada, Oxfam Canada and Interagency Coalition on AIDS and Development. 2003. Letter to Hon. Allan Rock, Minister of Industry. *Letter*, September 23.

Canadian HIV/AIDS Legal Network (CHLN), Médecins Sans Frontières (MSF) Canada, Oxfam Canada, and Interagency Coalition on AIDS and Development, Conseil Canadien de Surveillance et d'Accès aux Traitements (CCSAT), Canadian Treatment Action Council (CTAC), and Canadian Council for International Cooperation (CCIC). 2004. Joint Letter to Prime Minister and Key Ministers. *Letter*, January 13.

Chase, S. 2003. Poor-Nation Drug Bill: Liberals Table it, but Admit it's Not Ready. *Globe and Mail*, November 7.

Department of Foreign Affairs and International Trade (DFAIT). 2003. Government of Canada Introduces Legislative Changes to Enable Export of Much-Needed, Lower-Cost Pharmaceutical Products to Developing Countries. *News Release*, November 6.

Dunfield, A. 2003. PM Introduces Bill to Allow Cheaper Drugs for Poor Nations. *Globe and Mail*, November 6.

Elliott, R. 2003. Canada Can Carry Much More. *Globe and Mail*, September 23.

Fagan, D., H. Schoffield, and S. Chase. 2003. Ottawa Scrambles to Meet AIDS-Drug Pledge: A Key Initiative Shapes up in Public View and the Government Rushes to Keep Up. *Globe and Mail*, October 4.

Médecins Sans Frontières (MSF) Canada. 2004. Bill C-9: How Canada Failed the International Community, *Press Release*, April 28.

New Democratic Party of Canada (NDP). 2003. New Democrats Committed to the Lewis Legacy, *Press Release*, November 6, 2003.

Parliament of Canada (PoC). 2003. *Bill C-56. An Act to Amend the Patent Act and the Food and Drugs Act*. Available at: http://www.parl.gc.ca/37/2/parlbus/chambus/house/bills/government/C-56/C-56_1/C-56_cover-E.html [Accessed January 18, 2006].

——. 2004a. *Bill C-9. An Act to Amend the Patent Act and the Food and Drugs Act.* Available at: http://www.parl.gc.ca/37/3/parlbus/chambus/house/bills/government/C-9/C-9_1/C-9_cover-E.html [Accessed January 18, 2006].

——. 2004b. *An Act to Amend the Patent Act and the Food and Drugs Act (The Jean Chrétien Pledge to Africa).* Available at: http://www.parl.gc.ca/37/3/parlbus/chambus/house/bills/government/C-9/C-9_4/C-9_cover-E.html [Accessed January 18, 2006].

Rubec, S. 2003. Martin Set to Trim Fat, PM-to-be Lays Out Agenda in Election-Style Book. *Toronto Sun*, November 16.

Scoffield, H. and S. Chase. 2003. Ottawa Heeds Call on AIDS. *Globe and Mail*, September 26.

World Trade Organization (WTO). 1994. *Agreement on Trade-Related Aspects of Intelectual Property Rights.* Geneva: WTO. Available at: http://www.wto.org/english/docs_e/legal_e/27-trips.pdf [Accessed January 15, 2006].

——. 2001. *Declaration on the TRIPS Agreement and Public Health. Ministerial Conference.* Ministerial Conference. Fourth Session. Doha, November 9–14. Geneva: WTO. Available at: http://www.wto.org/english/thewto_e/minist_e/min01_e/mindecl_trips_e.pdf [Accessed January 16, 2006].

——. 2003. Implementation of Paragraph 6 of the Doha Declaration on the TRIPS Agreement and Public Health: Decision of the General Council of August 30. Geneva: WTO.

22 Placing access to essential medicines on the human rights agenda

Brook K. Baker

This chapter starts with an overview of multilateral efforts to codify a basic human right of universal and affordable access to essential medicines, focusing on access to HIV/AIDS medicines. After introducing the basic framework, the chapter also presents the most trenchant critiques that argue that a so-called right to health is ill-suited to accomplish its desired goals in a real world of material deprivation and social exclusion.

The chapter continues with a description of the ongoing, human rights-based campaign for access to affordable ARV medicines led by an international coalition of treatment activists. Although much has been accomplished – ARV drug prices have plummeted to a penny on the dollar, funding for procurement has multiplied tenfold, and anti-retroviral medicines are finally beginning to reach a measurable portion of the poor – much more remains undone. Thus, the campaign continues, organized around the bedrock principle that the human right to health, to essential medicines, and to life itself trumps intellectual property rights, trading regimes, and donor practices that otherwise perpetuate a system of pharmaceutical apartheid.

The chapter ends by demonstrating the interrelatedness of the formal rights regime and activism on the ground that they are mutually constituitive. The conclusion also outlines a way forward for human rights and for the access to medicine campaign.

The mainstream human rights, access to essential medicines paradigm

The international community has recognized a basic human right to health since the formation of the United Nations (UN 1946) and more particularly since the adoption of the Universal Declaration of Human Rights shortly thereafter (UN 1948). A human right to health is fundamental to being human; it is universal; and it supports both positive and negative claims of entitlement, defining what governments (and non-state actors) can do, cannot do, and should do (IFRC&RCS 1999). In a moral sense, a human right to health is considered to be absolute, immutable, and inalienable, meaning that it has priority over completing claims. However, the formal human right to health is also subject to qualifications and limitations, and its enforceability is less than robust. Nonetheless, the formal content of the human right to health has been clarified through a long series of UN documents, many of which have focused broadly on addressing the social determinants of health and illness while others have focused more narrowly on the right to medical care and the right of access to essential medicines, particularly those used to treat HIV/AIDS.

The Universal Declaration of Human Rights (UDHR), the founding document of the international human rights regime, recognizes that every person has a right to a standard of living adequate for his or her health and medical care, the right to share in scientific achievements, and the right to a social and international order in which the Declaration's rights can be fully realized (UN 1948). Although the realization of these rights is clearly underachieved and although many nations ignore their stated obligations to actualize a human right to health, the UDHR has achieved the formal status of customary international law. Therefore, it is at least theoretically, legally binding on *all* nations (Cann 2004). The skeletal framework of a human right to health has been further specified in a long series of international law instruments (UN 1975a and 1975b; 1993; 1999; 2001a and 2001b; WHO 1978), culminating in the International Covenant on Economic, Social and Cultural Rights (ICESCR), which represents an attempt to transform declared, paper rights into more binding treaty obligations (UN 1966).

In Article 12, the ICESCR guarantees the right of everyone worldwide to "the highest attainable standard of physical and mental health" and requires state parties to take steps necessary for "the prevention, treatment and control of epidemic, endemic, occupational and other diseases" and to provide "conditions which would assure to all medical services and medical attention in the case of sickness." This skeletal right to health provision received further clarification when the Committee on Economic, Social and Cultural Rights (CESCR) issued General Comment No. 14 (UNCESCR 2000) addressing the right to the highest attainable standard of health and concluding that it extends not only access to timely and appropriate healthcare but also to underlying determinants of health, including adequate food, housing, water, and sanitation, safe working conditions and environments, and access to health-related education and information (UNCESCR 2000). Although the General Comment recognizes that the precise nature of facilities, goods, and services delivered will vary according to numerous factors, including levels of development, there is a basic obligation to ensure *availability* of adequate health facilities, a trained and adequately resourced corps of healthcare workers, and a sufficient quantity of essential medicines (UNCESCR 2000). Using these resources, governments must actually deliver basic health services, treat prevalent disease, and supply affordable medicines (UNCESCR 2000). Healthcare delivery, facilities, goods, and services have to be *accessible* to all without discrimination, especially for the most vulnerable and marginalized, and it must be *affordable* as well, so that poorer households are not disproportionately burdened by health expenses (UNCESCR 2000). In sum, universal access to essential medicines is a core, non-derogable duty of all member states, as is preventing, treating, and controlling epidemic and endemic diseases (UNCESCR 2000).

The General Comment also clarifies that member states have clear obligations to take "deliberate, concrete and targeted" steps "toward the full realization of the right to health" by *respecting*, *protecting* and *fulfilling* the right to health (UNCESCR 2000).

The obligation to *respect* requires States to refrain from interfering directly or indirectly with the enjoyment of the right to health. The obligation to *protect* requires States to take measures that prevent third parties from interfering with art. 12 guarantees. Finally, the obligation to *fulfil* requires States to adopt appropriate legislative, administrative, budgetary, judicial, promotional and other measures toward the full realization of the right to health. (UNCESCR 2000)

In the trade arena, the failure of a state to account for "the right to health when entering into bilateral or multilateral agreements with other States, international organizations and other entities, such as multilateral corporations" is an express violation of the obligation to respect the right to health (UNCESCR 2000). Likewise, a state's failure to regulate corporations to prevent them from violating others' right to health and its failure to protect consumers from practices detrimental to health is a breach of the obligation to protect the right to health (UNCESCR 2000).

Noting that "gross inequality" in health status between people in developed and developing countries is "politically, socially and economically unacceptable," the General Comment emphasizes the obligations of powerful states "to take steps, individually and through international assistance and cooperation, especially economic and technical, towards the full realization of … the right to health" (UNCESCR 2000). Not only are rich countries obliged to share their technical and financial resources, they are also obligated "to respect the right to health in other countries" by preventing third parties, including private sector multinational corporations, from violating the right of health in other countries and by ensuring that their own international agreements do not adversely impact on the right to health (UNCESCR 2000).

Although the General Comment primarily addresses the obligations of sovereign states, it also emphasizes that both the private business sector and international financial institutions have responsibilities regarding the realization of the right to health (UNCESCR 2000). Thus, a violation of the right to health, in this context, can occur through the direct action of private entities insufficiently regulated by a state and through the lending and structural adjustment policies of the World Bank and IMF (Monshipouri 2001).

Further crystallizing the right to treatment, UNAIDS and the UN High Commissioner for Human Rights held a consultation on HIV/AIDS and Human Rights and issued a revised Guideline 6: Access to prevention, treatment, care, and support declaring that:

States should enact legislation to provide for … safe and effective medication at an affordable price. States should also take measures necessary to ensure for all persons, on a sustained and equal basis, the availability and accessibility of quality goods, services and information for HIV/AIDS … treatment…, including antiretroviral and other safe and effective medicines, diagnostics and related technologies for preventive, curative and palliative care of HIV/AIDS and related opportunistic infections and conditions. (UNCHR/UNAIDS 2003)

In its Recommendations for Implementation of revised Guideline 6, UNAIDS and the CHR specified that states should implement and support policies allowing purchase of cheaper generic medicines, diagnostics, and related technologies (UNCHR/UNAIDS 2003), and that they should amend domestic legislation to incorporate, to the fullest extent possible, any safeguards and TRIPS-compliant flexibilities for promoting and ensuring access to medicines (UNCHR/UNAIDS 2003). Other states, particularly developed countries, were instructed to avoid taking measures that would undermine access to HIV/AIDS treatment, including medicines, and to ensure that bilateral, regional, and international agreements involving intellectual property issues do not impede access to treatment including anti-retroviral and other medicines (UNCHR 2001; UNCHR/UNAIDS 2003).

The enforceability of these human rights norms is a complicated topic, well beyond the scope of this paper. However, in general terms, the mechanisms for formal, binding enforcement of the right of access to essential medicines within the UN system are quite limited. Only the Security Council can impose sanctions and other coercive measures, though other bodies can pass resolutions denouncing human rights violations. The UN also has powers to promote human rights by setting standards and interpreting norms, by creating awareness, and by strengthening national institutions. In addition, the UN can protect human rights through monitoring, reporting, and complaint procedures.

Criticism of the traditional human rights paradigm

The human rights paradigm, originating within a liberal conception of universal, negative, and pre-existing rights, has not been accepted uncritically either in its countries of origin or in the global South (Alexander, Borgen, and McAnnany 2004). Critics from both the North and the South have noted that traditional rights discourse assumes a nation/state framework and a set of individual and collective relationships that look more or less exactly like liberal democracies. Formal government structures, including a separation of powers and an independent judiciary, the invisibility of economic institutions, and a state of perpetual conflict between an over-reaching bureaucratic state and an autonomous individual are constituent components of the classic human rights paradigm, particularly with respect to the first-generation political and civil rights. Moreover, by constructing a universe based on formal equality, the rights paradigm risks obscuring the ubiquitous experience of inequality and the source of that inequality within the structures of the global economy.

The major critics of rights discourse from the legal academy have emphasized its excessive rigidity, ultimate indeterminacy, and excessive individualism; in addition, they have criticized the anti-democratic effects of rights and the failure of rights discourse to address shared social duties (Sunstein 1995). In the critics' view, rather than acting as "trump cards" that obliterate all competing values, rights are always defeasible, even when their core meaning(s) can be ascertained. More commonly, however, the exact meaning of an alleged right is found to be uncertain. Taking a different tack, Northern critics of rights talk have also complained that rights-talk reflects and reifies individualism at the expense of social solidarity and more complicated forms of human connection. They are joined in this critique by proponents of communitarianism – the middle ground between individual and collective rights and between rights and associated duties (*Rights and the Common Good* 1995). Other critics have noted that the selective enforcement of particularized human rights, including access to medicines, risks increasing inequality and human deprivation in other more neglected arenas, especially in a era of increasing global inequality and pervasive resource deprivation.

Echoing and even transcending these often esoteric, postmodernist critiques, Eastern and Southern intellectuals have also challenged the universality, indeed the cultural relativism and specificity of human rights discourse (Lewis 2000). Critics from Asia argue that they have a different structure of rights within which higher priority is given to a citizen's duties and to collective responsibility than to individual claims against the group (Van Ness 1999). Africa too is said to privilege communal needs and duties over the solipsistic rights of the individual, a moral ethic captured in the word *ubuntu*. Third World critics have also pointed to the deployment of human rights discourse by states, like the United States, and institutions, like the IMF and the World Bank, that are most identified with erecting and implementing the political, economic, and cultural structures that have perpetuated inequality and prolonged human misery.

The human rights campaign for access to anti-retroviral drugs

Communities, NGOs, and activists have fought for recognition of human rights, including the right to health, since the inception of the UN system first by contributing to the drafting of the UDHR (Korey 1998) and later by demanding essential primary healthcare at Alma-Ata, and increased reproductive healthcare services at the International Conference on Population and Development, 1994, and the Fourth World Conference on Women, 1995. The AIDS movement has most catalyzed global debate and global progress in realizing the right to health, most recently by focusing on issues of global justice, including access to essential AIDS medicines, particularly in developing countries (Siplon 2002).

Activists claim that there is a human rights-based right of access to pharmaceutical products, including generic versions of patented medicines, which has provoked a conflicting claim of right by developed countries and by the research-based pharmaceutical industry. Thus, rich country claimants in the global North seek to protect and extend the intellectual property rights of the proprietary pharmaceutical companies that research, develop, and market patented medicines claiming that supracompetitive profits are necessary to secure research and development into the next generation of life-saving medicines. In the other camp, people living with and affected by HIV/AIDS and their allies claim that it makes no moral sense whatsoever to deny cheaper medicines to poor people simply to guarantee monopoly-priced sales to the few rich people who can afford drugs.

The pro-intellectual property rights team has worked for 20 or more years to strengthen national and international intellectual property regimes (Drahos and Braithwaite 2003), especially via the WTO Agreement on the Trade Related Aspects of Intellectual Property Rights (TRIPS) (WTO 1994). Even after consolidating a worldwide baseline of intellectual property protections via the TRIPS Agreement, the U.S. has continued to threaten developing countries with trade sanctions when they propose using TRIPS-compliant means, such as parallel importation and compulsory licensing, to access more affordable medicines ('t Hoen 2002). In response, developing countries and their NGO supporters pushed health issues back onto the multilateral trading agenda, resulting in the Doha Declaration on the TRIPS Agreement and Public Health that clarified that TRIPS should be interpreted "in a manner supportive of WTO members' right to protect the public health and, in particular, to promote *access to medicines for all*" (WTO 2001).

Despite the Doha Declaration, for almost two years the U.S. unilaterally blocked efforts to address the problem facing the majority of developing countries that lack sufficient domestic capacity to manufacture medicines efficiently (Baker 2004). Likewise, despite trade authorization legislation, 19 U.S.C. § 3802(b)(4)(C), and Executive Order 13155 (2000), USTR continued to seek TRIPS-plus intellectual property protections in trade negotiations with developing countries, including Central American and Andean nations, Thailand, and Southern Africa Customs Union countries (Baker 2004). There is a strong argument that these efforts violate international human rights norms that require countries to protect rights to health in their bilateral and plurilateral trade agreements (Canadian Legal Network 2001).

Human rights activists in the global South and their international allies champion the human right to health and the corollary right of access to life-saving medicines for diseases that are decimating their poverty-stricken populations (Csete 2002). This pragmatic human rights strategy promotes robust generic production by a sufficient number of manufacturers at meaningful economies of scale so that medicines of assured quality can be accessed at the lowest possible cost. Activists have also promoted in establishing funding structures such as the GFATM and have agitated for greatly enhanced bilateral and multilateral donations so that there are reservoirs of purchasing power sufficient to provoke generic entry and to finance purchase of large quantities of medicine.

In the U.S., the ongoing campaign (Health GAP) includes demands against the federal government for greatly increased bilateral and multilateral aid for comprehensive HIV/AIDS prevention, care, and treatment in developing countries. It includes demands for debt cancellation and for an end to ruinous trade policies that privilege pharmaceutical profits over human life. Activist campaigns also target pharmaceutical companies demanding unconditional, deeply discounted prices, non-exclusive voluntary licenses for generic producers, and relaxation of patent rights in developing countries. Even more recently, the campaign has made successful demands on multinational corporations that they provide treatment for their workers and workers' dependents overseas. Finally, to enable future treatment scale-up, activists are turning their attention to capacity-building in the healthcare sector, demanding that public sector spending limits imposed by the World Bank and IMF be lifted, that odious debt burdens be eliminated, and that donor countries invest resources for training, recruiting, and retaining a greatly expanded corps of healthcare workers.

Activists in the South are even more intensely engaged in similar campaigns, often with a broader base including labor, religious leaders, and organized civil society.

The Treatment Action Campaign (TAC) in South Africa is the best example, having successfully completed a four-year campaign for prevention of mother-to-child transmission of HIV, culminating in the Constitutional Court's 2002 condemnation of the government's hesitant, pilot-project approach (*Minister of Health v. TAC* 2002). More recently in 2003, TAC launched a civil disobedience campaign against the ANC government for its failure to adopt a national treatment plan resulting six months later in the announcement of South Africa's Operational Plan for Comprehensive Treatment and Care for HIV and AIDS (South African Cabinet 2003). In addition, TAC has joined the government in beating back a lawsuit by the pharmaceutical industry, demanded price reductions from Pfizer on Diflucan, and filed a successful claim before the South African Competition Commission challenging excessive pricing by the patent drug industry. Supplementing its local focus, TAC has urged TRIPS reform and has helped forge a continental coalition, the Pan-African HIV/AIDS Treatment Access Movement, which has become increasingly active in demanding an end to governmental lethargy in African countries, many of which have failed to mount credible responses to the escalating crisis.

One by one, activists have attacked structural and legal barriers to access and have imagined and then advocated for new institutional arrangements and new practices that might make treatment a reality. By promoting generic competition, they have helped push the cost of anti-retroviral drugs in developing countries from US$10,000–12,000 per year in 2000 to as little as US$132 per year in 2005. By demanding greatly increased bilateral and multilateral spending, they have raised global resources for AIDS tenfold, from US$800 million in 1999 to nearly US$8.1 billion in 2005. Although they have relied on a rhetoric of a human right to health, to access to medicines, and indeed to life itself, they have implemented that rhetoric with sophisticated campaigns aimed at removing structural impediments and leveraging resources to actually increase access to medicines on the ground.

Conclusion: the emergence of an alternative "communal" right to health practice

The most compelling reformulation and expansion of the human rights paradigm, one most relevant to the right to health and the right of access to affordable, essential medicines, focuses on communal rights for collective needs and on the interconnectedness between all social, economic, and cultural rights issues (Felice 1996). This communal perspective should not result in losing focus on the corrective effects of mainstream "individual" human rights in restraining the stern disciplines of public health, population-based measures. But responding to urgent global health crises takes more than thinking of the immediate needs of individuals to core medical interventions when they are most vulnerable to illness or most dependent on treatment and care. Achieving lasting gains in health will require thinking about global structures and about the gradients of injustice, deprivation, and oppression that produce poor health for entire populations. It will require bold thinking and concrete action to dismantle systemic barriers to good health and to healthcare services, including the sustainable delivery of affordable medicines of good quality. And it will require implementation of new mechanisms for marshaling the material, social, cultural, and intra-psychic ingredients that produce healthy healthcare systems, healthy people, and healthy societies.

The field of public health offers important insights for formulating a communal human rights perspective appropriate to expanding treatment access and access to medicines because it "begins with the population perspective and with the effort to measure and improve the health status of populations" (New Ethics for the Public's Health 1999). The theoretical groundwork for integrating public health and more traditional human rights perspectives was set in Jonathan Mann's outline of the "triangular" relationship between human rights and public health:

- health policies and programs are recognized as having a major potential impact on human rights, both beneficial and adverse;
- human rights violations lead directly and indirectly to adverse health impacts; and
- the promotion of human rights and the practice of public health are complementary and indivisible approaches to protecting and advancing the well-being of people (London 2002).

As valuable as Mann's contributions were, the public health/right to health project now requires us to reduce collective vulnerability, to increase communal public health knowledge, to mobilize material, technical, and psychosocial resources on a massive scale, and to provide pragmatic and proportionate support to communities over-burdened with disease and on the verge of collapse.

Even so, human rights-based campaigns may ultimately prove inadequate in provoking radical transformation of the fundamental structures of the global economy. If the global South cannot invest in the infrastructures of social life – in schools, clinics, and roads – then capacity to provide medical care and to deliver medicines will be nonexistent. Even eliminating structural adjustment programs that restrict spending in the healthcare sector will not help if poor, "undeveloping" countries lack essential resources to invest in social infrastructure. Likewise, human rights discourse and a demand for medicines are inadequate to engender proper utilization of medicines by individuals in the absence of public health education and community-based treatment literacy, in the absence of support structures for long-term, high-level treatment adherence, and in the absence of cultural changes that reduce communal- and self-stigmatization and discrimination.

Can human rights discourse, even further refined, help us demand dramatically higher commodity prices? Can it help us build sustainable and sustaining rural economies? Can it increase material rewards and security for all of the feminized labor in homework and childrearing? Can it reduce migration to unhealthy mega-city shanty towns, and so on and on? If not, progress on human health and on access to medicines will be glacial at best.

References

Alexander, J., R. Borgen, and K. McAnnany. 2004. The Role of the Powerful in the Global AIDS Pandemic: The Collective Right to HIV/AIDS Treatment (unpublished) (on file with the author).

Baker, B. 2004. Arthritic Flexibilities for Accessing Medicines: Analysis of WTO Action Regarding Paragraph 6 of the Doha Declaration on the TRIPS Agreement and Public Health. *Indiana International & Comparative Law Review* 14: 613–715.

Canadian Legal Network. 2001. Canadian HIV/AIDS Legal Network and AIDS Law Project South Africa. *TRIPS and Rights: International Human Rights Law, Access to Medicines and the Interpretation of the WTO Agreement on Trade-Related Aspects of Intellectual Property.* Available at: http://www.aidslaw.ca/Maincontent/issues/cts/briefs/TRIPS-human-rights-briefPDF.pdf [Accessed June 20, 2005].

Cann, Jr., W. 2004. On the Relationship between Intellectual Property Rights and the Need of Less-Developed Countries for Access to Pharmaceuticals: Creating a Legal Duty to Supply under a Theory of Progressive Global Consitutionalism. *Pennsylvania Journal of International Law* 15: 755–944.

Csete, J. 2002. Several for the Price of One: Right to AIDS Treatment as a Link to Other Human Rights. *Connecticut Journal of International Law* 17: 263–272.

Drahos, P. and J. Braithwaite. 2003. *Information Feudalism: Who Owns the Knowledge Economy.* New York, W. W. Norton.

Felice, W. 1996. *Taking Suffering Seriously: The Importance of Collective Human Rights.* New York: State University of New York Press.

The Final Act of the Conference on Security and Cooperation in Europe. 1975. 14 I.L.M. 1292.

Health GAP (Global Access Project). Available at: http://hhealthgap.org/index.html [Accessed June 20, 2005].

International Federation of Red Cross and Red Crescent Societies and François-Xavier Bagnoud Center for Health and Human Rights (IFRC&RCS). 1999. Human Rights: An Introduction. In *Health and Human Rights: A Reader*, edited by Jonathan Mann et al., 21–28. New York: Routledge.

Korey, W. 1998. *NGOs and the Universal Declaration of Human Rights: A Curious Grapevine.* New York, St. Martin's Press.

Lewis, H. 2000. Reflections on "BlackCrit Theory": Human Rights. *Villanova Law Review* 45: 1075–1090.

London, L. 2002. Human Rights and Public Health: Dichotomies or Synergies in Developing Countries? *Journal of Law, Medicine & Ethics* 30: 677–688.

Minister of Health v. Treatment Action Campaign, 10 B.C.L.R. 1033 (S.A. Con. Ct. 2002).

Monshipouri, M. 2001. Promoting Universal Human Rights: Dilemmas of Integrating Developing Countries. *Yale Human Rights & Development Law Journal* 4: 25–61.

New Ethics for the Public's Health. 1999. Edited by D. Beauchamp and B. Steinbock. New York: Oxford University Press.

Rights and the Common Good: The Communitarian Perspective. 1995. Edited by Amitai Etzioni. New York: St. Martin's Press.

Siplon, P. 2002. *AIDS and the Policy Struggle in the United States.* Washington, DC: Georgetown University Press.

South African Cabinet. 2003. *Statement for Treatment Plan for HIV and AIDS.*

Sunstein, C. 1995. Rights and Their Critics. *Notre Dame Law Review* 70: 727–768.

't Hoen, E. 2002. TRIPS, Pharmaceutical Patents, and Access to Essential Medicines: A Long Way from Seattle to Doha. *Chicago Journal of International Law* 3: 27–46.

Treatment Action Campaign (TAC). Available at: http://www.tac.org.za/ [Accessed June 20, 2005].

United Nations (UN). 1946. *Charter of the United Nations.* 26 June 1945, TS 67.

——. 1948. *Universal Declaration of Human Rights.* G.A. Res. 217A (III), UN GAOR, Res. 71, UN Doc. A/810.

——. 1966. *International Covenant on Economic, Social and Cultural Rights*. G.A. Res. 2200 (XXI), UN Doc. A/6316.

——. 1975a. *The Declaration of the Rights of Disabled Persons*. U.N. GAOR 3447 (XXX).

——. 1975b. *Declaration on the Use of Scientific and Technological Progress in the Interests of Peace and for the benefit of Mankind*, U.N. GAOR 3384 (XXX).

United Nations World Conference on Human Rights (UN). 1993. *Vienna Declaration and Programme of Action*. U.N. Doc. A/CONF 157/23.

United Nations (UN). 1999. *Declaration on the Right and Responsibility of Individuals, Groups and Organs of Society to Promote and Protect Universally Recognized Human Rights and Fundamental Freedoms*, U.N. GAOR No. 53/144. U.N. Doc. A/RES/53/144.

——. 2001a. *Declaration of Commitment on HIV/AIDS ("Global Crisis – Global Action")*. Res. A/RES/S-26/2.

——. 2001b. *United Nations Millennium Declaration*. Res. A/RES/55/2.

United Nations Committee on Economic, Social, and Cultural Rights (UNCESCR). 2000. *General Comment 14: The right to the highest attainable standard of health (Art. 12)*. U.N. Doc. E/C.12/2000/4.

United Nations Commission on Human Rights, Sub-Commission on the Promotion and Protection of Human Rights, Economic and Social Council (UNCHR). 2001. *The impact of the Agreement of Trade-Related Aspects of Intellectual Property Rights on Human Rights: Report of the High Commissioner*. E/CN.4/Sub.2/2001/13.

United Nations Office of the United Nations High Commissioner for Human Rights and Joint United Nations Programme on HIV/AIDS (UNCHR/UNAIDS). 2003. *HIV/AIDS and Human Rights: International Guidelines: Third International Consultation on HIV/AIDS and Human Rights (revised Guideline 6)*. UNAIDS/02.49E.

Van Ness, P. 1999. *In Debating Human Rights: Critical Essays from the United States and Asia*. Edited by Peter Van Ness. New York: Routledge.

World Health Organization (WHO). 1978. *Declaration of Alma-Ata, International Conference on Primary Health Care*. Available at: http://www.who.int/hpr/NPH/docs/declaration_almaata.pdf [Accessed June 20, 2005].

World Trade Organization (WTO). 1994. *Agreement on Trade-Related Aspects of Intellectual Property Rights (TRIPS), Marrakesh Agreement Establishing the World Trade Organization, Annex 1C, Art. 8(1). 33 I.L.M. 81*.

——. 2001. *Declaration on the TRIPS Agreement and Public Health*. WT/MIN(01)/DEC/2.

Yamin, A. 2003. Not Just a Tragedy: Access to Medications as a Right under International Law. *Boston University International Law Journal* 21: 325–371.

Part VII

National responsibilities

Part VII

Social reproduction today

23 Producing affordable medicines in South Africa

João L. Carapinha

At a press conference in Pretoria on January 15, 2004 the Minister of Health of SA, Dr Manto Tshabalala-Msimang, informed the media of the contents of the draft Regulations Relating to a Transparent Pricing System for Medicines and Related Substances made in terms of the Medicines and Related Substances Control Amendment Act 90 of 1997. The MoH stated:

> These regulations are a major development in our effort to ensure that South Africans have access to affordable, good quality medicine. You will recall that when this Act was passed in 1997, it was strongly opposed by pharmaceutical companies. It took these companies almost four years to withdraw their court action in 2001 and finally accept the legitimacy of our efforts and genuineness of our respect for the international trade treaties that we are party to.
> (Tshabalala-Msimang 2004)

This statement was made in an environment when the relationship between the MoH and the multinational pharmaceutical industry was already on tenterhooks. The multinational pharmaceutical industry challenged the MoH in the courts of SA for provisions included in the Medicines and Related Substances Control Act that allowed the minister to parallel import medicines and issue compulsory licenses. Since 2001 the tenuous interaction between the multinational pharmaceutical industry and the government concerning the need to establish a means of providing medicines to the public at affordable prices, has opened other exciting debates that deserve attention in this paper.

The Business Day (a newspaper for the business community in SA. Available at: www. bday.co.za) reported on measures the MoH would use to pave the way for cheaper medicines. Here mention was made of the establishment of a Pricing Committee with a clear mandate to start a transparent pricing system, examining the prices of drugs in other countries, advising the MoH on parallel importation of medicines and sourcing cheaper medicines from outside SA, amongst others (Kahn 2003).

The precursor to the changes initiated by the MoH is contained in the NDP (DoH 1996). In it the health, economic, and national development objectives of SA were discussed. Two policy interventions of direct interest to this paper are first, to reduce the cost of drugs in both the private and public sectors, and second, to support the development of the local pharmaceutical industry and the local production of essential drugs.

Romano Prodi, then PEC, has shed some light on the urgency of making medicines more affordable. On April 28, 2003, he emphasized, during his address to the RTAM, that:

> Increased availability of and access to pharmaceuticals for developing countries population is today a key challenge for the developing countries and for their partners. This is a challenge which entails reducing the gap on the one hand between population needs, and on the other hand supply. It means reconciling needs, demand and supply at affordable prices. Hence, it means adapting, encouraging and it might even mean, sometimes, directing the market in a more socially responsible direction. Whichever of these applies, what is clear is that doing nothing is not an option. (Prodi 2003)

Such statements by leading figures in SA and the European Commission contribute to the perennial debate of making medicines more affordable for patients. Furthermore, Prodi's comment is clearly in support of governments in developing countries intervening in the market to correct market failures.

Competing priorities – the local context

However, government-led initiatives to enable the delivery of affordable medicines is often undermined by competing priorities, limited resources, ever-increasing expenses within the health sector, and increasing mortality and morbidity. For example, medical inflation has persistently run above the overall CPIX (see Table 23.1). Such trends place additional pressure on policymakers to release additional resources to deal with pressing health priorities, e.g., HIV/AIDS, TB, malaria, and diabetes.

Table 23.1: Health component of CPIX vs. CPIX Medical by financial year

	1997/98	1998/99	1999/00	2000/1	2001/2	2002/3
CPIX	7.8	12.3	6.9	7.8	6.6	9.8
CPIX Medical	17.5	12.3	10.2	10.5	10.9	12.1

Source: South African Health Review (2003/04).

Table 23.2: Provincial health spending trends by economic classification

Expenses	2001/2	2002/3	2003/4	2004/5	2005/6	Annual change
Personnel	20614	20402	21226	21556	21810	0.9%
Other current	9128	9888	10002	10801	11073	6.5%

Source: South African Health Review (2003/04).

In addition, provincial hospitals have taken the lion's share of funding from the national health budget and it is projected to decline from 68 per cent to 61 per cent between 1999/2000 and 2005/6 (Blecher and Thomas 2003). But, provincial health spending on medicines (other current expenses) is expected to grow above personnel expenditure (see Table 23.2).

The private sector is not immune to these phenomena observed in the public sector. Medical scheme contributions have increased by 12.4 per cent in real terms (i.e., over and above inflation) in 2001, and 7.1 per cent in 2002 (Blecher and Thomas 2003). Administration fees, managed care services, reinsurance, broker fees and bad debts (non-health expense), and private hospitals costs represent two major cost drivers of private health (Harrison 2003). These increases place additional pressure on the level of disposable income of the privately insured life and also result in a progressive decrease in private health coverage. Of greater concern is that the net operating surplus (including investment income) of medical schemes was R2.5 billion in 2002, an increase of 72 per cent on the previous year, and average medical scheme costs per beneficiary now exceed the total expenditure of government per capita, for all its functions and departments:

> In nominal terms, medical scheme contributions per beneficiary were R6214 per annum in 2002, while total government expenditure on the main budget (including all national and provincial functions and transfers to local government) amounted to R5364 per capita. (Harrison 2003)

Addressing such matters requires firm, government-led interventions to balance competing health priorities, containing increasing healthcare expenses, allocating resources based on sound policies, and improving health status. The introduction of generic medicine policy to improve generic medicine consumption is a strategy available to government. Likewise, deciding to produce pharmaceuticals locally, if conditions are favorable, may present an opportunity to deliver affordable medicines to patients.

The global context

As long ago as August 1976, the Fifth Conference of Heads of State or Government of Non-aligned Countries met in Colombo, Sri Lanka to resolve amongst other matters issues related to the status of the pharmaceutical industry in each member country. Patel (1983a) noted that the Non-Aligned Movement had already in place an "Economic Declaration" calling for further strengthening of economic cooperation amongst developing countries, and that studies were conducted by UNCTAD into major issues in the transfer of technology to the developing countries. At this conference, Resolution 25 was passed, which asserted the need to encourage "the establishment by each developing country of its own pharmaceutical industry as appropriate, beginning with formulation and packaging and building up to more complex production activities" (Peretz 1983).

At an early stage the UNIDO and UNCTAD stated that developing countries could improve their supply of pharmaceuticals by establishing their own pharmaceutical production concerns. In 1980, the First Consultation Meeting on the Pharmaceutical Industry organized by UNIDO in Lisbon, representatives of developing and developed countries, along with representation from the pharmaceutical industry, discussed matters related to the local manufacture of pharmaceuticals. An extract quoted by Peretz from the meeting's transcripts placed on record the industry's "willingness to expand further under mutually fair and acceptable terms, its contribution to industrial growth in the Third World and its sympathy with the general UNIDO objectives of raising the developing countries' share of world industrial output" (Peretz 1983).

The goals of industrialization and providing affordable medicines to patients are not always compatible. Stated during the First Consultation Meeting on the Pharmaceutical Industry was the point that "local manufacture does not necessarily produce cheaper drugs – indeed the reverse is often true, especially after taking into account the heavy capital investment in new plant and equipment" (Peretz 1983). Relatedly, Melrose (1982) emphasized that many countries are not in a position to set up local production mostly because of a lack of skilled administrators and the necessary market information to operate an efficiency purchasing system. Moreover, it was noted that patent laws prevented countries from purchasing generic alternatives or sourcing the necessary technology to produce the drugs themselves.

The Recommendations of the Inter-Agency Task Force on Pharmaceuticals (1979) argued that the formulation of new laws and policies concerning industrial policy are not in themselves a guarantee of success (Patel 1983b). New legislation should be introduced to strengthen domestic technological development, as well as to ensure effective quality control and consumer protection. This requires adequate institutional mechanisms for implementation of any legislation, affecting pharmaceutical procurement, production, and technological development. The harmonization among developing countries of their laws and regulations concerning industrial policy and the establishment of suitable cooperative institutional mechanisms for implementation are important steps toward ensuring smoother development of the pharmaceutical sector.

The UNDP also recognized the importance of "cooperating with the pharmaceutical companies, to provide access to affordable essential drugs in developing countries" (UNDP 2005) when their intention was formalized as one of their targets in the eight MDG. The MDG represents the UNDP's ambitious agenda for reducing poverty and improving lives in an unequal world. The report published by the ILO in 2004, Economic Security for a Better World speaks to this inequality. It highlights differences in basic economic security support, which is a measure of political democracy, civil liberties, government spending on social security, work-related securities and income security. The report made several observations:

- Globalization has not been associated with a dramatic increase in economic growth, as its advocates claimed it would, and indeed has been associated with a slowing of growth in many countries, with the major exceptions of China and India.

- There has been a rapid, and relatively unanalyzed, growth in private regulation of economic activity and policy.
- Social security systems have become less universal, less solidaristic, less protective and more differentiated, contributing to the growth of inequality and economic insecurity. Conditionalities for entitlement to state benefits have been tightened.

Each of the findings of the ILO report points to one overarching concern; that the world's population will be under increasing pressure to remain healthy in an environment with gapping disparities in economic security. Such differences in basic living conditions will test the political will of governments to implement policies to protect the health of its citizens. Consequently, government policy will be closely scrutinized to assess its ability to make medicines more affordable.

The developmental state

Industrial and trade policy has an important role to play in the development of the local pharmaceutical industry. To what extent should government be involved in the formulation and implementation of industrial and trade policy? Over the past two decades the dominant paradigm in economic thinking has been toward a significant diminution of the government's role as an economic player. The neoclassical view opposes the notion of the developmental state and seeks to entrench the dominance of the market as the prime means of addressing inefficiencies, and also asserted the lack of capacity and competence of the developmental state. However, countries such as South Korea and Taiwan have shown how an interventionist government can result in substantial growth rates. Selective intervention of this type is strongly opposed by free marketers. It is argued that the government bureaucracy is ill equipped to make decisions as to the appropriate development path of the economy. However, Wade (1990) held that government intervention was an important factor, but only insofar as it promoted exports and offset market failures. He argued that is was a certain kind of government role in the economy that made for a new and more effective way of putting the institutions of industry together.

Government, together with industry, may select components of industry that show signs of potential growth and are likely to contribute positively to the expansion of the economy, as with the pharmaceutical industry. A more tenable formulation is a synergistic connection between a public system and a mostly private market system, the outputs of each becoming inputs for the other, with the government setting the rules and influencing decision-making in the private sector in line with its views of an appropriate industrial and trade profile for the economy (Wade 1990). With the help of government grants and loans, and the cooperation of the banking sector, large new investments can be made in advanced new production equipment. Should the product be in need of technological innovation, government may subsidize R&D or alternatively fund such initiatives from the fiscus. The government should aim to reorient the structure of industry to allow it to compete effectively in the global economy. That is, government should act in support of industries with actual or potential comparative advantage.

Through policies, government may create competitiveness through rapid productivity increases that result from learning. Supply-side policies are important in shaping the pattern of investment, in changing the industrial structure and in the development of human resources. Another key instrument of industrial policy is the availability of long-term capital on a concessionary basis to targeted sectors. Government may decide what form concessionary finance can take. Apart from trade measures, various forms of subsidy can include cash transfers, R&D funding, tax concessions such as accelerated depreciation allowances, loan guarantees, subsidized credits, capital grants, state procurement policies, and marketing assistance.

The principle of selective support for certain sectors of the economy raises a host of problems. The skewing of incentives to favor certain industries places costs on other less favored sectors and this implies that the government has some vision of the direction of the future development of the economy and that this vision is in some sense appropriate (Black 1993). If one is seeking to create new areas of comparative advantage through government intervention, assistance needs to be targeted at a limited number of sectors and must be based on the principle of reciprocity, with stipulated requirements in performance objectives, productivity gains, export targets, new investment, and employment creation (Black 1993).

There are six neoclassical roles of government (Wade 1990). Government should first, maintain macroeconomic stability; second, provide physical infrastructure especially that which has fixed costs in relation to variable costs; third, to supply public goods; fourth, contribute to the development of institutions for improving the markets for labor, finance and technology; fifth, offset or eliminate price distortions, which arise in cases of demonstrable market failure; and sixth, redistribute income to the poorest in sufficient measure for them to meet basic needs.

Some believe that the government's intervention should be restricted to the provision of non-discriminatory and non-discretionary industrial promotion policies for the set of infant industries (Wade 1990). Furthermore, the views of neoclassicists maintain that the government's role is to plan the physical, social and psychological environment of private agents rather than to plan what these agents are supposed to do. However, Taiwan and South Korea are good case studies to illustrate that governments did intervene more positively to offset distortions caused by policies and those remaining from government failure to change distortion-inducing institutions. Wade (1990) termed it the "governed market." In relation to the newly industrialized countries, the "governed market" is due to a combination of very high levels of productive investment, making for fast transfer of newer techniques into actual production; more investment in certain key industries than would have occurred in the absence of government intervention and exposure of many industries to international competition.

Producing affordable medicines

SA's pharmaceutical manufacturing sector will benefit if it learnt from these experiences and commenced a process of instituting the measures used by newly industrialized countries to turn around their economies. The governments of these countries guided the market by redistributing agricultural land in the early post-war period; controlling the financial system and making private financial capital subordinate to industrial capital; maintaining stability in some of the main economic parameters that affect the viability of long-term investment, especially the exchange rate, the interest rate, and the general price level; modulating the impact of foreign competition in the domestic economy and prioritizing the use of scarce foreign exchange; promoting exports; promoting technology acquisition from multinational companies and building a national technology system.

SA needs to reorient its growth path toward one more in harmony with the redistributive principles of an interventionist government, while at the same time establishing a more stable basis for growth in the pharmaceutical manufacturing sector. Investments should be encouraged and the government should be careful not to crowd out private investment. Wade (1990) quotes Colin Bradford on the matter related to investments and concludes that the possibility of newly industrialized countries' growth and export performance in manufactures has been accelerated by public policies that have lowered the cost of investment goods. These policies could have been in the form of domestic monetary policy affecting interest rates and credit allocations to industrial investors and borrowers or in the form of direct subsidies affecting the rise of domestically produced investment goods. Such monetary and fiscal policies would have the effect of stimulating greater demand and supply of investment goods, which in turn spurs capital accumulation, industrialization and structural change.

To this end, the DTI published a document entitled *Accelerating Growth and Development: The Contribution of an Integrated Manufacturing Strategy*, in April 2002. Therein, it is emphasized that enterprises of all types and sizes will have to become adaptive, innovative, and internationally competitive. In addition, the manufacturing sector must build on a platform of infrastructure and logistics, competitive input prices, skills, technology and innovation, partnerships, efficient regulation and effective government offerings. Consumers must have access to safe, competitively priced quality goods and services in a non-exploitative system that encourages producers to respond to consumer needs, while providing effective recourse mechanisms where abuses do occur. Although the DTI's document speaks in general terms of an industrialization strategy required to turn around the competitiveness of the manufacturing sector, the same principles are applicable to the pharmaceutical manufacturing sector – a critical contributor to the manufacturing sector.

The DBSA and the DTI jointly commissioned a report on the pharmaceutical sector called the Pharmaceutical Investment Analysis. The report identified the components of the pharmaceutical sector, the drivers that influence investment decisions, and aimed to correlate these with those areas that could be both attractive and sustainable with regard to attracting foreign investment to SA. It is worth noting that the report included microeconomic elements in its final analysis – cost of supplies, raw material integration, capacity, technology advancement and intensity, information management, labor and critical skills, productivity, capital and finance strategy, pricing, quality of supply, spatial integration, and many more. For example, one of the findings of the report notes that the large number of mergers and acquisitions in recent times has resulted in the decrease of manufacturing sites maintained by multinational firms. This trend inevitably impacts the demand for specialized skills needed for the manufacturing of pharmaceuticals. In addition, SA has a relative lower level of academic qualification compared to other manufacturing countries, especially in higher levels of management.

Conclusion

The opening remarks in this chapter by the MoH of SA and the PEC is a reminder that ensuring the availability of affordable medicines is an important matter that requires concrete interventions. This chapter has argued for an interventionist government – the developmental state, to intervene in the pharmaceutical manufacturing sector and direct it to producing affordable medicines. Locally and globally there are constraints placed on governments of developing countries to design and implement policy interventions that aim to achieve the production of affordable medicines. What is certain is that adopting a *laissez-faire* approach to policy interventions is inadequate and will inevitably worsen the socioeconomic status of the population. Furthermore, the political will of governments will be tested in their ability to deliver affordable medicines to patients.

References

Black, A. 1993. The Role of the State in Promoting Industrialisation: Selective Intervention, Trade Orientation and Concessionary Industrial Finance. In *State and Markets in Post-Apartheid South Africa,* edited by M. Lipton and C. Simkins, 203–234. Johannesburg: Wits University Press.

Blecher, M. and S. Thomas. 2003. Health Care Financing. In *South African Health Review*, edited by C. Day and A. Ntuli, 269–290. Durban: Health Systems.

Bradshaw, D. and N. Nannan. 2003. Health Status. In *South African Health Review*, edited by C. Day and A. Ntuli, 45–58. Durban: Health Systems Trust.

Department of Health (DoH). 1996. *National Drug Policy*. Pretoria: DoH.

Department of Trade and Industry (DTI). 2002. *Accelerating Growth and Development: The Contribution of an Integrated Manufacturing Strategy*. Pretoria: DTI.

Harrison, S. 2003. Medical Schemes. In *South African Health Review*, edited by C. Day and A. Ntuli, 291–298. Durban: Health Systems Trust.

International Labour Organisation (ILO). 2004. *Economic Security for a Better World*. Geneva: ILO. Available at: http://www.ilo.org/public/english/protection/ses/index.htm [Accessed October 6, 2004].

Kahn, T. 2003. Health Minister Paves Way for Cheaper Medicines in SA. *Business Day*, August 19.

Melrose, D. 1982. *Bitter Pills: Medicines and the Third World Poor*. Oxford: Oxfam.

Patel, S. J. 1983a. Special Resolutions on Pharmaceuticals by the Non-aligned Countries (1976 and 1979). In *Pharmaceuticals and Health in the Third World*, edited by S. J. Patel, 291–292. Oxford: Pergamon Press.

——. 1983b. Recommendations of the Inter-Agency Task Force on Pharmaceuticals (1979). In *Pharmaceuticals and Health in the Third World*, edited by S. J. Patel, 293–296. Oxford: Pergamon Press.

Peretz, S. M. 1983. Pharmaceuticals in the Third World: The Problem from the Suppliers' Point of View. In *Pharmaceuticals and Health in the Third World*, edited by S. J. Patel, 271–279. Oxford: Pergamon Press.

Prodi, R. 2003. Speech at the Round Table of Access to Medicines. Brussels, April 28.

Tshabalala-Msimang, M. 2004. *Pricing of Medicines.* Speech at a Press Conference. Pretoria, South Africa, January 15.

United Nations Development Programme (UNDP). 2005. *Investing in Development: A Practical Plan to Achieve the Millennium Development Goals.* New York: UNDP. Available at: http://www.unmillenniumproject.org/goals/goals02.htm#goal6 [Accessed July 24, 2003].

Wade, R. 1990. *Governing the Market: Economic Theory and the Role of Government in East Asian Industrialisation.* Princeton, NJ: Princeton University Press.

White, E. 1983. Cooperation among National Drug Manufacturers: Asociacion Latinoamericana de Industrias Farmaceuticas (ALIFAR). In *Pharmaceuticals and Health in the Third World,* edited by S. J. Patel, 271–279. Oxford: Pergamon Press.

World Health Professions Alliance (WHPA). 2004. *International Health Professional Poll Puts Heart Disease, Obesity and Cancer as Top Health Problems.* Available at: http://www.whpa.org/pr07_04.htm [Accessed June 9, 2004].

24 National responsibility in the provision of basic medicines

Kinsley Wilson, Laura Esmail, and Jillian Clare Cohen

Governments have the responsibility to ensure access to essential medicines; they are increasingly regarded as a public good, and access to them, a fundamental human right. Essential medicines are not ordinary commodities that can be left subject solely to market forces; they have curative and therapeutic qualities and can control the spread of disease. Furthermore, international law places attendant obligations upon states to ensure that good quality drugs are available physically and economically (UNCESCR 2000).

Despite these obligations, government failures are identified consistently as a major barrier to drug access (Reich 2000; Leach, Paluzzi, and Munderi 2005). Healthcare systems are severely underfunded in many developing countries. Private spending on pharmaceuticals is the principal source (71 per cent) of drug expenditure in low-income countries (WHO 2004a), which has obvious implications for drug access, especially for the poorest of the poor. Inadequate regulatory capacity is widespread, the main problem being the lack of qualified human resources (Ratanawijitrasin and Wondemagegnehu 2002). These weaknesses drain public resources and decrease the effectiveness of already strained healthcare systems.

Corruption in the pharmaceutical sector is particularly a problem in developing countries, as weak institutions and a lack of transparency are common. The World Bank (1994) reports that some developing countries only benefit US$12 for each US$100 that the public sector spends on drugs due to inefficiencies or corruption in the prescription, storage, and use of drugs. This value is disputed, but emphasizes that government pharmaceutical expenditures may not be used effectively. Specific characteristics make the pharmaceutical system prone to corruption; wide information asymmetries exist; economic interests and the size of the pharmaceutical market serve as incentives for fraudulent behavior; poorly defined and documented procedures, inappropriate or skewed incentive structures, and the difficulty of distinguishing inefficiency from corruption. Government responsibility lies in reducing opportunities for corruption through good governance. Leisinger (2004) defines good governance as encompassing transparency, accountability, institutional pluralism, participation, and rule of law. To achieve an efficient pharmaceutical system, a government must apply all five principles forcefully.

The following sections follow the framework developed by Cohen, Cercone, and Macaya (2002) to discuss government responsibilities in facilitating a robust pharmaceutical system and access to essential medicines. The discussion begins with national drug policies, followed by responsibilities in registration, selection, procurement, distribution, and service delivery. The discussion concludes with policy considerations.

National drug policies

The development and dissemination of a national drug policy can facilitate comprehensive, structured and transparent government pharmaceutical decision-making (WHO 2001). Although the evidence on their effectiveness is still inconclusive (Ratanawijitrasin, Soumerai, and Weerasuriya 2001), "piecemeal" approaches to addressing problems in the pharmaceutical sector have been found to leave major issues unresolved (WHO 2001). An NDP should clearly define the country's goals, strategies to achieve them, and the roles and responsibilities of actors involved (WHO 2004a). Policy coordination is crucial to ensure that industrial goals do not undermine public health objectives (WHO 2004a).

By 1999, 108 countries had developed an NDP while 69 had yet to draft an implementation plan (WHO 2004a). Each country should take careful steps to plan and prioritize its implementation in correspondence with national priorities (WHO 2001). Prioritization is often based on balancing the severity of the problem, the likelihood in achieving the objective, and the potential impact possible with existing resources (WHO 2001). In the context of good governance, Cohen, Cercone, and Macaya (2002) suggest that resources should be funneled to the weakest link in the pharmaceutical system, to decrease the likelihood of poor investments.

Policy implementation may require multiple interventions simultaneously to ensure the policy's intended effects and decrease the likelihood of undesirable effects (Ratanawijitrasin, Soumerai, and Weerasuriya 2001). This requires monitoring and evaluation of intermediate policy indicators and communication with relevant stakeholders to reach policy goals. Significant coordination required at the implementation step is difficult to achieve given the layers of bureaucratic agencies usually involved (Ratanawijitrasin, Soumerai, and Weerasuriya 2001). Achieving such coordination is even more challenging for developing countries that suffer from inadequate institutional and administrative capacity.

Registration

A sound regulatory system is an essential element of a nation's pharmaceutical policy (Seiter 2005). The primary role of the registration process is regulation and protection of public health (Hill and Johnson 2004). As registration involves drug approval, including evaluation of efficacy, safety, and adverse effects, the process can be an important barrier to entry in the pharmaceutical market (Cohen, Cercone, and Macaya 2002). Not only are restrictions determined for labeling, marketing, and prescribing, but also essential to registration is the dynamic process of re-evaluation of older drugs, post-marketing and product surveillance (Hill and Johnson 2004).

Since governments are responsible for drug registration (Cohen, Cercone, and Macaya 2002), robust institutions and the appropriate skills are necessary to ensure patient health protection. Therefore, legislation and regulations that outline the rights, responsibilities, and qualifications of the involved parties must be devised and implemented (Seiter 2005). Procedures for obtaining regulatory approval must aim to protect patient safety and be applied equitably and straightforwardly (Leach, Paluzzi, and Munderi 2005).

Britain's DFID stresses two key obstacles within regulatory systems of developing countries. First, a lack of political support begets inadequate legislative framework, financial resources, inconsistent application processes, as well as corruption (Hill and Johnson 2004). These legislative and political needs are critical for national and regional cooperation to increase access to essential medicines by ensuring better systems and policies are in place. The second obstacle, if political will is established, is the insufficient capacity to govern, administer, and operate an efficient system, as scientific and administrative capacity is often lacking (Hill and Johnson 2004). Regulators must have technical skills in evaluating the pharmacological evidence base of essential medicines. The process of evaluation should be transparent to facilitate independent monitoring, quick identification of inefficiencies or unwanted practices, and solicit public trust in the pharmaceutical system. Penalties can deter the unethical practices of bribery to state officials to buy market time as well as officials seeking payment from applicants (MSH 1997).

Furthermore, a proficient drug registration process must ensure marketing licenses are bestowed only to effective and good quality products. Even in a competent system, however, it is possible to find quantities of substandard drugs as errors and fraud allows pharmaceutical products that are not identical to those licensed to be distributed (Seiter 2005). Semine and colleagues (2004) have estimated that in Cambodia up to 65 per cent of quinine may be fraudulent, while further information from Asia, Africa, and South America reveals that 10–50 per cent of prescription medications may be counterfeit (Rudolf and Bernstein 2004). Therefore, a monitoring system should be implemented to check adherence of imported or locally produced drugs at both market entry and dispensing levels (Seiter 2005).

Nations can either assess the quality, efficacy, and safety of new drugs after provision of scientific dossiers by manufacturers, or the assessment may be based on internationally accepted authorities, such as the WHO pre-qualification list or a foreign DRA (Seiter 2005). While most high-income nations support a DRA that evaluates complete dossiers, middle- and low-income countries are limited both financially and technically. However, developing nations must at a minimum have the capability to assess a generic dossier if a local pharmaceutical industry exists, or if market approval is requested from other developing countries (Seiter 2005). This involves assessing quality, good manufacturing practice compliance, good laboratory practice, good clinical practice, and bioequivalence. To assist nations in the development of scientific and regulatory capacity, the WHO and its pre-qualification project play a substantial role training and advising governments on quality assurance of pharmaceuticals (WHO 2005).

The DFID suggests that current barriers should be met by coordinated policies at the country and regional level. Regional coordination can ensure development of scientific capacity to assess and register new products as well as to perform clinical trials to establish safety and efficacy for new drugs of neglected diseases (Hill and Johnson 2004). International standards such as the Declaration of Helsinki or CIOMS may serve as models for governments to protect participants' safety in clinical research. Hyder and colleagues (2004) found that of over 200 developing country researchers, one-quarter did not have their research approved by an ethics board, IRB, or Ministry of Health. Strengthening such institutions is crucial to protect research participants, given the increase in clinical trials being conducted in developing countries.

Selection

Selection is the second decision point in the pharmaceutical system and is primarily a prioritization process (Cohen, Cercone, and Macaya 2002). Government selects drugs to meet the most important health needs of the population and cover the country's disease profile. Selection is critical in an NDP as it largely determines the goals for the health system (WHO 2002). Appropriate selection can lead to improved healthcare, management of medicines, and cost-effectiveness, all of which can result in improved access (Quick 2003).

It is common for governments to establish an EDL. The WHO suggests that EDLs be based on quality evidence and balance efficacy, safety, quality, and cost-effectiveness (WHO 2004a). The WHO essential medicines list, which covers basic pharmaceuticals for the most common diseases (Cohen, Cercone, and Macaya 2002) can inform this process (WHO 2004b); however, the government is ultimately responsible for selecting the drugs most suitable for its population. A number of factors should be considered. The country's disease pattern, population genetics, and demographics inform the clinical dimension (WHO 2002). Practically, local storage facilities, distribution capacity, service delivery factors, and local environmental conditions may restrict which drugs can be included (WHO 2002). Human resource availability, training, and experience are important, as some drugs require specialized expertise or more clinical attention than others.

Ideally, the EDL should be developed alongside clinical practice guidelines, drug donations, and local medicine production (WHO 2002), but coordination can be difficult. National EDLs can be used to guide drug reimbursement schemes, and provide education and procurement practices (WHO 2002). Ensuring agreement between the procurement scheme and EDL is challenging and can result in waste of resources if not executed appropriately (Laing 2003). Procurement staff should be involved in the development of the EDL to ensure stocks are managed effectively (Laing 2003).

Cost-effectiveness analyses should be employed to effectively use scarce resources. Price and effectiveness information is accessible via the Internet, through databases such as the WHO Essential Medicines Library (Laing et al. 2003). The database provides internationally applicable measures of effectiveness, but if they are unsuitable, and resources permit, local trials may be necessary (Laing et al. 2003). If the drug is not yet available in the country, international prices may have to be used (Laing 2003). Buffer funds for unexpected drug needs or limited supply products may be useful, but caution should be exercised as such undefined circumstances can be vulnerable to misuse (Laing, Hogerzeil, and Ross-Degnan 2001).

Corruption at the selection stage can include bribes or misinformation to public officials from manufacturers or importers (Cohen, Cercone, and Macaya 2002). Ensuring strong and appropriate incentives for honest behavior, such as good salaries, may reduce the likelihood of such occurrences. Manufacturers benefit greatly if their drug is added to an EDL or national formulary; therefore, government responsibility includes ensuring a transparent and objective EDL development process (Cohen, Cercone, and Macaya 2002). Explicit criteria for selection should be used and open consultation with end-users (health providers, patients, and NGOs) may increase the likelihood of acceptance (WHO 2002). Conflicts of interest should be minimized; therefore, industry and other actors with similar interests should not be involved in the consultative process (Laing, Hogerzeil, and Ross-Degnan 2001).

A requisite for the selection process is having sufficient staff with the appropriate technical skills to select the appropriate drugs (Cohen 2003). Ideally, skills should encompass usage of evidence-based resources, critical evaluation of evidence, and knowledge of adverse drug reactions, "morbidity profile shifts", and pharmacoeconomic evaluations. Usually, physicians and pharmacists fill this role, along with other relevant local consultants (Cohen 2003).

Once established, implementation of the EDL is the next challenging step. To increase the likelihood of successful uptake, the EDL should be disseminated widely to all stakeholders including providers, NGOs, and the public (WHO 2002). Consultation with end-users and regular review and update may also help facilitate acceptance (WHO 2002). However, lack of human resources, skilled personnel, and poor management practices may hamper effective implementation.

Procurement

Effective procurement strategies enable the availability of quality pharmaceuticals in the appropriate quantity at reasonable prices. While drugs may be acquired through purchase, donation or manufacture (MSH 1997), the processes that characterize the interface between the public system and drug suppliers primarily include purchasing and resource allocation (Cohen, Cercone, and Macaya 2002).

When purchasing drugs, the type and/or combination of procurement strategies a government uses will impact the amount of supplier competition (MSH 1997). Competition within the local market is created through generic tendering, while within therapeutic classes negotiation or equity pricing can be used to reduce the cost of patented medicines (WHO 2004b). The commonly referred to "rule-of-five" for pharmaceutical pricing maintains that, with a minimum of five generic substitutes on the market and with at least five tendering bids per item, generic prices and prices in tendering systems are at their lowest, respectively. Therefore, healthcare programs typically use a competitive bidding program, except for single-sourced drugs, small volumes, or emergency purchases. Procurement should follow formal written procedures with explicit criteria to maintain transparency and avoid corruption. The World Bank's *Standard Bidding Document on Health Goods* aims to assist governments' tendering processes; however, these procedures have faced criticism by developing countries.

Bulk and pooled procurement mechanisms can reduce drug prices substantially. The pooled procurement practices of the ECDS reduced unit costs for pharmaceuticals more than 50 per cent during its first procurement cycle (Huff-Rouselle and Burnett 1996). Also, the Delhi model used a pooled procurement system for hospitals and health facilities, through a CPA, saving nearly 30 per cent of annual drugs cost for the government and improving availability more than 80 per cent (Chaudhury et al. 2005).

Countries with few resources may contract procurement agents to ensure pharmaceutical quality (Seiter 2005). Therefore, if a government's capacity to secure procurement is poor, specialized bulk procurement suppliers and UN agencies acting as suppliers can be a source of quality, low-cost medicines. They perform bulk or pooled procurement guaranteeing quality and low prices while charging a fixed percentage fee. The GDF program aims to increase access to quality TB medications for DOTS implementation using an international drug procurement system. The GDF includes a web-based system for placing orders and tracking shipments that details orders on the Internet to assist with DOTS program planning. GDF claims their average cost per patient, at US$11, is approximately 30 per cent cheaper than other suppliers (GDF 2005).

Studying the Costa Rican pharmaceutical sector, Cohen and colleagues (2002) found the procurement segment of the value chain the most vulnerable to corruption where poor transparency and governance have significant effects on the quality of services. Therefore, regardless of the procurement measure, governments have a responsibility to assure good pharmaceutical procurement practices when acquiring essential medicines for its public. Cost-effective drugs need to be purchased in the appropriate dosage forms and volume, and the selected suppliers should comply with GMP (Leach, Paluzzi, and Munderi 2005).

Regular reports should be filed on procurement performance indicators to measure performance data over time against set targets. The ratio of volumes purchased to those consumed, negotiated prices to average international prices, as well as the average supplier lead-time and service level are all such key indicators. Also important is the stock level of drugs at all stages of the supply chain. To ensure procurement practices are economical, efficient, and in the interest of the public, offices should be audited annually by an independent professional body (MSH 1997; Cohen, Cercone, and Macaya 2002).

Low-income countries with poor administrative capacity can seek technical assistance to manage the procurement process (Leach, Paluzzi, and Munderi 2005). Strengthening regulatory bodies and judicial systems is critical, as provision of counterfeit or substandard drugs can harm the public and should be penalized. To further eliminate substandard suppliers from the tendering process, both pre- and post-qualification procedures can be utilized. While these procedures may also aid in ensuring the expeditiousness of tenders, they are not without the risk of corruption.

The WHO pre-qualification project can assist officials as a reliable international reference of quality drug sources, primarily ARVs, to countries procuring essential medicines. In order to improve access to quality and affordable medicines, more than half of the drugs on the list are generic (WHO 2005). The project also boasts its assistance in country capacity-building to produce quality medicines. However, in May 2005, MSF called for the strengthening of the currently understaffed and underfunded project (Raja 2005). In November 2004, seven ARV drugs manufactured by the Indian pharmaceutical company Ranbaxy were removed from pre-qualification (WHO 2004c). While patients were advised to continue treatment until alternatives were suggested, MSF argued the project must expand its list in order to be a reliable source for countries and international funds.

Distribution

Distribution involves costly transportation, storage, and inventory control; therefore, efficient management of this process can substantially reduce final drug costs. While governments should facilitate prompt distribution of the appropriate quality and quantity of pharmaceuticals to health facilities and dispensing points, opportunities for the diversion of goods are available at all stages. Unlike other goods, pharmaceuticals can be damaged by poor handling and inappropriate storage conditions, and they are susceptible to theft during the course of transport (Cohen, Cercone, and Macaya 2002). Pharmaceutical storage facilities with functional refrigeration units are critical to preserve the integrity of the products. Central and regional warehouses as well as pharmacies and service floors all participate in this process, and require efficient communication and flow of information to ensure that the movement and deposit of inventory is monitored and controlled.

Furthermore, anti-diversion measures should be implemented. Efficient clearance of drugs through customs is often hindered by unnecessary regulations or poor systems and procedures employed by authorities. Delays at ports with poor storage conditions result in reduced shelf-life, loss of drug potency, an increase in the probability of theft, and the imposition of storage fees (Cohen, Cercone, and Macaya 2002). Therefore, the movement of pharmaceutical products should be managed from the source to the end-user efficiently and inexpensively, such as professional storage management that involves limited access at all points in the distribution system.

Many distribution models exist, including a government-owned and financed "central medical store," more flexible "autonomous supply agency," government tendered and privately supplied "direct delivery system," and separate source and supply contracts in "prime vendor system," as well as "fully private supply system" (Cohen, Cercone, and Macaya 2002). Countries may also use mixed approaches for distribution involving the public and private sector, as well as NGOs (WHO 2004b). In developing countries NGOs and charitable organizations play a crucial role in the provision of essential medicines. In 1999, MSF launched the Campaign for Access to Essential Medicines, an international project targeting services to rural, urban poor as well as mother and child populations (MSF 2005). Therefore, it is important for governments to encourage the growth and development of these organizations (MSH 1997).

Finally, to monitor need of essential drugs reliable consumption records and morbidity and mortality data are required. Stock records are the core of an inventory management system and are the primary source of information for reordering and reporting. As such, the implementation of an information system is necessary to monitor demand, drug expiration dates, inventory levels, and the flow of inventory through the distribution chain. This monitors and forecasts supply needs, prevents product loss, and helps to reduce corruption (Cohen, Cercone, and Macaya 2002). Once implemented, adjustments can be made on a case-by-case basis for past surpluses or shortages as well as for an expected change in programs (MSH 1997).

One promoted tool is the Clinton Foundation HIV/AIDS Initiative Anti-retroviral (CHAI ARV) Procurement Forecast Tool. This is intended to assist program managers to quantify and budget a program's ARV needs during the initial 12-month phase of scale-up. It combines patient targets with clinical assumptions on drug toxicity and treatment failure to calculate the number of units required to meet demand (CHAI 2005). Unfortunately, many developing countries do not have complete consumption data or the data do not reflect the need as the supply chain has never been full. Therefore, in initial phases of procurement programs, technical assistance may be useful to gain understanding of the appropriate methodology (MSH 1997).

Service delivery

Service delivery is the interface between the healthcare system and its patients where the ultimate goal is effective treatment of health problems. This decision point encompasses inpatient and outpatient care, drug administration or dispensing and counseling, ADE monitoring, and patient compliance.

Irrational drug use is a significant issue at the service delivery stage; it can result in increased morbidity and mortality, antimicrobial resistance, decreased health facility attendance rates, and decreased confidence in the health system (WHO 2001). Furthermore, as an inefficient allocation of resources, it results in waste and shortages of drugs. Policies in this area target a wide range of actors, such as prescribers, dispensers, patients, manufacturers, and drug sellers (WHO 2001). Responsibilities include measures to promote rational prescribing, dispensing and use, ethical promotion and information materials, pharmaco-vigilance, and public education.

Changing provider prescribing behavior is complex, given the many social, cultural, economic, and local factors involved (WHO 2001). Many conflicting interests are implicated, including the manufacturer's business interests, physicians' interests in autonomy and status, and the common belief that government only wants to cut costs (WHO 2001). Any method to improve prescribing must address these issues, and often multiple approaches are needed. Interventions that standardize treatment, such as clinical practice guidelines, monitoring of prescribing practices, and DUR are among common methods employed. To facilitate appropriate use, coordination between the EDL, treatment guidelines, procurement practices, teaching curricula, and evaluation procedures is key (Laing, Hogerzeil, and Ross-Degnan 2001).

Irrational prescribing can be from either corrupt practice or poor drug therapy decision-making. Providers may charge patients informal prescription fees or write false or multiple prescriptions to sell the drugs on the black market. Informal fees and diversion of products can also occur at the dispensing stage (Cohen, Macaya, and Cercone 2002). Dispensing restrictions and monitoring mechanisms may reduce the likelihood of such practice.

Unethical patient behavior is also a concern. Examples include bribing providers or dispensers to receive specific products, speeding up the receipt of the drug, faking illness to receive medication for another individual, or receiving multiple prescriptions from different facilities for resale on the black market.

The physician–industry interface is particularly vulnerable to unethical practice. Wazana (2000) observed that physician–industry interaction was associated with more requests for drugs on hospital formularies and changes in prescribing behavior. Providers in developing countries are especially vulnerable, as updated treatment information is often unavailable, forcing reliance on industry drug information (WHO 2001). Currently, only one in two countries regulates drug promotion (Quick 2003). Unethical promotion practices can include expanding indications for use, exaggerating therapeutic efficacy, and underplaying risks and side-effects (Menkles 1997; Gulhati 2004). Corrupt marketing practices include offering gifts or monetary incentives for prescribing a product. Guidelines, such as the WHO's 1998 *Ethical Criteria for Medicinal Drug Promotion*, may provide policy guidance, but it is ultimately up to governments to ensure appropriate monitoring and enforcement through law and regulation. Participation of civil society and the media are essential in assisting the identification of corrupt practice.

Protection of patient safety remains a responsibility at service delivery. Post-marketing surveillance systems aim to monitor, collect, and evaluate ADEs to identify long-term or unknown safety issues. Most developing countries lack the resources to make pharmaco-vigilance a priority; therefore, international data can help inform national DRA decisions (WHO 2001).

Lastly, public education on drug use is often neglected (WHO 2001). Patient non-compliance, informally purchased prescription drugs, and self-medication are common and increase the potential for misuse, increased morbidity, and drug resistance. Therefore, educating the public on appropriate drug use is critical to achieve public health goals (WHO 2001). This includes information on specific therapies and common inappropriate drug use. Regulation of DTC advertising may reduce the biased or inaccurate drug information the public receives.

Policy considerations

The pharmaceutical system cuts across a number of sectors; therefore, governments must ensure policy coordination to prevent conflicting programs and goals. As governments face the challenge to balance priorities with limited resources, thoughtful resource allocation is crucial. There is a variety of different interest groups placing competing pressures on governments. When considering pharmaceuticals, both health and industrial policy must be considered jointly (Jacobzone 2000). Ultimately, each country must consider its local social, cultural, political, economic, and environmental circumstances to determine whether a policy is appropriate within its specific context.

Policy must also address human resources at all decision points. Human resources are an aspect of healthcare that is often neglected but that can be a formidable barrier to drug access. Shortages of healthcare providers and chronic oversupply, inadequately trained staff, low worker motivation, and poor human resource management are critical issues (Martinez and Collini 1999). Policy should include strategies on the development, training, and retention of professionals in the pharmaceutical and healthcare sector (WHO 2001), as neglecting this can significantly hamper pharmaceutical sector reforms (Bach 2000).

To determine the vulnerable areas of the pharmaceutical system to corruption, governments should assess the institutional robustness of core decision points, while improving transparency across the system will reduce information asymmetries and may facilitate the identification of corrupt practices. To encourage ethical practice, incentives to public officials must outweigh the risks of corruption (Cohen, Cercone, and Macaya 2002). Governments must hold individuals accountable for their actions and impose penalties when necessary. Sufficient regulation should ensure that firms practice ethical behavior. Ultimately, individual governments have the responsibility to enact and implement policies and processes, which encourage ethical behavior and punish firms and/or individuals for any corruption.

Coordination needs to be implemented at both the national and regional level to develop adequate scientific, regulatory, and administrative capacity. Also, NGOs assistance in delivering essential medicines to under-served populations is indispensable. Therefore, it is crucial for the national authorities to foster the growth of these organizations. Drug donations, aid, and loans may provide short-term alternatives (WHO 2001). However, policies may be incongruent or may compete, which will affect the policy options at a government's disposal. Additional constraints can be imposed by loan conditions from international financial organisations or while servicing debts (Leach, Paluzzi, and Munderi 2005). This can also reduce the autonomy of governments to address their population's health needs.

References

Bach, S. 2000. *HR and New Approaches to Public Sector Management: Improving HRM Capacity.* Paper presented at the Workshop on Global Health Workforce Strategy, Annecy, France.

Chaudhury, R. R., R. Parameswar, U. Gupta, S. Sharma, U. Tekur, and J. S. Bapna. 2005. Quality Medicines for the Poor: Experience of the Delhi Programme on Rational Use of Drugs. *Health Policy and Planning* 20: 124–136.

Clinton Foundation HIV/AIDS Initiative (CHAI). 2005. *ARV Procurement Forecast Tool: User's Manual.* Quincy: Clinton Foundation HIV/AIDS Initiative.

Cohen, J. C. 2003. *Government and Market Failures in the Pharmaceutical System: Partial Explanations Towards Understanding the Troubling Drug Gap.* Paper presented at the Intellectual Property and International Public Health Conference, Washington, DC.

Cohen, J. C., J. A. Cercone, and R. Macaya. 2002. *Improving Transparency in Pharmaceutical Systems: Strengthening Critical Decision Points Against Corruption* (unpublished). Washington, DC: World Bank.

Cohen, J. C., M. Gyansa-Lutterodt, and K. Torpey. 2004. *Increasing Access to Medicines: Policy Options for Ghana.* London: DFID.

Global TB Drug Facility (GDF). 2005. *Higher Quality TB Drugs Cost Less.* Geneva: GDF.

Gopalakrishnana, S. and R. Murali. 2002. India: Campaign to Tackle Unethical Promotion. *WHO Essential Drugs Monitor,* No. 31.

Gulhati, C. 2004. Marketing of Medicines in India. *British Medical Journal* 328: 778–779.

Hill, S. and K. Johnson. 2004. *Emerging Challenges and Opportunities in Drug Registration and Regulation in Developing Countries.* London: The DFID Health Systems Resource Centre.

Huff-Rousselle, M. and F. Burnett. 1996. Cost Containment Through Pharmaceutical Procurement: a Caribbean Case Study. *International Journal Health Planning and Management* 11: 135–157.

Hyder, A. A., S. A. Wali, A. N. Khan, N. B. Teoh, N. E. Kass, and L. Dawson. 2004. Ethical Review of Health Research: A Perspective from Developing Country Researchers. *Journal of Medical Ethics* 30: 68–72.

Jacobzone, S. 2000. *Pharmaceutical Policies in OECD Countries: Reconciling Social and Industrial Goals.* Labour Market and Social Policy. Occasional Paper No. 40. Paris: OECD.

Laing, R. 2003. *Personal Reflections on 25 Years of the WHO Model List for Essential Medicines.* WHO Essential Drugs Monitor, No. 32: 16.

Laing, R., H. V. Hogerzeil, and D. Ross-Degnan. 2001. Ten Recommendations to Improve Use of Medicines in Developing Countries. *Health Policy and Planning* 16: 13–20.

Laing, R., B. Waning, A. Gray, N. Ford, and E. t'Hoen. 2003. 25 years of the WHO Essential Medicines Lists: Progress and Challenges. *Lancet* 361: 1723–1729.

Leach, B., J. E. Paluzzi, and P. Munderi. 2005. *Prescription for Healthy Development: Increasing Access to Medicines*: UN Millenium Project Task Force on HIV/AIDS, Malaria, TB and Access to Essential Medicines.

Leisinger, K. M. 2004. Overcoming Poverty and Respecting Human Rights: Ten Points for Serious Consideration. In *International Social Science Journal* 180: 313–320, published on behalf of UNESCO. Oxford: Blackwell Publishing.

Management Sciences for Health (MSH). 1997. *Managing Drug Supply: The Selection, Procurement, Distribution and Use of Pharmaceuticals.* Bloomfield, CT: Kumarian Press.

Martinez, J. and L. Collini. 1999. *A Review of Human Resource Issues in the Health Sector: Briefing Paper.* London: DFID Health Systems Resource Centre.

Médecins Sans Frontières (MSF). 2005. *The Campaign for Access to Essential Medicines.* Geneva: MSF. Available at: http://www.accessmed-msf.org [Accessed August 11, 2005].

Menkes, D. B. 1997. Hazardous Drugs in Developing Countries: The Market May be Healthier than the People. *British Medical Journal* 315: 1557–1558.

Quick, J. D. 2003. Essential Medicines Twenty-Five Years On: Closing the Access Gap. *Health Policy and Planning* 18: 1–3.

Raja, K. 2005. MSF Criticises WHO's Weakness in Drug Prequalification Project. *Third World Network Health*, No. 3. Geneva, 18 May.

Ratanawijitrasin, S., S. Soumerai and K. Weerasuriya. 2002. Do National Medicinal Policies and Essential Drug Programs Improve Drug Use? A Review of Experiences in Developing Countries. *Social Science & Medicine* 53: 831–844.

Ratanawijitrasin, S. and E. Wondemagegnehu. 2002. *Effective Drug Regulation: a Multicountry Study.* Geneva: WHO.

Reich, M. 2000. The Global Drug Gap. *Science* 287: 1979–1981.

Rudolph, P. M. and I. B. G. Bernstein. 2004. Counterfeit Drugs. *New England Journal of Medicine* 350: 1384–1386.

Seiter, A. 2005. *Pharmaceuticals: Drug Regulation in Low and Middle Income Countries.* Health, Nutrition and Population Brief No. 4. Washington: World Bank.

Semine, A., S. Phanouvong, L. Chanthap, R. Tsuyuoka, N. Nivana, and N. Blum. 2004. *Antimalarial Drug Quality in Mekong Region.* A poster presentation at the International Conference on the

Use of Medicines, March 30–April 2, Chiang Mai, Thailand. Available at: http://www.uspdqi.org/pubs/other/AntimalarialPoster.pdf [Accessed August 10, 2005].

United Nations Committee on Economic, Social and Cultural Rights (UNCESCR). 2000. General Comment No. 14, *Substantive Issues Arising in the Implementation of the International Covenant on Economic, Social and Cultural Rights*, E/C.12/2000/4, August 11, 2000. Geneva: CESCR. Available at: http://www.unhchr.ch/tbs/doc.nsf/(symbol)/E.C.12.2000.4.En?OpenDocument [Accessed March 24, 2005].

Wazana, A. 2000. Physicians and the Pharmaceutical Industry: Is a Gift Ever Just a Gift? *JAMA* 283: 373–380.

World Bank. 1994. *Better Health in Africa*. Washington, DC: World Bank Publications.

World Health Organization (WHO). 2001. *How to Develop and Implement a National Drug Policy*. 2nd edn. Geneva: WHO. Available at: http://whqlibdoc.who.int/publications/924154547X.pdf [Accessed August 3, 2005].

——. 2002. *The Selection of Essential Medicines*. WHO Policy Perspectives on Medicines, No. 4. WHO/EDM/2002.2. Geneva: WHO.

——. 2003. Access to Essential Medicines: a Global Necessity. *Essential Drugs Monitor* 32: 13.

——. 2004a. *The World Medicines Situation*. Geneva: WHO. Available at: http://w3.whosea.org/LinkFiles/Reports_World_Medicines_Situation.pdf [Accessed November 21, 2005].

——. 2004b. *Equitable Access to Essential Medicines: A Framework for Collective Action*. WHO Policy Perspectives on Medicines No. 8. Geneva: WHO.

——. 2004c. *Ranbaxy Withdraws All Generic ARVs from WHO Prequalification*. Geneva: WHO. Available at: http://mednet3.who.int/prequal/press_and_media.htm [Accessed August 11, 2005].

——. 2005. *Key Facts About the WHO Prequalification Project*. Geneva: WHO. Available at: http://www.who.int/3by5/prequal/en/ [Accessed August 5, 2005].

25 Pharmaceutical cost-effectiveness pricing: developing and protecting a global ideal form

Thomas A. Faunce

This chapter explores policy options concerning a hitherto largely unexamined threat to global public goods in the area of universal access to essential medicines. This is the use of industry lobbying, particularly facilitated by trade agreements, to undermine regulatory systems involving scientific, cost-effectiveness evaluation of allegedly "innovative" pharmaceuticals prior to government reimbursement. As a response to this challenge, it makes recommendations for strategically developing and protecting progressively realized ideal elements (including supporting scientific knowledge) of a global, socially responsive, cost-effective pharmaceutical pricing system.

Cost-effectiveness evaluation and the global problem of ensuring universal access to essential medicines

Essential medicines are defined by the WHO (2004) as "those that satisfy the priority health care needs of the population … selected with due regard to public health relevance, evidence on efficacy and safety and comparative cost-effectiveness." The important point is that, for this authoritative international public health body, "comparative cost-effectiveness" evaluation (or relative value to a community) is an integral part of the basic conception of an "essential" medicine.

The provision of universal or equal access (regardless of income or private insurance status) to essential medicines may be classified as a global public good in that it is systematically underprovided by private market forces and imposes international externality costs on third parties (Maskus and Reichman 2005). Further, it carries non-excludable benefits, as to regard "patients" primarily as rivalrous "consumers" of necessarily scarce commodities involves utilitarian logic at odds with basic virtues and principles of medical professionalism (Faunce and Gatenby 2005; Shaffer 2005). Providing universal access to such medicines may also be appropriately designated a "merit" good for public conscience, because such a policy presumptively appears of critical importance to foundational social virtues of justice, fairness, and (particularly with regard to international human rights) respect for human dignity (Birkett, Mitchell, and McManus 2001; Faunce 2005a). My initial contention here is that similar arguments should apply to government-coordinated pharmaceutical cost-effectiveness analysis.

Today over one-third of the world's population lacks "affordable" access to essential medicines. For developing nations in Africa and Asia, the figure is over 50 per cent and such patients (apart from humanitarian assistance through non-governmental agencies) must pay for these basic pharmaceuticals themselves, without assistance from government reimbursement (WHO 2006). Essential medicines can be classed as unaffordable when a course of peptic ulcer treatment costs twice the monthly wage of a government employee, the situation, for example, in Cameroon. This means that in 2005 there were over 40 million unnecessary deaths ("international externality costs" or "market diminishing events" in the language of corporate globalization), particularly from infectious diseases (WHO 2006). With aging demographics, patients in developed countries will also experience significant and increasing health problems related to the unaffordable cost of medicines (Bloor, Maynard, and Freemantle 1996).

A profusion of normative systems support "affordable" access to essential medicines as a global public good. The UN Millennium Target 17 requires that, in cooperation with pharmaceutical companies, states shall provide access to *affordable* essential drugs in developing countries (UN 2005). The indicator related to this involves the collection of data on the proportion of a studied population with access to affordable essential drugs on a sustainable basis. UNESCO's Universal Declaration on Bioethics, specifically applying to public and private corporations (Article 1.b), requires that progress in science and technology should advance access to quality healthcare and essential medicines (Article 14) (UNESCO 2005; see also Faunce 2005b) Articles 7.1 and 7.2 of the Rome Statute of the International Criminal Court lists amongst "Crimes against Humanity", "the intentional infliction of conditions of life, inter alia the deprivation of access to food and medicine, calculated [broadly defined] to bring about the destruction of part of a population" when "committed as part of a widespread or systematic attack [similarly broadly defined] directed against any civilian population with knowledge of the attack" (Lee 2001: 81–4). Also relevant are states' obligations to progressively realize the international right to health as specified in Article 12 of the International Covenant on Economic, Social and Cultural Rights (Article 25 of the UDHR) (Leary 1994).

Amongst the industry-based reasons for the problem of access to essential medicines (increased pharmaceutical patent rights; lack of R&D targeted at neglected or unprofitable diseases) one area has been less explored academically. This involves the emerging threat by manufacturers of so-called "innovative," brand-name pharmaceuticals, to science-based cost-effectiveness reimbursement pricing. Left deliberately vague by industry, the concept of "innovation" circles with corporate values disguised by advertising, round the more explicitly public good-oriented concept of essential medicines scientifically evaluated for community benefit.

The pressured varieties of pharmaceutical price controls and cost-effectiveness analysis

A variety of different techniques are being employed or investigated, without much regional or international coordination, by governments to control the escalating price of so-called "innovative" medicines. These include regulatory processes encouraging generic competition and substitution by prescribers and pharmacists (Denmark, Germany, Australia) as well as compulsory licensing of patented products to generic manufacturers in public health crises (Brazil, South Africa, South Korea). Other strategies investigated include cost-shifting by rising fixed or percentage patient co-payments (Australia), limits on pharmaceutical industry profits and marketing expenditure (UK and Spain), tendering (New Zealand), parallel importation of exported products now priced lower after monopsony negotiations (U.S. from Canada), and Ramsey optimal pricing differentials (Bloor, Maynard, and Freemantle 1996; Danzon and Towse 2005).

Use of expert cost-effectiveness analysis linked to government monopsony buying power has been linked with positive or negative government reimbursement lists. One important aspect of such a process is therapeutic reference pricing (the government reimbursing the average, or lowest, price in a therapeutic grouping of products) (Lopez-Casasnovas and Puig-Junoy 2000). In the U.S., cost-effectiveness analysis proceeds in a largely covert manner and is often linked with confidential discounts (as with managed care or Veterans Affairs purchasers) (Siegel 2005).

Cost-effectiveness evaluation prior to government reimbursement, however, was not developed primarily as a cost-containment strategy. Generally lacking a capped budget, it seeks to ensure that a government has value (or quality use) for reimbursement expenditure. No country currently requires evidence of pharmaceutical cost-effectiveness as a criterion for licensing approval and marketing; hence it is technically not a barrier to trade (Bloor, Maynard, and Freemantle 1996). Cost-effectiveness analysis is a scientific process, building on the widespread program of constructing clinical medicine on evidence-based practice (Cochrane 1972). It is, however, currently evolving in a somewhat random manner, this both facilitating and being an outcome of industry pressure.

The global development of cost-effectiveness evaluation of allegedly "innovative" pharmaceuticals, since the early 1990s, indeed has been characterized by much opportunistic improvization (from its socially-minded creators) and tactical variation (imposed by industry lobbying on governments). The Canadian province of British Columbia, for example, was a leader in the early development of pharmaceutical reference pricing, despite strong contrary industry pressure. Since 2004, however, BC has moved from a universal access system to one fully subsidizing only the lowest income earners (called "Fair PharmaCare") (Morgan, Bassett, and Mintzes 2004). Reference pricing in BC now is unable to expand beyond existing limited categories. The populous province of Ontario gained industry leverage through binding price volume agreements (coupled with fixed reimbursement prices and imposed price-drops on the first 30 per cent, and subsequent 10 per cent, generic market entrants) (Morgan, Bassett, and Mintzes 2004). Equally influential Quebec (the location of most Canadian pharmaceutical companies), however, adopted a strangely "parasitic" system that automatically adopted the lowest price developed through (the thereby inhibited) cost-effectiveness analysis processes in other Canadian jurisdictions (Morgan, Bassett, and Mintzes 2004).

The Canadian provinces (with the exception of Quebec) have now pooled resources to create a common drug review (through the independent CEDAC operating under the not-for-profit CCOHTA). The review factors transparent (public) cost-effectiveness estimates, derived from systematic reviews, back to provincial cost-effectiveness committees (such as Ontario's DQT) for local pricing and reimbursement decisions. This system suffers by its lack of association with the negotiation clout of a single national buyer (CCOHTA 1994; Laupacis 2005).

At the Federal level, the PMPRB sets an upper limit for each patented "new active substance" and existing patented medicine, after determining the median price for medicines in seven nominated developed jurisdictions (including the UK, France, Germany, and the U.S., but not Australia) and, for existing products, taking into account changes in the CPI (PMPRB 2004). The extent to which CEDAC-type cost-effectiveness analysis merely inefficiently replicates that used in this PMPRB process is debatable (Laupacis 2005).

Cost-effectiveness analysis has remained under-utilized in the U.S., except for areas such as VHA and, confidentially, with managed care programs (Siegel 2005). Such reluctance has been ascribed in part to methodological problems with cost-effectiveness analysis (Drummond and Sculpher 2005). The most likely reason, however, is fierce lobbying against it by a brand-name pharmaceutical industry that has permeated all major sectors of the Federal government (Angell 2005).

Many OECD countries have reimbursement processes that make evaluations of pharmaceutical prices in other countries (Jacobzone 2000; WHO 2004). The UK PPRS links control over manufacturer profits (taking into account the company's expenditure on R&D as well as marketing) with a negative (non-reimbursed) list and cost-effectiveness guidance from NICE. NICE sets its own agenda, usually on classes of drugs, utilizing a strong outcome measure (cost/quality of life year gained by the new product) (UKP 2005).

Australia's cost-effectiveness evaluation system has evolved under the National Health Act 1958 (Cth) since relevant guidelines were issued in 1993. It is now regarded as an international benchmark process, combining the advantages of rigorous multi-centered cost-effectiveness analysis by independent experts with monopsony buying power by the Federal government. Under this system, a new prescription pharmaceutical must be approved for marketing by the TGA, on quality and safety grounds. Then, a pharmaceutical manufacturer ("sponsor") seeking to have a drug listed for government reimbursement on the PBS, makes a submission to the PBAC specifying a disease indication and a putative listing price based on the pharmaceutical company's assessment of the best relevant available data on clinical effect (Birkett, Mitchell, and McManus 2001).

The sponsor's application is passed on to expert reviewers (both in an independent expert economic subcommittee and in academic centers based at particular universities), who consider the cost-effectiveness of the product proposed for listing against comparative substances in the relevant therapeutic class, or the standard medical (non-drug) treatment. They may create simulations to assess outcomes such as the incremental cost-effectiveness ratio (the additional cost for an additional beneficial effect, or QALYs gained), rather than simply a pharmacological effect (lowered cholesterol or blood pressure). The reports of these experts are reviewed by the PBAC along with industry responses. The process is designed to take six weeks and follows guidelines set out on the PBS website.

The pharmaceutical manufacturer may be claiming a pricing premium because of a claimed additional benefit (that is, improved effectiveness, a better adverse-event profile or delivery system) conferred by the new product over its therapeutic rivals. If no such benefit is established, the PBAC process is known as "cost minimization" and involves a recommendation for therapeutically equivalent doses and prices (Birkett, Mitchell, and McManus 2001). Once a decision is made to recommend listing of the drug for government reimbursement, the PBPA then evaluates the requested price against an international benchmark price and the clinical and cost-effectiveness data from the PBAC.

PBS reference pricing linked with scientific cost-effectiveness evaluation before government reimbursement, on the other hand, saves the Australian government at least A\$1 billion a year (Sainsbury 2004). Yet, the PBAC agenda is wholly set by the pharmaceutical industry (through individual product submissions). This, combined with limited staffing and financial resources, currently restricts the PBAC from achieving greater savings through cost-effectiveness reviews on old listings. Further, its members have to make many evaluations on surrogate outcomes (such as blood levels measuring LDL cholesterol) because the industry has difficulty producing published data with hard outcome comparisons (quality of life years gained) (Henry, Hill, and Harris 2005).

Finally, it should be noted that many developing countries lack officials with the requisite pharmaco-economic expertise or access to information, sufficient to permit rational negotiation over medicines prices (WHO 2004). The WHO (1999) World Drug Situation Survey 1999 showed that of 135 countries surveyed, 40 per cent had no regulation of medicines prices at all.

Crucial, then, to the provision of essential medicines to the developing world (where government regulation and industry in many countries are disrupted by armed conflict), is the WHO EML. Originally produced in 1977, the WHO EML now contains over 300 products. By 1998, 140 countries had developed their own national lists of essential drugs.

The relevant WHO guidelines require that information on cost and cost-effectiveness should refer to average generic world market prices as listed in the International Drug Price Indicator Guide, an essential medicines pricing service provided by the WHO and maintained by MSH. If this information is not available, other international sources, such as the WHO, UNICEF, and MSF price information service, can be used. Information is also required by the WHO on the comparative cost-effectiveness presented as range of cost per routine outcome (that is, cost per case, cost per cure, cost per month of treatment, cost per case prevented, cost per clinical event prevented, or, if possible and relevant, cost per QALY gained). Although originally intended for developing countries, an increasing number of developed countries have adapted the WHO's Essential Medicines cost-effectiveness pricing mechanism (Laing et al. 2003).

U.S. pharmaceutical industry's challenge to cost-effectiveness analysis

In 2003 a group of Democrat and Republican Congressmen, proposed a Bill to authorize US\$50 million for the NIH and US\$25 million for the AHRQ to conduct the studies comparing the cost-effectiveness of different medications. The draft legislation was supported by the AARP. It was extensively criticized, however, by the PhRMA, particularly for encouraging the government to develop "a single determination on the comparative value of different medicines" (Moynihan 2003).

Under the Medicare Prescription Drug Improvement and Modernization Act 2003 (USC 2003), however, the U.S. government was specifically prohibited from using its bulk buying power for Medicare beneficiaries to negotiate medicines prices on cost-effectiveness grounds. Section 1123 of the legislation also commissioned a study by the USDoC.

The resultant report claimed to have established that pharmaceutical cost-effectiveness "price controls" in 13 OECD nations cost American drug purchasers US$5–$6 billion each year. It argued that American drug prices should serve as a benchmark for deregulated prices, despite the fact that they were 18–67 per cent *higher* than those in the relevant OECD countries (USDoC 2004). The study was critical, for example, of how the FMSAE jointly agree on pricing decisions. It attacked the reference pricing system reintroduced in Germany in 2004 and the German government requirement that pharmaceutical companies pay a 6 per cent mandatory rebate to statutory health funds. It criticized the UK PPRS for regulating manufacturers' profits, promotional spending, and the prices for medicines sold to the National Health Service (USDoC 2004). The next step is likely to be an investigation and lobbying within the OECD about how cost-effectiveness systems can be made more responsive to "innovation."

Another mechanism used to effect this global assault on pharmaceutical cost-effectiveness pricing may be bilateral trade agreements. The AUSFTA, which entered into force on January 1, 2005, was notable here because it was the first such bilateral FTA to include provisions directly targeting the pharmaceutical cost-effectiveness reimbursement pricing mechanism of another nation (Faunce et al. 2005).

The AUSFTA's challenge to PBAC cost-effectiveness

The U.S. Trade Act 1972 required AUSFTA negotiators to facilitate the "elimination of government measures such as price controls and reference pricing which deny full market access for United States [pharmaceutical] products" (USC 2002, 107–210 §2102 b.8.D). Official comments supported the position that the AUSFTA would make Australian consumers pay more for the R&D costs of U.S. pharmaceuticals and set a precedent for "eliminating" a pharmaceutical cost-effectiveness pricing system (Shiner 2004).

Australian negotiators were told that even the limited promised access to the U.S. manufacturing and agricultural markets would be closed unless the PBS was part of the deal (Drahos and Henry 2004). Yet, at the conclusion of negotiations Australia's reasonable and legitimate expectation, as expressed in public by its Prime Minister and Trade Minister, was that the core elements of the PBAC cost-effectiveness would remain intact; there would be no amendment to section 101 of the National Health Act 1958 (Cth).

The AUSFTA contains approximately 50 provisions in four areas relevant to Australia's pharmaceutical sector: Annex 2C (Pharmaceuticals); the side-letters between the

Australian Trade Minister and U.S. Trade Ambassador; Chapter 17 (Intellectual Property Rights); and Chapter 21 (Dispute Resolution Procedures) (Faunce 2005c). All of these in different ways have the capacity to impact on pharmaceutical cost-effectiveness pricing (Faunce et al. 2005). Chief amongst them, however, is Annex 2C.

Annex 2C (1) articulates one overarching principle – that the parties to the agreement are "committed to facilitating high quality health care and continued improvements in public health for their nationals" (AGDFAT 2005). It then mentions four subsidiary principles which emphasize, in that public health context, the importance of innovation, and research and development.

Other measures in the provisions of Annex 2C, and in the associated "exchange of letters," require process changes in relation to transparency: hearings prior to PBAC meetings, a review process, and public summary documents of PBAC decisions. Annex 2C requires the creation of a "Medicines Working Group" with health officials from each country in dialogue about such matters, though not the mechanisms of cost-effectiveness pricing. Annex 2C(5) permits a pharmaceutical manufacturer to disseminate information about pharmaceutical innovation via the Internet, in what appears to be the precursor, after the inevitable persistent industry lobbying, of DTC advertising, the conceptual arch-rival of cost-effectiveness analysis.

On the face of it, and as argued by the Australian government (Davies 2004), the provisions of the AUSFTA represent procedural changes rather than substantive reform to current regulatory arrangements. Further, within the principles of Annex 2C, "innovation" is uniquely linked with "high-quality healthcare," "affordability," "accountability," and "objectively demonstrated therapeutic significance."

Nevertheless, it appears that pharmaceutical industry lobbyists in Australia may already be using ambit claims about the impact of the AUSFTA PBS-related provisions on "innovation" to push for favorable governmental and bureaucratic decisions. Claims related to cost-effectiveness may include that the PBAC process should be more willing to break the therapeutic groupings of reference pricing for new products on pharmacologic, rather than health outcome data.

The constructive ambiguities in Annex 2C may be definitively settled only under the AUSFTA dispute resolution chapter 21, by an unelected panel of three nominated trade lawyers (Article 21.7). Perhaps of great importance for the PBS in this context is Article 21.2(c). This is what is known in international trade law as an NVNB clause. NVNB provisions allow dispute resolution proceedings to be commenced where only the "spirit" of the treaty had been broken or, more technically, the "legitimate expectations" have been nullified or impaired (no technical violation) by a "measure" of the other party.

Reflections on developing an ideal pharmaceutical cost-effectiveness pricing system

Those wishing to protect and enhance pharmaceutical cost-effectiveness evaluation in the face of the challenges outlined above are hindered by the lack of academic and regulatory attention hitherto paid to developing a definitive gold standard. Some reasons for beginning to think systematically about developing an ideal form are now set out:

1. This global public good is critically dependent on the provision of large amounts of reputable scientific data. An ideal system should encourage the creation by researchers lacking relevant conflicts of interest, of public databases of large-scale, randomized, double-blind clinical trials involving head-to-head comparisons, using therapeutically equivalent dosage forms, for the most commonly prescribed pharmacological analogues or non-drug therapies for the same indication. Transparent sharing of evaluations should also be facilitated.
2. The outcomes of effectiveness increasingly should be clinically relevant measures such as deaths prevented or QALYs gained, rather than mere pharmacological outcomes.
3. The process should increasingly include evaluation of opportunity costs of government reimbursement (for social justice and human dignity reasons) in the health system as a whole.
4. Attempts could be made to systematically evaluate the social benefits of linking cost-effectiveness analysis not only with reference pricing, but government controls over industry-level profit and promotional expenditure, price-volume agreements, and competitive tendering.
5. Regulators could have the capacity to make binding health outcome agreements with industry and to reduce or remove reimbursement price premiums if ongoing research shows the promised benefits failed to materialize.
6. Industry funding of cost-effectiveness evaluation officials could be resisted as potentially creating a client-type relation with regulators which compromises objectivity.
7. Regulators may be encouraged to work towards links between every prescription of a pharmaceutical to a health outcome. This could ultimately be done by electronic linking of prescription data with hospital records. Privacy and confidentiality concerns would need to be overcome, but are not insuperable.
8. Leverage may gradually be obtained to discuss principles on commercial-in-confidence (not set unilaterally, not to endanger public health or unduly restrict transparency) and revealing local and international marginal costs of production for each drug.

Conclusion: protecting the ideal

This chapter has argued that cost-effectiveness evaluation of medicines, despite widespread normative, bureaucratic and political support, is an endangered global public good. This is so not only because of threats posed by corporate multinationals, but because those operating it lack a systematic global vision for its long-term enhancement.

In a world where globalized economies are exquisitely susceptible to trade pressure, the best way of protecting any systematic evolution of such an ideal may be to make it the subject of a multilateral treaty, or provisions in strategically significant bilateral trade agreements. Such arrangements would not be caught by prohibitions on restricting intellectual property rights emerging from the TRIPS Agreement. They would facilitate a trade in academic services from nations with relevant expertise and be a capacity-building measure offering genuine leverage on key regulatory issues with a globalizing industry where licensing agreements, takeovers, and mergers are making generic and brand-name players largely indistinguishable. Such a bilateral provision might read along the following lines:

> The parties agree to establish a committee [or some more convenient operational process] comprising officials and pharmacoeconomic experts nominated by the respective Ministers, to develop and enhance for the purpose of improving public health in their respective nations, the process of scientific cost-effectiveness evaluation and objectively demonstrated therapeutic significance of pharmaceuticals.

Such a treaty or provisions also facilitate recognition that the evolving process of scientific cost-effectiveness analysis is best placed to normatively legitimize claims for pharmaceutical "innovation," by gatekeeping, as a global public good, entry to the class of truly "essential" medicines.

Acknowledgment and disclaimer

The author is Project Director and a Chief Investigator under an Australian Research Council Grant to investigate the impact of international trade agreements on access to medicines in Australia. The ARC was not involved in the preparation of this chapter.

References

Angell, M. 2005. *The Truth about the Drug Companies. How they Deceive Us and What to Do About it.* Victoria, Australia: Scribe Publications.

Australian Government, Department of Foreign Affairs and Trade (AGDFAT). 2005. *Australia–US Free Trade Agreement (AUFSTA).* Barton, ACT. AGDFAT. Available at: http://www.dfat.gov.au/trade/negotiations/us.html [Accessed November 26, 2005].

Birkett, D. J., A. S. Mitchell, and P. McManus. 2001. A Cost-Effectiveness Approach to Drug Subsidy and Pricing in Australia. *Health Affairs* 20: 104–114.

Bloor, K., A. Maynard, and N. Freemantle. 1996. Lessons from International Experience in Controlling Pharmaceutical Expenditure III: Regulating Industry. *British Medical Journal* 313: 33–35.

Canadian Coordinating Office for Health Technology Assessment (CCOHTA). 1994. *Guidelines for Economic Evaluations of Pharmaceuticals.* Ottawa, Canada: CCOHTA. Available at: http://www.ccohta.ca [Accessed November 5, 2005].

Cochrane, A. L. 1972. *Effectiveness and Efficiency: Random Reflections on Health Services.* London: Nuffield Provincial Hospitals Trust.

Danzon, P. M. and A. Towse. 2005. Theory and Implementation of Differential Pricing of Pharmaceuticals. In *International Public Goods and Transfer of Technology Under a Globalized Intellectual Property Regime*, edited by K. E. Maskus and J. H. Reichman, 425–456. New York: Cambridge University Press.

Davies, P. 2004. *Health Impacts of the AUSFTA*. Australian Department of Health and Aging: Woden, ACT. Available at: http://www.apec.org.au/docs/fta04Davies.pdf [Accessed November 28, 2005].

Drahos, P. and D. Henry. 2004. The Free Trade Agreement Between Australia and the United States undermines Australian Public Health and Protects US Interests in Pharmaceuticals. *BMJ* 328: 1271–1272.

Drahos, P., T. Faunce, M. Goddard, and David Henry. 2004. *The FTA and the PBS. Submission to the Senate Select Committee on the US-Australia Free Trade Agreement Canberra*. Canberra: Australian Senate. Available at: http://evatt.labor.net.au/publications/papers/126.html [Accessed November 26, 2005].

Drummond, M. and M. Sculpher. 2005. Common Methodological Flaws in Economic Analysis. *Medical Care* 43, no. 7: 5–14.

Faunce, T. A. 2005a. *Pilgrims in Medicine: Conscience, Legalism and Human Rights*. Leyden: Martinus Nijhoff.

——. 2005b. The UNESCO Bioethics Declaration "Social responsibility" Principle and Cost-Effectiveness Price Evaluations for Essential Medicines. *Monash Bioethics Review* 24, no. 3: 10–19.

——. 2005c. Global Intellectual Property Protection for Innovative Pharmaceuticals. Challenges for Bioethics and Health Law. In *Globalization and Health*, edited by B. Bennett and G. F. Tomossy. Dordrecht: Springer.

Faunce, T. A. and P. Gatenby. 2005. Flexner's Ethical Oversight Reprised? Contemporary Medical Education and the Health Impacts of Corporate Globalization. *Medical Education* 39: 1066–1074.

Faunce, T. A., E. Doran, D. Henry, P. Drahos, P. Searles, B. Pekarsky, and W. Neville. 2005. Assessing the Impact of the Australia–United States Free Trade Agreement on Australian and Global Medicines Policy. *Globalization and Health* 1, 1–15. Available at: http://www.globalizationandhealth.com [Accessed November 3, 2005].

Henry, D. A., S. Hill, and A. Harris. 2005. Prescription Drug Prices and Value for Money. The Australian Pharmaceutical Benefits Scheme. *JAMA* 294 (20): 2630–2632.

Jacobzone, S. 2000. *Pharmaceutical Policies in OECD Countries: Reconciling Social and Industrial Goals*. Paris: OECD.

Laupacis, A. 2005. Incorporating Economic Evaluations into Decision-making. The Ontario Experience. *Medical Care* 43, no. 7: 15–19.

Laing R., B. Waning, A. Gray, N. Ford, and E. 't Hoen. 2003. 25 Years of the WHO Essential Medicines Lists: Progress and Challenges. *Lancet* 361: 1723–1729.

Leary, V. A. 1994. The Right to Health in International Human Rights Law. *Health and Human Rights* 1: 24–32.

Lee, R. S. 2001. *The International Criminal Court. Elements of Crimes and Rules of Procedure and Evidence*. New York: Transnational Publishers.

Lopez-Casasnovas, G. and J. Puig-Junoy. 2000. Review of the Literature on Reference Pricing. *Health Policy* 54: 87–123.

Maskus, K. E. and J. H. Reichman. 2005. The Globalization of Private Knowledge Goods and the Privatization of Global Public Goods. In *International Public Goods and Transfer of Technology Under a Globalized Intellectual Property Regime*, edited by K. E. Maskus and J. H. Reichman, 3–45. New York: Cambridge University Press.

Morgan, S., K. Bassett, and B. Mintzes. 2004. Outcomes-Based Drug Coverage in British Columbia: A Unique Approach to Public Drug Coverage That Uses Academic Advisers and Saves Money. *Health Affairs* 23: 269–276.

Moyniham, R. 2003. US Politicians Want Federal Funding to Discover Cost-Effectiveness of New Drugs. n.p.

Patented Medicines Prices Review Board (PMPRB). 2004. *Annual Report Health*. Ottawa: PMPRB. Available at: http://www.pmprb-cepmb.gc.ca [Accessed November 5, 2005].

Sainsbury, P. 2004. Australia-United States Free Trade Agreement and the Australian Pharmaceutical Benefits Scheme. *Yale Journal of Health Policy Law Ethics* 4: 387–99.

Shaffer, G. 2005. Recognizing Public Goods in WTO Dispute Settlement: Who Participates? Who Decides? The Case of TRIPS and Pharmaceutical Patent Protection. In *International Public Goods and Transfer of Technology Under a Globalized Intellectual Property Regime*, edited by K. E. Maskus and J. H. Reichman, 884–908. New York: Cambridge University Press.

Shiner, J. 2004. Evidence to Committee on Finance Subcommittees on Health Care and International Trade, United States Senate, Washington, DC, April 27.

Siegel, J. E. 2005. Cost-effectiveness Analysis in U.S. Healthcare Decision-making. Where is it Going? *Medical Care* 43, no. 7: 1–4.

United Kingdom Parliament (UKP). 2005. *The Influence of the Pharmaceutical Industry*. London: TSO. Available at: http://www.publications.parliament.uk/pa/cm200405/cmselect/cmhealth/42/4202.htm [Accessed October 20, 2005].

United Nations. 2005. Human Development Report. Available at: http://hdr.undp.org [Accessed May 24, 2005].

United Nations Education, Scientific and Cultural Organization (UNESCO). 2005. *Universal Draft Declaration on Bioethics and Human Rights*. Draft 33 C22. Paris: UNESCO. Adopted October 2005.

United States Congress (USC). 2002. *Trade Act 2002, 107–210 §2102 b.8.D*. Washington, DC: USC.

——. 2003. *Under the Medicare Prescription Drug Improvement and Modernization Act 2003*. Washington, DC: USC. Available at: http://www.cms.hhs.gov/medicarereform/ [Accessed November 29, 2005].

United States Department of Commerce (USDoC). 2004. *Pharmaceutical Price Controls in OECD Countries. Implications for US Consumers, Pricing, Research and Development and Innovation*. Washington, DC: U.S. Department of Commerce.

World Health Organization (WHO). 1999. *World Drug Situation Survey 1999*. Geneva: WHO.

——. 2004. *The World Medicines Situation*. Geneva: WHO.

——. 2006. *Commission on Intellectual Property Rights, Innovation and Public Health*. Available at: http://www.who.int/intellectualproperty/en/ [Accessed May 24, 2006].

Notes on the contributors

Brook K. Baker is Professor of Law at Northeastern University, IL. He studied economics at Harvard College and Law at Northeastern University. He has consulted and published widely on access to medicines issues and the global AIDS pandemic, focusing in particular on intellectual property, free trade agreements, and multilateral and bilateral global health initiatives. He is policy advisor to Health Global Access Project.

B. Burciul is a Research Program Manager at Dignitas International, a medical humanitarian organization developing and implementing community-based care for people with HIV/AIDS in the developing world. He has worked with the Drugs for Neglected Diseases Initiative (DNDI), and has studied humanitarian issues extensively in the PhD program in Political Science at the University of Toronto.

João L. Carapinha is involved with various governmental and non-governmental health organizations. With a first degree in pharmacy, he is currently registered for his Doctorate in Public and Development Management at the Graduate School of Public and Development Management, University of the Witwatersrand.

Jillian Clare Cohen is the Director of the Comparative Program on Health and Society and an Assistant Professor at the Leslie Dan Faculty of Pharmacy, University of Toronto. She received her BA and MA in Political Science from McGill University and her PhD in Politics from New York University. Cohen has advised a myriad of governments on pharmaceutical policy issues including the governments of Brazil, Bulgaria, Ecuador, Ghana, Haiti, India, Ontario, and Romania. She is a frequent lecturer and media commentator on pharmaceutical policies in Canada and elsewhere. Her research and teaching are focused on drug access issues for the global poor, the comparative politics of international pharmaceutical policy, and ethics and corruption in pharmaceutical systems.

Richard Elliott is Deputy Director of the Canadian HIV/AIDS Legal Network (www.aidslaw.ca), a leading advocacy organization working on the legal and human rights issues raised by HIV/AIDS. He is a founding member of the Global Treatment Access Group (GTAG), a coalition of Canadian civil society organizations.

Laura Esmail is a doctoral student at the Leslie Dan Faculty of Pharmacy, University of Toronto. Her research focuses on the use of compulsory licensing for the production and export of pharmaceuticals to developing countries. In 2005, she was a research intern for Médecins Sans Frontières.

Thomas A. Faunce holds a joint appointment as senior lecturer in the College of Law and Medical School at the Australian National University. His PhD was awarded the Crawford Prize at the ANU in 2002. He is currently Project Director of a three-year Australian Research Council grant investigating the impact of international trade agreements on Australian medicine policy.

Nathan Ford has worked for Médecins Sans Frontières for the past eight years, focusing on increasing access to medicines for medical programs in resource-poor settings. He is currently working with MSF's HIV/AIDS program in Khayelitsha, South Africa.

Lisa Forman qualified as a lawyer in South Africa with a BA and LLB from the University of the Witwatersrand. She received a Masters in Human Rights Studies from Columbia University, and received her SJD from the University of Toronto, Faculty of Law in 2006. Her dissertation explores the role of human rights in increasing access to AIDS medicines, focusing on South Africa as a case study. She is also a research fellow at the Munk Center for International Studies, Comparative Program on Health and Society, exploring links between human rights on health and trade law and policy on medicine. Forman has published and presented various aspects of her research.

Robert A. Freeman is a 20-year veteran of the global pharmaceutical industry, having led public policy and health economics groups for a number of companies. He is currently Principal of the Freeman Group LLC, a consultancy to the pharmaceutical, biotechnology, and medical device industries. He has widely published in the fields of pharmaceutical policy, industry economics, and technology assessment, and holds adjunct faculty appointments at the Thomas Jefferson University Department of Health Policy and The University of Maryland Center on Drugs and Public Policy.

Michael Gorman is a Professor in the Department of Science, Technology & Society at the University of Virginia. His research interests include experimental simulations of science, described in his book *Simulating Science* (Indiana University Press, 1992) and ethics, invention, and discovery, described in his book *Transforming Nature* (Kluwer Academic Press, 1998). He has co-authored a book with M. M. Mehalik and P. H. Werhane, *Ethical and Environmental Challenges to Engineering* (Prentice-Hall, 2000), and has edited a volume on *Scientific and Technological Thinking* (Lawrence Erlbaum Associates, 2005).

Aidan Hollis is Associate Professor of Economics at the University of Calgary and a Research Fellow of the Institute of Health Economics. His principal research interests are competition and innovation policies in pharmaceutical markets.

Søren Holm is Professorial Fellow in Bioethics at Cardiff Law School, and Professor of Medical Ethics at the University of Oslo. He has written extensively on genetics and justice, and is currently preparing a book on these topics under the working title "Bioethics in an Unjust World."

Warren Kaplan is presently Assistant Professor of International Health, Center for International Health & Development, Boston University School of Public Health. Kaplan was trained as a field biologist and has worked extensively in Peru, Brazil, and Ecuador on a variety of ecological projects relating to the Amazon rainforest and climate change. He is also an intellectual property attorney and was Assistant General Counsel, IP at Biogen, Inc. in Cambridge, MA. He is co-author, with Richard Laing at the WHO, of "Priority Medicines for Europe and the World," a Dutch-funded study on priorities for pharmaceutical R&D for diseases common to developed and developing countries.

Joel Lexchin is an Associate Professor in the School of Health Policy and Management at York University and a practicing emergency physician in Toronto. He has been a consultant on pharmaceutical issues for the governments of Ontario, Canada, and New Zealand as well as the World Health Organization and the Australian National Prescribing Service.

Donald W. Light is Professor of Comparative Health Care at the University of Medicine and Dentistry of New Jersey. Trained in organizational and economic sociology, he served on the working group organized for the Gates Foundation on "making markets" for vaccines in poor countries. He is conducting a series of studies on the foundations of pharmaceutical policies and will be a fellow at the Institute for Advanced Study in the Netherlands in 2006–7. Light is a founding fellow of the Center for Bioethics at the University of Pennsylvania.

Florencia Luna is Adjunct Researcher at CONICET (National Scientific and Technological Research Council), Argentina. She is Director of Bioethics at FLACSO and is Co-director, with Ruth Macklin, of a research training grant of the NIH (U.S.) and was President of the International Association of Bioethics (IAB) (2003–2005).

Kristina M. Lybecker is an Assistant Professor of Economics at Lake Forest College, Illinois. She earned a BA from Macalester College, with a double major in Economics and Latin American Studies, and received her PhD in Economics in 2000 from the University of California, Berkeley. Her research analyzes the difficulties of strengthening intellectual property rights protection in developing countries, specifically the problems related to pharmaceutical counterfeiting and the response of the pharmaceutical industry. Current areas of interests also include the recent changes in pharmaceutical policymaking in Latin America, the balance between pharmaceutical patent protection and access to essential medicines, and the intersection of innovation and antitrust policy.

Adam Mannan is a PhD student in law researching pharmaceutical innovation and the incidence of the pharmaceutical patent on pharmaceutical innovation. Concurrently he is also researching infectious diseases. He read physics at Bristol and Manchester Universities, before reading English and French law at the Universities of Kent and Paris I (Panthéon Sorbonne) respectively.

Ian E. Marshall studied political science and economics at Carleton University, Ottawa, and law at Queen's University, Kingston, Ontario. He is currently an international business consultant specializing in anti-corruption work, corporate governance, and country investment risk. Before that, he was Associate General Counsel at an international mining company where he co-authored their *Code of Business Conduct* and worked in 16 different countries. He has served on the board of directors of Transparency International Canada for eight years.

Steven H. Miles is Professor of Medicine, University of Minnesota Medical School, Minneapolis. He served as President of the American Association of Bioethics and was awarded the Distinguished Service Award of the American Society of Bioethics and Humanities. He served on President Clinton's Bioethics Working Group on Health Care Reform.

Ann Mills is Assistant Professor in the Center for Biomedical Ethics, University of Virginia, where she is co-director of the Program on Ethics and Policy in Healthcare Systems.

James Orbinski is a research scientist and clinician at St. Michael's Hospital, Toronto, and an Associate Professor of Medicine and Political Science at the University of Toronto. He received his MD degree from McMaster University in 1990, and completed a Masters degree in international relations at the University of Toronto in 1998, before becoming international president of Médecins Sans Frontières (MSF) from 1998 to 2001. His research interests are focused on access to healthcare, medicines, and other health technologies; medical humanitarianism in war and social crisis, and global health policy.

Kevin Outterson is a Professor of Law at West Virginia University. He is the author of numerous articles on global pharmaceutical markets and innovation. Outterson read law at the University of Cambridge (LLM) and Northwestern University (JD).

Wendy E. Parmet is George J. and Kathleen Waters Matthews Distinguished University Professor of Law at Northeastern University School of Law, Illinois. A graduate of Cornell University and Harvard Law School, she has published numerous law review and medical journal articles on law, bioethics, healthcare, and public health. She recently co-authored with Patricia Illingworth *Ethical Health Care* (Prentice-Hall).

Thomas Pogge studied philosophy at Harvard. He has published widely on Kant and in moral and political philosophy, including various books on Rawls and global justice. He is Professor of Political Science at Columbia University, Professorial Fellow at the Australian National University Centre for Applied Philosophy and Public Ethics, and Professor II of Philosophy at the University of Oslo. He is editor for social and political philosophy for the *Stanford Encyclopedia of Philosophy* and member of the Norwegian Academy of Science.

David B. Resnik studied philosophy at the University of North Carolina at Chapel Hill, NC and Law at Concord University. He has published over 100 articles on various topics in philosophy and bioethics, and is the author of six books. He serves on several editorial boards and is an Associate Editor of the journal *Accountability in Research*. Resnik is Vice-Chair of the NIEHS IRB.

Michael J. Selgelid is a Senior Research Fellow in the Centre for Applied Philosophy and Public Ethics at the Australian National University. He was previously the Sesquicentenary Lecturer in Bioethics at the University of Sydney and a Lecturer and Postdoctoral

Research Fellow at the University of the Witwatersrand, Johannesburg. He received his PhD from the University of California, San Diego.

Eline M. Sepers recently completed a Masters degree in Biomedical Science at the University of Amsterdam. Her work on this volume was undertaken during an internship with the Unit for History and Philosophy of Science at the University of Sydney.

Alan Story studied law in Canada and the United States. He worked as an investigative reporter and political journalist before going to the UK to teach law. He is currently a lecturer in the Kent Law School, University of Kent.

Patricia Werhane is Wicklander Chair of Business Ethics in the Department of Philosophy, and Director of the Institute for Business and Professional Ethics, at DePaul University. She holds a joint appointment as the Peter and Adeline Ruffin Professor of Business Ethics and Senior Fellow of the Olsson Center for Applied Ethics in the Darden School at the University of Virginia. Werhane has published numerous articles and is the author or editor of 16 books, including *Ethical Issues in Business* (with T. Donaldson and Margaret Cording, seventh edition), *Persons, Rights and Corporations*, *Adam Smith and His Legacy for Modern Capitalism*, *Moral Imagination and Managerial Decision-Making* (Oxford University Press) and *Employment and Employee Rights* (with Tara J. Radin and Norman Bowie) (Blackwell). Werhane's current research projects include an examination of best practices in American corporations and a study of women in leadership.

Kinsley Wilson is a doctoral student at the Faculty of Pharmacy, University of Toronto. Her research focuses on the role of technology transfer in the local production of patented anti-retrovirals for the treatment of HIV/AIDS. Wilson also has spent time working with the healthcare management consulting firm Sanigest Internacional in Costa Rica and Slovakia on pharmaceutical policy-related issues.

Index

Compiled by Sue Carlton

schistosomiasis (bilharzia) 112, 117, 118, 121, 142
Semine, A. 262
sertraline 15
sexual dysfunction 81, 89, 93
side-effects 16, 18–19, 67, 100–1, 102, 103, 143
see also safety issues
sildenafil (Viagra™) 18, 81, 85, 180
Singer, Peter 104
'skunkworks' 48
sleeping sickness 12–13, 109, 112, 113, 117, 118, 119, 121, 142
smallpox 77, 82, 117
and bioterrorism threat 83
vaccine 79
Smith, R. 78
SmithKlineBeecham 17–18
social phobia 17–18
South Africa 146, 157, 182, 196
access to ARVs 164, 245
access to medicines 126, 251–3, 256–8
competing priorities 252–3
drug pricing system 251–2
and government intervention 256–8
South Korea 255, 256
'spaghetti organization' 48
SSRIs (Selective Serotonin Reuptake Inhibitors) 14, 81
Staphylococcus aureus 180
stavudine (d4T) 42
Stein, P. 172–3
Stevens, P. 131
Surfaxin™ 215, 218
Swazey, J.P. 221
syphilis 156

TAC (Treatment Action Campaign) 245
Taiwan 255, 256
TB (tuberculosis) 88, 112, 117, 121, 154–5, 196
directly observed therapy 81
multi-drug resistance strains (MDR-TB) 80–1, 83, 155
and R&D activity 12, 53, 69, 109, 110, 118–19, 121
TDR (Special Program for Research and Training in Tropical Diseases) 121–2
Temple, Robert 218
tetanus 156

TGA (Therapeutic Goods Administration) 275
Thembalami Pharmaceuticals 170
tobacco-related illness 83
Towse, A. 51
trading zones 36–8, 39
and developed world 38
and developing world 37–8
triazolam 18–19
TRIPS (Trade-Related Aspects of Intellectual Property Rights) 19, 33, 36–8, 46, 95–6, 144–5, 182–3, 186, 187, 190–2, 243–4
calls for reform of 131, 245
and Canadian activists 228–32
and compulsory licences 169–71, 185, 194, 227–8
India and 47, 185
minimum IP standards 190, 191
and right of first refusal 232
TRIPS-plus standards 190, 192–3, 196, 229, 231, 232, 244
and voluntary licences 232–3
see also intellectual property rights (IPR); patent system
tropical diseases 142
drug development 12–13, 109–10, 117, 118, 121, 146, 156, 204
trypanosomiasis
African *see* sleeping sickness
South American *see* Chagas disease
Tshabalala-Msimang, Manto 251
Tufts Center for the Study of Drug Development 27

Uganda 196, 207, 216
UNAIDS (Joint United Nations Program on HIV/AIDS) 35, 88, 241–2
UNCESCR (United Nations Committee on Economic, Social and Cultural Rights) 240–1
UNCHR (United Nations Commission on Human Rights) 241–2
UNCTAD (United Nations Commission for Trade and Development) 253–4
UNDP (United Nations Development Program) 254
UNESCO (United Nations Education, Scientific and Cultural Organization) 209, 273
Unger, Peter 104